The Colonial Revival in America

The Colonial
Revival in America

EDITED BY

Alan Axelrod

PUBLISHED FOR

The Henry Francis du Pont Winterthur Museum

WINTERTHUR, DELAWARE

W·W·Norton & Company

NEW YORK   LONDON

Published simultaneously in Canada by Penguin Books Canada Ltd, 2801 John Street, Markham, Ontario L3R 1B4.
Printed in the United States of America.

The text of this book is composed in Electra, with display type set in Garamond. Composition and manufacturing by The Maple-Vail Book Manufacturing Group.

First Edition

Library of Congress Cataloging in Publication Data
Main entry under title:

The Colonial revival in America.

"Published for The Henry Francis du Pont
Winterthur Museum."
Includes index.
1. Colonial revival (Art)—Addresses, essays,
lectures. 2. Arts, Modern—19th century—United
States—Addresses, essays, lectures. I. Axelrod,
Alan, 1952–. II. Henry Francis du Pont
Winterthur Museum.

ISBN 0-393-01942-X

W. W. Norton & Company, Inc., 500 Fifth Avenue, New York, N.Y. 10110

W. W. Norton & Company Ltd., 37 Great Russell Street, London WC1B 3NU

1 2 3 4 5 6 7 8 9 0

Contents

Preface

"Our age is retrospective. It builds the sepulchres of the fathers," Ralph Waldo Emerson wrote in 1836. That year has long since elapsed, and the age of which Emerson wrote has passed, but his observation still rings true. And so we discover that it is more accurate an appraisal of place than of time: Our nation is retrospective.

America was very much a new world in 1836. Its origins, at least its origins as the United States, were still recent history then. Yet even with the passage of time and the widening of the gulf between 1776 and the present, the country has remained strangely and stubbornly new. The Civil War created a new nation, industrialization and urbanization yet another, and immigration still another. If this seemingly perpetual and perpetually augmented newness has offered promise to some, it has posed threat to more, who, turning to the past, have built against the forces of change the sepulchres of the fathers. Thus the colonial revival is more than an isolated aesthetic or even cultural phenomenon. Its foundation is sunk more deeply than the self-congratulatory nationalism of the Centennial in Philadelphia, and its structure rears itself well beyond the early twentieth century, reaching our own day and promising to outlast even it. To study the colonial revival is to examine aspects of our past, present, and future selves.

The fourteen essays collected here explore the motives, forms, and consequences of national retrospection. Museum curators, architectural historians, art historians, a literary historian, a historic-preservation scholar, and other students of material culture present their research and analysis of the colonial revival as it has figured in urban planning, public-garden restoration and reconstruction, architecture, the decorative arts, painting, and popular literature. The issues investigated are aesthetic, historical, and social. What we learn most emphatically is that the colonial revival cannot be dismissed as a mere byway of popular culture, the province of the idle rich or the fantasy of the acquisitive parvenu. It emerges instead as a multifarious and often urgent response to social stress and crisis: war, urban rootlessness, mass immigration, and economic depression. Of particular importance is how, especially in difficult times, cultural myths and idylls come into conflict with social conscience and historical consciousness. While the writers represented in this volume bring to bear the expertise and methods of their diverse disciplines, all address themselves to discussions of vividly representative episodes in the evolution of national identity.

Alan Axelrod

The Colonial
Revival in America

Introduction
Kenneth L. Ames

The papers in this volume grew out of two conferences on the colonial
revival sponsored by Winterthur Museum in 1981 and 1982. The
"Winterthur Conference on the Colonial Revival in America" brought
together more than two dozen speakers in addition to a musician and a
pair of dancers for two very busy and rewarding days in November 1981.
The second conference, a lively one-day exploration titled "Colonial
Revival Gardens: Real and Romanticized," was organized by Winterthur's coordinator of gardens education programs Philip G. Correll and
took place in March of the following year. Together, these two programs were probably the most extensive and diversified examination
ever undertaken of the colonial revival theme in American material
culture.

Why study the theme so thoroughly? Ideally, of course, inquiry into
any episode of the past yields valuable lessons about the human condition, but study of the colonial revival offers even more specific and
direct rewards. The colonial revival is not simply another historic episode locked into the past, but a phenomenon that continues with
impressive vitality into the present day as an ongoing part of our own
culture. The colonial theme has, to use a word fashionable nearly two
decades ago, "relevance" matched by few other historic phenomena.
The colonial is of the past, but it is also very much of the present. We
can hardly fail to miss it in the modern environment.

It is a public phenomenon fraught with autobiographical connections. I believe that colonial aspects of America's material culture are
important because I encounter them so frequently. In my own (admit-
tedly impressionistic) examination of the landscape—both public and

domestic—I have been struck by how common colonial forms are. I would not go so far as to say that colonial revival structures constitute the majority of what I see—they are clearly less prevalent in some periods and in some places than in others—but they are remarkably common. They may not be uniform in appearance, but they draw upon a common, fluid and flexible, language of colonial design. Under the colonial rubric we can find extraordinary varieties and digressions as well as regional interpretations with startlingly different visual effects, all of which nevertheless embody some notion of the colonial.

Visions or versions of the colonial past can be found on a remarkable range of structures, including supermarkets, gas stations, shopping centers, post offices, governmental structures of many kinds, ice-cream parlors, churches, and a surprising number of other forms wherever building has taken place in the last century. But the American home, particularly the suburban single-family home, is the major vehicle for the expression of colonial ideas in building. Indeed, the colonial seems to have become a dominant paradigm for domestic architecture in the United States.

Like millions of Americans, I live in a colonial revival tract house. I cannot say exactly that I ended up there by choice, since most of my options were other colonial tract houses. Delaware unquestionably has demographic and historical peculiarities that play a large role in shaping the kind of housing available, but similar situations prevail elsewhere, especially east of the Mississippi. When I leave my colonial tract house in the morning, I drive by about fifteen miles of other colonial houses, some older, some newer, some cheaper, some significantly more expensive (one of my favorites is a replica of Mount Vernon), and go to work at Winterthur Museum. Winterthur is many things, but chief among them it is a monument to one person's fascination with the American colonial past, and it is a generator and perpetuator of interest in things colonial.

Moving from the exterior landscape to the domestic interior, the visibility of the colonial actually increases. I have seen few homes without some touches of the colonial; I have seen many with little else. As with domestic architecture, the variety of colonial furnishings is great. To call a group of furnishings colonial is not even to hint that the individual items look the same. We do not see superficial resemblance to some fixed notion of the colonial when we survey furnishings over many years;

rather, we find a shifting understanding of ways to express colonial qualities within changing patterns of preferences and even changing definitions of the term *colonial* itself. Concept, not form, provides the continuity.

We study this topic, then, because it is an ongoing epic, a part of our everyday world. We study it for the very reason that it seems familiar and unexceptional; anthropologists remind us that the commonplace is the best means by which to understand central values and assumptions of a culture. I will not claim that exploring the colonial revival will crack the riddle of the meaning of American life, but I do think that colonial objects, icons, and ideas are more imbedded in American culture than may at first seem apparent.

In the call for papers that went out a year or so before the November 1981 conference we asked for speakers willing to discuss some aspects of the "colonial revival in America." We decided that it was possible to interpret the phrase in at least two different—although overlapping—ways. The colonial revival could be viewed in the conventional and relatively narrow sense of a discrete phase of American architectural and furnishings history usually thought of as beginning about the time of the Centennial and dying out with the advent of the modern movement in the early twentieth century. But the phrase could also be given broader meaning, encompassing virtually any variety of artifactual interaction with visions of colonial America. Defined in this broader sense, the colonial revival might be seen less as a time-bound episode in American cultural history and more as a persisting and pervasive component of American culture with antecedents reaching surprisingly far back into the American past. Some of the conference papers, including a number of those developed for inclusion in this volume, fit within the first (more conventional) definition, but others investigate issues and artifacts dating from before 1876, and still others concentrate on events many years after the Centennial, charting varying interactions with the colonial past well into the twentieth century.

As originally planned, the 1981 and 1982 conferences aimed at three interlocking goals, which have been attained in this collection of papers with considerable if varied success. First, we tried to put together programs sufficiently rich and diverse in people, topics, and viewpoints to generate a body of resource material and ways of thinking about the material that would be useful to anyone studying references to the colonial past in American material culture. In short, our most basic goal was to generate and record a significant and suggestive body of research. I think this goal has been amply achieved in these papers.

The second goal was to move beyond exposition to examine ways objects or events might be related to larger cultural issues. This has been accomplished here with a good deal of success through both direct and indirect means. Some essays are directly conjectural, speculating about the meanings of their material and its relationship to other cultural activities. Others venture less conjecture, but even these prod us toward analysis indirectly by offering accounts of artifacts and events that seem, at least at first glance, off the beaten paths of colonial revival or even material culture study. Particularly as they are juxtaposed with the other papers, these essays help us to reexamine some of our compartmentalized and complacent ways of arranging the past in our minds and discourse.

Indeed, one of the great values of this collection of papers is its diversity of theme and method, which produces a healthy confusion about the topic that should convince most readers that the whole business is neither simple nor clear. I cannot claim that these essays are the keys to understanding and explaining all the ways Americans have recorded, collected, restored, displayed, replicated, emulated, celebrated, manipulated, or otherwise interacted with the colonial American past, but surely they constitute a major aid to thinking about these issues.

The third goal, frankly, was not one that we actually expected the conferences—or this volume—to meet. Nevertheless, it is fair to say that these essays are means toward this final goal. Through an understanding of the ways people in this country made the past into usable history, we hoped to contribute—however tentatively—to material culture and historical theory. The truth is that both material culture and historical study at present tend to operate in a theoretical vacuum. While this volume does not dramatically change the situation, thoughtful readers will find richly implicit theoretical assumptions here on which to construct their own conceptual apparatus to help us grapple more productively with human behavior and, more specifically, with human behavior that involves objects from the past or relating to the past.

My own thinking about the assumptions implicit in these papers has yielded a provisional list of ten observations on the nature of the colonial revival. I offer these as a spur to further thought and as generalizing cement to bind the particularistic essays more tightly together.

1. The interactions with the colonial past chronicled here are extraordinarily complex. Given episodes may be readily comprehensible by themselves, but as we begin to pile one on top of another our view of the subject blurs. We soon learn that this matter cannot easily be encompassed, and if the subject cannot be thought about easily, it cannot be explained easily either.

2. Colonialism is not a surface phenomenon, a thin veneer over the real body of American life, but a network of communications and linkages that reaches deep into American experience and behavior. No single pivotal event generates these interactions with the colonial past; no solitary origin can be discovered. The motivations are many and complex, inextricably intertwined with fundamental aspects of life in America and the modern world.

3. If the colonial revival defies easy conceptualization and suggests complicated origins, its meanings also refuse to fall into clear and predictable patterns. Like classicism, the colonial has no fixed symbolic content but serves instead as a nearly bottomless pool of possibilities, sometimes surprising in the range of needs it fulfills. Occasional consistencies emerge among these needs, but we are frequently startled by the fertility of the imagination in creating meanings from the unprotesting past. As an image or experience recedes into the past, certain features are effaced and others are accentuated, depending on the new conditions that affect our present and, therefore, affect our way of looking at the past. Over time one image of the past is erased and replaced by newly generated images informed and shaped by supplementary and altered conceptions and definitions.

4. Since the process of reinterpreting, revising, rethinking, or reevaluating the past may go on continuously, propelled by newer information or exigencies, it sometimes happens that whatever actually occurred, whatever an object or an environment originally looked like may not be important for a given group at a given moment. The requirement to possess a past as we need it is often more pressing than any motive of historical accuracy. What one age deems as historical accuracy a later one sees as naiveté or self-deception. The transformation of images to meet historical needs takes place not only in the mind

but in the material world as well. The physical past can be shaped or reshaped to fit a society's requirements. It is therefore true that even manifestly authentic materials are hardly immune to alteration or destruction solely by virtue of their design or structural integrity. If they fail to fit current needs, the most pristine remnants of the past may fall prey to demolition. In some of the essays in this volume we see how what might have actually existed at some point in the past is of little significance at a later point. Williamsburg (treated by Charles B. Hosmer, Jr., in "The Colonial Revival in the Public Eye: Williamsburg and Early Garden Restoration") and Litchfield (studied in William Butler's "Another City upon a Hill: Litchfield, Connecticut, and the Colonial Revival") are only particularly obvious cases. While ideas about the past depend heavily on objects for their survival, it is also possible to arrange or modify objects to suit a particular idea or to make an idea appealing.

5. The process of making history is subject to complexities and contradictions. History is an artificial, fragmented, and biased production. The apparent but illusory directness of our language and the way certain emphases are made to seem not only correct but also inevitable disguise the ambiguity of the entire venture. Material culture history, still in its infancy, is a special case within the larger realm of history, replete with a distinctive group of rarely acknowledged problems. Among the most crucial is that objects have no single past but an unbroken sequence of past times leading backward from the present moment. Moreover, there is no ideal spot on the temporal continuum that inherently deserves emphasis. In selecting one past moment we necessarily shut out the possibility of other past moments—at least for a time. In elevating or admiring one piece of the past, we tend to ignore and devalue others. One reality lives at the expense of countless others.

Repeatedly we see just this happening, sometimes with unsettling, even grotesque results. One variety of this selective vision is found in conjunction with collecting and is noteworthy both for the cognitive machinations involved in it and for the frequency with which it recurs. We see such selectivity most blatantly in the behavior of some of the early collectors of colonial artifacts and even in collectors today who look for the same "good luck" their early counterparts enjoyed. Indeed, to read accounts of early collecting is to discover a remarkable fusion of exquisite sensibility for objects and incredible insensitivity to human beings. As Beverly Seaton reminds us in "A Pedigree for a New Century: The Colonial Experience in Popular Historical Novels, 1890–1910," some of the early collectors saw themselves as rescuing old china and other historic items from people too ignorant to value them. Such collectors had little sympathy for the "rustics" from whom they attempted to buy objects at grossly undervalued prices, and they had no interest in the meanings of the objects in the lives of those who had owned them. Exploitation and predation, although obviously operative, are less significant here than the process of redefinition involved in transforming the objects from old things in country homes to prized attributes of gracious living in sophisticated settings. In this process what is uncontestably known about the objects—their association with the rustics—and just as uncontestably unappreciated may be eagerly forgotten in favor of unverifiable but much more appealing assumptions about old-time craftsmanship, the piety and patriotism of the original owners, and the moral superiority of an earlier age. A similar process occurs whenever a structure or object is restored and whenever a neighborhood is gentrified. The social complexity and ambivalence to which gentrification gives rise constitute a good shorthand for grasping the essentials of the process. Questions we might ask as we watch colonial revivalism at work now or in the past address problems of determining the values and assumptions underlying the celebration of the colonial at the expense of subsequent times and people.

6. That all objects from the past are also of the present is an observation derived predictably if also somewhat paradoxically from the preceeding one. This dual nature gives objects the special qualities and properties they possess. If we look back again for a moment at our early collectors we see that it is past associations that make the objects into collectible artifacts; nevertheless, age and authenticity are necessary rather than sufficient sources of value. For the early collectors it was also vital that the objects could be possessed and moved, bought and sold. In spite of being objects from the past, then, they were—and are—also part of present economic exchange systems. We might even argue that their role as present commodities outranks their historical roles. For the predatory collector the principal function of history is to help limit the pool of comparable objects and to add a degree of difficulty and chance to the process of acquisition. Although allegedly an exercise in historical study, collecting can be ahistorical if not downright antihistorical.

If we allow observations 5 and 6 a degree of validity, we see how emphasis on a moment in the past or in the present is at odds with emerging historical interest in process, in the ongoing sequence of events, behavior, will, and actions that leave some imprint on a place or an object. An object altered admits to the passage of time, to changes in attitudes, ideas, needs, and uses. If objects emit mixed signals, it is with the resulting confusion, the cacophony of indicators, that the historian should try to chart changing mentalities and conditions. Yet to some who deal with objects, mixed and jumbled signals are anathema because they admit to the existence of significant activity between the desired time, usually at or near the beginning of the object in question, and the present. When we admit to the passage of time and to alternative visions and values, objects lose their clear programmatic role, and those who behold the objects are cast adrift on the seas of complex historical actuality. Antiques and deliberately restored buildings or environments tend to be frozen ahistorical objects outside the flow of time and human action. But an unaltered building in an environment marked by pronounced change may be judged ahistorical in itself even though it serves as an index to the change all around it. As Hosmer notes in "The Colonial Revival in the Public Eye," early dialogues with the colonial have just begun to concern those historians who study historical process and shifting patterns in values and attitudes.

7. The decision to colonialize is always an act of choice—an effort grounded in intention—and a choice necessarily made over other choices. Because the essayists were invited to focus on colonializing, it is only appropriate that they devote their greatest attention to that subject, and no one will suppose them ignorant of the larger world of choices lying beyond the focus of their essays. But readers will profit by attempting to place the events and objects described here into a fuller setting. People are motivated as much by negative drives as they are by positive; the desire to reject and dissociate from may be as strong as the desire to accept and affiliate with. The two kinds of behavior can be reciprocal, and we may find cultural activities generated by positive and negative motivations simultaneously. To put the matter more prosaically, many cultural accomplishments have been propelled by a strong desire *not* to be confused with or associated with other people. Some episodes of the colonial revival fall into this category, often with the kind of xenophobic implications explored centrally in William B. Rhoads's "Colonial Revival

and the Americanization of Immigrants" and investigated more peripherally elsewhere in this volume.

8. What happens in the episodes gathered in these essays is in no way the natural, predictable, or inevitable turn of events. We fail to seize a productive approach to this material if we slip into the comfortable habit of seeing in it the normal or obvious order of things. In order to crack the cultural meaning of a phenomenon—particularly one that does *seem* the regular order of things—we profit from obtaining the perspective of an outsider. As long as we can maintain a sense of being startled by what we see, even an inclination to believe we have stumbled onto truly weird behavior, we have a better chance of appreciating how a phenomenon actually functions in our culture or in a culture of the past. Once we begin to think that what we encounter is perfectly reasonable and inevitable, we are no longer efficient analysts, and deeper meanings of the phenomena we confront are likely to elude us.

9. Objects play a central role in the processes of the colonial revival. This may seem self-evident or a self-fulfilling prophecy. Yet it is no foregone conclusion that the processes of the colonial revival should be so deeply grounded in objects. Nevertheless, if we were to turn the problem around and start with an inquiry into the nature of the colonial revival and the forms it takes, we would probably come up with much the same conclusion: in these processes objects are crucial. It is difficult to follow the strand of the colonial very far without reference to objects. As Celia Betsky's "Inside the Past: The Interior and the Colonial Revivial in American Art and Literature, 1860–1914" and Seaton's "Pedigree for a New Century" demonstrate, the colonial revival has literary manifestations, and the colonial surely ripples through other forms of verbal behavior, but the mind runs out of suggestions fast if we exclude material culture. We can partially explain this situation by recalling the double role that objects so frequently play: they are expressions of the culture, and they are the medium that reinforces the culture or that creates some new culture. Material culture has always been one of the major means of controlling or shaping society. Whether the intention that motivates the manipulation of objects is judged benevolent or malevolent is of secondary significance. It is more important merely to realize that objects have social impact. And such impact is a leitmotiv running through these papers, all of which closely relate objects to the dynamics of human interaction.

10. One final observation summarizes and encapsulates the previous ones and brings us back into confrontation with the relationship between material artifacts and the study of history: the past is most evocatively preserved in physical surroundings. As Maurice Halbwachs noted in *The Collective Memory* (1950; reprint ed., New York: Harper & Row, 1980), collective memories (or what we generally think of as history) unfold within spatial frameworks. The legitimacy of these memories (or histories) is irrelevant; the critical issue is that ideas, events, and people endure because objects do. It seems to me that this underlies the entire set of papers and explains the centrality of objects in a retrospective phenomenon like the colonial revival.

If the multifaceted engagements with the colonial charted here have no single cause or impetus, we can at least identify some of the major forces that seem to propel them. These might be divided into two general groups: *persisting* and *changing*.

The persisting forces include fundamental and recurring impulses, like ancestor worship and the need to generate myths of beginnings. Neither of these (in actuality facets of the same irrational emotional needs) is often acknowledged in discussions of the colonial revival. For that matter, neither is often entertained explicitly in general literature about America, as if such behavior, appropriate for "less civilized" peoples in some other part of the world, were cause for embarrassment among us here. At least some of the colonial revival gestures discussed in this volume can be viewed as variations on these ubiquitous—if rarely discussed—themes.

Not far remote from such forces as ancestor worship and myths of origin are myths of a golden age. These too are persisting impulses, capable of emerging in any social setting, particularly one undergoing dynamic change. In golden-age myths the colonial dimension is largely a product of circumstance, as it is with ancestor worship and myths of origin. Different ancestors and different origins would have inspired other settings for visions of a golden age.

In opposition to persisting forces are more specifically historical movements, most of which seem to cluster in three sets: (1) responses to modernization, (2) expressions of nationalism, and (3) strategies to cope with America's social and cultural diversity. The first two of these represent American variations on international themes, but the third is particularly an American case.

What tend often to be ignored in looking at the American colonial revival are its parallels with behavior in other parts of the world. A narrow obsession with American exceptionalism obscures the strands that tie American cultural experience to concurrent, antecedent, or subsequent behavior elsewhere. This is particularly true if we examine colonializing behavior as a response to modernization. However one defines it, modernization is a complex international phenomenon that originated in western Europe—Britain in particular—then spread to this country, and is still dawning on other areas of the world. Sweeping changes on many levels, incorporating technological, industrial, social, demographic, economic, cultural, and other transformations, bring both a profound sense of gain and an equally profound sense of loss. The sense of gain is largely reflected in an increased sentiment of material well-being; the sense of loss is generated by the disappearance of once-familiar objects or events that are no longer required in the modernized society. Social reaction to loss takes many forms. We may see a rise of interest in folklore and folkways at the very moment when such lore and such ways are becoming obsolete. Or we may witness the cultural reevaluation of preindustrial labor and handicraft, both of which were taken for granted before the industrial age made handicraft a vanishing folkway and thereby endowed it with new meanings. Perhaps ironically, those whose livelihoods and fortunes are based on industrialism are often those who most enthusiastically sing the praises of preindustrial ways and who become most deeply committed to their preservation.

Central elements of the response to modernism are an orientation toward either preindustrial times in the past or nonindustrial alternatives in the present, an emphasis on handicraft, an antiurban bias—which usually translates into an emphasis on rural life—and an inclination to stress simple rather than complex social structures, homogeneous, cooperative folk rather than diverse, competitive people. These are the reverse of the most dominant features of modernism. Similar patterns with only minor variations can be found in most western European nations.

That modernization was more critical in generating the colonial revival in America than motivations grounded in political history, for example, is attested to by the curious but readily documentable fact that *colonial* was loosely used well into the twentieth century to mean the period before about 1840. That is, it described the period before the onset of

Victorianism, which in America is virtually interchangeable with modernization. In this country, *colonial* can be seen as a code word for anti- or non-Victorian, anti- or nonmodern.

A subset of these antimodern sentiments is an emphasis on domesticity. By no means do all of these papers address the colonial revival in a domestic setting, but home life is a most salient dimension of the phenomenon. As my earlier comments suggest, the domestic sphere may well be the major focus of colonializing activity. While it is not clear that the nineteenth-century American emphasis on domesticity can be seen wholly as a response to modernization, some links seem likely. Certainly, the changing configurations and furnishings of the home consume an inordinate amount of time and energy and take curious forms. The period room is a forceful reminder of the evocative power of domesticity and of the nineteenth-century inclination to think both literally and metaphorically in terms of rooms. Premodern relics play central roles in period rooms, so that we find it possible to recite a list of objects high in symbolic content, as Betsky has done in "Inside the Past."

Another instance in which the response to modernism tended to focus on domesticity is the extraordinary emphasis on the kitchen as a conveyor of multiple values and meanings. The so-called New England kitchens that were so much a part of early colonial revival activities are particularly telling manifestations of this interest. As Rodris Roth's "New England or 'Olde Tyme' Kitchen Exhibit at Nineteenth-Century Fairs" demonstrates, these allegedly rural, preindustrial spaces set up in the most thoroughly urbanized areas of the industrial North were decked out with heavily evocative artifacts like spinning wheels and tall clocks. The kitchens pulled together a number of anthropologically and sociologically charged themes. As kitchens they acknowledged the significance of foodways as cultural carriers and implements of social bonding. As areas in the home normally associated with women, kitchens also provided spaces for female activities that may be seen as equivalents to the heroic male events and accomplishments of the older time, fitting nicely within mid nineteenth-century notions of separate spheres of influence for men and women. The kitchens also offered a bit of social irony and inversion. In them, elegant folk escaped from some of the social dogma and decorum of their own day to dine and chat in nonformal spaces radically different from the heavily ritualized rooms in which their dining activities normally took place. What these people might never have done in the kitchens of their own homes or in those of their social peers was both enjoyable and acceptable in these short-term inversions of the modern world. The appeal of the New England kitchens was pervasive, and the exhibits outlived the fairs that spawned them. As Melinda Young Frye suggests in "The Beginnings of the Period Room in American Museums: Charles P. Wilcomb's Colonial Kitchens, 1896, 1906, 1910," they were the origin of the period room, still a popular museum-installation type today.

Is nationalism part of modernization, or are the two merely coexistent? For most of the Europeanized world during the nineteenth century, nationalism was an important political and cultural force. Part of nation-building is the need to create a central national experience and a central core of myths and values. Repeatedly in the accounts of American colonial revival efforts we find that patriotism is perceived as a major motive for preservation or restoration. Early examples, like Mount Vernon or Washington's Headquarters at Newburgh, New York, were explained almost wholly in patriotic terms. Today these expressions of patriotic fervor seem somewhat quaint and naive, and we may be inclined to view the patriotic impulses as historic artifacts themselves. The evidence of the past, including the not-so-distant past, demonstrates that people realized the necessity of preserving relics in order to keep ideas and ideals alive. The most abstract cultural values need to be grounded in some tangible and verifiable truths. Some of these relics, like Mount Vernon, were unique but were given widespread impact through such strategies as designing a governing board with representatives from all states. But some artifacts, particularly house styles and household furnishings, could be replicated readily, making it possible to spread patriotic thoughts and feelings to almost any place in the nation. That the colonial became the vehicle for national identity is again largely an accident of history, since any objects associated with the formative years of nation-building probably could have been transformed into positive and potent icons of that period.

The third cluster of themes, which I have identified as responses to cultural diversification, might be seen as a particularly American problem within the larger context of nationalism. One of the distinguishing characteristics of this country, and an important part of its international image, is its role as a home for people of many nationalities. While an ethnically heterogeneous citizenry fostered America's image as a land of prosperity open to all, it created significant social tensions, both among the older stock, which felt threatened on many levels by the newcomers, and among the newcomers themselves, the "uprooted," who sometimes found social and cultural change excruciatingly difficult. Here the role of the colonial revival was to expedite acculturation and socialization. Rhoads treats this role explicitly in terms of Americanization. That the language for Americanization was colonial is, again, a historic accident, but this did not reduce its effectiveness as a central core around which a cohesive society might be fabricated from disparate parts.

This core of beliefs, values, and even rituals has sometimes been called a civil religion, although it is not at all clear that viewing such behavior as religious leads to productive insights. All societies need shared symbols and values; without them they are only an agglomeration of people. Although there are parallels between the colonial revival and religion—in functional and structural properties and because such systems ultimately rest on untestable articles of faith—it is more significant to note that every society evolves the rules by which it will operate and the symbols it will honor, and to describe these universal processes of social coherence as religion stretches the word beyond useful meaning. Better to see the extraordinary success of the colonial revival into our own day as evidence of a need to continue to reaffirm in nonverbal terms certain tenets and values perceived as central to American life and the American experience.

The most fundamental question this collection of essays raises is whether deep immersion into the past can be read as a positive, affirmative action or whether it might be seen more accurately as an act of cultural desperation. The evidence does not support a rosy view of the colonial revival, which strikes me first and foremost as the product of a reactive stance. In the majority of the cases outlined in this book, the colonial is more an instance of cultural retaliation than a positive statement of social outreach. Healthy organisms live in the present; those who live mostly in the past cannot or will not deal with the present. This is true for both individuals and societies. My judgment is that while a little colonial revival may be a good thing, a great deal of it is a sign of personal or group disorder. I am perfectly willing to be persuaded to the contrary, but such persuasion is not to be found in these essays. I am curious to know what others will think after reading this volume and reflecting on its testimony.

Another City upon a Hill: Litchfield, Connecticut, and the Colonial Revival
William Butler

This paper analyzes the changing image of the New England village and how it became a national symbol during the colonial revival. Litchfield, Connecticut, a stereotypical town that popular sentiment perceives as a realistic representation of an eighteenth-century colonial village, is in fact an idealized interpretation of what elite society during the late nineteenth and early twentieth centuries thought was colonial.[1]

A typical New England town in the modern landscape is a nucleated village of white clapboard houses lining elm-shaded streets, with a simple Congregational church, a general store, and a small schoolhouse surrounding a parklike green (fig. 1). We perceive this classic setting as

[1] The term *colonial* in the context of this study requires an explanation. When I document and interpret the colonial landscape of Litchfield I am referring to 1719–80, or roughly from the town's first English settlement to just before the close of the Revolution. *Colonial* is used popularly and loosely today to describe the style and epoch of the eighteenth century, particularly the years surrounding the Revolution. During the colonial revival, popular culture thought of the colonial period as starting in 1620, with the landing of the Pilgrims, and ending around 1840, with the beginnings of industrialization. Some architectural historians during the colonial revival were aware of the inexact use of this word: C. Matlack Price coincidentally raised this issue in "Historic Houses of Litchfield," *White Pine Series of Architectural Monographs* 5, no. 3 (June 1919): 13–14. Also in this article (and for the first time in the monograph series), Price discussed the stereotypical image of the New England town, using Litchfield as an example.

Fig. 1. Village Green, Litchfield, Conn., March 1982. (Photo, William Butler.)

a monument to colonial America, a monument unchanged since the eighteenth century. We assume that Puritans, in search of religious freedom, founded this typical settlement in the midst of a hostile wilderness. Small-town boys grew up here, fought for our nation's independence, and then became famous statesmen. This village is steeped in Yankee tradition and conservatism; it is the home of town-meeting democracy and the "American experience." Most of the inhabitants are genteel farmers living in houses built by their Revolutionary ancestors. George Washington *must* have slept here.

But the New England town has not always evoked such stereotypes and has undergone significant alterations since the earliest English settlements. Even contemporary geographers and architectural historians have perpetuated the stereotype of the New England town, basing their conclusions on romanticized tradition, misconceptions, and erroneous town histories. Geographer John Brinckerhoff Jackson is perhaps the first scholar to raise questions about the accuracy of popular as well as scholarly images of the archetypal New England town. In "Several American Landscapes" Jackson cautions his readers that "no landscape has ever changed so profoundly and so swiftly as ours; not merely within the recent past but from its very beginning. So completely did the Colonial landscape vanish during the nineteenth century that aside from a few monuments nothing remains of it." Despite doubts such as these, scholars have never sufficiently analyzed the rethinking and—more important—the reshaping of the New England town during the colonial revival.[2] An understanding of these processes of transformation requires an accurate documentation of the colonial, or pre-Revolutionary, landscape as well as a brief history of the New England village and its changing role in American ideology.

Boston, the first community in the Massachusetts Bay Colony, was intended to be a compact agricultural village planned around a meetinghouse and governed by a Christian covenant that promoted unity and equality. This fabled "city upon a hill," however, like similar Puritan settlements, began to break down after its first generation of establishment. By the mid seventeenth century most New Englanders did not live in compact villages, but rather on dispersed farmsteads.[3] Those

[2] J. B. Jackson, "Several American Landscapes," in *Landscapes: Selected Writings of J. B. Jackson*, ed. Ervin H. Zube (Amherst: University of Massachusetts Press, 1970), p. 43. For the transformation of the natural landscape of the New England town during the late nineteenth century, see J. B. Jackson, *American Space: The Centennial Years, 1865–1876* (New York: W. W. Norton, 1972), pp. 87–136; David P. Handlin, *The American Home: Architecture and Society, 1815–1915* (Boston: Little, Brown, 1979), pp. 93–116; and Jay Cantor, *The Landscape of Change: Views of Rural New England, 1790–1865* (Sturbridge, Mass.: Old Sturbridge Village, 1976). For further reading on the New England town in American ideology, see D. W. Meinig, "Symbolic Landscapes: Some Idealizations of American Communities," in *The Interpretation of Ordinary Landscapes*, ed. D. W. Meinig (New York: Oxford University Press, 1979), pp. 164–88; and Page Smith, *As a City upon a Hill: The Town in American History* (New York: Alfred A. Knopf, 1966).

[3] For an excellent study of the geographic transformation of the New England town from 1630 to 1830, see Joseph S. Wood, "The Origin of the New England Village" (Ph.D. diss., Pennsylvania State University, 1978). For a general study of Connecticut towns, see Bruce C. Daniels, *The Connecticut Town: Growth and Development, 1635–1790* (Middletown, Conn.: Wesleyan University Press, 1979); and Anthony N. B. Gar-

who did live within the boundaries of a town built town or village centers that contained nothing more than a meetinghouse, a school, a tavern, and a few houses.

The nucleated village did not emerge in New England until after the Revolution, when our nation experienced commercial, transportation, and general economic expansion.[4] The hill villages of northwestern Connecticut and Massachusetts particularly enjoyed a "golden age" between 1780 and 1830; several became modern urban villages, prospering with stylish architecture, new industry, and increased business.

During the next generation, however, many New England hill villages suffered from a steady decline in manufacturing, commerce, and population. Their difficult mountainous geography prevented the establishment of a railroad network, thereby cutting off substantial trade. Agriculture, in turn, diminished as farmers either relocated on more productive land in the West or moved to large cities for factory work. This change especially altered the colonial character of the New England landscape as river and coastal towns, with more powerful water sources, gradually became industrial cities, while once-prosperous hill villages gracefully aged as fashionable Victorian summer resorts.

Wealthy city folk were largely responsible for transforming colonial urban villages, essentially barren of natural vegetation, into "picturesque" or countrified towns. They formed Village Improvement Societies, which decorated streets with towering shade trees and inviting parks. These summer residents broke away from classical tradition to build stylish Gothic and Italianate cottages that better harmonized with the natural colors of the landscape. Beautification and architectural changes in resorts such as Stockbridge, Massachusetts, or Litchfield, Connecticut, in no way recreated America's historical past. Most of elite society during the mid nineteenth century were modernists, too

---

van, *Architecture and Town Planning in Colonial Connecticut* (New Haven: Yale University Press, 1951). For the social, political, cultural, and demographic changes of the colonial New England town, see Richard L. Bushman, *From Puritan to Yankee: Character and Social Order in Connecticut, 1690–1765* (New York: W. W. Norton, 1970); Kenneth A. Lockridge, *A New England Town: The First Hundred Years, Dedham, Massachusetts, 1636–1736* (New York: W. W. Norton, 1970); and Darrett B. Rutman, *Winthrop's Boston: Portrait of a Puritan Town, 1630–1649* (Chapel Hill: University of North Carolina Press, 1965).
[4] Wood, "New England Village," p. 5.

preoccupied with the progress of the present to think about the past.[5] Our nation had written histories, celebrated patriotic anniversaries, and formed historical repositories, but because our nation was so new, we interpreted our heritage as an index of how far we had come, not as what we should revert to.

By the 1860s, however, Americans were becoming increasingly bewildered by the effects of industrialization, urbanization, and immigration. Society became increasingly stratified culturally, economically, and politically, at last fighting a civil war. Disillusionment with the war, discontentment with reconstruction, and a severe financial panic in 1873 prompted Americans to reminisce about what seemed a more stable and less complicated past. The centennial celebration of 1876 extolled the advancement of modern machinery while at the same time it encouraged Americans to appreciate their national heritage. Writing in 1877, architect Robert Swain Peabody observed that with the Centennial we "discovered that we too have a past worthy of study. . . . Our Colonial work is our only native source of antiquarian study and inspiration."[6] A new historical consciousness had indeed been discovered as a better source of inspiration for the present and the future. A colonial revival resulted.

Architecture was the most effective material manifestation of the colonial revival. As an early chronicler of the movement wrote, "Architecture is crystallized history . . . it represent[s] the life of the past in visible and enduring form."[7] New England–style architecture tended to dominate taste during most of the colonial revival. Just as New England monopolized biased American histories, so too did it monopolize architecture. Architects thought that New England buildings were the oldest American buildings and therefore the most truly American. The prevailing taste for colonial New England, furthermore, represented Northern

---

[5] David Lowenthal, "The Place of the Past in the American Landscape," in *Geographies of the Mind*, ed. Martyn Bowden and David Lowenthal (New York: Oxford University Press, 1976), pp. 106–9.

[6] [Robert S. Peabody], "Georgian Houses of New England," *American Architect and Building News* 2 (October 20, 1877): 338; also quoted in William B. Rhoads, "The Colonial Revival and American Nationalism," *Journal of the Society of Architectural Historians* 35, no. 4 (December 1976): 242

[7] Harold D. Eberlein, *The Architecture of Colonial America* (Boston: Little, Brown, 1915), p. 1.

supremacy to a society recently recovering from a war between its states.

William B. Rhoads has pointed out that patriotic sentiment was one of the appealing forces behind colonial-style architecture. Native Americans restored historic buildings and built modern colonial revival structures as a sign of nationalism.[8] In addition, these structures could function as symbols of ancestry and social status. Immigrants, although living in cities, could at least identify themselves with colonial revival buildings because the immigrant was himself a "modern colonial" in the American landscape.

During the last three decades of the nineteenth century, the intensification of industrialization, urbanization, and immigration threatened the identity of white Anglo-Saxon Protestants. Individual colonial or colonial revival buildings standing alone did not satisfy the ideological needs of elite WASP society, which began to search for a comprehensive colonial environment. It sought refuge in the venerable New England town. Here history pervaded; one found a higher concentration of colonial structures as well as inhabitants of "superior native stock." The wealthy upper class could easily escape the poverty, filth, and overcrowding in cities to summer in the Arcadian hills of New England. Elites further transformed the urban village (became Victorian resort) into an emblem of what they thought best symbolized colonialism: stability, morality, and democracy. In many popular novels, writers such as Harriet Beecher Stowe—born and raised in Litchfield—romanticized life in New England towns at the turn of the nineteenth century.[9] The widespread "country life movement" of the Progressive Era monumentalized the colonial New England village as an archetype for all of rural America to emulate. Vachel Lindsay, poet and promoter of rural improvement, suggested in one of his widely circulated "proclamations" that the United States become a new "New England of ninety million souls." By the early twentieth century the ubiquitous New England village was a popular subject for art, literature, and advertising and had become a stereotype in the American mind. It was a treasured

---

[8] Rhoads, "Colonial Revival," pp. 239–54.

[9] Harriet Beecher Stowe idealized the town of Litchfield in her widely acclaimed novel *Pogonuc People* (New York: Fords, Howard, and Hulbert, 1878). Stowe's brother, Henry Ward Beecher, partially based *Norwood: Village Life in New England* (New York: Charles Scribner, 1869) on Litchfield. During the last quarter of the nineteenth century many prominent writers and local town historians wrote short stories and novels about earlier life in New England towns.

image so familiar to people everywhere that Thornton Wilder did not
use a scenic backdrop, but just a few evocative lines, to recreate Grov-
er's Corner, New Hampshire, in *Our Town*.[10] Even the possessive
pronoun in the title further suggested that the landscape was distinctly
American and symbolic.

Certain New England villages figured more prominently than others
as archetypes during the colonial revival. Writers continually praised
Stockbridge, Massachusetts, for having the first Village Improvement
Society in America. Places such as Old Lyme, Connecticut, and Cornish, New Hampshire, were noted as exclusive artists' colonies. Deerfield, Massachusetts, gained admiration for its "untouched" charm.
Wallace Nutting, like many writers and travelers, favored the hill country of northwestern Connecticut. Nutting boldly proclaimed in *Connecticut Beautiful* that this state was "a museum of late seventeenth and
early eighteenth century American life. Her numerous historical societies have done far more than Massachusetts, or indeed, than any other
state in keeping for us the examples and the records of what is very old.
. . . Connecticut landscapes are more definitely defined as early American scenes than any other part of our land."[11]

Litchfield, Connecticut, was one of the most admired New England
villages during the colonial revival. Local tradition records that Sinclair
Lewis once said that the "only street in America more beautiful than
North Street in Litchfield was South Street in Litchfield."[12] Photographs of this village accompanied numerous national advertisements
for everything from white paint to old-fashioned candy. During the late
nineteenth and early twentieth centuries, American architectural history books, academic journals, and popular periodicals featured articles
and measured drawings of the town's colonial architecture. Litchfield
furthermore attracted worldwide recognition in 1913 as the first town in
America to remodel its historic landscape comprehensively in the colonial style.

[10] Vachel Lindsay, "Proclamation of the New Time for Farmers and the New New
England," *Rural Manhood* 4, no. 6 (June 4, 1913): 186. For an interpretation of *Our
Town*, see Meinig, "Symbolic Landscapes," p. 174.

[11] Wallace Nutting, *Connecticut Beautiful* (Garden City, N. Y.: Garden City Publishing Co., 1923), p. 7.

[12] Mrs. Ludlow S. Bull, interview with William Butler, Litchfield, June 1980. Sinclair
Lewis first said this to Ludlow Bull in the early 1920s, and the statement has been widely
quoted since in articles about the town.

The legacy of a landscape like Litchfield's persists into modern times. The "typical" New England village still answers to the aspirations and normative values of Americans. In the prologue to their McCarthy-era book, *Frontier of Freedom: The Soul and Substance of America Portrayed in One Extraordinary Village, Old Deerfield, Massachusetts,* Samuel Chamberlain and Henry Flynt saw the New England village as an answer to Communist anti-American propaganda:

there is a legion of . . . replies to the vilification of the Communists, and they do not need to be couched in calumny or hollow phrases. They can even be expressed pleasantly. Visual truth speaks louder than words in contradicting propaganda. A graphic picture of one of a hundred phrases of American life— a state university, a western farm, a New England village—can be the most eloquent response to the strident falsehoods poisoning the air today. We have chosen the symbol of a specific village street. Among many others, it demonstrates the calm strength of America today.[13]

Chamberlain demonstrated the strength of the New England village and perpetuated its image in popular culture by publishing between 1930 and 1975 several photographic-essay books, postcard series, and calendars featuring his favorite towns. Litchfield appears to have been the epitome of the stereotype, Chamberlain ennobling its Congregational Church on the cover of his 1962 book, *The New England Image.*

During the colonial revival most of the inhabitants of Litchfield believed that they were living in a unique city upon a hill that accurately recreated the look of colonial times. Wooden houses painted an "old-fashioned" white with dark-colored blinds, towering elm trees arching over streets, a well-manicured village green, and a classical Congregational church were the most important elements of this idyllic setting. The homogeneity of the landscape and the pristine quality of the architecture suggested perfect eighteenth-century order. The conventional historical interpretation of Litchfield's settlement relied on the a priori assumption that its first inhabitants had cleared a "pioneer wilderness" and bravely established a nucleated village around a meetinghouse. The

[13] Samuel Chamberlain and Henry N. Flynt, *Frontier of Freedom: The Soul and Substance of America Portrayed in One Extraordinary Village, Old Deerfield, Mass.* (New York: Hastings House, 1957), p. 1.

community remained church-oriented and compact throughout the seventeenth and eighteenth centuries.[14] Until the Revolution, most families lived in crude log cabins. After the war, a newly rich mercantile class built fashionable homes in Litchfield, and the town became part of the sophisticated "polite world." Litchfield deliquesced into an isolated but dignified backwater in the nineteenth century, only to be restored to its "colonial" grandeur during the early part of the present century.

It is true that Litchfield's comprehensive restoration did not convince everyone. An early skeptic remarked: "The village looked more colonial in 1930 than it *ever* did in the colonial era."[15] But this response was exceptional; few people had doubts about the appearance of Litchfield's contrived landscape during the late nineteenth and early twentieth centuries. The town's first history, printed in 1845, relied almost exclusively on tradition and one man's memory of the past, rather than on documented facts. Subsequent histories, down to this day, expand upon and perpetuate Litchfield's mythology. In order to understand the misconceptions and idealizations embodied in the colonial revival landscape we must begin with an unromanticized documentation and interpretation of colonial Litchfield.

Third-generation New Englanders established Litchfield in 1719 as part of the late frontier settlement of northwestern Connecticut. This wilderness community in the foothills of the Berkshire Mountains was 30 miles west of Hartford and 102 miles northwest of New York City. The original town measured 10 miles square; its nucleus contained a mile-long plateau of large farm lots. Litchfield was a speculative or proprietary settlement, and about half of its original investors, or approximately thirty heads of households, actually lived in the town. Only about ten families permanently settled within the nucleus; the rest lived on dispersed farms.

During the first generation of settlement most families lived in one- or two-room unpainted plank structures (fig. 2). A Congregational meetinghouse in the "plain" style stood on common land in the center of the village. A few houses and three large garrisons were the only other

---

[14] For a more detailed discussion of the conventional interpretation of the New England town, see Wood, "New England Village," pp. 1–57.

[15] Harmon Poole, interview with Butler, Litchfield, June 1980.

Fig. 2. Anonymous, two-room house, Litchfield, ca. 1790. Pencil on paper. This house type was built in the town between 1719 and 1760. (Litchfield Historical Society.)

structures within the nucleus. By the 1740s, land records indicate that inhabitants built larger two- and four-room houses, presumably in the latest style.

In 1751 Litchfield became the shiretown for Litchfield County and grew in area and population. The first recorded population was 1,366 in 1756. Although the town was an important administrative center, a map drawn by Ezra Stiles in 1762 (fig. 3) indicates that while some 220 families owned farms or mill sites on the outskirts of town, only about 30 lived within the nucleus, mainly rich attorneys, physicians, and merchants, a schoolteacher, a clergyman, and several tavernkeepers. These "professional gentlemen" built fashionable five-bay houses (fig. 4) painted shades of red, brown, green, and blue—if they were painted at all.[16] Such houses usually had rear additions of a kitchen ell, a sink

[16] I am indebted to Sara B. Chase, of the Society for the Preservation of New England Antiquities, and Richard Candee, preservation consultant, for sharing with me their research and knowledge of eighteenth-century paint colors.

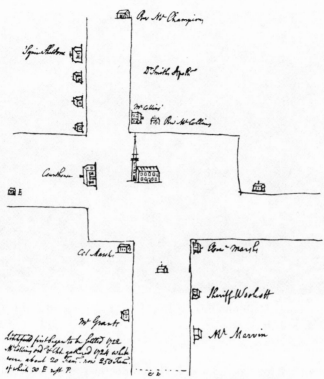

Fig. 3. Ezra Stiles, map of Litchfield, 1762. Pen and ink on paper. The small structure in the middle of the road just below the center is a Sabba-day house of the type that was built between 1719 and 1790. (Litchfield Historical Society.)

room, a wood house, and a stable. Interior rather than exterior shutters prevailed. Most houses did not have front lawns; they abutted unshaded dirt streets. Pigpens, poultry yards, vegetable gardens, an outhouse, and several barns were close to the main house.

"Sabba-day," or nooning, houses, common in the eighteenth century, were extinct by the early nineteenth. These buildings were small one- or two-room impermanent structures that farmers who lived on

Fig. 4. Thomas Catlin house, Litchfield, ca. 1760. (Courtesy Litchfield Historical Society.)

the outskirts of town used for warmth and noonday meals between religious services on the Sabbath. They also functioned as town houses when a farmer conducted extended business in the village center. The town allowed farmers to build Sabba-day houses on common land, the most popular place being the middle of a street (see fig. 3).

When Ezra Stiles drew his map the second Congregational meetinghouse was an unpainted structure less than a year old. It was not "coloured" until ten years later. In all likelihood, the original color was a stone red. This conclusion is based on microscopic analysis of Ralph Earl portraits, which reveals that although the steeple of the meetinghouse was white, the rest of the structure was red. A sketch by Mary Anne Lewis also shows that this meetinghouse was red as late as 1817 (fig. 5).[17] A classic white Congregational church did not appear in

[17] See, for example, Ralph Earl's painting *Mrs. Benjamin Tallmadge* (1790) at Litchfield Historical Society. The Mary Anne Lewis sketch of the second Congregational meet-

Fig. 5. Mary Ann Lewis, Congregational meetinghouse, ca. 1780. Pencil and watercolor on paper.
(Litchfield Historical Society.)

Litchfield until the 1820s, perhaps as late as the third church structure
of 1829.

Meetinghouse, courthouse, jail, tavern, and schoolhouse stood in
the middle of Litchfield's main intersection. There was no parklike green

---

inghouse was rediscovered at Litchfield Historical Society in June 1980. Because it shows
a red structure, this sketch was rarely used in historical studies of the town. For a seminal
study of the prevailing use of colors other than white on colonial meetinghouses, see
Peter Benes, "Sky Colors and Scattered Clouds: The Decorative and Architectural Painting of New England Meetinghouses, 1738–1834," in *New England Meeting House and
Church, 1630–1850,* ed. Peter Benes (Boston: Boston University, 1979), pp. 51–69.

with ornamental rows of trees in the town's village center during the colonial period. Writers referred to this location as an open "area," "square," or "space," containing market stalls, hitching posts, and animal pens in addition to garbage heaps and woodpiles. Until the revolutionary war, there were no more than fifty buildings within Litchfield's nucleus. The town essentially was a milling and agricultural settlement.[18]

During the Revolution, however, Litchfield became a strategic crossroads for travelers en route to Boston, Hartford, Albany, or New York. Craftsmen, merchants, and innkeepers began building up the village center. The town played a renowned role in our nation's struggle for freedom. Gov. Oliver Wolcott, a signer of the Declaration of Independence and a brigadier general of the Connecticut militia, came from an old Litchfield family. Ethan Allen was a native son. Folklore has it that the famous Regiment of Horse—led by Col. Elisha Sheldon of Litchfield—was George Washington's favorite corps. Washington also visited Litchfield on several occasions. The town served as an important outpost for supply storage and maintained a secret prison for British spies. The most famous event occurred when the Sons of Liberty tore down the lead equestrian statue of King George III from its pedestal on Bowling Green in New York City and then secretly shipped it to Litchfield, where it was melted down for bullets. Such people and events, of course, were glorified during the colonial revival.

After the war Litchfield enjoyed a "golden age of prosperity" as a commercial and industrial urban village. The town was noted as a center for progressive education. In 1784 Judge Tapping Reeve founded the first private law school in America, training future vice-presidents, senators, congressmen, and, among others, John C. Calhoun, John M. Clayton, Horace Mann, Noah Webster, and Samuel F. B. Morse. Sarah Pierce started the first female academy in America, attracting a distinguished group of young ladies from all over the United States. Miss Pierce's school pioneered education as well as equal rights for women. The reputation of these academic institutions combined with a growing mercantile economy to foster a new prosperity in Litchfield.

The stark urban appearance of northwestern Connecticut's hill vil-

[18]Marquis de Chastellux, *Travels in North America in the Years 1780, 1781 and 1782,* trans. Howard C. Rice, vol. 1 (Chapel Hill: University of North Carolina Press, 1963), p. 81; "A Traveller Observes," *Litchfield Monitor* (June 29, 1803).

lages impressed travelers during the colonial period. Sensitive observers particularly admired the stylishness of Litchfield's federal architecture. William Martin, a well-traveled southerner, remarked that Litchfield was "one of the most beautiful towns in the world with houses that were large and elegant, neatly arranged and all painted." Several writers commented on the "impressive size and very elegant fashion of the meetinghouses." Timothy Dwight felt that the county courthouse was "handsomer than any other in the state." The contrasting countryside also attracted the attention of numerous visitors, J. P. Brissot de Warville referring to the region as the "paradise of the United States."[19] Ralph Earl perhaps best captured Litchfield's fashionable buildings and lush countryside. Wealthy families such as the Wolcotts and the Tallmadges proudly commissioned him to paint their portraits with their new homes, the Congregational Church, and rolling hills as the background. It was Litchfield's landscape that inspired Earl to be among the first formally trained American artists to paint sitters in a local rather than a classical setting.

During the golden age of New England's hill villages, homes and shops built close together in a congested nucleus on treeless wide-open streets were positive signs of modernity and "civilized advancement." In the late 1780s when Oliver Wolcott, Jr., planted thirteen sycamore trees in honor of the thirteen original colonies, town elders criticized him for obstructing progress by reforesting the streets that the town's founding fathers had worked so hard to clear. By colonial standards, treeless streets represented order and man's dominance over the landscape. In *Greenfield Hill* (1794) Timothy Dwight described a "flourishing" village as one where "industry resounds." Dwight's poem, like Earl's paintings, was a fitting tribute to America's distinctive landscape. As Kenneth Silverman has postulated, *Greenfield Hill* was the first *lengthy* poem in America consciously written for a native audience.[20] Both Dwight

---

[19] William D. Martin, travel journal from South Carolina to Connecticut, 1809 (typed transcript), Litchfield Historical Society; Timothy Dwight, *Travels in New England and New York*, ed. Barbara Miller Solomon, vol. 2 (1821–22; Cambridge, Mass.: Harvard University Press, Belknap Press, 1969), pp. 257–59; J. P. Brissot de Warville, *New Travels in the United States of America*, 1788, trans. Mara S. Vamos and Durand Echeverria (1791; Cambridge, Mass.: Harvard University Press, Belknap Press, 1964), p. 117.

[20] *Litchfield Monitor* (January 3, 1788). There were some decorative landmark trees along Litchfield's streets during the late eighteenth and early nineteenth centuries, but these were not regimented rows of arching elms; instead, townspeople planted clusters of

and Earl provided Americans with some of the earliest images that eventually contributed to the stereotype of the ideal New England village.

By 1810 Litchfield was the fourth largest settlement in Connecticut, with a population of 4,639. There were over 400 farmsteads on the outskirts of town, in addition to the following mills and manufactories: 4 iron forges, 5 large and 5 small tanneries, 1 nail, 1 cotton, and 2 comb manufactories, 5 gristmills, 18 sawmills, and 1 slitting, 1 oil, 1 paper, and 6 fulling mills. Litchfield's nucleus now contained over 125 houses, shops, and public buildings, including 2 churches, 1 court-house, 3 schools, 2 bookstores, 10 taverns, 2 brickyards, 1 post office, 1 bank, and 1 jail as well as structures occupied by 1 newspaper, 2 hatters, 2 carriagemakers, 11 justices of the peace, 7 attorneys-at-law, 8 physicians, 1 surgeon, 11 merchants, 3 goldsmiths, 19 house carpenters and/or joiners, 4 cabinetmakers, 3 saddlers, 3 blacksmiths, 3 potters, and 3 clothiers.[21]

There was no separate business district in Litchfield's village center during the colonial period. What *later* became sprawling residential streets during the colonial revival were congested commercial streets throughout the late eighteenth and early nineteenth centuries. An individual had either a shop or an office in his home or, if he was wealthy, built a separate building adjacent to his residence. Prosperous merchant Julius Deming lived in a house and store similar to that of Elijah Boardman (fig. 6). Deming made most of his money in the China trade as well as in several industrial enterprises that developed after the revolutionary war. He commissioned William Sprats to design his house in 1793, one that reflected the latest, "most elegant" style of architecture (fig. 7).[22] Accordingly, it was painted white, an uncommon color in Litchfield during the last decade of the eighteenth century. Deming's

oak, beech, horse chestnut, and Lombardy poplars. Such trees, however, often died before attaining substantial height. Timothy Dwight, *Greenfield Hill: A Poem in Seven Parts* (Greenfield, Conn.: By the author, 1794), pt. 2, lines 1–80. Kenneth Silverman analyzes this poem in *Timothy Dwight* (New York: Twayne Publishing, 1969), pp. 43–67.

[21] James Morris, *A Statistical Account of Litchfield, Connecticut* (n.p., 1810).

[22] The Elijah Boardman house was built in New Milford, Conn., in 1792. Both Boardman and Julius Deming came from the same mercantile background and class; the similarity between their homes is important for my discussion of the new federal style of architecture in Litchfield.

Fig. 6. Ralph Earl, *The Elijah Boardman House*. New Milford, Conn., 1796. Oil on canvas; H. 48″, W. 54″. (Cornelia Boardman Aldridge Service.)

fashionable house most likely stood out as a significant symbol of social status and economic wealth.

Recent research on the original colors of eighteenth-century New England structures shows that white was not popular. Only as part of the later neoclassical or federal aesthetic did light yellow ochers, pale pearl grays, and various shades of off-white become fashionable. Shades of white reached their peak in popularity between roughly 1810 and 1840, but these shades varied from a stone gray to a buff brown. The stark white so familiar to us today was, in fact, first produced during the colonial revival.[23]

[23] Again, I am indebted to Sara Chase and Richard Candee for this information on paint colors.

Fig. 7. William Sprats, facade and south elevation, Julius Deming house, Litchfield, 1793. Photo, 1875. (Collection of Mrs. Ludlow S. Bull, Litchfield.)

Litchfield reached the peak of its golden age during the 1820s when tradesmen, merchants, and professional gentlemen served a population of more than 4,600. Enrollment in both the Tapping Reeve Law School and Miss Pierce's Female Academy also reached a record high. The Reverend Lyman Beecher served the Congregational Church and directed an overwhelming religious revival. Rebecca Couch, a student at the academy, captured the prosperity of Litchfield at this time in a watercolor (fig. 8), and Benjamin Silliman, on his travels through New England in 1820, described the town in this way: "Litchfield Hill is a beautiful spot. One principal street extends more than a mile and contains a collection of very handsome houses with gardens and courtyards. The houses and appendages are generally painted white. And it is rare to see so considerable a number of houses in a country town where nearly all

Fig. 8. Rebecca Couch, *View of Litchfield, Connecticut*. Litchfield, ca. 1820. Watercolor and ink on wove paper; H. 12⅞", W. 16½". (Abby Aldrich Rockefeller Folk Art Collection.)

apparently belong to gentry . . . it presents a very interesting and gratifying spectacle."[24] Such a depiction made a lasting impression on Litchfield's residents. This classical image of the early nineteenth century, rather than the pre-Revolutionary pioneer appearance of the eighteenth, served as the archetype to which people looked when they "restored" the town during the colonial revival.

Beginning in the 1830s, Litchfield's political, educational, and economic structure drastically changed with the closing of the Tapping Reeve Law School, which yielded to competition from larger, more metropolitan law schools at Harvard and Yale universities. Litchfield lost its reputation as an influential legal center, along with a substantial

[24] Benjamin Silliman, *Geology, Mineralogy, Scenery, etc. in the Counties of New Haven and Litchfield* (New Haven, 1820), p. 27.

amount of related business and trade. As a means of recovery, a few entrepreneurs built larger mills and manufactories, only to find that Litchfield's rivers could not supply sufficient waterpower. Commercial activity drastically declined when the railroad bypassed the hill-top village. The population dropped below 4,500 as laborers, craftsmen, and merchants sought better work in the more industrial cities of Hartford, Waterbury, Danbury, New Haven, and Bridgeport.[25]

Agriculture also decreased substantially during the 1830s and 1840s as families abandoned their farms in Connecticut and moved to more competitive farming regions in the West. Such moves were familiar to Litchfield's agricultural population because Connecticut farmers had been in the forefront of settling the Western Reserve in Ohio since the late eighteenth century. During the later migration, farmers moved to Iowa, Illinois, and Michigan, taking their Connecticut culture with them. Each of these states has a town named after Litchfield. Settlements in Ohio often copied the plan and classical architecture of their native New England counterparts. Litchfield's Congregational Church, for example, inspired the Congregational Church in Tallmadge, Ohio, a tribute more than appropriate because the church's first minister was from Litchfield, Connecticut. Indeed, the town itself was named for Benjamin Tallmadge of Litchfield, a major land speculator on the Western Reserve. Such transmission of style was an important contribution to the West's stereotypical image of the New England village.

Although Litchfield experienced a rapid depopulation and dismantling of industry in the 1830s, it did not become a decadent backwater. Many of the wealthy "professional gentlemen" retired and continued to live in Litchfield as part of the landed aristocracy. A few lawyers and doctors moved to New York for career advancement but maintained their ancestral homes in Litchfield as country summer residences. The high price of real estate came down, and other well-to-do New Yorkers quietly began buying or building second homes in Litchfield. Year-round inhabitants welcomed these summer folk because they came from social, cultural, and economic backgrounds similar to those of the Litchfield natives and were, like them, descendants of old American families. Summer residents also brought increased revenue for the

[25] Clive Day, *The Rise of Manufacturing in Connecticut, 1820–1850* (New Haven: Yale University Press, 1935); John C. Herbst, "Hill Town—Valley Town: Goshen and Torrington, Connecticut" (M.A. thesis, Syracuse University, 1950).

townspeople and a new desire to create a more pastoral village. Along with the support of permanent Litchfield residents, summer residents planted trees and created a central park in 1835. Beautification efforts continued for another ten years, and the once-barren colonial village became a carefully landscaped Victorian resort. Residents planted irregular, overgrown greenery after Andrew Jackson Downing's "picturesque" fashion. Colonial picket fences were torn down so that the entire village would resemble a rambling park. Residents demolished most of the eighteenth-century shops, offices, and outbuildings and built asymmetrical, polychrome cottages in their place. Owners of colonial homes updated their houses with earth-tone color schemes and bracketed architectural details. Litchfield kept pace with the times, enjoying the transition from a commercial urban village to a residential country town.

By the mid nineteenth century several other towns in the Berkshires were summer retreats for old-money New Yorkers and Bostonians, influential figures who formed Village Improvement Societies that planned landscape beautification more carefully. The Reverends Horace Bushnell and B. G. Northrop (both of whom were born and raised in Litchfield County) as well as A. J. Downing promoted rural and village improvement nationwide. They suggested planting trees, ivy, and shrubbery that would grow to please the present generation and—more important—those of the future. This type of beautification did not evoke a sense of the past. Instead, as Downing stated, such improvements were a "powerful means of civilization . . . and progress."[26] *Improvement*, in this particular mid nineteenth-century context, meant modernization. Picturesque landscaping updated the old-fashioned bare streets. "Beautification is a town's prosperity" was a popular slogan for Village Improvement Societies, and *prosperity* meant modern advancement.

Progress and prosperity, in a sense, preoccupied the minds of most individuals in nineteenth-century America. We regarded ourselves as an abundant, superior, and unique nation; only in the United States,

[26] A. J. Downing, *The Architecture of Country Houses* (New York: D. Appleton, 1850), pp. xix–xx; A. J. Downing, "On the Improvement of Country Villages," *Horticulturalist* 3, no. 12 (1848): 545–49. See also David Schuyler's excellent review of David P. Handlin, *The American Home: Architecture and Society, 1815–1915*, in *Winterthur Portfolio* 16, no. 4 (Winter 1981): 350–51.

the land of opportunity, could the bucolic country town so successfully coexist with the industrial city. But not all Americans shared positive feelings about progress in the mid nineteenth century. There were some antimodernists who were skeptical of our nation's rapid industrial and urban expansion. Congregational theologian Horace Bushnell consequently advocated a stronger religious understanding of progress, modernization, and village improvement. In his nationally circulated essay *The Age of Homespun* (1851) Bushnell described Litchfield County's smooth transition from a primitive wilderness to a civilized culture, elevated through the advancement of industry, commerce, government, and education. He admonished unbelievers to have faith in God and his influence over the future.[27] Skepticism from all levels of society increased nonetheless as the next generation faced dramatic social changes in industrial cities and as our nation became politically and culturally divided in the Civil War.

During the postwar centennial celebration and subsequent colonial revival, America's new interest in the past prompted Village Improvement Societies to beautify towns in a different style. As cities and industry expanded uncontrollably, antimodernism intensified, and these societies began to historicize the landscape in what they thought was a proper colonial fashion.

In Litchfield people looked back not to the "age of homespun" as a colonial source, but to the golden age of prosperity, the period of the stylish white house that expressed order, balance, rationality, and security. Residents did not rely on documentary evidence for their colonial restorations, but based their work instead on traditions and memory, romanticizing, sentimentalizing, and idealizing the image of the colonial style, copying only the most elite features. Eager residents wanted what they perceived as an accurately reproduced colonial house, but they did not want the outbuildings, stables, shops, animal pens, and vegetable gardens that had originally gone along with such a house. The residents of Litchfield wanted the look of the flourishing federal village minus the signs of the period's commercialism and industrialism. They wanted to create what they deemed a more refined and dignified colonial setting. Home owners preferred flower to vegetable gardens, white

---

[27] Horace Bushnell, *The Age of Homespun* (Hartford: Edwin Hunt Publishing, 1851); also reprinted nationwide during the latter half of the nineteenth century in newspapers and collections of Bushnell's speeches and discourses.

to red houses. Elm-shaded streets were based on sparse historic references to sporadic tree plantings.

The Litchfielders, like so many of the colonial revivalists that were
to follow their example, worked less to achieve strict historical accuracy
than to create a generalized colonial conceit. In a recent article on
R. T. H. Halsey as curator of the original American Wing of the Metropolitan Museum of Art, Wendy Kaplan observed that "idealization of
the past [was] a reaction to fears of foreign contamination, industrialization, and irrevocable change in American life." She cited the observation of anthropologist Ralph Linton "that such idealization leads to
ancestor worship, whereby 'the society's members feel that by behaving
as the ancestors did they will, in some usually undefined way, help to
recreate the total situation in which the ancestors lived.' "[28] Having lost
a national sense of innocence after a shattering civil war, faced with a
bewildering influx of immigrants, and surveying the disintegration of
American agrarianism, the Litchfielders sought asylum in the idealized
New England village, commencing its elevation to the status of national
symbol.

Litchfield was at the forefront of a new phase of village improvement.
The town's first "colonialization" project preserved and labeled the
remains of thirteen sycamore trees planted by Oliver Wolcott, Jr. For
the Centennial, the Village Improvement Society replaced the ran-
domly planted mixture of trees along the town's streets with regimented
rows of American elms, having chosen this type of tree for its distinctive
native branching pattern. In addition, the planners knew that the elm
grows very quickly in Litchfield's climate so that it would take only
about fifteen years for the trees to arch over the village streets, creating
a homogeneous "colonial" appearance. Such tree formations also suggested an important spiritual security, people readily associating overarching branches with the all-embracing arms of God.[29]

[28] Wendy Kaplan, "R. T. H. Halsey: An Ideology of Collecting American Decorative
Arts," *Winterthur Portfolio* 17, no. 1 (Spring 1982): 51.
[29] William Solotaroff, *Shade Trees in Towns and Cities* (New York: John Wiley and
Sons, 1911); Charles L. Pack, *Trees as Good Citizens* (Washington, D.C.: American Tree
Association, 1922). During the 1820s when he was stationed in Litchfield, the Reverend
Lyman Beecher preached about the spiritual significance of trees, which inspired a small
tree-planting movement. His children, Henry Ward Beecher and Harriet Beecher Stowe,
discussed the moral and patriotic value of trees in several of their writings during the latter
half of the nineteenth century.

Most of the funding for Litchfield's beautification projects came from private sources. The town legislature, however, provided the manual labor. It required all locally jailed prisoners to water and mow both public and private lawns. The townspeople believed that this was one of the best ways to rehabilitate criminals and turn them into patriotic, law-abiding, and conscientious citizens.

In the early 1880s Litchfield's Village Improvement Society initiated an important architectural project. Prior to this time the townspeople had taken pride in their colonial homes but had directed more attention to the historic events and people associated with houses rather than to the age and architecture of the buildings themselves. Their interest shifted to the physical structures during the colonial revival. Litchfield was most likely the first town in America to sponsor a campaign to date and placard its historic houses. Litchfield's colonial homes, in a sense, *needed* designation because about 65 percent of the town's houses were in the competing Gothic style. A building marked with a colonial date, then, acquired a special significance and function. As one writer observed, "the passerby would gain a sense of history, security, patriotism and stability when he encountered a doorway bearing an eighteenth-century date."[30]

Litchfield's secluded rural setting helped to determine the persistence of a strictly colonial American style. Residents in the town did not build what Henry James called "white elephants, with their affront to proportion and discretion," homes indigenous to seaside summer resorts such as Newport and generally not found along restrained village streets. In *A Backward Glance* Edith Wharton remarked on how extravagant summer residences ruined the colonial character of Newport. Wharton even described her joyous "escape" from an ugly Tudor house in Newport, "a vapid watering-place," to a colonial revival home in the Berkshire Mountains, "the *real* country."[31]

[30] Newspaper accounts from the period strongly suggest that Litchfield was the first town to placard houses. In checking with other American towns, I have not yet found an earlier occurrence. For the quotation, see "Beautiful Litchfield," *Litchfield Enquirer* (May 3, 1882).

[31] Henry James, *The American Scene* (1907; reprint ed., Bloomington: Indiana University Press, 1968), p. xx; Edith Wharton, *A Backward Glance* (New York: D. Appleton-Century Co., 1934), pp. 107–24. James also praises in *The American Scene* the simple life and classic architecture of the inland New England village as among the most virtuous features of the landscape.

Litchfield also did not attract any of the ostentatious "nouveaux riches," as Newport did. Litchfielders often referred to the Newport "400" as "un-American hybrids."[32] In contrast, Litchfield appealed to old-money families with impeccable ancestral attachment to the town. Most year-round residents lived in colonial houses or on land owned by their fore-bears. Many summer residents were either descended from old Litch-field stock or from ancestors who once attended school there. Lucretia Deming, a great-granddaughter of merchant Julius Deming, was typical of Litchfield's residents. She posed for a photograph wearing an approx-imation of a colonial dress and a locket miniature of her grandfather as she pours tea from his armorial set of Chinese export porcelain (fig. 9). Miss Deming was just one of thousands of "aboriginal aristocrats" in Litchfield, influentials who initiated a comprehensive restoration of the town in the colonial or "ancestral" style that was in full force by the mid 1880s. The security—but, more important, the social and cultural status—of living in a colonial home became a self-conscious concern for Litchfield's elite. These townspeople went to great lengths to create what they perceived and idealized as the colonial style of architecture.

The most common way of achieving a colonial look was to perpetu-ate the tradition of the white house with black or dark green shutters. The John Collins house (fig. 10), for example, was built in 1782 and was first painted red; it was not painted white until 1815, during the height of Litchfield's golden age. Exterior shutters most likely were added at this time, too, the building originally having had interior shutters. This house remained white throughout the rest of the nineteenth cen-tury. During the colonial revival no one doubted that the house had always been white. The owners relied on tradition, believing that they were restoring the correct colonial appearance of the house by painting it white.

A second way that a home owner could create the colonial look was to take an eighteenth-century structure such as the Julius Deming house (see fig. 7) and make it an even grander statement of the colonial style (fig. 11). Architect E. K. Rossiter duplicated the original Palladian facade on a new and larger projecting portico on the south elevation. He added colonial dormer windows to a raised roof and romantic bay windows to the ground floor of the south elevation. Enlarged chimney stacks dis-

---

[32] "Litchfield Roads," *Litchfield Enquirer* (August 24, 1899).

Fig. 9. Anonymous, *Miss Lucretia Deming*. Litchfield, ca. 1890. Photograph. (Collection of William
Butler.)

played the dates 1793 and 1888, commemorating both the original construction and the later colonialization.

The coveted colonial style could also be achieved in several other
ways. During the late nineteenth century, it was common to take a
polychrome Victorian house and render it "colonial" by painting it white
(fig. 12). Even though this type of house had no characteristically colonial architectural elements, it could at least match Litchfield's classic
color scheme. The house pictured here underwent a more dramatic
change during the 1920s when the owner totally transformed it into a

Fig. 10. John Collins house, Litchfield, 1782. (Collection of Nan F. Heminway, Litchfield.)

gambrel-roof colonial-style structure (fig. 13). Many Victorian homes were subjected to such a character change. In order to create a more authentic colonial appearance, architects made exact copies of details from genuine colonial structures or period design books. Several houses in Litchfield had meticulous reproductions of moldings, doorways, and columns from Asher Benjamin source books. Colonial revival architect and critic Aymar Embury II often found it difficult to distinguish between colonial and colonial revival details. Any type of house could be colonialized during the late nineteenth and early twentieth centuries. Academic and popular journals, as well as advice books, offered helpful hints for turning even the "smallest eyesore of a structure into a Colonial jewel."[33]

[33] Aymar Embury II, Introduction to *Asher Benjamin* (reprint of five of Benjamin's architecture books) (New York: Architectural Book Publishing Co., 1917), pp. 1–2; Emily Post, *The Personality of a House* (New York: Funk and Wagnalls Co., 1930), pp. 90–119.

Fig. 11. South elevation, Julius Deming house, showing 1888 alterations by Rossiter and Wright. (Collection of Mrs. Ludlow S. Bull,
Litchfield.)

A final way of achieving the colonial look was to commission a New
York architect to design a "modern colonial" home. This came in two
distinct styles. The first copied local architecture from Litchfield's golden
age. On the Mary Perkins Quincy house (fig. 14) architects Howells
and Stokes combined the overall Georgian form of the 1775 Benjamin
Tallmadge house with the Palladian window and doorway of the Julius
Deming house. The Quincy house was painted a pale yellow and had
olive-green shutters. Complete with a white picket fence, it stood in
perfect harmony with the surrounding colonial houses.

The second "modern colonial" style was a bit more romantic: it evoked
a familiar and erroneous stereotype of the Southern plantation (fig. 15).
Even though this style had never been a part of Litchfield's colonial
building tradition, it was nonetheless a tasteful architectural interpretation. The use of this style in Litchfield was appropriate because it, too,
suggested a significant golden age, the very reverse of post–Civil War

Fig. 12. Lamb house, Litchfield. Photo, ca. 1905. (Litchfield Historical Society.)

Northern supremacy: the age of the antebellum South and white supremacy. As one resident of Litchfield remarked in a discussion of the potential immigrant threat in the United States, "with a rise in white supremacy comes the rise of white pillars."[34]

By the turn of the century, Litchfield's colonial and colonial-looking homes, situated behind green sloping lawns and nestled under canopies of elms, rendered a peaceful, homogeneous appearance. Litchfield was noted throughout the United States as a white city upon a hill. The townspeople took great pride in their village. An active Daughters of the

[34]Charles T. Payne to Ludlow S. Bull, September 17, 1923, collection of Mrs. Ludlow S. Bull, Litchfield. During the colonial revival, popular culture associated large classical porticoes supported by colossal columns with Southern plantation-style architecture; this is yet another erroneous stereotype (see Lewis Mumford, *Sticks and Stones* [1924; reprint ed., New York: Dover Publications, 1955], p. 54). Several residents of Litchfield even organized tours to the South to get ideas for their homes. How the costume of the Civil War–era stereotypical Southern belle was discussed by Gretchen A. Schneider of Colonial Williamsburg in "Minuets, Martha Washington Tea Parties, and Landings of the Forefathers: Colonial Revival Styles and Meanings in Social Ritual" (Paper delivered at the 24th Winterthur conference, November 13–14, 1981).

Fig. 13. Lamb house, showing 1920s colonialization. (Litchfield Historical Society.)

American Revolution sponsored historical exhibits in concert with the town's historical society. The Village Improvement Society offered several lecture series on American architecture in conjunction with their beautification projects. Individuals tried to approximate the way of life of their ancestors by holding colonial teas, costume balls, musicales, and historical pageants. Mrs. Shepherd Knapp donated her large colonial farm to the Fresh Air Fund so that poor New York City children could come to the country for a "breath of our great democracy" and be "moulded into upright and honored citizens."[35] Newspaper accounts of the period praised the congenial rapport between the city summer folk and the year-round residents. Merchants gladly catered to the needs of the upper classes. Litchfield had a harmless immigrant population of Irish who were mainly servants and caretakers for the wealthy. The townspeople did not feel threatened by the Irish, who were small in

[35] "Opening of Shepherd Knapp Memorial Home," *Litchfield Enquirer* (July 6, 1905).

Fig. 14. Howells and Stokes, Mary Perkins Quincy house, Litchfield, 1904. (Litchfield Historical Society.)

number, knew their place in society, and were honest Catholics. In addition, their fair features did not make them look too foreign, and they shared at least a similar language.

The residents of Litchfield delighted in showing off their ideal town while making it virtually inaccessible to the common folk. The wealthy elites forbade both the railroad and the trolley from coming through, primarily to discourage tourism. They did not want any of what they called "unworthies" spoiling their "utopia." This act also represented a conscious rejection of a modern intrusion that would lead to commercialism and industrialism. A trolley was for the evil city, not the virtuous country. Merchants in other towns objected to being cut off from wealthy customers living in Litchfield. For more than a decade Litchfield publicly fought surrounding towns for its privacy. In an argument printed in a local paper one merchant from nearby Torrington accused Litchfielders of being too proud to associate with commoners and speculated that they spent all of their time tracing their ancestry. Such accu-

Fig. 15. Samuel Edson Gage, Underwood house, Litchfield, 1898. (Litchfield Historical Society.)

sations only pleased the inhabitants of Litchfield, who were not ashamed of their insular prejudices. Litchfielders honestly believed that they were serving their country by preserving and isolating their unique village. It was in all seriousness and with a due sense of patriotism that one of the town's leading citizens proposed sending a model of Litchfield to the Saint Louis exposition as an example of the ideal New England town, the defender of democracy.[36]

In 1923 Thorstein Veblen observed that "the country town is one of the great American institutions; perhaps the greatest, in the sense that it has had and continues to have a greater part than any other in shaping public sentiment and giving character to American culture."[37] Veblen might not have made such a powerful statement had Americans not so

[36] "Litchfield Trolley," *Litchfield Enquirer* (November 12, 1903); "Torrington Objects," *Litchfield Enquirer* (November 19, 1903); "Litchfield the Only," *Litchfield Enquirer* (July 24, 1902).
[37] Thorstein Veblen, *Absentee Ownership and Business Enterprise in Recent Times* (1923), as quoted in Max Lerner, ed., *The Portable Veblen* (New York: Viking Press, 1965), p. 407.

self-consciously shaped the character of their idyllic country towns during the preceding years of the colonial revival. The early twentieth century witnessed our nation's most concerted efforts to preserve its country towns. In 1908, as a direct response to the adverse effects of industrialization and to the concomitant desertion of farms throughout the United States, Theodore Roosevelt initiated the Country Life Movement, which more seriously reevaluated social, economic, and cultural conditions in rural America. In addition, this movement helped to establish our nation's first state forests and parks as well as preserve our natural resources. New England's colonialized villages and restored farms served as inspirational models for rural towns all over America.

Rural Manhood and *The Village Magazine*, primarily published for Western farmers, carefully detailed the improvements of New England's towns and farming regions. Articles in such periodicals made a universal impression on the landscape. In *Main Street* Sinclair Lewis said of Mankato, Minnesota, that it is "not a prairie town, but in its garden-sheltered streets and aisles of elms is white and green New England reborn." The future stability of farms and villages in the West depended on the ideal appearance and survival of the New England archetype. As Lewis Mumford assured society: "In what other part of the world has such a harmonious balance between the natural and the social environment been *preserved?* . . . [T]he New England village reaches a pretty fair pitch of worldy perfection; and beneath all the superficial changes that affected it in the next century and a half [a reference to the dramatic changes of the nineteenth century] its sturdy framework held together remarkably well."[38]

Beginning in 1913 Litchfield played its most important role as a national archetype and symbol. In this year the Village Improvement Society, directed by Ludlow S. Bull and Charles T. Payne, proposed a townwide project to remodel in the "purely" colonial style all of Litchfield's public and commercial buildings as well as the village green. With the completion of this project, Litchfield would become America's first comprehensive restoration of our colonial past. Newspapers nationwide praised the town by reporting that "while practically every boro, village, and town in the United States is seeking twentieth-century improvements and zealously working for a position in the march

[38] Sinclair Lewis, *Main Street* (1920; reprint ed., New York: New American Library, 1961), pp. 11–12; Mumford, *Sticks and Stones*, pp. 28–29.

of progress, Litchfield thru the choice of its people, after standing aloof
and looking on, is about to turn the other way."[39]

That Litchfield proposed such colonialization plans in 1913 is no
accident of history. The townspeople's deliberate rejection of modern
design coincided with the opening of the Armory Show in New York
and America's official introduction to "modern art." Many of Litchfield's summer elite disliked the show but had to be careful in what they
said about it because many of their social and cultural peers accepted
the new styles. A candid interview with two of Litchfield's oldest and
most prominent residents revealed that many townspeople disliked the
foreign high style of the show because it competed with the native
American colonial style. Some residents, furthermore, resented the
prominent Jewish families who patronized this art, a prejudice that only
strengthened Litchfield's colonial crusade.[40]

Depictions of villages and village life, ironically, were in fact exhibited at the Armory Show. American artists such as Anne Goldthwaite,
Childe Hassam, and Maurice Prendergast featured abstract works
depicting New England genre scenes. French artist Maurice de Vlam-
inck exhibited the most abstract painting in this vein, a scene entitled
Village, depicting Rueil, France. In this composition the artist reduced
white houses, black shutters, green trees, and a village church to mere
patches of color.

Litchfield was not interested in such abstraction. The Village
Improvement Society commissioned architects A. P. F. Adenaw, of
LaFarge and Morris, and F. B. J. Renshaw to design all of the colonialization plans, which were first exhibited in private apartments and
clubs in New York City and then in Litchfield for public approval. A
lecture series on colonial American architecture accompanied each
exhibition. The Village Improvement Society personified antimodern-
ist sentiments; the society wanted to camouflage all signs of industry
and commerce, leaving not "the slightest vestige of modern design."[41]

[39] "Litchfield's Transformation Back to Colonial Styles," *Waterbury Republican*
(Waterbury, Conn.) (March 2, 1913). Similar articles appeared in newspapers both
nationally and worldwide.

[40] Interviews with Butler, Litchfield, March 1982 (the individuals wish to remain anonymous). For a scathing article on anti-Semitism in Litchfield, see Willson Whitman, "O
Little Town . . . (Restricted)," *Nation* (December 25, 1943): 751–54.

[41] Village Improvement Society, *Colonial Plans for Litchfield Connecticut* (Litchfield:
Privately printed, 1913), p. 1.

It is not surprising, then, that their first project involved transforming the railroad depot and a series of Victorian storefronts into domestic-looking colonial structures. The society had white wooden cornices, pediments, doorways, quoins, and pilasters custom made and then attached to the buildings. In some cases, wooden clapboards were placed completely over the brick exterior of a structure. The society similarly changed the courthouse, thought to be in the style of "utilitarian ugliness," to a more colonial-looking icon of justice and democracy.

One of the most important symbols in Litchfield, the village green, also underwent a total transformation at this time. The Village Improvement Society hired John Charles Olmsted and Frederick Law Olmsted, Jr., to relandscape this chaotic plot of land. The green had been graded and planted several times during the last half of the nineteenth century but had never had a complete overhaul. Even though there was no grassy green in eighteenth- or early nineteenth-century Litchfield, the Olmsted brothers "restored" one based on an idealized composite of several noncolonial New England greens. Their product, a symmetrical, tree-shaded park, harmonized with the colonial uniformity of the town down to the smallest detail: lamp posts and benches even copied colonial designs. Litchfielders justified the existence of such a green by arguing that if Litchfield had had a village green in colonial times, it most surely would have resembled the Olmsteds' work.[42]

Other important persons contributed to colonializing and preserving Litchfield's landscape in 1913. A group of ambitious ladies formed the town's first Garden Club of America chapter, with membership limited only to those women already in the DAR. With true patriotic zeal they promoted new colonial-style gardens. They idealized the past and planted "old-fashioned, English flower gardens" rather than the more authentic herb and vegetable gardens. As a direct result of Theodore Roosevelt's Country Life Commission, Alain C. White established a 4,000-acre conservation reservation in Litchfield. In 1913 this was one of the country's largest privately supported public trusts. White contributed more land over the next few decades, buying abandoned farms, scenic lookouts, waterfalls, and mountains. What eventually totaled well over 6,000 acres of prime land formed the basis of Connecticut's parks and forest

[42] Extemporaneous remarks of John C. Olmsted, 1913 (typescript), Litchfield Historical Society; Frederick Law Olmsted, Jr., to F. Kingsbury Bull, March 15, 1913, collection of Mrs. Ludlow S. Bull.

system. The residents of Litchfield enjoyed the security of knowing that their lush countryside would never be destroyed.

The year 1913 was a landmark for village improvement generally. P. T. Farwell published in that year a comprehensive book on the movement, citing the New England town as the model American community. Farwell perpetuated the myth of the nucleated tree-shaded village, identifying environmental protection and town beautification with the colonial way. He reminded readers that

> it is worth remembering that the old Puritan settlers must have had some deep sense of the value of natural beauty, else they would not have surrounded these commons and planted them, here and there, with the graceful elms, now in their majestic old age. . . . The old Puritans were not without their appreciation of beauty, and oftentimes in town-planning they showed more forethought than has been accredited to them, and more than the builders of the newer towns have usually exercised.[43]

Also in 1913 many cities instituted beautification projects based on the New England village archetype. Frederick Law Olmsted, Jr., chaired the National Conference on City Planning, campaigning for better-landscaped cities, new building codes, and improved sanitary conditions. These plans were interrupted, however, by our nation's entrance into its first world war and an even more intense period of nativism and insecurity.

Although Litchfield's architectural colonialization abated during World War I, the town still served as an important symbol of Americanism. Many New York City families, not necessarily previous summer residents, moved to this isolated village for a sense of security and protection. Rather than spend money on cosmetic colonial remodelings, these people instead founded small hospitals for wounded soldiers, prepared bandages, and packaged supplies just as their Revolutionary ancestors had done.

After the war the Village Improvement Society undertook its final and most arduous project, the restoration of the Congregational Church. Richard Henry Dana, Jr., a New York architect and Litchfield summer resident, supervised this ten-year "restoration," which may be more accurately termed a reconstruction. The first step was particularly dras-

---

[43] Parris Thaxter Farwell, *Village Improvement* (New York: Sturgis and Walton, 1913), p. 143.

tic. The parishioners demolished the existing Gothic-style church built in 1873, rejecting Victorian taste in favor of the colonial style.[44] The next step required salvaging what was left of the 1829 Congregational Church, which by the 1920s was gutted, having been used variously as a cow barn, a warehouse, a movie theater, and a gymnasium. The sparse remains of this structure were moved to a site overlooking the village green. Dana totally redesigned the interior, basing it on early nineteenth-century architectural design books. Everything but a new mahogany pulpit was painted white. Dana reconstructed a steeple as well as other exterior ornaments, and by 1929 the church had assumed the classical appearance we still see today (see fig. 1). With the completion of this icon and the romantic restoration of the Tapping Reeve Law School during the following year, the residents of Litchfield had created their ideal image of a "colonial" New England town for Americans to admire and adopt. For a nation experiencing the uncertainties and hardships of the Great Depression, Litchfield's landscape served as an even greater symbol of survival, stability, and democracy.

Other New England towns, particularly rural summer resorts, underwent similar transformations during the colonial revival, but Litchfield was at the forefront of the colonialization process. The town furthermore served as a source of inspiration for establishing the later museum villages of Colonial Williamsburg, Old Sturbridge Village, and Historic Deerfield.[45] The visual plan of Litchfield during the colonial revival, like the spiritual plan of John Winthrop's Boston, was to create an ideal city upon a hill. Winthrop's plan, however, was unsuccessful, and Americans did not fashion an ideal image of a New England townscape until the late nineteenth and early twentieth centuries. It is the romantic colonial revival image of the New England town rather than the authentically Puritan or historically accurate colonial image that has become a fixed stereotype in the American mind and has made a lasting material mark on the American landscape.

---

[44] As Kenneth L. Ames has contended in courses on Victorian material culture given at Winterthur Museum, elites in the 1920s rejected Victorian artifacts and architecture because they were products of a time that significantly altered and, more important, threatened their society. Elites favored the colonial style because it suggested to them a more stable and refined era.

[45] Mrs. Ludlow S. Bull, interview with Butler, Litchfield, November 1982. Mrs. Bull recalls that the founders of these museum villages made several trips to Litchfield to get ideas for planning their restorations.

The Colonial Revival in the Public Eye: Williamsburg and Early Garden Restoration
Charles B. Hosmer, Jr.

The first efforts to recreate the gardens of the colonial era for exhibition purposes began in the later 1920s with large private and public projects. When John D. Rockefeller, Jr., agreed to undertake the restoration of Williamsburg, Virginia, he launched a number of important initiatives in the field of historic preservation: city planning, commercial rehabilitation, architectural training and research, historic archaeology, and the study of colonial landscape design. By the early 1930s the National Park Service undertook projects of its own that involved research into eighteenth-century gardens, and the Civilian Conservation Corps program brought park service professionals into many large restorations. Landscape architects were no better prepared for these challenges than their colleagues in the fields of history and architecture. Their training did not equip them for the development of accurate historical museum exhibit areas. Administrators of historical restorations believed that visitors should see an essentially beautiful picture of the past, and this outlook inhibited efforts to produce historically accurate garden settings. The landscape decisions made at Williamsburg were repeated at private and public restorations all over the United States in the 1930s.

The first colonial revival gardens in museum restorations were only settings for larger pictures, never ends in themselves. While research had to be done for these plantings, the primary goal was to produce a "frame" for attractive views of the past. The plantings were rarely historically accurate revivals of eighteenth- and nineteenth-century landscapes. Trained in twentieth-century concepts of design, landscape architects became artists who helped to perpetuate the idea that the life of the past was always blissfully harmonious. There was a conscious refusal to accept the conclusions of research reports that implied colonial gardens had been simple, functional, and even somewhat bare. Perhaps the tendency to such refusal became a form of patriotism as the Great Depression generation searched for a stable past to alleviate the stresses of an uncertain present.

In almost every instance where professionals worked on restorations the landscape architect was a fairly influential figure in the decision-making process. At Williamsburg, for example, noted landscape architect Arthur A. Shurcliff was able to create a great many garden settings and played a significant role in all planning decisions, but the project was an architectural enterprise, and naturally building—not landscape—architects had more to say about what was done. Within the territory staked out for them the landscape architects did act boldly, but they often showed only a rudimentary knowledge of the original garden plans that they were supposed to reproduce.

The research efforts that supported garden restorations should have been carried out by professional archaeologists along with the landscape architects, but in most cases trained archaeologists were only able to provide minimal data about walls, outbuildings, paths, and watercourses. They did not have the right training to interpret postholes and fragments of fences or tools that appeared in their trenches. It would be fair to say that pioneer restorers of the 1920s and 1930s did try to find documentary evidence for their garden plans, and they did travel as much as their museum budgets would permit. But the result of this kind of research was an impressionistic approach to colonial revival gardens. There were usually only a handful of surviving plants to give restorers an idea of where different species should be placed. In one case there might be a few old trees, and in another the testimony of former slaves to help lay out a kitchen garden.

There is evidence that restoration planners debated the correctness of colonial revival gardens. Often landscape architects found themselves facing criticism from historians and architects alike, but almost always the landscape experts managed to win the arguments. The colonial revival gardens usually ended up the way they were originally planned. The historians and architects believed they had documentary proof that the landscape architects were ignoring important evidence. They claimed that the garden restorations were too ornamental and too extensive to be in character with known eighteenth- and nineteenth-century practice. But such critics rarely convinced the administrators of the restoration projects that the garden plans were wrong.

In spite of the debates, or possibly because of them, we should now view these restored gardens as important artifacts of the twentieth century. The colonial revival gardens from the decade of the depression reflect an important development in the evolution of landscape design and research. It is true that Rockefeller's penchant for neatness caused the Williamsburg gardens to look like picture postcards all year long. Although much of Shurcliff's work still exists, there are a few signs of a return to the kind of maintenance that would have been practiced before 1800 in Virginia's capital.

Three specific garden restorations will serve to illustrate the character of the programs in the 1930s: Colonial Williamsburg, Stratford Hall in Westmoreland County, Virginia, and Mission La Purisima Concepcion in Lompoc, California. The purpose of each of these restorations is an important indication of how the gardens were to be developed. In the case of Williamsburg it is essential to know that the real decision makers—John D. Rockefeller, Jr., and William Archer Rutherfoord Goodwin—had idealized views of the past. Their goal was to recreate an attractive picture of the eighteenth century, and they often used terminology in their correspondence that bordered on the artistic. The idea of painting a picture for visitors was a means of bringing back the past. Rockefeller's interest in Williamsburg was based on his conviction that the eighteenth century was far more beautiful than the twentieth, which very well may be true. This sensitivity to beauty would influence many decisions that had to be made about garden plans.

The Williamsburg restoration was an architectural project staffed and run by architects. A private architectural firm, Perry, Shaw, and Hepburn of Boston, carried out the program. They had been hired by W. A. R. Goodwin acting on behalf of John D. Rockefeller, Jr. The principal decisions of the architectural staff were debated by an advisory committee of architects. Only later did Rockefeller eventually add advisory committees for furniture, history, and landscape architecture. He read the minutes of these committees carefully so that he could understand how his project was viewed in the professional world. Since these minutes have been preserved we have a unique picture of the decision-making process in the Williamsburg program. Moreover, Rockefeller's chief administrator at Williamsburg in the middle 1930s was Kenneth Chorley, who spent most of his time in New York City to be near his patron, which meant that there was also considerable correspondence within the Williamsburg organization over each step in the restoration process.

The key figure in the Williamsburg garden development was Arthur A. Shurcliff (he changed his name from Shurtleff about 1930) (fig. 1). A graduate of both Massachusetts Institute of Technology and Harvard University, he did work with the Boston Park Commission and had been involved in town planning during World War I when Emergency Fleet Corporation had to construct ship-building towns. He was an advisor to the metropolitan district commissioner in Boston, had an office on Beacon Street, and had worked with Perry, Shaw, and Hepburn. When Goodwin asked the project architects for the name of a landscape architect, they replied on January 30, 1928: "We have done work for Mr. Shurtleff, and are at present associated with him on work in the neighborhood of Boston and also in the south. Mr. Shurtleff is the type of man with whom it is an inspiration to work. He is clear, simple, direct, energetic and personally, very charming. His work is of the highest order and he appeals to us particularly since he has a personality which is most adaptable to collaboration with others."[1] Shurcliff's power of persuasion must have been considerable, for he usually got his way (see fig. 2). Eager to carry out his plans, he approached the executives at Williamsburg with the momentum of a tidal wave.

Shurcliff was particularly clear in stating his research methods at a conference of Williamsburg executives on December 11, 1928:

> When we come to laying out a certain lot in Williamsburg, we try to find out the way the lot was arranged in the old days. The sources of information are the Frenchman's map [drawn by a French surveyor in 1781], which is sometimes usable and many times not at all usable; the actual surveys which

[1] William G. Perry to W. A. R. Goodwin, January 30, 1928, General Correspondence, Administration—Architects and Engineers, Colonial Williamsburg Foundation Archives, Williamsburg, Va. (hereafter cited as CWFA).

Fig. 1. Arthur A. Shurcliff, 1937. (Colonial Williamsburg Foundation.)

have been made showing the boundary lines and location of the buildings; then we go over the ground and add to the survey a detailed location of a rosebush or a boxbush and all the different trees, naming them carefully. Then we have a certain amount of book knowledge regarding the way those things were arranged in the old days. Then we go to the old owners and get all the information we can from them, and we have occasionally gotten an extraordinary amount of information. We also examine the insurance maps. When we have gotten all that data together, we can't still go ahead without knowing something about the way things were actually done in the South in the old days, and that has led me in particular to go around the South to a good many places. I have gone around visiting such places as Claremont, upper Brandon, Shirley, Westover, the old University of West Virginia [Shurcliff must have meant the University of Virginia], Monticello, and I am going to visit more places this week.

Fig. 2. Arthur A. Shurcliff, garden, Williamsburg, Va. Created 1930s.
(Colonial Williamsburg Foundation.)

Further on in the same meeting Shurcliff revealed his philosophy of
garden restoration.

In these estimates that I have made, I have kept this point in mind: That
there are two dangers that we can run into in laying out these places, aside from
their archaeological perfection and their convenience. One is putting in and
planting the whole scheme too poorly and poverty looking, and the other is
making them look very flossy. It seemed to me that certainly in the beginning,
when we first show our cards, as it were, to the public, it would be a mistake to
go to the extreme of making the grounds too good looking, too much boxed,
too many flowers, too many trees, because they wouldn't be appropriate to the
simple, little weather-beaten and rather poor looking houses, and the small

amount of money that we knew the old people living in those houses spent in
the old days, so in making these estimates I have tried to err on the side of
making those places look a little bit thin. You know how rundown at the heel
those old Virginia houses look, and I think we are safer in the first year's work
in running the risk of going to that extreme.[2]

Perhaps Shurcliff was setting a reasonably conservative goal for his
plantings while he indulged in some New England condescension in
discussing Virginia gardens. After all, the citizens of Williamsburg tended
to view the arrival of the Perry, Shaw, and Hepburn crew from Boston
as a second Yankee invasion.

Although as late as 1935 Colonial Williamsburg did not have a staff
historian, there was a vigorous director of the Office of Research and
Record. Harold R. Shurtleff (no relation to Arthur Shurcliff) was a trained
architect who gradually moved into the field of written history. By 1935
he had begun graduate work in history at Harvard. Like other historians
of his day, Shurtleff began to do battle with the more or less poetic
concepts proposed by landscape architects. He warned Andrew Hepburn in the Boston office about new ideas coming from Williamsburg's
landscape office.

I see an intimation in the minutes of the February 6th meeting that it is
Arthur Shurcliff's intention to continue his elaboration of the Palace lay-out,
and even to carry it on into the so-called "Park." I think this is a good moment
to inform you that looking at it from the Research Department's point of view
there is no remote possibility that this "Park" area was ever used for anything
except a cow pasture. So any attempt to landscape it would seem to me to rob
the Palace lay-out of a good deal of verisimilitude, as well as to take away a
good deal of its 18th century plantation character.

In going over these same minutes of February 6th meeting, I find my mind
suddenly focusing on something that has been bothering me for quite a while,
owing to the fact that there were allusions in these minutes to projects already
accomplished or proposed projects which were either frankly unauthentic or of
very dubious authenticity. There were eight of these, of which five had to do
with the Palace.[3]

[2] Minutes of the Williamsburg Meeting held at 61 Broadway, New York City, December 11, 1928, pp. 62–63, General Correspondence, Conferences—Minutes and Reports,
CWFA.
[3] Harold R. Shurtleff to Andrew H. Hepburn, February 16, 1935, Perry, Shaw, and
Hepburn (Boston) Files—Research Department, CWFA.

One of the severest arguments erupted when Shurcliff proposed to fill an area in the palace garden with a maze (figs. 3, 4). He told Perry, Shaw, and Hepburn in December 1934 that he had studied mazes in England, citing old engravings and the popular maze of Hampton Court. Unable to find a clear record of a maze in Virginia, Shurcliff was disarmingly frank: "I think the authenticity of mazes in England at our period is a more important matter for us to consider than mazes in Virginia at that time." The new addition to the palace garden would have the advantages of economy and popularity. It would be easy to install, and the visitors would soon learn to love it. Even before Shurtleff condemned the new schemes at the palace, William Perry told Shurcliff that the maze needed to be based on proven precedent.

The Maze, attractive as the idea is and attractive to visitors as it would be, seems to be based upon neither documentary nor three dimensional evidence so far as Williamsburg is concerned. We believe presumptions to be strong that a Maze was in the minds of the garden planners in accordance with the points brought out in your letter but we are of the definite opinion that it would be wise to postpone this matter until building, landscape work and furnishings for which there is definite information, are more fully carried out.[4]

Shurtleff was even more pointed in his criticism of plans that appeared to be totally at variance with known garden practices in Williamsburg. He told Kenneth Chorley, the president of the restoration, that some future "young architectural thesis-writer—to whom we cannot very well refuse access to the files" might want to create a reputation for himself by showing the great inconsistencies in the palace garden.[5]

But the final result was predictable. Shurcliff prevailed, and the maze was planted. He managed to convince Chorley to agree to the proposal by pointing out (1) that the mazes did indeed exist in eighteenth-century England, a source for design ideas in the New World, (2) that a maze would be cheap to install and maintain, (3) that the new maze would grow fast, and (4) that the public would come to love it. All of these arguments were valid, and the intervening years have shown the popularity of this feature of the Williamsburg garden restoration.

[4] Arthur A. Shurcliff to Perry, Shaw, and Hepburn, December 28, 1934, and Perry to Shurcliff, January 4, 1935, Perry, Shaw, and Hepburn (Boston) Files, Landscaping—Governor's Palace, CWFA.
[5] Shurtleff to Kenneth Chorley, February 16, 1935, General Correspondence—Research, CWFA.

Fig. 3. Garden, Governor's Palace, Williamsburg, Va. (Colonial Williamsburg Foundation.)

It is important to consider the element of personality in the planning of garden restorations in Williamsburg. The descriptions of Shurcliff taken from the diary of Mrs. George P. Coleman, the wife of the mayor, are especially instructive. The Colemans lived in the St. George Tucker house, which faces Market Square (fig. 5). At first Mrs. Coleman was very apprehensive about Shurcliff when the staff of Williamsburg Restoration began work on her home:

January 23, 1931. Today I was asked to go over the Tucker House yard with Mr. Arthur Shurcliff, the landscape artist of the Restoration, to discuss the laying out of brick walls, boxwood hedges, etc. I found him a very alarming person! Somehow the idea of changing the yard and garden is much more repellent to me than changing the house, and this is such a terribly enthusiastic man! He startled me the first time I met him, when he addressed the Garden Club on the subject of old gardens, and hoped that the modern species of flowers would be banned from the gardens here, and urged us all to grow red

Fig. 4. Arthur A. Shurcliff, topiary maze, Governor's Palace, Williamsburg, Va. (Colonial Williamsburg Foundation.)

geraniums in profusion! I have grave doubts as to the presence of red geraniums in Virginia in Colonial Days, and have no partiality for them at any time![6]

Her mood of apprehension did not improve during the spring of 1931. She also found that it was almost useless to resist the plans of the landscape architect.

May 22, 1931. Mr Shurcliff came down like a wolf on the fold again today. He rushed in and out several times with charts and plans for all sorts of alarming "landscapes" in our yard. He has boxwood on the brain. We are surrounded by it already. On the east and the north a perfectly marvellous hedged walk connecting the Courthouse Green with the old walk behind Miss Cora's house has been set out, and boxwood is to be set out across the road where Miss Howie-

[6] Mary Haldane Begg Coleman, "The Reminiscences of Mrs. George P. Coleman," transcript of interview, February 22, 1956, pp. 56–57, Oral History Collection, CWFA.

Fig. 5. Arthur A. Shurcliff, boxwood garden, Saint George Tucker house, Williamsburg, Va., spring 1958. (Colonial Williamsburg Foundation.)

son's house has been moved away, but Mr. Shurcliff is hurt and grieved by our lack of appreciation when we declare that we don't want more boxwood mazes and hedges all over our yard![7]

Perhaps Mrs. Coleman's diary illustrates the problems involved in the client-architect relationship. It certainly took time for a new garden to take shape in the eyes of the uninitiated. By the winter of 1932 her tone had changed slightly. Shurcliff's good taste and persuasive enthusiasm had helped to carry the day with her, as it had with the executives of Williamsburg Restoration.

February 22, 1932. Mr. Shurcliff appeared today filled with artistic zeal and a great desire to plant shrubs and trees all over the place, and had to be severely opposed by both George and me. We consented to the planting of Japanese Quince bushed from the backyard, on each side of the front steps, and a large spinea on front of the kitchen, but set ourselves with steadfastness bordering on rudeness against all other propositions. It is exquisite mild weather and we all sit around the steps and porches watching the transplanting and bricklaying. It is fascinating, and the idea of the yard as it will be is entrancing.[8]

[7] Coleman, "Reminiscences," p. 62.
[8] Coleman, "Reminiscences," p. 70.

Stratford Hall served as a memorial to Robert E. Lee and to a way of life. A group of women, the William Alexander, Jr., Chapter of the United Daughters of the Confederacy in Greenwich, Connecticut, set out to buy a large plantation. Soon May (Mrs. Charles) Lanier, the moving spirit of the enterprise, managed to form the Robert E. Lee Memorial Foundation. This organization saved Stratford Hall and its immediate surroundings as a sacred spot for southerners and for people who believed in the complete reunion of the North and the South.

As the research program developed, the ladies found that Stratford was also the symbol of a remarkable family that produced three generations of leaders for Virginia. Although the board of the foundation sought authenticity in the restoration program for the house and garden, their treasury did not permit the kind of professional staff that had been used at Williamsburg. Therefore, the administrative setup at Stratford was entirely different from that of the Williamsburg project. May Lanier, president of the foundation, was assisted by two other women who directed the research and restoration work. Lanier was the organizer and fund raiser. She was a great success in both endeavors: the $250,000 debt on the plantation was paid off by 1932. She had a way of finding some of the wealthiest and most influential women in America.

At Lanier's side was Ethel Armes, a journalist-historian who wrote a series of reports on the research program for Stratford. These culminated in a huge book, *Stratford Hall, the Great House of the Lees,* which appeared in 1936. A year earlier the staff of Perry, Shaw, and Hepburn had published in the *Architectural Record* for December a brief overview of the Williamsburg restoration, including short articles by William G. Perry (on the architecture) and Arthur A. Shurcliff (on the gardens). What a contrast between these brief statements and Armes's massive research report. The Stratford book contained an entire chapter on the history of the landscape developments at the plantation from the eighteenth century up through the restoration plans of the 1930s.

A third figure at Stratford was Mary van Deventer, who served as chairman of the restoration committee. She was instrumental in putting the whole program under the control of America's foremost architectural scholar of that time, Fiske Kimball of Philadelphia.

Although Shurcliff did offer free advice to the ladies at Stratford Hall on their garden plans, he was principally responsible for the excavations there funded not by Lanier's group, but by the Garden Club of Virginia, financed with profits from its 1930 tours. Following the excavations made in the summer of 1930 Shurcliff said:

> The findings have more than substantiated our early belief that Stratford was laid out with a generous hand and was one of the most interesting and imposing of the early places. Certainly we can say without hesitation that we are more strongly of the opinion now than before, that the restoration is worthy of the devotion which has been bestowed upon it already, and that the hopes which we have all had for the ultimate beauty will be realized if we are willing to continue our patient study of the actual facts of the old design before we attempt the restoration of the grounds.[9]

The foundation hired Morley J. Williams as its principal landscape architect. He was an associate of Shurcliff and carried out the final plan for an elaborate formal garden beside the house. Williams was a graduate of Toronto University. He was a bit younger than Shurcliff, having completed his formal training in 1925. He worked in Harvard's architectural school in the landscape department and was teaching there when he came to Virginia to plan the new gardens at Stratford.

In contrast to the restoration work at Williamsburg and Stratford, Mission La Purisima Concepcion in Lompoc, California, was a governmental reconstruction project. It was an effort on the part of the state of California and the federal government to recreate a complete Spanish mission complex. The site has become the only place in California where visitors can see a mission community as it existed in the first quarter of the nineteenth century. Civilian Conservation Corps (CCC) funds made it possible to use the professional staff of the National Park Service in cooperation with a local advisory committee.

Relationships among various levels of government made the administrative situation at La Purisima very complex. The CCC provided the labor—three companies of enrollees. The state of California bought the land under the guidance of Newton Drury, the acquisitions officer of the California Park Commission, who was soon to become director of the National Park Service. The park service provided the professional staff for research in history, art, archaeology, architecture, and landscape design. The park was to be turned over to the state as soon as it

---

[9] Ethel Armes, *Stratford Hall, the Great House of the Lees* (Richmond, Va.: Garrett and Massie, 1936), p. 503.

was judged to be completely developed as a mission community.

The historian was Russell Ewing, a recent doctoral graduate from the University of California. The landscape architect was Ed Rowe of Santa Barbara, a gardener who had done research on Spanish missions. He worked under the general supervision of Emerson Knight, National Park Service regional architect. There were consultants on the Purisima project like Rexford Newcomb, dean of the College of Fine and Applied Arts at the University of Illinois, and Ronald F. Lee, chief historian of the National Park Service. Actual construction at the mission site was supervised by architect Fred Hageman.

La Purisima was a tremendous operation involving six years of work on the part of the CCC companies, and the final dedication came inopportunely enough on the morning of December 7, 1941. The CCC enrollees had rebuilt the mission with adobe bricks fashioned the same way the Indians had originally made them. Even to this day tourists are amazed at the quietness of the site at Lompoc; the state had managed to buy enough land in the valley to preserve the sense of isolation that must have characterized the missions along the old royal highway (fig. 6).

In 1936 arguments erupted during the preparation of the garden plan for the mission. The disputes were often conducted through reports to the supervisors of the CCC projects in California. The historians and other professionals associated with the mission work were not gentle in their criticism of the ideas of the landscape architects. The first hint of disharmony came in a letter from regional officer Lawrence Merriam to the acting assistant director of the National Park Service in Washington. Merriam complained that the professional staff had been working with a local advisory committee that had gone off on its own.

Recently the Advisory Group employed a very competent landscape architect and prepared a plan for the Mission Garden. Unfortunately, this office was not officially advised of the action, and had no contact with the development of the plan until after it was completed. We do not in any way question the sincerity of the group. However, they rather expected that the State Park Division would accept the plan, which was very unfortunate, as both our historian and landscape architect assigned to the project for the study of the garden . . . disagreed with the plan as submitted.[10]

[10] Lawrence Merriam to Verne E. Chatelain, July 1, 1936, Proposed National Historic Sites, California o–36, Records of the National Park Service, Record Group 79, National Archives, Washington, D.C. (hereafter cited as NPS records).

Fig. 6. Restored residence building and garden with Civilian Conservation Corps camp in the background, Lompoc, Calif., spring 1938. (California Department of Parks and Recreation, La Purisima State Historical Park.)

Park service historian Ewing began a debate on the correctness of the Purisima landscape plan when he commented in 1936 on a proposal to build a wall in the garden. He was reporting to the regional office of the CCC, and he spoke from the viewpoint of a historian who wanted *some* documentary evidence of archaeological precedent for each step taken in the reconstruction of the mission, but he deferred to the knowledge of the park service landscape architect on big decisions of this type:

The Regional Historical Inspector strongly advises against the erection of a garden wall at the mission. Neither historical nor archaeological records have as yet revealed the former existence of such a structure at the site. A study of the physical remains at the site and an understanding of the original uses of the area between the monastery and the Indian dwellings rather conclusively point out the fact that there never was a garden wall in front of the monastery. . . . The Regional Historical Inspector feels that this matter should be left to the recommendations of Mr. Knight. . . . All that the historian requests is that simplicity and informality govern in devising appropriate landscaping plans for the mission.[11]

[11] Russell C. Ewing to Regional Officer, May 2, 1936, Federal Records Center, San Francisco, Calif.

Once more the first research efforts led to the conclusion that colonial revival gardens, whether English or Spanish, would be simpler than our own ideas of what might have been appropriate.

In the fall of 1936 noted architectural historian Rexford Newcomb came for a visit. He was an authority on the surviving buildings of the California missions, having published a book on the subject ten years earlier. Newcomb sent a long letter to the chairman of La Purisima Advisory Committee, giving his observations on the reconstruction program. At the end of his report Newcomb revealed his great concern over the new garden plan:

> The proposed mission garden does certain violence to the whole idea of a "working" museum of mission culture. Of course in opening up such a structure to the public certain concessions must be made to that public. . . . If you have visited any of the mission show places, you will have discovered that the crowds are never excessive. . . . Therefore the making of a garden with paths thirty or sixty feet wide is entirely unthinkable and unjustified. The old mission gardens were simple practical affairs, places where cherished plants, trees, etc. from Spain, Mexico, even Peru, could be protected and propagated. . . . The location and width of the paths were determined by the line of travel of the padres and their neophytes in going from building to building. Usually these were paths in the real sense—just pathways. . . . I do want to appeal to your committee to keep the gardens in the same spirit of the old mission buildings, and above all do not let the thing become the type of place that lovely old Capistrano (picturesque as it may be in some respects) has become.[12]

It appears that Newcomb's advice was not heeded. The ideas of the local committee had considerable visual appeal, and so a reasonably elaborate garden began to grow in front of the reconstructed residence building at La Purisima. In the summer of 1938 Guy Fleming of the California Division of Parks reported to his superiors that the garden was an "extremely doubtful restoration," and he recommended that the area be called an educational exhibit so that visitors would not look upon the site as a restoration of the original plantings. Later in the summer the regional historian for the National Park Service backed Fleming's conclusion. Olaf Hagen had a more radical solution to the problem of authenticity. He recommended that the "plant material in the area in front of the mission . . . be removed elsewhere." Other staff

[12] Rexford Newcomb to Wallace C. Penfield, September 17, 1936, Federal Records Center, San Francisco.

historians agreed with Hagen's proposal, but apparently no real effort to move the garden actually came about.[13]

But the debate continued while the plants grew each year, making the mission complex a very beautiful spot for visitors who happened to come by on the highway toward Lompoc. The most interesting statement of all came from staff landscape architect Rowe in his final report on the garden, dated August 1939. It would be difficult to equal the frankness of Rowe's approach to authenticity in presenting a garden of the colonial period:

> The design of the garden and plant material used today at Mission La Purisima Concepcion is in no sense a reproduction of the original surroundings of the mission at the time of its occupation by the Franciscan Order. . . . The area directly in front of the major buildings and adjacent to them was probably a bare, dusty space in which were the fountains, basins, a reservoir and a few trees. There are still two large pepper trees growing so close together they look like one. These trees are possibly of early mission planting. Other trees may have been scattered about, and have been destroyed for the lands have been farmed for many years, and nearly all evidence of the earlier occupancy has been obliterated. It is a question now whether it is advisable to restore these historic surroundings with their subsequent deserted and barren atmosphere, or whether to create a garden more or less of the design then in vogue wherever European culture and civilization had been established. . . . For purely historical reasons, the bare dusty area is the best treatment, but it will be of little interest to the majority of the visitors who come today. The historically-minded minority will question the present treatment. It is probable that if the missions had continued, some attempt would have been made to improve the amenities of the buildings. The gardens as now designed and planted are perhaps what might have happened under authority and guide of a mission padre interested in plants. During the year 1938, some 20,000 visitors came to the park, most of these have shown as much interest in the garden as in the buildings, and there has also been much appreciation of the educational value of the planting.[14]

In this brief passage Rowe outlined nearly all the important arguments that could be used to justify elaborate garden restorations. No

[13] Guy L. Fleming to A. E. Henning, June 17, 1938, La Purisima—Fleming, District Superintendent, California State Archives, Sacramento; Olaf T. Hagen to Regional Director, August 18, 1938, and V. Aubrey Neasham to Newton B. Drury, August 19, 1938, Tumacacori National Monument, 101—General, NPS records.

[14] E. D. Rowe, Report of the Gardens and Plants at La Purisima Mission, August 1939, Proposed National Historic Sites, California, o–36, NPS records.

one would want to see a bare and dusty area, even if it were authentic. Possibly a "historically-minded minority" would object to ornamental gardens, but such a group would be balanced by thousands of visitors who would find the site very educational. Then there was always the remote possibility that European culture could have been more "established" in California, or an occasional priest might have been very interested in plants. When the causes of history and aesthetics collided, beauty almost always won. Compromises had to be made, even in keeping the very old trees that might have been part of the original gardens. Perhaps landscape architects had learned how to argue their plans effectively. Certainly most executives charged with the supervision of restorations did not want to present something ugly to the public. The public needed refreshment, not desolation.

At Williamsburg the artistry and persuasive talents of Arthur Shurcliff fitted in well with the love John D. Rockefeller, Jr., had for ornamental gardens. The ideal of historical accuracy was important when architects dealt with restoring or reconstructing Virginia buildings. But, where gardens were concerned, the revival of the past was the creation of a picture of beauty, a romantic setting that would give pleasure. The historical research at Williamsburg and the archaeology done for the building operations only gave a shadowy view of the landscape of the town. The comments from the Department of Research did not convince Kenneth Chorley that accuracy was more important than questions of time, cost, and visitor comfort. At Stratford Hall Shurcliff was able to persuade the Robert E. Lee Memorial Foundation that the formal gardens around the plantation house were indeed grand in scale. There was some archaeological evidence for paths and terraces, and there was no person in the Stratford Hall project comparable to Harold Shurtleff to produce evidence that Thomas Lee did not have a great display of boxwood.

The arguments preserved in the files at La Purisima show that thousands of miles away from Williamsburg, National Park Service professionals argued in vain that the cause of historical accuracy would be harmed by an elaborate mission garden. Why did Rowe's reasoning succeed against the pleas of several historians and architects? Possibly one explanation is that La Purisima was to be a park, not a textbook. A park should educate and give pleasure. The reconstructed mission did not belong to the padres and Indians who built it originally. To some extent the reconstruction belonged to the CCC enrollees who worked on it for six years. But the people of California really owned the site, and their needs were paramount.

Today we face a reevaluation of many of these restorations, based on budgetary considerations and new research techniques. We have ample evidence that the restorers in the 1930s discussed their garden decisions in a clear and rational manner. Usually historians and architects were unimpressed with the ideas of the landscape fraternity, who nevertheless most often prevailed. Today we might well decide to present these gardens with greater simplicity. But now the plantings are fifty years old. They are not only decorative; they have become a part of the history of garden restorations. At least two generations of visitors have come to know these landscapes as historical exhibits. It should be said that the colonial revival gardens have finally become historical artifacts that deserve our care and respect.

Wilson Eyre and the Colonial Revival in Philadelphia
Edward Teitelman and Betsy Fahlman

Until recently, the colonial revival has too often been viewed as the creation of New York and Boston architects, but the contributions of those working in other parts of the United States must also be considered in order to achieve a balanced view of this movement. Other major cities were energetically exploring colonial styles. Philadelphia's importance was described in 1912 by C. Matlack Price: "Possibly no group of architects in this country has so thoroughly grasped the spirit of the Colonial style of architecture as the group in Philadelphia, whence have come of late years developments of the Revolutionary farmhouse as clever as they are excellent. Certain individuals and firms in New York have been successful in their studies in the style, but their work has lacked the logical consistency and the pleasant uniformity that characterize the Pennsylvania work."[1]

The distinctive character of the colonial revival in Philadelphia and the local specificity of that city's new architecture evoked considerable

[1] C. Matlack Price, "The Allusive Simplicity of Colonial Decoration: Some Examples of Pure Colonial Interiors by Philadelphia Architects," *Arts and Decorations* 2, no. 12 (October 1912): 426. Although Price was mainly considering the work of Mellor and Meigs; Duhring, Okie, and Ziegler; Thomas, Churchman, and Molitor; Savery, Scheetz, and Savery; and Baily and Bassett—architects who came after Wilson Eyre—his observations hold true for Eyre and his contemporaries as well.

discussion in the contemporary literature, as noted by an unidentified critic: "There has been evolved a type of country house which, quite unlike most American work, is a logical development—a type in which there is more local than borrowed precedent and in which local materials are frankly expressed in terms of honest craftsmanship." Even that romantic colonial revivalist Wallace Nutting perceived the singular character of southeastern Pennsylvania architecture, finding around Philadelphia "a more careful attention to the harmonizing of dwelling with country landscape. There is a quieter tone and a better taste generally manifest in this suburban district than we find in others. Furthermore, the stability and obvious attention of permanence conveyed by the Pennsylvania homesteads is most satisfying. Anything which makes for peace in a country landscape is of the highest importance, for that is what American life needs most. Anything that makes for permanence appeals to that sense of eternal which is so little exemplified by modern civilization."[2]

Rich but idiosyncratic, the Philadelphia tradition of colonial building made equally rich and idiosyncratic contributions to the national colonial revival movement. As much a colonial survival as a revival, the style began after the 1876 International Centennial Exposition but underwent its mature synthesis in the city during the first decades of the twentieth century through a body of architectural work characterized by a free and creative adaptation of old forms. The primary force in the creation of this new style was Philadelphia architect Wilson Eyre (1858–1944), whose continuation of regional traditions was fused with a new sophistication and eclecticism that grew out of late nineteenth-century architectural and cultural developments. Although the outstanding figure in the revival movement, he was in fact part of a communal effort to reinterpret the vernacular in light of new standards of comfort, taste, and scale as well as wider architectural knowledge. His colleagues Walter Cope, John Stewardson, and Frank Miles Day, as well as many other Philadelphia architects, including William L. Price and even Frank Furness, all contributed in different ways to this effort. Still, Eyre was

[2] "The Pennsylvania Type, a Logical Development: Recent Work by Mellor and Meigs, D. Knickerbocker Boyd, Duhring, Okie, and Ziegler," *Architectural Record* 32, no. 4 (October 1912): 307; Wallace Nutting, *Pennsylvania Beautiful (Eastern)* (1924; reprint ed., New York: Bonanza Books, n.d.), p. 8.

by far the most creative and most successful in establishing the new synthesis.

When figures of the next generation (such as Walter Mellor and Arthur Meigs, Edmund Gilchrist and Robert McGoodwin) became more literal in their recreation and reevocation of the colonial, it was still usually the local vernacular country and village structures that they chose for their models. There was a continuing emphasis on craft, informality, comfort, convenience, and the show of restraint—elements of the ongoing Philadelphia regional tradition.

In order to appreciate fully the character of Philadelphia's exceptional contribution to the colonial revival, it is necessary to consider the particular historical conditions that made the local farmhouse form possible and thus led to Philadelphia's distinctive country house architecture. The city and the surrounding fertile valleys settled by William Penn and his followers after 1682 appear to have been unique among the English settlements. The land and the Indians were for the most part hospitable, and sparse European habitation by Swedish, Finnish, Dutch, and English colonists had already occurred over the greater part of the preceding century. Penn's plantation attracted Welsh and English Friends, German Dutch Pietists, and many craftsmen and middle-class people to what quickly became a prosperous establishment. The building trades seem also to have benefited from the immigration of large numbers of workers who had gained experience in the rebuilding of London after the Great Fire but who were now unemployed. Local fieldstone (a handsome mica schist which weathers into shades of gray and brown) as well as brick clay and limestone were readily available. These materials, with which the immigrants were already familiar, fit into their established masonry building traditions.

A snowy yet temperate climate, a geography characterized by rolling hills and valleys, and the presence of a group of building traditions— several of which were highly sophisticated—led to the creation of buildings different from those developing either to the north or to the south. The farmhouses and country structures grew with an easy and informal ambience, often snuggled partly into the hills, never attempting a formal sense of dominance over nature (fig. 1). Walls were substantial plain surfaces of brick, stone, or pebble dash. Additions and changes to the structures reflected only a basic harmony of scale and an asymme-

Fig. 1. Farmhouse, Old York Road near Owen Wistar's house, Philadelphia; demolished. From John T. Farris, *Old Roads Out of Philadelphia* (Philadelphia: J. B. Lippincott Co., 1917), p. 262.

trical balance, retaining an overall cohesion within the diversity of individual parts. Specific elements, such as pent eaves, owed their origin to
Welsh and German sources. Queen Anne and Georgian were the dominant modes not only for the high-art city work but for the overall scale
and massing of the country structures as well. There was little of the
medieval style that flourished in New England.

The high-art efforts in the city reached a notable level of sophistication by the mid eighteenth century. These buildings were compatible
with the professional principles espoused by Carpenters' Company, among
others. If more clearly related to England, this work nevertheless had
local peculiarities and may also have reflected Philadelphia's German
heritage as well as the city's commercial associations with Southern
Europe and the West Indies. There is a heavier handling of detail as
well as a stronger simplification than in London work of the period.

By the time of the centennial exposition, Philadelphia was a center of heavy industry and commerce but still retained its "country heart" and its strong attachment to the leisured suburban life that had been Penn's original ideal. Many old Philadelphia families continued to live on the farms that had been their ancestral homesteads. Furthermore, much of the colonial city survived in downtown areas. That Philadelphia was no longer the political, commercial, or intellectual capital of the country was of little concern to its residents: for the essential values of the city were modest, stressing then—as even now—the primary importance of home, comfort, and quiet prosperity. Students of the city have, like Nathaniel Burt in 1963, commented on its "middleness," Burt questioning rather ruefully whether "Philadelphians hold to the past so long that they abandon it just when it is picturesque and fashionable elsewhere," thus always staying a bit behind fashion.[3]

But Cornelius Weygandt saw matters more as a Philadelphian and in 1938 affirmed the city's easy affection for the past: "We like to feel that we are very like our Colonial ancestors. We shrug our shoulders and let it pass when we are called 'stick-in-the-muds.' We have houses that are 200 years old, and we reproduce them in our homes. We have 200 year old trees on the lawns of our suburban homes. We hang onto our forebears' treasures, to Savery highboys, to Randolph chairs, to Peale paintings, and to Strickland prints, to Syng silver, and to Tucker china." It is just that, as is not the case in other American cities, Philadelphians do not proclaim their worship of the past loudly—as Horace Lippincott well understood: "Philadelphians do not feel a necessity or a propriety in shouting about their importance or usefulness. After all, it is enough to just *be it*."[4]

Spurred by the Centennial, patriotic, wealthy, and leisured patrons commissioned new and spacious colonial revival homes in Boston, Newport, and New York. As others began to revere and revive the colonial past, Philadelphia continued to do what it had always been doing while absorbing the new concerns and values. Eyre was the pivotal and

[3] Cornelius Weygandt, *Philadelphia Folks* (New York: Appleton-Century, 1938), p. 1; Nathaniel Burt, *Perennial Philadelphians: An Anatomy of an American Aristocracy* (Boston: Little, Brown, 1963), p. 35.

[4] Weygandt, *Philadelphia Folks*, p. xi; Horace M. Lippincott, *A Narrative of Chestnut Hill, Philadelphia, with Some Account of Springfield, Whitemarsh, and Cheltenham Townships in Montgomery County, Pennsylvania* (Jenkintown: Old York Road Publishing Co., 1948), p. 93.

most creative artisan influenced by the Philadelphia tradition as it was modified by the colonial revival.[5]

Although he was born in Florence, Italy, Wilson Eyre was the child of an old Philadelphia family, which numbered among its members Tobias Lear, secretary to George Washington during the Revolution.[6] Eyre was educated in Florence, then at a school in Newport, Rhode Island, and briefly at the Massachusetts Institute of Technology. In 1877 he became a draftsman in the Philadelphia office of James Peacock Sims (1859–82), an architect strongly influenced by English sources. Advancing quickly in the practice, Eyre appears to have helped to shift the character of the firm's work from high Gothic and a strong Shavian Queen Anne revival emphasis to a softer, more indigenous style exhibiting greater horizontality. An 1881 double house for the Sinn brothers in Germantown, a commission that Eyre probably brought into the office and that he apparently designed, reveals a new awareness of the possibilities of plain surfaces and the aesthetic qualities of the farmhouse.[7] While Vincent J. Scully, Jr., and James D. Kornwolf tend to emphasize Eyre's English sources and frequent use of English detail at

[5] Although William B. Rhoads in his seminal discussion of the colonial revival, *The Colonial Revival* (New York: Garland Publishing, 1977), included Eyre in his brief chapter on Philadelphia (thereby recognizing Eyre's importance to the colonial revival in the area), not all of his views on Eyre and Philadelphia can be supported. His claim that Eyre did not use colonial elements until the 1890s (*Colonial Revival*, p. 105) is refuted by Eyre's famous Charles Potter house of 1883 (see Vincent J. Scully, Jr., *The Shingle Style and the Stick Style* [1955; rev. ed., New Haven: Yale University Press, 1971], figs. 97, 98). The colonial gooseneck pediment placed over the Potter door reveals that Eyre had an interest in colonial motifs almost from the start of his independent practice. Other works, including those cited in this article, offer further contradiction. Rhoads's view that Eyre was influenced by Shaw and Godwin seems to have been taken uncritically from James D. Kornwolf, *M. H. Baillie Scott and the Arts and Crafts Movement* (Baltimore: Johns Hopkins University Press, 1972). A study of Eyre's total body of work refutes Kornwolf on this point. Further, Eyre was neither "academic and cold" nor "completely academic" by 1917. Neither was he ever a true advocate of "historical styles and Beaux Arts training." Although late in his life Eyre did express misgivings about his early work, writing superficially in favor of the Beaux-Arts approach by then dominant, there is no substantial evidence that his design methods or values changed significantly. Finally, Rhoads's claim that Philadelphia lost her preeminence in architecture "during the course of the nineteenth century" is simply not true (*Colonial Revival*, pp. 105, 106, 107, 104).

[6] Many colonial heirlooms descended in the Eyre family. See, for instance, Roger Caye, "The Office and Apartments of a Philadelphia Architect," *Architectural Record* 25, no. 1 (July 1913): 78–88. Eyre also possessed books on colonial architecture in his library and saved views of colonial and colonial revival structures in his office scrapbooks.

[7] See *American Architect and Building News* 9, no. 282 (May 21, 1881).

this time, local vernacular also appears in his work quite early and develops in parallel with his continuing interest in England, which was itself looking more and more to the early English vernacular structures that were in many ways similar to our own.

When Sims died suddenly in 1882, Eyre assumed the practice at the age of twenty-four. The W. Moylan Lansdale house (now totally rebuilt) in Chester County near Philadelphia followed two years later in 1884.[8] The structure was a free fantasy version of the Pennsylvania farmhouse with some allusions both to the shingle style and to Frank Furness's local William K. Rhawn house (Knowlton) of 1879–81. A great asymmetrical mass, the Lansdale house was covered by a group of gambrel and half-gambrel roofs. The detailing was Georgian, but its openness and sweep were clearly designed for a more leisurely style of life than would have been found on a working colonial farm. Surfaces were broad and largely unornamented, and the skill of the stone mason as well as the varied beauty of the fieldstone were stressed throughout.

Eyre worked during the next decade and a half in a variety of styles. These were never pure essays but often combined Queen Anne revival scale and detail with the broader masses and surfaces characteristic of the vernacular. He especially favored the gambrel roof, using it in 1885 on an otherwise rather Flemish city house in Camden, New Jersey, as well as on a contemporary steam plant and laundry for a nearby hospital. At the same time in Camden, he also altered (with shingle details) a modest, somewhat Greek revival vernacular Quaker meetinghouse, respecting and extending the original design.[9]

Camden's 1892 Howard M. Cooper house (fig. 2) was another revealing example of Eyre's efforts to expand the indigenous farmhouse tradition in combination with other elements. A free variation on the central-hall farmhouse, its plan was in fact asymmetrical and rather loose, perhaps even too contrived in its asymmetry. Set on the corner of a semi-suburban lot, the house had living and dining rooms that opened onto a back and side lawn with a large simple veranda. The formal parlor was done in a highly personalized version of the Georgian style. Indi-

[8] See *American Architect and Building News* 22, no. 606 (August 6, 1887).
[9] See Edward Teitelman, "Wilson Eyre in Camden: The Henry Genet Taylor House and Office," *Winterthur Portfolio* 15, no. 3 (Autumn 1980): 229–55, for some discussion of all of these commissions. See also Edward Teitelman, "A Queen Anne Quaker Meetinghouse: Newton Meeting, Camden, New Jersey," *Quaker History* 55, no. 2 (Autumn 1966): 104–10.

Fig. 2. Wilson Eyre, Diamond Cottage, Howard M. Cooper house, Camden, N.J., 1892; demolished. (Photo ca. 1900, collection of Edward Teitelman.)

vidually, the moldings might be regarded as correct colonial reproductions, but they were used here in combinations that would never have been found in a genuine colonial house. However, the central hall spoke clearly and invitingly of home, as did most of the other spaces. Simple Greek revival mantels saved from an 1831 family home were incorporated in several of the rooms, although these did not prevent Eyre from also employing Gothic motifs alongside the basically Greek antiques and colonial allusions.[10]

The Joseph Burroughs house in Chestnut Hill (1888) is an instructive transitional work. The round tower in the front might be Norman, yet it is attached to a stone and pebble-dash farmhouse. The kitchen porch (fig. 3) conveys a serene impression of artlessness and, viewed after nearly

[10] See Edward Teitelman, "The Howard Mickle Cooper House," *Camden County Historical Society Bulletin*, no. 35 (Spring 1983): 1–10.

Fig. 3. Wilson Eyre, kitchen porch of Joseph Burroughs house, Philadelphia, 1888. (Photo, Edward Teitelman.)

a century of use, continues to evoke that sense of agelessness and human presence among genteel disorder and decay that was conspicuously part of both Philadelphia's cultural tradition and Eyre's domestic aesthetic. His interest in certain aspects of older buildings, whether in America, England, or other European countries, was largely due to the enduring quality of comfort found in gradual change over time, an agelessness that goes beyond specific period. However, while strongly imbued with this notion, Eyre always sought to make a contemporary building that met current needs and was well suited to the lives of his patrons.

In a city house and office of 1894 for Dr. Joseph Leidy, Eyre developed an inventive plan which included a small physician's office within a largely asymmetrical dwelling set behind a symmetrical Georgian facade.[11] Interestingly, it was built in studied relationship to Eyre's earlier, more French-flavored Clarence Moore house (1890) directly next door (with which it shares an inner wall) to form a varied but balanced composition. The concentration of ornament in the since-removed elaborate cartouche above the front door (also removed) was characteristic of Eyre's approach to external decoration, which he preferred to focus in specific areas. The Leidy house represents a relatively sophisticated work and marks Eyre's continuing free adaptation of the local vernacular in the process of arriving at a new comfortable form of-architecture.

Although most of Eyre's work in the colonial revival found expression in residences, an exception is the small banking house he designed for Charles L. Borie in 1893 (fig. 4). Described in 1903 as "a charming study in the Colonial,"[12] it is characterized by the sense of small scale that is found in his best public buildings. It is an example of his effort to reinterpret the Georgian with a new concentration on craft in combination with a baroque exuberance. Another city work, the J. Webster Dougherty remodeling of 1900 (fig. 5) is similar to the Borie bank in its simplification and distortion of Georgian detail and scale. A total reworking of two row houses, thus leading to urban variety, the structure breaks stylistically with its neighbors while keeping some of their proportions and placement of elements. The arrangement of the facade results in further dynamic visual tension. Despite its seeming correctness and symmetry, the final result is anything but pure colonial.

Although Eyre at times turned out some closer approximations of the colonial, the more "correct" he became, the less vital the design tended to be. These more imitative commissions are located primarily outside of the Philadelphia region (mostly in Connecticut and New York) and for clients not of Philadelphia origins.[13] One of the more successful of these was a summer house (1901) for William K. Bixby at Bolton Landing on Lake George, New York (fig. 6). Called Mohican Cottage, it

[11] See Teitelman, "Eyre in Camden," p. 252.

[12] Julian Millard, "The Work of Wilson Eyre," *Architectural Record* 14, no. 4, (October 1903): 285.

[13] Beyond those commissions discussed are, for example, the Z. Bennett Phelps house in Binghamton, N.Y. (1901), the Frances A. Phelps house in Wilkes-Barre, Pa. (1900), and the Melbert B. Cary house in Ridgefield, Conn. (1908).

Fig. 4. Wilson Eyre, Charles L. Borie Bank, Philadelphia, 1896. (Photo, Edward Teitelman.)

took its inspiration from the building demolished for its erection, a genuine colonial tavern, then thought to be one of the oldest buildings on Lake George.

Critics and architects did not always have a clear conception of regional differences in various colonial styles, often condensing several geographical areas into one. As one writer inaccurately noted of Mohican Cottage, "the house is treated in the style characteristic of country residences of Colonial New York and New England."[14] Although the Bixby

[14] " 'Mohican Cottage,' Bolton-Landing-on-Lake-George, New York," *House and Garden* 3, no. 1 (January 1903): 28.

Fig. 5. Wilson Eyre, perspective, J. Webster
Dougherty house, Philadelphia, 1900. (Architectural Archives of the University of Pennsylvania.)

house more closely approximates proper academic form than most of
Eyre's other work does, the strange placement of the corner columns
framing the open porches, the odd bay window jarringly positioned under
a portico, the general horizontal arrangement, and the jumble of rooms
at the rear continue to remind one of comfortable, rambling, old Philadelphia country houses.

A similar sort of work was Ashford, the 1900 Frank Squier house

Fig. 6. Wilson Eyre, Mohican Cottage, William K. Bixby house, Bolton Landing, Lake George, N.Y., 1901. (Photo, Edward Teitelman.)

high on a hill outside of Greenwich, Connecticut.[15] *American Architect* in 1905 classed this structure with McKim, Mead, and White's James L. Breese house (1898), the Orchards, in Southampton on Long Island. Both were seen as more suitable for wealthy families such as the Astors than the copies of Florentine palazzi they usually favored.[16] The Squier house is a close approximation of correct Georgian only in spots;

[15] See " 'Ashford,' Belle Haven, Connecticut, Designed by Wilson Eyre, Jr.," *House and Garden* 1, no. 1 (August 1901): 65–70. It is also illustrated in Alfred Morton Githens, "Wilson Eyre, Jr., His Work," in *Architectural Annual*, ed. Albert Kelsey (Philadelphia: Architectural Annual for the Architectural League of America, 1900), p. 128. An unusual detail in sketches found at Avery Library and at University of Pennsylvania is Eyre's delineation technique: streaking white lines on dark paper to make the clapboards read as strongly horizontal. This method of drawing is also used in a sketch Eyre made of Mount Vernon about the same date (University of Pennsylvania).

[16] *American Architect and Building News* 87, no. 1523 (March 4, 1905): 74, as quoted in William B. Rhoads, "The Colonial Revival and American Nationalism," *Journal of the Society of Architectural Historians* 35, no. 4 (December 1976): 244. Eyre admired colonial revival buildings by his contemporaries, including two by McKim, Mead, and White—the Breese house and Sherrewogue, the house of Devereaux Emmett at Saint James on Long Island (see Sherwin Hawley, "Good Taste in County Houses, Two Dozen

numerous accommodations to comfort are evident, including two por-
ticoed porches that allude to T. U. Walter's Greek revival riverfront
wing at Andalusia.

It was about this same time, in 1901, when Eyre was well established
in the profession, that he and two other Philadelphia architects—Frank
Miles Day (1861–1918) and Herbert Clifton Wise (1873–1945)—founded
and edited the magazine *House and Garden*.[17] One of the main purposes of the periodical was to bring to a tasteful and educated readership
the point of view of architects. Their philosophy was that the house and
garden should be considered equally in design, a notion that furthered
the development of the country house in America.

In its early years, the magazine concentrated on architecture and was
aimed at those with interests similar to the editors' own. It summed up
the genteel electicism of Philadelphia and in so doing gave prominence
both to actual colonial buildings and to the colonial revival. Still, *House
and Garden* did not champion a single architectural style but pressed
more generally for high standards of design, practicality, and comfort.
By avoiding out-and-out polemics but exposing the colonial widely in a
context appealing to a broad range of sensitive readers, it may have done
more to increase the popularity of the colonial revival than if it had
been more deliberately slanted toward that style. In this broad appeal,
it differed greatly from, for example, *The Craftsman*, which more nar-
rowly sponsored the mission style and the arts and crafts movement.

In the first several years of publication, for instance, *House and Garden* featured Cope and Stewardson's farmhouse-related efforts at Aubury
(fig. 7) along with the colonial revival work of Eyre, Day, Charles Platt,
and others, as well as colonial homes in New York, New England, and
Philadelphia. Henry Chapman Mercer's experiments in reviving the
technique of making Moravian tiles were illustrated with Eyre sketches

---

American Country Houses Chosen by Four Successful Architects—What They Considered to be Representative—a Diversity of Styles," *Country Life in America* 10, no. 6
[October 1906]: 611–24).

[17] See Patricia Heintzelman Keebler, "The Life and Work of Frank Miles Day" (Ph.D.
diss., University of Delaware, 1980). Keebler indicated that Day "referred to Wise as an
expert in Colonial architecture" (p. 277), and, indeed, Herbert Wise later coauthored
(with H. Ferdinand Beidleman) *Colonial Architecture for Those about to Build* (Philadelphia: J. B. Lippincott Co., 1913). For Day's involvement with *House and Garden*, see
Keebler, "Frank Miles Day," p. 199. See also Richardson Wright, "How *House and
Garden* Began," *House and Garden* 50, no. 1 (July 1926): 68–71, 116.

Fig. 7. Cope and Stewardson, Aubrey, Edward Toland house, White-marsh, Pa., ca. 1895. From *House and Garden* 1, no. 2 (July 1901): 19.

of Mercer's converted farmhouse as well as with photographs of tiles and some of the Pennsylvania German firebacks on which the designs were based. A story about the Delaware River town of New Castle, Delaware, was extensively illustrated by Eyre (fig. 8) and featured the colonial buildings still standing in what had been a Dutch and Swedish settlement and a major urban center of Penn's Lower Provinces.[18] The picturesque, adaptive way Eyre saw the old becomes evident when one compares the sketches with the buildings themselves.

During the last twenty years of his career, Eyre arrived at a new synthesis of contemporary needs and allusions to the old which brought a quality of low-art timelessness and charm to a high-art high. Such large country houses as John W. Pepper's second Fairacres, dating from 1904

[18] See H. L. Carncross, "The Old Town of New Castle, Delaware," *House and Garden* 1, no. 2 (July 1901): 9–15.

Fig. 8. Wilson Eyre, sketch, Immanuel Episcopal Church, New Castle, Del., ca. 1901. Built eighteenth century. From *House and Garden* 1, no. 2 (July 1901): 31.

(demolished), had English and vernacular farmhouse characteristics while emphasizing the exquisite craft of the mason, a combination worked into largely timeless forms.[19] Typical of Philadelphia's big places, it was unpretentious, large, and comfortable—clearly a home of importance, but, above all, a home.

Montrose, the John Townsend house (1912) in Radnor, is another work in local stone which brings both English and American farmhouse forms together.[20] The Palladian motif in the French door and the details of the stonework and the unpainted wood provide the main ornamentation. Ageless permanence and artistry are seen again in the Howard Henry house (1904 and 1911) set unpretentiously in the hillside beneath George Washington's fortifications north of Philadelphia (fig. 9). Even what might be called the quintessential Philadelphia country seat, Hunting

[19] See Frederick Wallick, " 'Fairacres' and Some Other Recent Country Houses by Wilson Eyre," *International Studio* 40, no. 158 (April 1910): xxix–xxxiv.

[20] See "The Townsend House, Radnor, Pennsylvania," *Architectural Record* 44, no. 4 (October 1918): 376ff. Drawings for this commission are to be found at Avery Library.

Fig. 9. Wilson Eyre, Little Orchard Farm, Howard Henry house, Fort Washington, Pa., 1904 and 1911. From *American Architect* 97, no. 1797 (June 1, 1916): n.p.

Hill Farm, a 2,500-acre estate built for Walter Jeffords in 1914 which included a ballroom for a thousand, was underplayed, fairly informal, and displayed Eyre's highly personal sense of design.[21] Built around a small 1780 farmhouse, the original farmhouse fabric was left intact outside and in, the extensive additions built as two wings half buried in a hillside. The entrance feels informal and unassuming and does not hide the old structure.

At Sunnybrook, the Isaac Clothier, Jr., house in Radnor (1923) (fig. 10), Eyre balanced earlier additions made by Arthur Brockie about 1907 and 1913 to an 1813 farmhouse. Eyre kept the structure close to the road, behind a high wall. Its rear aspect opens onto a high sheltering

[21] The Jeffords estate is located near Media, Pennsylvania, and is now Ridley Creek State Park. Drawings for this commission are to be found at University of Pennsylvania. Eyre and John Gilbert McIlvaine (1880–1939), who was then his partner, received the first Gold Medal of the Philadelphia Chapter of the American Institute of Architects for this commission.

Fig. 10. Wilson Eyre, elevations, Sunnybrook, Isaac Clothier, Jr., house, 1923 additions to an altered 1813 farmhouse, Radnor, Pa. From *Yearbook of the Twenty-sixth Annual Architectural Exhibition* (Philadelphia: Philadelphia Chapter A.I.A. and T-Square Club, 1923), n.p.

hillside. He added a gambreled form, leaving a long, rambling composition eminently comfortable, if large, which embodies the Philadelphia colonial at its most appealing.

But the vernacular regionalism of Wilson Eyre and Philadelphia is best seen in smaller houses that are closer to the farmhouse in scale and whose restraint and understatement are most concentrated. Perhaps Eyre's most sublime house was designed in 1907 for William Turner in Germantown (fig. 11). Set along a drive at an edge of the property, it appears to be a farmhouse built close to a rural lane. Its subtly articulated expanse, massive chimney, and interlocking surface planes provide the main focus of ornamentation, with the exception of two simple lead lanterns which had hung on the corners along the entrance drive. Before the house was altered and added to as a retirement home for ministers, the view from the back revealed a comfortable, contemporary country spread— verandas, sleeping porches, and patios for summer living close to the land. A studiously picturesque barn and garage were also included and remain. Interior detail harmoniously uses colonial elements, combined

Fig. 11. Wilson Eyre, Lycoming, William Turner house, Philadelphia, 1907. From *American Architect* 94, no. 1719 (December 2, 1908): n.p.

in new ways with Mercer tiles and other manifestations of contemporary craft. In the Charles Ladd house of 1905 in Ardmore, which uses a site partway down a hillside for both protection and drama, Eyre again revealed how comfortable he was working within the restrained Pennsylvania farmhouse tradition while still supplying creative new forms for contemporary life.

C. Matlack Price called Eyre and his work the "neutral brown" thread that mellows all the others in the web of American architecture.[22] Certainly Eyre used Philadelphia's colonial traditions to establish his mature residential style, which was founded on the local pre-Revolutionary vernacular. An asymmetrical, strongly articulated, and yet comfortable and almost timeless style, it has continued to be the stimulus for the work of the generations that followed in making Philadelphia an outstanding

[22]C. Matlack Price, "The Development of a National Architecture, the Work of Wilson Eyre—Fifth Article," *Arts and Decoration* 3, no. 1 (November 1912): 16.

center of residential architecture. Idiosyncratic and perhaps more a survival than a revival, the colonial style was, in Eyre's hands, at once inventive and quiet, artistic and yet without artificiality. This is a different sort of colonial revival than that found in Boston or New York. Specifically local, individual, yet strongly communal, Eyre's work is at once rich and ageless.

Toward a National Style of Architecture: The Beaux-Arts Interpretation of the Colonial Revival

Mardges Bacon

The belief in progress and the desire for order which dominated late nineteenth-century American thought also guided the search for a national style of architecture. In the years following the Philadelphia centennial exhibition of 1876, architects began to discover and revive an American building tradition, producing what is now known as the colonial revival. Between 1890 and the depression, practitioners of the colonial revival were predominantly educated in Paris at the Ecole des Beaux-Arts or in America at schools that reflected Beaux-Arts methods and principles. Although their architecture was broadly labeled "Beaux-Arts," it embraced a variety of stylistic categories, among which the colonial revival most ardently expressed a growing need for national identity.[1]

Research for this paper was made possible by a Trinity College Junior Faculty Department Grant. I would like to thank John A. Chewning, Samuel Haber, William H. Jordy, and Sarah Bradford Landau for their assistance in the preparation of this manuscript.

[1] William B. Rhoads accounts for the historical use of the terms *colonial* and *colonial revival* in the preface to his work *The Colonial Revival* (New York: Garland Publishing, 1977), pp. xxxvi–xxxxiv. Other studies on the colonial revival include Vincent J. Scully, Jr., *The Shingle Style* (New Haven: Yale University Press, 1955); Richard Guy Wilson, "The Early Work of Charles F. McKim: Country House Commissions," *Winterthur Portfolio* 14, no. 3 (Autumn 1979): 235–67. For a discussion of the search for national

In their search for nationalism during the late nineteenth century, Beaux-Arts architects applied the discipline of their French education to restore order to a century dominated by what they perceived as a chaos of revival styles. Two central and inextricably linked objectives characterized the Beaux-Arts search for order. First, architects applied a "scientific" working method—the academic Beaux-Arts method—to design. Second, they promoted an evolutionary approach to historical style. Beaux-Arts architects eschewed the recent past, preferring to restore seventeenth- and eighteenth-century French and American classicism. In effect, they propelled the Renaissance into modern times.

A Beaux-Arts education was considered scientific because it consisted of a rigid curriculum, a specific working method or procedure for design, and a set of design principles. Louis Sullivan believed that the school had taught him "the concrete value of logical thinking" and later helped him to develop his own "scientific system of thought and expression." Training in the Beaux-Arts system was conducted on two fronts: internally, during the course instruction, and externally, through a student's affiliation with an atelier, or studio. The curriculum was comprehensive, students receiving instruction in mathematics, perspective, architectural composition, construction, and scientific subjects. The academic year was divided into a series of long and short design projects for which students received credits or points *(valeurs)* leading to promotion and, after 1867, a diploma.[2]

The Ecole des Beaux-Arts taught a method or procedure of design beginning with a preliminary sketch *(esquisse)* and ending with the final project *(projet rendu)* submitted to a jury. Each step in the design process was informed by principles of composition based on an architectural repository of past styles, fundamentally concentrating on Renaissance classicism. In his *Eléments et théorie de l'architecture* (1901–4), Julien Guadet, professor of theory at the Ecole des Beaux Arts, summarized many aspects of late nineteenth-century architectural theory, defining

identity, see William B. Rhoads, "The Colonial Revival and American Nationalism," *Journal of the Society of Architectural Historians* 35, no. 4 (December 1976): 239–54.

[2] Claude Bragdon, "Letters from Louis Sullivan," *Architecture* 64, no. 1 (July 1931): 8. Sullivan spent from 1874 to 1875 first preparing for the entrance exams and then as a student at the Ecole des Beaux-Arts. The school's curriculum was modified slightly during the nineteenth century. See Richard Chafee, "The Teaching of Architecture at the Ecole des Beaux-Arts," in *The Architecture of the Ecole des Beaux-Arts*, ed. Arthur Drexler (New York: Museum of Modern Art, 1977), pp. 77–109.

the path to architectural design through his notions of composition and character. Composition was "the solution to the program"; character was what Guadet called "legitimate variety" based on historical precedents, a quality "between the architectural impression and the moral impression of the program." Moreover, he identified specific principles of composition, among them the role of the plan as the generating factor of a composition such that exterior volumes would express interior functions. Guadet's principles of composition also included the importance of axes, distinctions between circulation and noncirculation, hierarchy of parts, procession of spaces, symmetry, balance, and variety. Variations of these principles were stated in a number of architectural treatises. Americans were less than meticulous about following the principles faithfully, so that aberrant forms of French classicism resulted. But for Guadet, the process of composition which began with historical prototypes was intended to be rational and scientific. "As method," Guadet maintained, "I will always endeavor to go from the simple to the compound, from the known to the unknown; I aspire to show that in architecture all proceeds from deduction."[3]

In place of composition and character, other nineteenth-century architectural theorists defined the path to architectural design as a function of *parti*—a term derived from *prendre parti*, literally "to take a side" or to "make a choice."[4] The architect exercised choice, the subjective component of architecture. Thus, for some theorists, the degree to which the Beaux-Arts method was "scientific" remained relative, for the architect was still free to choose what architectural models and what historical evidence or documents to present while manipulating design to express an academic rationale.

[3] See J[ulien] Guadet, *Eléments et théorie de l'architecture*, vol. 1 (1901; reprint ed., Paris: Librairie de la Construction Moderne, 1909), pp. 8, 132, chap. 3, "Main Rules of Composition," pp. 117–36, 9. In 1894 Guadet assumed the post of professor of theory. His lectures were later published as this four-volume work. For an extensive discussion of the working method taught at the Ecole des Beaux-Arts, see Chafee, "Teaching of Architecture," pp. 77–109. David Van Zanten analyzed the role of composition in his "Architectural Composition at the Ecole des Beaux-Arts from Charles Percier to Charles Garnier," in Drexler, *Architecture of the Ecole*, pp. 111–15; see also David Van Zanten, "le système des Beaux-Arts," *Architecture d'Aujourd'hui* 182 (November–December 1975): 97–106. For a list of Beaux-Arts architectural treatises, see Van Zanten, "Architectural Composition," p. 505, note 3. For a discussion of American aberrant forms, see Jean Paul Carlhian, "Beaux Arts or 'Bozarts'?" *Architectural Record* 159 (January 1976): 131–34.

[4] See Van Zanten's analysis of composition and *parti* in "Architectural Composition," pp. 112–15.

Beaux-Arts architects proposed a scientific explanation, not just a working method, to justify Renaissance classicism as a national style. Style, they argued, should be the product of evolution. Thomas Hastings and Ernest Flagg, two self-appointed spokesmen for the Beaux-Arts movement in America, articulated these notions, denouncing the revival styles which had dominated American architecture during most of the nineteenth century: Greek, Gothic, Romanesque, Queen Anne.[5] Hastings and Flagg maintained that these styles were anachronistic because they were unsuited to life in nineteenth-century America. For example, Hastings argued that Gothic architecture was suitable only for a cloister or a monastery because it expressed a "feverish and morbid aspiration peculiar to such mediaeval life." But Hastings and Flagg agreed that, in contrast to the Middle Ages, the Renaissance had produced a style that had survived and evolved for four centuries. "With the revival of learning . . . with the birth of modern science and literature . . . with this modern world," Hastings wrote in 1894, "there was evolved what we should now recognize as the modern architecture, the Renaissance." In identifying the evolution of style, Hastings was a true Darwinian. "The laws of natural selection and of the survival of the fittest," Hastings argued, "have shaped the history of architectural style just as truly as they have the different successive forms of life." If France was the immediate heir to the Italian Renaissance, then America was the distant heir. But a break from the proper Darwinian evolution of classical principles had occurred in the early nineteenth century. Flagg argued that the break began in America when the Greek and later the Gothic revival replaced colonial architecture: when "invention gave place to copying" and architects "abandoned their national style." Even France had suffered an analogous break, which Flagg maintained had occurred when "the horrors of the Empire" replaced the style of Louis XVI.[6]

<hr />

[5] Thomas Hastings, "The Relations of Life to Style in Architecture," *Harper's New Monthly* 88, no. 528 (May 1894): 959, 961; Ernest Flagg, "American Architecture as Opposed to Architecture in America," *Architectural Record* 10, no. 2 (October 1900): 178–80; Ernest Flagg, "Influence of the French School on Architecture in the United States," *Architectural Record* 4, no. 2 (October–December 1894): 214–15; Ernest Flagg, "The Truth about American Architecture," Ernest Flagg Papers, Avery Library, Columbia University.

[6] Hastings, "Relations of Life to Style," p. 960; Flagg, "Truth about Architecture," pp. 7–8.

Hastings and Flagg were joined by other proponents of the evolutionary concept of style. Guadet used this argument to justify classicism: "where progress was continued perfection, evolution, not revolution." Joy Wheeler Dow, an American architect trained outside the Beaux-Arts system, also called for a national style of architecture. In his book *American Renaissance*, Dow identified the Renaissance as the fountainhead of American architecture. Yet he saw the nineteenth-century styles, Greek revival among them, as a continuation of the Renaissance rather than a break with it. He believed that national style was the product of evolution and endurance.[7]

To Hastings, Flagg, and other Beaux-Arts architects, the eighteenth century represented the highest point in the evolution of classical principles toward a national style. Thus Hastings and Flagg embraced colonial and federal architecture in America and eighteenth-century architecture in France as ways of recapturing both the lost principles of the Renaissance and America's lost national style. By applying the scientific rigor of French theory and practice to American buildings, these and other Beaux-Arts architects hoped that the advance of classicism might result in a new style, both national and modern. Hastings and Flagg thereby encompassed the colonial revival within the broader context of a national style based on Renaissance classicism.

When Flagg called for a new national style, he applied his "scientific" argument, stipulating that a national style be "architectural" and not "archaeological." Unlike the nineteenth-century revival styles, which he considered archaeological, the new national style would not imitate foreign buildings divorced from the cultures that produced them. Rather, the national style should make use of "all the resources which modern science has placed at the disposal of the architect, which, if used logically that is, with the aid of reason, will call for new, fresh forms." But to provide a loophole in such rigid dogma, Flagg, like other Beaux-Arts architects, also embraced the notion of *parti*. Thus a national architecture, which Flagg called a *parti* for America, would not rely on one particular style, but could embrace a number of different directions or historical components. For Hastings, Flagg, and the other Beaux-Arts practitioners, this justified what has been called academic eclecticism

---

[7] Guadet, *Eléments et théorie de l'architecture*, 1:134; Joy Wheeler Dow, *American Renaissance* (New York: William T. Comstock, 1904), pp. 149–55.

or, more recently, "scientific eclecticism."[8] The *parti* most often reflected a synthesis of Renaissance classicism, French and American principally, and also English, Italian, and Spanish. Yet in the formation of a national style, their use of eclecticism was ultimately flawed by a paradox: how to be at once "modern" and "Renaissance."

Whether in architecture or planning, new construction or restoration, regardless of building type or program, Beaux-Arts architects applied their scientific working method and evolutionary understanding of historical style to design problems. A few case studies will illustrate the way in which Beaux-Arts methods conditioned the colonial revival after 1890.

The Senate Park Commission plan of 1901 for Washington, D.C. (fig. 1) illustrated both a scientific restoration and the evolution of the city's original eighteenth-century plan. It also confirmed America's search for nationalism. To celebrate the centennial of the nation's capital in 1900, the American Institute of Architects and its secretary, Glenn Brown, began a study of the city's plan and principal government buildings. The following year the Senate authorized a committee to study the improvement of the city and its park system. The Senate Committee on the District of Columbia was headed by Michigan senator James McMillan, whose secretary, Charles Moore, became the committee's spokesman. By April 1901 the committee had organized a group of professionals to study the problem and make recommendations. The Senate Park Commission—or McMillan Commission, as it became known—included four principals: Daniel Burnham and Charles McKim, who had collaborated earlier on the Chicago fair as master planner and Beaux-Arts architect respectively; the landscape architect, Frederick Law Olmsted, Jr.; and the sculptor, Augustus Saint-Gaudens. The commission had two tasks: to prepare a plan for the park system by recovering and developing the eighteenth-century plan for Washington and to locate future public buildings.[9]

[8] "A Letter by Ernest Flagg," in *The Architectural Annual*, ed. Albert Kelsey (Philadelphia: Architectural Annual for the Architectural League of America, 1900), pp. 31–32; Richard Guy Wilson, "Scientific Eclecticism," in *The American Renaissance, 1876–1917* (New York: Brooklyn Museum, 1979), pp. 57–61. Historians also shared a scientific working method and an evolutionary approach to their discipline. In his attempt to apply a scientific method to the study of history, Henry Adams helped to shape the so-called New History. Because he emphasized documentation rather than a narrative of events and heroes, Adams has been called a "scientific historian" (see William H. Jordy, *Henry Adams: Scientific Historian* [New Haven: Yale University Press, 1952], pp. 1–22).

[9] The Senate Park (McMillan) Commission plan of 1901 has been the subject of recent investigation. See John W. Reps, *The Making of Urban America* (Princeton: Princeton

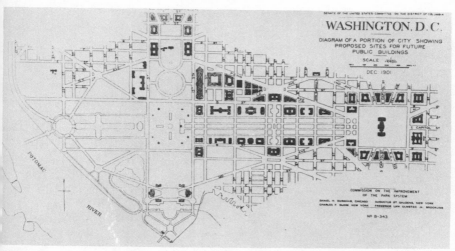

Fig. 1. "The Senate Park Commission Plan for Central Washington, D.C.: 1901." From Charles Moore, ed., *The Improvement of the Park System of the District of Columbia* (Senate Report no. 166, 57th Cong., 1st sess., 1902), fig. 302.

It became clear from their deliberations that the original 1791 plan for Washington (fig. 2), designed by the French artist and engineer, Maj. Pierre Charles L'Enfant (with Andrew Ellicott's assistance), had in the Senate Committee's words, "stood the test of a century" and "met universal approval." The commissioners vowed "to restore, develop, and supplement" L'Enfant. But their views had not been shared by the previous generation of architects, which had neglected, and in some

University Press, 1965), pp. 502–14; Frederick Gutheim, *The Federal City: Plans and Realities* (Washington, D.C.: Smithsonian Institution Press, 1976); and Thomas Walton, "The 1901 McMillan Commission: Beaux Arts Plan for the Nation's Capital" (Ph.D. diss., Catholic University of America, 1980). Augustus Saint-Gaudens, who was recommended by McKim, did not join the commission until June 1901 (see Charles F. McKim to Daniel H. Burnham, June 1, 1901, Charles Follen McKim Papers, Library of Congress, Washington, D.C.). The formation of the commission is chronicled in the "Report of the Senate Committee on the District of Columbia," in *The Improvement of the Park System of the District of Columbia*, ed. Charles Moore (Senate Report no. 166, 57th Cong., 1st sess., 1902), pp. 7–10. For comments on the commission's two tasks, see Charles Moore, *The Life and Times of Charles Follen McKim* (Boston and New York: Houghton Mifflin Co., 1929), p. 182; and "Report of the Senate Committee," p. 10.

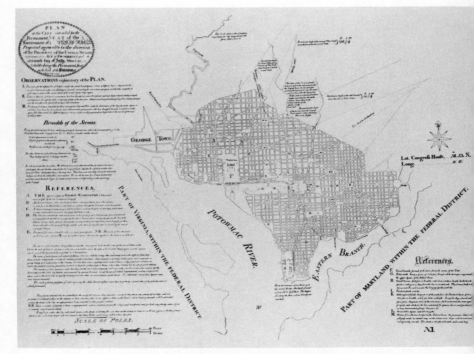

Fig. 2. Pierre Charles L'Enfant, plan for Washington, D.C., 1791. Facsimile made by the Coast and Geodetic Survey in 1887. From Werner Hegemann and Elbert Peets, *Civic Art* (New York: Architectural Book Publishing Co., 1922), fig. 1192.

cases deliberately sabotaged, the city's federal plan. By 1900 the formal clarity of the L'Enfant scheme had eroded to the point of chaos. First the Mall had come under the influence of the picturesque movement and its proponents, James Renwick and Andrew Jackson Downing; then the railroad station and tracks of the Baltimore and Potomac had intruded into the site. "The departures from that [L'Enfant's] plan are to be regretted," wrote the Senate Committee in its report, and "wherever possible, remedied."[10] If the L'Enfant scheme had "stood the test of a

[10] "Report of the Senate Committee," p. 10; "Report of the Park Commission," in Moore, *Improvement of the Park System*, p. 35. Ellicott's role in the plan of Washington

century," it only meant that the plan was salvageable despite those persistent violations and intrusions.

McKim and the other commissioners envisioned a full-scale restoration, "carrying to a legitimate conclusion the comprehensive, intelligent, and yet simple and straightforward scheme devised by L'Enfant." Although most of the proposals brought before the American Institute of Architects convention in 1900 sought to clarify the layout of the existing city with formal treatments of government buildings, landscaping, and sculpture, these proposals honored the spirit, but not the central concept, of L'Enfant's plan. Cass Gilbert's proposal called for a complex grouping of buildings, including a new White House located considerably north of the existing one. Only Frederick Law Olmsted, Jr., who was later appointed to the commission, called for a restoration of L'Enfant's plan and Mall treatment.[11]

McKim and the commissioners adopted a Beaux-Arts methodology for their restoration. They researched the salient characteristics of the L'Enfant plan and made an extensive firsthand study of its antecedents at home and abroad, incorporating most of its constituent elements into the new McMillan Commission plan. They finished their task in January 1902 with a report and public exhibition of models and renderings which illustrated both existing conditions and the improvements they envisioned. The exhibition also featured plans and photographs of historical buildings and sites which influenced the commission plan.[12]

The commissioners interpreted L'Enfant's plan as an evolution of seventeenth- and eighteenth-century American and French classicism. Its gridiron and axes, its green flanked by prominent buildings, its broad

is discussed in Reps, *Making of Urban America*, pp. 242–56; and Richard W. Stephenson, "The Delineation of a Grand Plan," *Quarterly Journal of the Library of Congress* 36, no. 3 (Summer 1979): 207–24. Reps discusses conditions in Washington, D.C., during the mid to late nineteenth century and reproduces several lithographic views in *Making of Urban America*, pp. 254, 259, 260, 261, 505, figs. 151–53; see also "Report of the Senate Committee," pp. 14–15 (see p. 10 for the statement about regrettable departures from L'Enfant's plan).

[11] "Report of the Park Commission," p. 25. Cass Gilbert's proposal appears in *Papers Relating to the Improvement of the City of Washington*, comp. Glenn Brown (Senate Doc. no. 94, 56th Cong., 2d sess., 1901), pp. 78–82. Olmsted's call for a restoration of L'Enfant's plan is reported in Moore, *Life and Times of McKim*, pp. 182–83.

[12] The exhibition was held from January 15 to February 25, 1902, at the Corcoran Gallery of Art. Afterward it was displayed at the Library of Congress (see "Report of the Senate Committee," p. 18, note 1). See also Moore, *Life and Times of McKim*, pp. 201–3; and Charles Moore, "Memoirs," pp. 103–6, Papers of Charles Moore, Library of Congress, Washington, D.C. (hereafter cited as CMP).

diagonal boulevards linking the city's principal monuments with reciprocal views—these elements of formal baroque planning were to be found
in American colonial town planning, which had been influenced by
Andrea Palladio, Sir Christopher Wren, and French urban design. "The
very fact that Washington and Jefferson, L'Enfant and Ellicott, and
their immediate successors, drew inspiration from the world's greatest
works of landscape architecture and of civil adornment," the commissioners wrote, "made it imperative to go back to the sources of their
knowledge and taste in order to restore unity and harmony."[13]

The commissioners thus proceeded in a scholarly, scientific manner
to study "the sources." First they made a tour of towns and estates along
the Potomac and James rivers and the Chesapeake Bay, which, Moore
explained, supplied models to Washington and Jefferson, and "thereby
continued in this country the architectural traditions established by Inigo
Jones and Sir Christopher Wren in England." They visited the estates
of Stratford, Carter's Grove, Brandon, Westover, and Shirley. But their
visit to Williamsburg was particularly instructive. Here they recognized
the salient features of the Washington Mall: "the Capitol at one end of
the broad parkway, the College of William and Mary at the other end
of the main axis, and the Governor's Palace at the head of the cross-
axis, a location similar to that of the White House." To the commissioners these towns and estates demonstrated the principles of seventeenth-century planning, even though their treatments of landscape were
"meager and slight" in comparison to European models.[14]

Next they embarked in the summer of 1901 on a five-week trip to
eight European cities. Olmsted drew up the exhausting itinerary: Rome,
Venice, Vienna, Budapest, Paris, Frankfurt, Berlin, London, and their
suburbs. (Ambitious though it was, the tour had been in fact scaled
down from an earlier itinerary which included Saint Petersburg, a stop
vetoed by McKim, who abhorred the frantic pace of the tour and the
"madness" of so much rail travel.) The commissioners focused on the
work of André Le Nôtre, whom they considered L'Enfant's mentor.
They sought out examples of Le Nôtre's "mastery of landscape in connection with buildings," including Versailles, where L'Enfant's father

[13] "Report of the Park Commission," p. 25.
[14] Charles Moore described the commissioners' trip in *Daniel H. Burnham*, vol. 1
(Boston and New York: Houghton Mifflin Co., 1921), pp. 144–45; for commissioners'
comments, see "Report of the Park Commission," p. 25.

had been a court painter. They visited other sites with gardens by Le Nôtre and those attributed to or influenced by him: the Villa Aurora (American Academy) in Rome, Schoenbrun, Vaux-le-Vicomte, Versailles, Hampton Court, and Bushy Park. Equipped with a camera, a tripod, and a steel tape measure, Olmsted and the other commissioners studied and recorded these European sites. In so doing, Moore later explained, the commissioners were "tracing to their source the ideas and ideals which L'Enfant expressed not only in his plan of streets, avenues and circles, but also in his notes and writings." There were also daily discussions about the Washington improvements using maps of the district which Olmsted had brought. They considered their method scholarly.[15]

The commissioners' vision of the restored Washington, first crystalized in Williamsburg, was given further shape in Rome. But their subsequent visit to Paris toward the end of the tour was, as Moore wrote, the "critical moment of the trip." The commissioners saw in Paris the image of the future Washington. Only one small detail clouded their vision. Could they convince Alexander J. Cassatt, president of the Pennsylvania Railroad, to remove the existing station from the Mall? They resolved to bring Cassatt back to Paris and lead him to "the terrace overlooking the Place de la Concorde, to take note of the glories of a city designed as a work of art—the Palace of the Tuileries [Louvre] as the Capitol, the Tuileries Gardens as the Mall, the Obelisk in the crossing of two Paris axes as the Washington Monument centers the Capitol and White House axes; and then a Lincoln Memorial . . . comparable to the Arc de Triomphe de l'Etoile."[16]

The McMillan Commission plan addressed the concerns of landscape design more than architecture, but it did take into account the location of new public buildings "arranged according to a rational system of grouping." The new plan thus reflected what the commissioners

---

[15] For the veto of Saint Petersburg, see McKim to Charles Moore, May 10, 1901, CMP. For visitation of Le Nôtre sites, see Moore, *Life and Times of McKim*, p. 187; and Reps, *Making of Urban America*, p. 252. Charles Moore, "Makers of Washington," pp. 116, 122–24, CMP; Moore, *Life and Times of McKim*, pp. 187, 192; Charles Moore, "Speeches, 1871–1934," p. 4, CMP.

[16] Moore, "Makers of Washington," p. 121. For the comments on Paris, see Moore, *Life and Times of McKim*, p. 198. Werner Hegemann and Elbert Peets reproduced the Senate Park Commission Plan of 1901 for Washington and the plan of central Paris drawn to the same scale in *Civic Art* (New York: Architectural Book Publishing Co., 1922), p. 285, fig. 1193.

interpreted as L'Enfant's concept of parks "laid out as settings for public buildings." L'Enfant's plan articulated a formal mall flanked by prominent buildings and divided by a central roadway. With respect to architectural style, the commissioners fell under McKim's influence when they advocated Italian rather than French classicism. [17]

The Mall dominated the McMillan Commission plan, seen in a perspective rendering by Beaux-Arts architect Francis Hoppin (fig. 3). Its two principal landscape components—a green space and trees—reasserted L'Enfant's synthesis of seventeenth- and eighteenth-century French and American planning. The Mall's green space, a mile and a half long and 350 feet wide, stretched between the Capitol and the Washington Monument. Like the L'Enfant plan, the new Mall would be modeled after the French *tapis vert*—literally a green carpet or lawn—featured in Le Nôtre's garden designs. Charles Moore described the commissioners' reaction to Vaux-le-Vicomte: "From the terraces to the far horizon stretched the *tapis-vert* . . . on either side the endless vista was outlined with dense lines of tall trees." There the commissioners pictured what the Washington Mall would be when, according to Moore, "L'Enfant's design had been restored and American taste had worked its adornment—a far cry but by no means an impossibility." Although McKim and the commissioners studied many "grass carpets" in England, particularly those at Hatfield House, Bushy Park, and Hampton Court, they supported Olmsted's objection to a mall with a central roadway like the one at Windsor Great Park, England. Instead they recommended that walks, roads, and trees flank the green space as at Vaux-le-Vicomte. In the Beaux-Arts manner, they cited this and other Le Nôtre garden designs to justify their departure from L'Enfant. Yet, the commissioners recognized the decorative and functional advantages of water in L'Enfant's plan. Basins, canals, and fountains, like those they studied in Rome, Versailles, Fontainebleau, and Vaux-le-Vicomte, would complement the Mall. Versailles, with its Basin of Latona, *tapis vert*,

---

[17] "Report of the Senate Committee," p. 17; "Report of the Park Commission," p. 23. For analyses of the L'Enfant plan, see Reps, *Making of Urban America*, pp. 245–62, 505; H. P. Caemmerer, *The Life of Pierre Charles L'Enfant, Planner of the City Beautiful, the City of Washington* (Washington, D.C.: National Republic Publishing Co., 1950); and J. L. Sibley Jennings, Jr., "Artistry as Design: L'Enfant's Extraordinary City," *Quarterly Journal of the Library of Congress* 36, no. 3 (Summer 1979): 225–78. For advocacy of Italian classicism, see Moore, *Life and Times of McKim*, pp. 191–92.

Fig. 3. Francis L. V. Hoppin, *Bird's-Eye View, the Senate Park Commission Proposal,* 1902. (Commission of Fine Arts: Photo, National Archives.)

and canal, provided a comprehensive design prototype (fig. 4).[18]

The second component of the Mall would be elm trees "planted in formal procession four abreast" on either side of the green. "Examples of this treatment abound in England and on the Continent of Europe," the commissioners reported, "and also may be found in our own country in those towns, both North and South, which were laid out during the colonial era." They cited such French examples as Versailles, Fontainebleau, Compiègne, and Vaux-le-Vicomte as well as English models which presumably influenced colonial planning, including Bushy Park, Windsor Great Park, and Hatfield House. A rendering of Union Square (fig. 5) just west of the Capitol indicates the proposed treatment of elms. The commissioners compared the character of this square adorned with fountains and sculpture to the Place de la Concorde. For American prototypes, Moore identified the colonial towns of Old Hadley, Massachusetts, and Williamsburg. Hadley's West Street (fig. 6) provided the northern colonial model for a green of roughly the same dimensions as

[18] Moore, *Life and Times of McKim,* pp. 197, 199; "Report of the Park Commission," pp. 27–28.

Fig. 4. Basin of Latona and *tapis vert*, Versailles. From Glenn Brown, comp., *Papers Relating to the Improvement of the City of Washington* (Senate Doc. no. 94, 56th Cong., 2d sess., 1901), fig. 16.

the Washington Mall and flanked by drives and rows of elms. Williamsburg, with its similar drives and elm trees, furnished the Senate Park Commission with a southern colonial model illustrating Wren's influence in America. Olmsted and the commissioners selected the American elm for the character of its trunk and branch formation and because such trees continued to thrive in Washington's parks and on the grounds of the Capitol. Charles Bulfinch, for example, had planned to landscape the section of Maryland Avenue nearest the Capitol with a thousand trees. Requesting a Congressional appropriation in 1829, Bulfinch proposed "to plant the whole avenue with four ranges of forest trees," estimating the cost at $1,000.[19]

[19] "Report of the Park Commission," pp. 41–42, 44–45. For an 1895 plan of Hadley, Mass., see *Hadley* (Northampton, Mass.: Picturesque Publishing Co., 1895), n.p. Reps illustrates a 1782 plan of Williamsburg which indicates rows of trees flanking the street leading up to the Governor's Palace (see Reps, *Making of Urban America*, p. 112, fig. 64). For the Bulfinch proposal, see "Appropriation for the Public Buildings," Committee

Fig. 5. C. Graham, *Union Square, the Senate Park Commission Proposal*, exhibited in 1902. (Commission of Fine Arts.)

In their exhibition of 1902, the commissioners displayed twenty-four photographs originally grouped in a section entitled "Typical American Elms."[20] In addition to photographs of Old Hadley, there were illustrations of elms on the grounds of the Capitol, Lafayette Square facing the White House, Boston Common, Harvard University, and Central Park. The survival of elms from previous generations, and even from the colonial and federal periods, symbolized a link with the past and the endurance of a new country. The American elm became an icon of the colonial revival.

During the course of their research and travels and through their plans, models, and diverse experiments, the Senate park commissioners

Report (House of Representatives Report no. 69, 20th Cong., 2d sess., 1829), p. 3; Harold Kirker, *The Architecture of Charles Bulfinch* (Cambridge, Mass.: Harvard University Press, 1969), p. 339, fig. 155.

[20] "Catalogue of Drawings and Designs, Illustrating the Report of the Commission on the Improvement of the Park-System of the District of Columbia, Corcoran Art Gallery, Washington, D.C., January–February, 1902," pp. 159d–e, nos. 118–42; this undated exhibition list, containing 142 photographs, follows a letter from McKim to Moore, December 24, 1901, CMP. The list that accompanies the Senate Report has 179 items; most of the photographs on the McKim list appear in the Senate Report. See "Report of the Senate Committee," p. 18, note 1, and app. F, pp. 147–54.

Fig. 6. West Street, Hadley, Mass. From *Hadley* (Northampton, Mass.: Picturesque Publishing Co., 1895), n.p.

were attempting a scientific restoration. Yet only certain aspects of the McMillan Commission plan constituted a period restoration. In proposing alterations or additions—the substitution of driveways along the edge of the green in place of a central roadway, the terraced and colonnaded treatment of the Washington Monument, the addition of the Lincoln Memorial with its formal canal—the commissioners viewed their work as a modern extension of L'Enfant's original plan and its sources in Italian and French classicism. They regarded their designs, both physically and symbolically, as an evolution of federal planning— from Washington, Jefferson, L'Enfant, Ellicott, and Bulfinch—to modern times. In his biography of McKim, Charles Moore wrote: "That he [McKim] followed so tenaciously both the L'Enfant plan and the work done later by Bulfinch was due to his recognition of the mastery of those earlier men and his respect for noble precedents. He strove not for originality but for perfection."[21] Beaux-Arts architects like McKim used

[21] Moore, *Life and Times of McKim*, p. 185.

historical research to justify eclecticism on academic grounds. In so doing, they confirmed their faith in progress and the evolution of style.

This application of Beaux-Arts methods and principles to urban design paralleled turn-of-the-century developments in colonial and federal revival architecture. In his design for Portland City Hall of 1909–12 (fig. 7), Thomas Hastings practiced a Beaux-Arts interpretation of the colonial revival. In order to establish a style that would be both national and modern, and at the same time to develop Renaissance classicism, Hastings devised a hybrid of eighteenth-century French and American forms. Portland City Hall specifically recalls a "French" landmark of the federal period. Its forecourt, projecting wings, Louis XVI neoclassicism, and cupola pay homage to New York City Hall of 1802–12 by Joseph François Mangin and John McComb, Jr. (fig. 8). Like the L'Enfant plan, New York City Hall was a symbol of French classical influence in America. In fact, Flagg and Hastings used it as a high-water mark in the evolution of classicism against which to judge the changing tide of style toward revivalism in both America and Europe. Its design reflected the collaboration of Mangin, a Frenchman who worked in New York as an architect and engineer, and McComb, a native-born architect. New York City Hall was predictably eclectic. Hastings observed that it was as much colonial as it was characteristic of the period of Louis XVI, which he called "the last distinctive epoch in the history and development of style"—he meant, of course, the Renaissance style. If architects would follow the example of Mangin and McComb and "endeavor to do new work without mere copying and adapting, yet studying applicable precedents," Hastings maintained that the question of a national style would be resolved.[22]

The Mangin and McComb design summarized the prevailing taste for late colonial Palladianism, Louis XVI neoclassicism, and English influence. Strongly identified with French *hôtels de ville*, New York City Hall reflected not only the strategic eclecticism that Hastings sought but also Beaux-Arts principles. Aside from the overt Frenchness of its style and ornament, it indicated the way a plan might generate the elevation and section. New York City Hall's discrete volumes—vestibule, tower, staircase rotunda—are expressed on the exterior. The stair-

[22] Thomas Hastings, "Architecture and Modern Life," *Harper's New Monthly* 94, no. 564 (May 1897): 404, 406.

Fig. 7. Carrère and Hastings (Stevens and Stevens, associate architects), Portland City Hall, Portland, Maine, 1909–12. (Photo, Mardges Bacon.)

case reveals the same electicism of American and English Palladianism, as well as French neoclassicism.[23]

Intended to be viewed in perspective, Portland City Hall was also modeled in the colonial image. Its courtyard plan recalled eighteenth-century American Palladianism. More specifically, its parapet gables with clustered chimney stacks, and its *corps-de-logis* defined by a central tower and quoins shared features with Independence Hall, Philadelphia, begun in 1731 (fig. 9). Aside from those elements common to eighteenth-century public buildings, Portland City Hall also recalled American domestic architecture. The planarity of its facade and the use of triangular and segmental pediments above the second-story windows

Fig. 8. Mangin and McComb, New York City Hall, 1802–12. (Prints and Photographs Division, Library of Congress.)

are quotations from Georgian buildings in America. Moreover, its discrete central block, parapet gables, and dormer windows closely resemble such domestic colonial models as Massachusetts Hall of Harvard University (1718) and the McPhedris-Warner House, Portsmouth, New Hampshire (1718–23).

Like Carrère and Hastings's earlier Paterson City Hall (1893–94) and Worcester City Hall (1896), the plan, composition, and scale of Portland City Hall also reveal a late nineteenth-century Beaux-Arts treatment. The interior is dominated by a vestibule, a staircase, and a transverse hall leading to offices, reception rooms, and an auditorium. An elliptical staircase at Portland City Hall takes its cue from New York City Hall, but also from such eighteenth-century buildings as Ange-Jacques Gabriel's Petit Trianon at Versailles. The spatial planning, however,

Fig. 9. Alexander Hamilton, Independence Hall (originally Pennsylvania State House), Philadelphia, 1731–36 (tower design by Edmund Woolley added 1750–53). (Prints and Photographs Division, Library of Congress.)

lacks both the clarity and the hierarchy of New York City Hall, or Carrère and Hastings's own Worcester City Hall.[24] Portland City Hall conveys the superficial image of the New York model more successfully than it embodies the underlying principles of French classicism.

In a freestanding town house for Mrs. Alfred Corning Clark, heir to the Singer Manufacturing Company fortune, Ernest Flagg demon-

[24] Montgomery Schuyler published a perspective rendering of Portland City Hall in "Notes and Comments," *Architectural Record* 27, no. 3 (March 1910): 272. See also "The City Hall, Portland, Maine," *American Architect* 102, no. 1918 (September 25, 1912): 109–14, with additional plates. John Calvin Stevens and John Howard Stevens were associate architects for the building. Curtis Channing Blake analyzed the relative merits of three Carrère and Hastings's city halls in "The Architecture of Carrère and Hastings" (Ph.D. diss., Columbia University, 1976), pp. 268–75, pls. 181–87.

strated a synthesis of colonial forms and French architecture of the late sixteenth and early seventeenth centuries during the reigns of Henry IV and Louis XIII. The Clark house (fig. 10) also revealed the infusion of colonial elements into an existing tradition of Manhattan town houses in the 1880s and 1890s called *châteaux*. Built on a generous corner site on Riverside Drive at 89th Street, the Clark house (1898–1900; demolished) was aptly recognized by the editors of *Architecture* as "a good illustration of French Renaissance adapted to American conditions."[25]

The Clark house looked nominally colonial or federal in style. Its blocklike mass of red brick and white trim recalled the town houses of Charles Bulfinch or Samuel McIntire. As in such federal houses, the proportions of the three floors diminished from the ground level to the attic, and the whole was capped by a balustrade. But there were other aspects of the Clark house for which eighteenth-century American models could not account. Its scale and siting, its plan, composition, and ornament, reflected the fundamental principles of Beaux-Arts design. The size of the Clark house (70 by 80 feet) and the scale of its ornament firmly placed it within the late nineteenth century.

Flagg's use of red brick with stone quoins and decorative trim recalled two Fifth Avenue town houses, one by Richard Morris Hunt, the other by Hunt's student, George B. Post. Montgomery Schuyler described Post's Cornelius Vanderbilt II house, between 57th and 58th streets, (1880–82; demolished) as a "French château" which had been "classicized." Flagg, a cousin of Vanderbilt, was especially familiar with the architecture of this house. Hunt, who had assisted Post in designing a tower addition (1892–94), adopted the characteristics of the "French château," including its red brick and stone trim, for his Elbridge Gerry house at 61st Street (1891–94; demolished). Although the materials and French elements were similar, the Post and Hunt houses were comparatively picturesque, lacking the formal symmetry and blocklike massing of Flagg's Clark house.[26]

---

[25] *Architecture* 2, no. 7 (July 15, 1900): 252.

[26] Montgomery Schuyler, "The Vanderbilt Houses," in *American Architecture and Other Writings*, ed. William H. Jordy and Ralph Coe, vol. 2 (Cambridge, Mass.: Harvard University Press, 1961), p. 495; Mardges Bacon, "Ernest Flagg: Beaux-Arts Architect and Reformer" (Ph.D. diss., Brown University, 1978), p. 16; Schuyler, "Vanderbilt Houses," pp. 493–99; Montgomery Schuyler, "The Late Works of Richard M. Hunt," in Jordy and Coe, *American Architecture*, 2:538–40. See also Paul R. Baker, *Richard Morris Hunt* (Cambridge, Mass.: MIT Press, 1980), pp 340–45.

Fig. 10. Ernest Flagg, Mrs. Alfred Corning Clark house, New York, 1898–1900; demolished. From *Architectural Record* 11, no. 4 (April 1902), fig. 47.

The central-hall plan of the Clark house, with rooms axially disposed on either side, demonstrated an evolution from eighteenth-century antecedents. It contained little of the intricacy of spatial experience, charged movement, and asymmetry which characterized Adamesque federal plans. Further, unlike such plans, the public spaces of the Clark house were confined to the first floor. The dominant features of the Clark house plan were the size of the public rooms, the specificity and variety of its room functions, and the degree to which the exterior expressed interior spaces. The grand dimensions of the library and drawing room, each 22 feet wide, were expressed on the exterior. These were characteristics of Beaux-Arts planning. Flagg rotated the Clark house on its irregular site to accommodate a driveway leading to a porte-cochere and to take advantage of the view along a bend in Riverside Drive. A projecting wing contained diverse functions. Unlike wings of shingle-style houses which functioned as servants' quarters, Flagg's Clark house wing contained two indispensable components of the leisure estate, circa 1900: a conservatory and a bowling alley.

In a further departure from federal models, the Clark house facade was organized by its windows, which for the most part were linked not only vertically but also horizontally through banding. The use of marble quoins and banding against patterned red brick emphasized planarity and suggested constructional polychromy. The Clark house strongly reflected Henry IV and Louis XIII masonry architecture such as that of the Pavillon, Place des Vosges, Paris (fig. 11) begun in 1605. In looking to French architecture of the late sixteenth and early seventeenth centuries, Flagg also paid homage to Eugène-Emmanuel Viollet-le-Duc, the French theorist and archaeologist. Viollet-le-Duc admired the period of Henry IV and Louis XIII not only for its Gallic qualities but also for what he considered its structural rationalism, meaning a reasoned approach to architecture as decorated structure. The architecture of this period, he argued, "became reasonable, chastened, and modest in its ornamentation, and in structure severe and studied. . . . Construction was the main element of design." Flagg may also have wanted the Clark House to recall the spirit of Viollet-le-Duc's project for a *hôtel*, or town house (fig. 12), which Viollet-le-Duc published in the second volume of his *Discourses on Architecture* in 1872. Both designs specified brick walls detailed with stone quoins and window moldings linked horizontally and vertically. Materials were legibly combined and structurally defined as in their French Renaissance models, although, more likely, Flagg was actually adopting a style widely employed in France during the Third Republic. Viollet-le-Duc's use of the "butterfly" plan in the town house was also reflected in the Clark house plan, whose recreational wing defined one edge of its site.[27] In his search for a national

[27] Eugène-Emmanuel Viollet-le-Duc, *Discourses on Architecture*, trans. Henry Van Brunt, vol. 1 (Boston: James R. Osgood, 1875), p. 245. For the butterfly plan, see Alan Colquhoun, "The Beaux-Arts Plan," *Architectural Design* 17 (1979): 62–65, figs. 6, 7. The English use of the butterfly plan is the subject of several discussions (see Jill Franklin, "Edwardian Butterfly Houses," *Architectural Review* 157, no. 938 [April 1975]: 220–25; and Jill Franklin, *The Gentleman's Country House and Its Plan, 1835–1914* [London: Routledge & Kegan Paul, 1981], pp. 232–37). See also Andrew Saint, *Richard Norman Shaw* (New Haven: Yale University Press, 1976), p. 332. Plans of the Clark house are reproduced in *Architectural Record* 11, no. 4 (April 1902): 51, fig. 48.

Fig. 11. Pavillon, Place des Vosges (Place Royale), Paris, begun 1605. (Photo, Giraudon.)

style that would be the product of historical evolution, Flagg demonstrated the same aspirations that Viollet-le-Duc advocated in his writings and projects.

Other Beaux-Arts architects shared Hastings's and Flagg's views on French and American classicism. Two of them were Isaac Newton Phelps Stokes, who studied in an atelier of the Ecole des Beaux-Arts, and his partner, John Mead Howells, who received a diploma from that school in 1897. Howells was the son of the highly respected writer and editor, William Dean Howells. When Yale University proposed a new administration building to celebrate its bicentennial in 1901, it selected the

Fig. 12. Eugène-Emmanuel Viollet-le-Duc, perspective, *hôtel* (town house). From Eugène-Emmanuel Viollet-le-Duc, *Discourses on Architecture*, trans. Benjamin Bucknall, vol. 2 (Boston: Ticknor, 1889), pl. 33.

architectural firm of Howells and Stokes. In an age of patronage, the award seem predestined. Stokes's brother, Anson Phelps Stokes, Jr., was secretary to the university. Moreover, the *Yale Alumni News* reported matter-of-factly that Stokes's two philanthropist aunts, Olivia Egleston Phelps Stokes and Caroline Phelps Stokes, simply "gave the hall."[28] It

[28] Stokes studied in the preparatory atelier of Godefroy and Freynet and later transferred to the atelier and office of Jean-Henry Duray, remaining in Paris from 1894 to 1897 (see I. N. Phelps Stokes, *Random Recollections of a Happy Life* [rev. ed.; New York, 1941], p. 98; and Roy Lubove, "I. N. Phelps Stokes: Tenement Architect, Economist, Planner," *Journal of the Society of Architectural Historians* 23, no. 2 [May 1964]: 75). John Mead Howells entered the Ecole des Beaux-Arts in 1892 as a student of Jules-Alexis Godefroy (see E. Delaire, *Les Architectes élèves de l'Ecole des Beaux-Arts, 1793–1907* [Paris: Librairie de la Construction Moderne, 1907], p. 295). For information on the donors, see "Woodbridge Hall Dedication," *Yale Alumni Weekly* (January 1902): 170.

was named after the Reverend Timothy Woodbridge, one of Yale's founders and an ancestor of the Stokeses.

In a dramatic departure from the Ruskinian High Victorian architecture of Yale's nineteenth-century campus, exemplified in Russell Sturgis's Farnum Hall of 1869–70, Woodbridge Hall (fig. 13) signaled a new direction for a new century. Constructed of buff-colored Indiana limestone, Woodbridge Hall is totally unlike the polychromed architecture of the rest of the campus. It contains elements of French classicism: a blocklike mass with a terminating balustrade as well as an abundance of seventeenth- and eighteenth-century classical details, including paired pilasters and swags set in low relief, similar to the ornament of New York City Hall and Louis Le Vau and J. H. Mansart's garden facade of the château of Versailles. Yet at its dedication in 1901, Woodbridge Hall was broadly proclaimed to be both "Georgian" and "colonial." The Palladianism of its central pediment marks its ancestry back to the Georgian architecture of eighteenth-century America. For example, a central pediment with paired pilasters and a balustrade at Woodbridge Hall are features shared by Charles Bulfinch's Perez Morton house (fig. 14), Roxbury, Massachusetts (1796; demolished).[29]

To reinforce the connection between past and present, between colonial America and the Progressive Era, Stokes incorporated architectural fragments of earlier houses. Black and gold marble mantels in the president's and the secretary's offices came from "the old Rogers House in New Haven" and "a colonial residence in New York." Similarly, the mahogany doors of the offices were "taken from private houses in Greenwich Village." Although they are of mid nineteenth-century origin, these doors were identified, not surprisingly, as examples of "the best colonial period."[30]

Like Portland City Hall and Flagg's Clark house, Woodbridge Hall is a hybrid of French and American classicism. It was ostensibly an example of academic eclecticism conditioned by the Beaux-Arts method, yet Stokes quoted Georgian Palladian architecture and adaptively reused

[29] [Donald Grant Mitchell], "Mr. Mitchell's Address," *Yale Alumni Weekly* (January 1902): 170. I would like to thank Elizabeth Mills Brown for referring me to Mitchell's dedication speech. A drawing of Woodbridge Hall accompanies Flagg's "American Architecture," p. 187. The Perez Morton house is discussed in Kirker, *Architecture of Bulfinch*, pp. 135–40.

[30] "Description of Woodbridge Hall," *Yale Alumni Weekly* (January 1902): 180.

Fig. 13. Howells and Stokes, Woodbridge Hall, Yale University, 1900–1901. From *American Architect and Building News* 81, no. 1439 (July 25, 1903): pl. 1439.

architectural fragments which he believed to be colonial. Woodbridge Hall illustrates the revival and survival of colonial forms appropriate to its bicentennial character and the ancestry of its patrons and principal architect.

The Beaux-Arts fusion of eighteenth-century American and French classicism endured until the depression. A late example is Bushnell Memorial Hall in Hartford, Connecticut (fig. 15). It was built between 1928 and 1930, although its architect, Harvey Wiley Corbett, had submitted plans and a model a decade earlier. Land and funds for the hall were donated by Dotha Bushnell Hillyer in memory of her father, the esteemed Congregationalist preacher and reformer, Horace Bushnell (1802–76). In designing the hall, Corbett took three factors into account. First, Dotha Hillyer had requested the "Neo-Colonial" style because it would symbolize Bushnell's life and his colonial ancestors who, in Corbett's words, "founded this great country on its principles of sincerity and honesty." Second, Corbett needed a design solution for the hall to

Fig. 14. Charles Bulfinch, Perez Morton house, Roxbury, Mass., 1796; demolished. From *American Architect and Building News* 20, no. 571 (December 4, 1886): n.p. (Photo, Society for the Preservation of New England Antiquities, Boston.)

complement "its imposing surroundings."[31] Proposed for a prominent corner location across from Bushnell Park and Richard M. Upjohn's State Capitol (1872–79), the Bushnell would be within sight of two important Beaux-Arts buildings: Donn Barber's State Library (1908–10) and Benjamin Wistar Morris's State Armory (1909). Third, the hall was planned as a cultural center for meetings, concerts, plays, and opera.

The image of Bushnell Memorial Hall is part meetinghouse, part

[31] "Minutes of the Meeting of October 25, 1920," Horace Bushnell Memorial Hall Corporation, Hartford, Conn.; Helme, Corbett, and Harrison, "Horace Bushnell Memorial Hall" (statement read at the laying of the cornerstone, October 16, 1928), Archives, Horace Bushnell Memorial Hall, Hartford, Conn.; "The Bushnell Memorial Building," *Architectural Record* 68, no. 4 (October 1930): 279.

Fig. 15. Helme, Corbett, and MacMurray, Horace Bushnell Memorial
Hall, Hartford, Conn., 1928–30. (Photo, Mardges Bacon.)

theater. Its red brick exterior, pedimented portico, tower, and cupola
recall examples of Georgian and federal architecture in New England.
A preliminary design of 1920 called for a larger building with a particularly Gibbsian treatment of its exterior and interior. The monumental
scale of its pedimented portico was an example of Palladianism trans-
ported into the twentieth century along with a cupola lifted from the
roof of Mount Vernon. Julien Guadet would have sanctioned its eclecticism. The design Corbett finally executed was more restrained and
characteristic of New England architecture. It suggested two federal
buildings in Hartford, Charles Bulfinch's Old State House (1793–96)
and Center Church (1807), attributed to Daniel Wadsworth.[32]

But there are also decorative and compositional elements that stamp

[32] Corbett's plans are dated October 23, 1920, Archives, Horace Bushnell Memorial
Hall; Michael R. T. Mahoney, "Bushnell Memorial: The Monument Takes Form,"
Bushnell Prompter 25, no. 7 (April 1980): 14.

the building "Beaux-Arts." Aspects of the hall's decoration and massing are identifiably French and specifically recall theater design. The scoring of its limestone base and a row of paterae above the entrances are classical details which Corbett recombined from eighteenth-century French antecedents such as Marie-Joseph Peyre and Charles de Wailly's Comédie-Française (Théâtre de l'Odéon) in Paris (1778–82). Moreover, its sequence of spaces—lobby, foyer, auditorium, stage—is fully articulated. Each spatial grouping of the program is a legible volume expressed on the exterior. In designing this logical organization, Corbett followed the example of Charles Garnier's Opera (1861–75).[33] The hall's image was primarily that of the colonial meetinghouse, but its program and spatial development derived from the French theater. Corbett's Beaux-Arts interpretation of the colonial revival was a means for demonstrating architecturally those "principles of sincerity and honesty" to which the Bushnell Memorial Hall was dedicated.

In their search for nationalism and order, these Beaux-Arts architects—McKim, Hastings, Flagg, Stokes, Howells, and Corbett—were motivated by two principal objectives. First, they sought to apply the scientific rigor and discipline of their French training to problems of contemporary architecture and planning. Second, they wanted to promote an evolution of the Renaissance style by reviving French and American classicism. These architects attempted to transmit to America the ideas that had been percolating in the ateliers of the Ecole des Beaux-Arts during their student years. Moreover, all of them belonged to an organization, part social, part professional, called the Society of Beaux-Arts Architects. Officially founded in New York in 1894, the organization published its goals: "to cultivate and perpetuate the associations and principles of the Ecole des Beaux-Arts of Paris."[34] The club's objectives

---

[33] Peyre and de Wailly's Comédie-Francaise (Théâtre de l'Odéon) is illustrated in Allan Braham, *The Architecture of the French Enlightenment* (Berkeley and Los Angeles: University of California Press, 1980), p. 102, fig. 130. For the Garnier source, see Mahoney, "Bushnell Memorial," pp. 14–15.

[34] In 1893/94 McKim and Flagg served as vice-president and as treasurer of the Society of Beaux-Arts Architects. In 1894 they were made trustees. Flagg was elected president for two terms in 1911/12 and 1912/13. Hastings was a member of the Committee on Education in 1897/98. Stokes was elected to the society in 1906 as an associate member. Howells joined in 1905. Corbett was a member of the Committee on Education in 1907/8 and served as vice-president in 1908/9. See *Society of Beaux-Arts Architects. Incorporated January, 1894* (1916), pp. 4, 37, 50, 52, 53, 55. I am grateful to Richard Chafee for providing me with details regarding Stokes's and Howells's memberships in the society.

were largely ideological, its influence substantial.

When McKim and the other commissioners were charged with designing a new plan for Washington, they thought that they were continuing the tradition of L'Enfant. They set about their evolutionary task in a scholarly and methodical manner by studying abroad and adopting Beaux-Arts principles of scientific planning. Hastings and Flagg also wanted to separate their architecture and planning from what they perceived to be the irrational and unscientific recent past. They wanted to found a national style that would be both modern and native to America. But by the 1890s to be modern was to be scientific and to be scientific was to be "French." Nevertheless, Beaux-Arts practitioners of the colonial revival thought that they were creating an enduring American style because it was a continuation of the Renaissance. Yet, even though an undercurrent of the colonial revival survived, it was nearly eclipsed by the modern movement of the 1930s. Like the nineteenth-century styles these Beaux-Arts architects vehemently rejected, the colonial revival went the way of all other revivals. Life in the nineteenth century was not Greek, Gothic, Romanesque, or Queen Anne; but life in America from 1890 to the depression was also not colonial.

A Georgian Renascence
in Georgia: The Residential
Architecture of Neel Reid
Catherine M. Howett

As the nineteenth century drew to a close, most of the South was still struggling to overcome the devastating economic consequences of the Civil War. But in Atlanta, an overgrown town of 75,000 that the railroads had made "Gate City of the South," the mood among the leading citizens of the business community was one of extravagant confidence and boosterism, even in the teeth of recent severe financial instability. These bold entrepreneurs successfully planned and promoted the Cotton States and International Exposition of 1895, a $2 million regional fair with aspirations to an international audience of buyers and investors. They even brought Frederick Law Olmsted, landscape architect of that great prototype, the 1893 World's Columbian Exposition at Chicago, to consult on the laying out of the fairgrounds.[1]

Henry Woodfin Grady, the grandiloquent editor of the *Atlanta Constitution,* had earlier been chief propagandist for this group, coining the phrase "New South" to describe the rebirth of commerce and culture which was transforming both the city and the region. In an address before a banquet meeting of the New England Society of New York on December 21, 1886, at which one of the guests was William Tecumseh

[1] Olmsted's plan for the fair was never actually implemented; he withdrew from the project when the decision to begin work was postponed beyond what he considered a reasonable time, and a local engineer was hired to do the design.

Sherman—the Union general who had begun his infamous "march to the sea" by putting Atlanta to the torch—Grady went so far as to proclaim that the new generation of Atlantans were in fact "Georgia Yankees," and that "from the ashes [Sherman] left us in 1864 we have raised a brave and beautiful city; that somehow or other we have caught the sunshine in the bricks and mortar of our homes, and have builded therein not one ignoble prejudice or memory."[2]

At the auspicious turning of the century, then, Atlanta was a city deliberately seeking to lay aside the bitterness, humiliation, and sense of helplessness that had been the legacy of war and reconstruction throughout most of the South. It was a new city, after all, just as Grady suggested, its official symbol a phoenix rising out of flame over the motto Atlanta Resurgens. And it had a new merchant aristocracy as well, many of whom had been drawn from other states by the sense, which the exposition was designed to foster, that Atlanta was a boom town in which fortunes were being rapidly made—as indeed they were. The rest of the state might go on sleeping, brooding over the past, cherishing the old values of kinship rooted in place and the social and physical forms through which those values had traditionally been expressed; Atlanta had turned its back on that past and sought instead a new identity based on national and, especially, Northern models. Grady would boast, "This is the city that is oftenest cited as a 'Northern city in the South.' "[3]

Peachtree Street, the central commercial axis of modern Atlanta, had been the first nexus of upper-class residential development in the 1870s and 1880s and was lined on either side by the stately Victorian homes, on large landscaped lots, of the city's business and professional elite. But downtown Atlanta's flourishing enterprises already cast a shadow on this handsome tree-lined boulevard, and suburban development was well under way by 1890, drawing not on indigenous residential models, but on the latest developments from the North. Joel Hurt had engineered Atlanta's first electric street railway to link his Inman Park—Atlanta's first planned suburb—with the downtown Equitable Building, the South's first skyscraper, commissioned by Hurt and designed by

[2] Quoted in Mills Lane, "Introduction: The New South in Georgia," in *The New South: Writings and Speeches of Henry Grady*, ed. Mills Lane (Savannah: Beehive Press, 1971), pp. 7–8.
[3] Quoted in Lane, *New South*, p. 119.

John Welborn Root of Chicago's Burnham and Root. It was Hurt who first brought Olmsted to Atlanta as consultant in the design of a second subdivision, Druid Hills, which was to be the South's first "ideal residential suburb" in the tradition of Olmsted's famous plan for Riverside, Illinois. Although financial difficulties, delays, and frustrations with shareholders later forced Hurt to sell his interest in this development, the character of Druid Hills was substantially determined by the Olmsted firm's early involvement. Furthermore, the legacy of Olmsted's style— curving roads nestled into natural topography, sensitive siting of structures, and creation of a visually rich complex of canopy trees, shrubs, and broad expanses of lawn—influenced the later development of Ansley Park just north of the city limits and, much farther out, Paces Ferry-Tuxedo Park.[4]

Although no single architectural style equivalent in dominance to Olmsted's landscape planning offered itself as a model for Atlanta's suburban developers, a dominant typology was operative for the new builders and their clients, that of the suburban "villa," or country house. While both the type and the terminology bring to mind the commentary of such mid nineteenth-century practitioners as Andrew Jackson Downing and Calvert Vaux, the sense of the terms and the stylistic canon to which they were applied underwent significant change in the opening decades of the twentieth century. In marked contrast to the flamboyant eclecticism of the earlier tradition, the "modern" house of this type was characterized by a restrained classicism. Fiske Kimball recognized this evolution and described the new fashion in his now classic essay of 1919, "The American Country House," in which he observed that "the central body of forms in American style of the present is beyond dispute the academic vocabulary of the Italian Renaissance, of Palladianism and classicism in France, England, and the early American republic, and their more vernacular expression in Georgian England and the American colonies."[5] Kimball embellished his remarks on current practice in country house architecture with illustrations from the work of a number of major firms; among these are several interior

[4] Elizabeth A. Lyon, "Frederick Law Olmsted and Joel Hurt: Planning for Atlanta," in *Olmsted South: Old South Critic–New South Planner*, ed. Dana F. White and Victor A. Kramer (Westport, Conn.: Greenwood Press, 1979), p. 116.

[5] Fiske Kimball, "The American Country House," *Architectural Record* 46, no. 4 (October 1919): 334.

and exterior views of Atlanta houses designed by the local firm of Hentz, Reid, and Adler. Neel Reid was the principal residential architect for this firm.[6] Between 1909 and 1926 he was more than any other person responsible for introducing to Atlanta's elite new suburbs an architectural idiom reflecting the most discriminating national standards even as it responded exquisitely to the needs of his clients, needs rooted in the peculiar ethos of their own place and time.

Reid was born and raised in Alabama, but in 1903, at eighteen, moved with his family to Macon, Georgia, about ninety miles south of Atlanta. Most of what is known of his life before he established his architectural practice in Atlanta comes from recorded oral history, the recollections of family members, colleagues, and friends. One story identifies his encounter with an architect hired to remodel the family's new house in Macon as the origin of Reid's career, which commenced with a brief architectural apprenticeship in Macon, followed by one year in the Atlanta office of Willis F. Denny. During this year Reid met Hal Hentz, who was superintendent of construction for the Candler Building, latest and most lavish of Atlanta's skyscraper office buildings. The two became close friends and resolved to pursue careers in architecture together, not by years of apprenticeship in local firms, but in New York City, at Columbia University's School of Architecture.

Since the days of New South editor Henry Grady, New York had been that "model city which all Atlantans hoped to pattern after."[7] Grady would have approved of these two "Georgia Yankees" heading north to prepare themselves properly for their chosen career. Hentz was officially enrolled at Columbia, while Reid apparently took classes without becoming a degree candidate. Hentz later recalled that his friend spent most of 1905 and part of 1906 studying with him in New York. Their exposure to architecture at Columbia evidently convinced the two men that they needed the rigorous discipline of the Ecole des Beaux-Arts, and in 1906 they set out for Paris. Reid spent the next year in the *atelier*

---

[6] Reid's partnerships during his years of practice were as follows: 1909, (G. L.) Norrman, (Hal) Hentz, and Reid; 1909–14, Hentz and Reid; 1915–26, Hentz, Reid, and (Rudolph) Adler. After Reid's death a young draftsman in the firm, Philip T. Schutze, won the Rome prize and returned in 1927 to assume Reid's role as principal designer (Hentz, Adler, and Schutze). Schutze had a long and distinguished career, which continued many of the directions begun during Reid's lifetime.

[7] Paul H. Buck, *The Road to Reunion, 1865–1900* (Boston: Little, Brown, 1937), p. 185.

libre of Laloux, sharing an apartment with Hentz in the Latin Quarter until his money ran out and he was forced to return to New York. After another year or so working in the office of Murphy and Dana, Reid went home to Macon, sending word to Hentz (who was still studying in Europe) that he should come back to Georgia and join Reid in a partnership. In 1909 they closed their Macon office and settled into practice in Atlanta.[8]

Neel Reid's period of formal education had been brief but intense; combined with the lessons of apprenticeship and a native genius for design universally acknowledged by his peers, it had prepared him to undertake the work that awaited him at home. On coming to Atlanta Hentz and Reid enjoyed a brief affiliation with the elderly Norwegian architect Gottfried Norrman, who at his death just a year later bequeathed to his young associates the mantle of his highly respected practice in the city. But the clients for whom Norrman had built in the Gothic, Romanesque revival, Queen Anne, and shingle styles were leaving the city now, moving into the country and into the new age, commuting by car, and searching for a new environment in the suburbs. They were ready for an architecture that looked as new to them as their lives were, and Neel Reid had a sure sense of what it ought to be.

It ought not to look *radically* new. Reid had been living on the Left Bank in Paris in the very year that Picasso had painted *Les Desmoiselles d'Avignon*. Eager student of architecture that he was, Reid must have been aware of the revolution that had swept out of the Middle West with the Prairie School architecture of Frank Lloyd Wright, whose splendidly innovative design for the Avery Coonley house of 1908 was built in Riverside, Illinois, Olmsted's paradigmatic suburban community. Wright called for an indigenous American architecture that rejected Beaux-Arts tradition, but Reid, a Southerner learning his trade in alien lands—New York as well as Paris—was not attracted to the avant-garde.

In 1908, when Reid was still working in New York, Wright lost the important commission to design the Lake Forest (Illinois) mansion of Harold and Edith Rockefeller McCormick when his clients chose instead the proposal of Charles Adams Platt, who created for them the sump-

[8] Stephanie A. Kapetanakos, "The Architecture of Neel Reid" (Master's thesis, University of Georgia, 1971), p. 2. Biographical information is from this source and from James Grady, *The Architecture of Neel Reid* (Athens: University of Georgia Press for the Peachtree-Cherokee Trust, 1973).

tuous Villa Turicum, a masterly American interpretation of Italian house and garden design. Reid admired the work of Platt, and if he chose to model himself on any architect of his generation, the urbane and aristocratic Platt, a "gentleman architect" who came to his profession late in life after having been overcome by the beauty of Italian villa design, might well have been his mentor. Probably the most important lesson Reid learned from Platt was that "the essential truth in country house architecture is that house and garden together form a single design. They cannot be separated."[9] Like Platt, Reid believed in the close integration of indoor and outdoor environments; given the opportunity, he preferred to conceive the entire site—house, garden, grounds, and even the interior furnishings—as a single design.

Perhaps men like Platt and Reid loved the past too well to embrace the new iconoclasm directed against Beaux-Arts supremacy. Whatever the case, it would be a mistake to allow historical hindsight to blind us to a proper appreciation of the excitement generated in the new age by what many considered vanguard work within the conservative tradition. The New York office of McKim, Mead, and White was of course the fountainhead of that tradition from the 1870s onward, and one of their major new directions clearly dazzled the imagination of Reid during the years that he was studying and working in New York. Colonial revival, which, according to Wayne Andrews, "may be said to have originated in the office of McKim, Mead, and White," would become an increasingly preferred style during the period of Reid's early practice in Georgia. Kimball recounted the famous story of the revival's genesis in the excursion of the partners to the coast of New England in the centennial year of 1876—what they would afterward refer to as their "celebrated trip," spent sketching and measuring surviving eighteenth-century American buildings in a fever of discovery: "Thus to the young Beaux-Arts élèves, with their portfolios full of high-roofed chateaux . . . came the impulse responsible for their first executed works of classic character, the revived Colonial houses of Newport and Lenox. It was the decisive impulse of the great movement which . . . has swept all before it."[10]

[9] Kapetanakos, "Architecture of Reid," p. 8; Platt quoted in Wayne Andrews, *Architecture, Ambition and Americans: A Social History of American Architecture* (New York: Free Press, 1964), p. 201.

[10] Andrews, *Architecture*, p. 193; Kimball, "American Country House," p. 334.

The revival of enthusiasm for the original American examples of the classicizing spirit followed the same evolution as the styles themselves. First there was a celebration of the properly Georgian buildings of the mid eighteenth century, the first "high style" tradition in the colonies, made possible by the emergence of a class of wealthy merchants and planters in New York, Boston, Newport, Philadelphia, Williamsburg, Annapolis, and Charleston, and on rural estates in New York, New England, and the Middle Atlantic colonies, stretching south to the Carolinas. There followed a broadening of interest in the vocabulary of federal forms, "whether the delicate Adam detail of Bulfinch and McIntire, or the more classic Jeffersonian porticoes of the South." Moreover, the movement that began as an effort to affect the look of the American past by a freewheeling and inventive combination of details borrowed from more than one place and period became increasingly academic, even occasionally rigorous, in its copying, laying the groundwork for the attempt at historic and archaeological accuracy in the Williamsburg restoration of the late 1920s. In Eastover, a house for G. S. Palmer in New London, Connecticut, Charles Platt "reproduced" Westover, the handsome James River plantation home of the Byrd family. A great number of Platt's earlier designs, however, were more casually derived from the colonial revival idiom. Indeed, Kimball observed that although the vogue of Platt's Italian gardens may have inspired a later shift from American colonial to Florentine villa design as a model for country house architecture, in the beginning Platt's Italianate gardens graced houses that were "almost purely Colonial or Georgian."[11]

In his introduction to the *Monograph of the Work of Charles Platt*, Royal Cortissoz made the point that the character of Platt's houses often makes one think "of the old American South, of the famous homes built long ago on the James under the influence of Georgian ideas."[12] It seems reasonable to suppose that the young Neel Reid, coming home to the South from New York and exposure to the colonial revival enthusiasms of Platt, McKim, Mead, and White, and others of the country house architects, saw the potential for capturing exactly this "Old South" image for the houses he was being asked to design in Atlanta's new suburbs. He was probably unaware of the irony in this; for Georgia, last

[11] *Monograph of the Work of Charles A. Platt* (New York: Architectural Book Publishing Co., 1913), pp. 51–60; Kimball, "American Country House," pp. 334, 336–39.
[12] Royal Cortissoz, Introduction to *Work of Platt*, p. vi.

founded of the original thirteen colonies, had but a brief colonial history. Founded in 1733, the colony lagged a full century behind New England and Virginia, and only a little less far behind neighboring South Carolina. Charleston was the thriving center of an urbane, cultured, and prosperous society when the English settlers in Georgia were still scratching out a living in frontier wilderness. Even at the end of the eighteenth century, Georgia had very few fine city houses or country estates to compare with those being built elsewhere in the New Republic.

This situation changed in the early decades of the nineteenth century with the westward expansion into the Piedmont of a plantation economy based on slavery and cotton, but even then Georgia architecture tended to lag. Federal-style building lingered longer in Georgia, and Greek revival came into ascendancy even as the fashion for it waned in the North. It would be fair to say that late federal and Greek revival forms represented Georgia's equivalent, a hundred years later, of colonial Georgian and federal styles—the first widespread and informed commitment to a "high art" tradition. So absolute was the commitment to the later styles that the white-columned temple-form house came almost to symbolize the values of the antebellum social order, and enough of these houses survived into the new century to act as haunting reminders of glories long gone. What was needed was a past more distant than this recent one—an innocent, mythic, American past older than the fall from grace. The need was answered by Reid's gracious neo-Georgian and federal houses, designed for suburbs in which nature itself had been carefully ordered to create the effect of a serene Eden.

In the course of his career Reid would design houses in other popular country-house styles—Tudor and English Georgian, Italian Renaissance and baroque—but his colonial revival houses predominated and shaped the character of the suburbs in which they were built.

Reid was just twenty-four when he and Hal Hentz established their office in Atlanta, and it is hardly surprising that some of his designs pay homage to powerful models with which he was familiar. He had been working in New York in 1906 when Stanford White designed one of the landmarks of colonial revival residential architecture, his house for James Breese at Southampton, Long Island, which clearly had been derived from George Washington's Mount Vernon. Reid's version was begun in 1914 for James Dickey on West Paces Ferry Road in Atlanta

Fig. 1. James Dickey house, 456 West Paces Ferry Road, N.W., Atlanta, 1914–17. (Photo, Dennis O'Kain.)

(fig. 1), a design that emulates the river facade of the Potomac mansion even more closely than White's had done. Reid exploited the full height of the two-story portico with its eight slender columns, repeated the triplicate dormers, and allowed the high arched glazing of the first-floor sun room to refer, almost like a brief musical quotation, to the framing arcades at Mount Vernon.

In the same year Reid built a home for himself in Druid Hills, becoming a neighbor to the many clients for whom he was designing houses in that area. A gesture of fealty to Charles Platt, Reid's shingled house on Fairview Road (fig. 2) is a fairly close copy of Platt's 1902 house for Frederick C. Culver at Hadlyme, Connecticut. Because the central block of Reid's house is somewhat smaller than Platt's, the imposing second-story Palladian window above the doorway seems out of scale, particularly since in both houses the low eave of the hipped roof cuts off the window. Reid even imitated the detail of the window

Fig. 2. Neel Reid house, 1436 Fairview Road, N.E., Atlanta, 1914. (Photo, Dennis O'Kain.)

box over the door, an inappropriate feature in an otherwise chaste Georgian facade—and a maintenance nightmare.

Three other large frame houses built in Atlanta's northwestern suburbs in the 1920s repeat the motif of the arcaded wing that Reid had used in the Dickey residence. They illustrate the degree to which he had absorbed the lessons of older masters like White and Platt. The Manry residence (fig. 3) was done for close friends, who allowed Reid to design the interior and the garden as well. The facade, with its imposing two-story pedimented portico, reveals a confident boldness in balancing forms, a boldness that is characteristic of Reid's work—the door off center, the recessed side porch and single second-story window of the right wing played against the three-over-three patterns of the central block and the left wing.

The Newman residence (fig. 4), built in the same year, similarly rejects a rigid balancing of forms, although here the five-bay facade is more formal, delicately articulated by attached columns supporting the

Fig. 3. Manry house, 2804 Habersham Road, N.W., Atlanta, 1921.
(Photo, Dennis O'Kain.)

central gable and by the central doorway with its sidelights and fanlight.
The Wright house of 1922 (fig. 5) reverts to a still simpler Georgian
massing of forms, which—except for the absence of a hipped roof with
dormers—strongly resembles the 1785 Benjamin Hall, Jr., house in
Medford, Massachusetts.[13] Both are clapboard houses with corner quoins
made from wood in imitation of stone, with the same stone effect repeated
inside the pilasters in the door surrounds, under dentiled pediments.
The dentiled roof cornices and the use of more elaborate cornices over
the first-floor windows are similar in both houses. In the Wright house
Reid elected to balance the arcaded wings, preserving the powerful simplicity of the late Georgian prototype.

In his earlier houses in Druid Hills Reid had manipulated details
from historic American models in a highly personal manner. The
Campbell house of 1914 (fig. 6) is eccentric in this way. In the insistent
verticality of its fenestration, in its balanced central chimneys, and in

[13] Carole Rifkind, *A Field Guide to American Architecture* (New York: New American
Library, 1980), p. 26.

Fig. 4. Newman house, One Cherokee Road, N.W., Atlanta, 1921.
(Photo, Dennis O'Kain.)

the handling of the pedimented doorway, it was perhaps remotely inspired
by such early houses as the one purchased in the 1730s by the Reverend
Jonathan Ashley of Deerfield, Massachusetts.[14] But the whole is made
to look lighter and later by the federal-style detailing—the vertical lights
framing the door, attenuated pilasters, and surface ornaments. Symmetry is achieved in a most unorthodox way, the entrance bay being
balanced against modern porches on both floors. Moreover, Reid liked
the look that many early American houses had of having been added
onto sequentially. His Prescott house and the house for Jesse Draper on
Clifton Road, both of 1915, deliberately strive for the appearance of
casual, additive massing—the look not of a great baronial manor, but
of a finely crafted, practical, country gentleman's house, rather republican in spirit. For the Draper house Reid designed a colonial box garden, rectangular beds edged with brick paths.

His work in the suburbs of northwestern Atlanta in the 1920s is generally more formal, the designs more ambitious. The splendid brick

[14] Samuel Chamberlain and Henry N. Flynt, *Historic Deerfield: Houses and Interiors*
(New York: Hastings House, 1965), pp. 22–23.

Fig. 5. Wright house, 2820 Habersham Road, N.W., Atlanta, 1922. (Photo, Dennis O'Kain.)

Alston house of 1923 (fig. 7) begins with a classic early Georgian central block, including hipped roof and dormers, to which are added symmetrical two-story recessed wings on either side. On the main floor these wings extend still farther and are fronted with matching tetrastyle Doric porticoes. James Grady has suggested that English architecture of the period around 1800, such as Sir John Soane's Moggerhanger House, may have inspired this design,[15] although one might see as well a kind of Jeffersonian ordering in the white temple-front pavilions flanking the horizontal axis of the brick house. The rhythm of advancing and receding planes and the complexity of the facade are masterfully controlled by Reid's deliberate balancing of the forms. The Witham house of 1926 (fig. 8) is another in the series of very substantial and elegant houses based on Georgian prototypes designed during the closing years of Reid's life. It bespeaks the same academic and archaeological enthusiasms that characterized Platt's plan for Eastover, a house with which it should be compared. The facade of Reid's last house, the Nixon residence of 1926, is a quite faithful copy in stucco of the facade of the 1774 Hammond-

[15] Grady, *Architecture of Reid*, p. 135; Dorothy Stroud, *The Architecture of Sir John Soane* (London: Studio Books, 1961), p. 108.

Fig. 6. Campbell house, 888 Oakdale Road, N.E., Atlanta, 1914. (Photo, Dennis O'Kain.)

Harwood house in Annapolis, but the plan and the other elevations are fresh inventions.

In most of these houses, interior furnishings were modeled on eighteenth-century American practice in New England and the Middle Atlantic colonies. Even in houses not based on colonial revival themes, Georgian and federal interiors were consistently preferred—a taste that has persisted well into the present time in Georgia. Kimball remarked in 1919 that the fashion for eighteenth-century interiors had largely given way to a preference for Italian decor, except that "such fashions are not adopted instantly or universally, and a number of fine Georgian and Adam or McIntire interiors are still being done, especially in regions of strong colonial tradition." Kimball specifically illustrated this obser-

Fig. 7. Alston house, 2890 Andrews Drive, N.W., Atlanta, 1923. (Photo, Dennis O'Kain.)

vation with photographs of Reid's interiors for the 1915 Montag house in Druid Hills, thereby perpetuating the historical myth that Georgia is a region of "strong colonial tradition."[16]

It is a half-truth at least. Georgians, like Southerners generally, prided themselves on a conservative view of life, history, and society. Having largely escaped the rapid industrialization and urbanization of the North, the sense of the past and even its physical vestiges lingered longer. For city dwellers in the new century, however, the actual historic past had been compromised; for the fervid prophets of a New South, Georgia's recent history was a shame to be overcome. They needed imaginatively to create for themselves a new past, and they responded enthusiastically to the image of a much earlier and unsullied American (rather than Georgian) past suggested in the colonial revival houses that Neel Reid designed for Atlanta's new suburbs and for similar neighborhoods throughout Georgia and the South. They decorated their homes with eighteenth-century furniture; they imitated the box-bordered parterres of Gunston Hall in a climate where boxwood was unable to thrive. Meanwhile, the passion for Greek revival, the nineteenth-century style

[16] Kimball, "American Country House," p. 387.

Fig. 8. Witham house, 2922 Andrews Drive, N.W., Atlanta, 1926. (Photo, Dennis O'Kain.)

preeminently identified with the region, went out of favor until the distance of years and the success of Margaret Mitchell's *Gone with the Wind* lent it a newly respectable resonance, a shift of mood not lost upon postwar developers building whole streets of Taras in the still more remote Atlanta suburbs and exurbs of the last quarter century.

Curiously, Reid himself, who used Greek revival elements sparingly in his houses, purchased in 1916 as his own home Mimosa Hall, an 1842 Greek revival mansion in Roswell, Georgia. He lived there until his early death, from a brain tumor, at the peak of his career. He remained productive during the whole period of his illness; the Nixon house was on the boards when he finally succumbed in 1926. An enormously admired and popular figure in his lifetime—handsome, urbane, conspicuously gifted—Reid left a body of work which is still widely known and appreciated in Georgia. He was a society architect of sorts, a man who made his reputation designing homes for people of new wealth in a city eager to catch up with the rest of the country. But he also loved great architecture and endeavored to make his own buildings as fine in their way, as responsive to the demands of contemporary life, as the best work of the past. And if he intuitively exploited a style which captured and bodied forth the right myth for his clients, inventing a past borrowed from another place, in the end he seems to have made peace with some part of the true past of the Georgia that he loved, coming home to die in Mimosa Hall.

The Tradition of the Old: Colonial Revival Silver for the American Home
Charles H. Carpenter, Jr.

Colonial revival, as a style in the decorative arts, is based on simpler earlier styles current in America and England in the seventeenth, eighteenth, and early nineteenth centuries. An unkind critic might suggest that colonial revival is a watered-down version of these earlier fashions. Nevertheless, it is one of the most durable styles in American silver, having originated well over a hundred years ago. It is *the* popular style of the twentieth century.

The colonial revival entered the mainstream of American silver craft about 1870. However, there are a number of pieces from the 1840–70 period that do mirror earlier forms, which would suggest either that "colonial" styles never completely died out or that there was some renewed interest in the earlier styles in the middle decades of the late century. Such pieces are not typical of American silver in the mid nineteenth century. These are proto-colonial-revival examples, which can be compared to the proto-art-nouveau American silver of the 1870s and 1880s, well before the heyday of art nouveau proper in 1895–1905. Most of these proto-revival wares are interpretations of earlier forms rather than simple reproductions. Many of these pieces are from New York and New England, although examples are also known in Southern silver.

New York silversmiths such as Eoff and Shepard and Boston makers like Newell Harding made objects in the 1840–70 period closely related

Fig. 1. Sugar basket, Obediah Rich. Boston, ca. 1840.
H. (handle) 7¼"; L. 6⅜". (Gebelein Silversmiths:
Photo, George M. Cushing.)

to those of the late eighteenth and early nineteenth centuries. Such
details as beading and engraving tend to be slightly heavier on the later
pieces.

The sugar basket in figure 1 was made by Obediah Rich, Boston,
about 1840. Although it is based on half-century-old classical forms,
Rich's basket is broader and fatter than earlier treatments of such forms.
The plain borders around the rim and on the foot give no hint of the
Victorian exuberance to come, although the handle has gentle curves
that might not have been present on a more austere ancestor.

The porringer shown in figure 2 is stamped with the maker's mark of
E. & J. Kelley, Nantucket. It is dated 1847. The handle of the Kelley

Fig. 2. Porringer. H. 2½", Diam. 5⅛". Mark on back of handle: PURE / COIN / E. & J. KELLEY. Possibly by another maker (see text). Engraved on handle: I and LBM / 1847. (Collection of Richard S. Sylvia.)

porringer is related to mid eighteenth-century porringer handles of such Boston silversmiths as John Burt, Thomas Edwards, and Paul Revere.[1] The Kelley handle is slightly more delicate and open than its earlier prototypes. A close examination of the body of the Kelley porringer reveals telltale spinning marks, indicating that it was made on a lathe. In the eighteenth century, porringer bodies were hand raised from flat pieces of silver by means of hammering on stakes or small anvils. Although the use of the spinning lathe was introduced in American silver manufacture in the 1830s, it was not commonly used in hollowware forms until after 1850.[2]

That the body of the porringer was spun on a lathe creates a problem in attribution. It seems unlikely that the Kelleys, who were primarily spoonmakers, would have had such a new and relatively sophisticated piece of machinery as a metal-spinning lathe on the island of Nan-

[1] Kathryn C. Buhler, *American Silver, 1655–1825, in the Museum of Fine Arts, Boston* (Boston: By the museum, 1972), pp. 153, 177, 390.
[2] Charles H. Carpenter, Jr., with Mary Grace Carpenter, *Tiffany Silver* (New York: Dodd, Mead, 1978), pp. 235–36.

tucket. This leads to the suspicion that the porringer body might have been purchased in Boston or Providence. Perhaps the porringer itself was produced by another maker. The Kelley mark on the porringer handle is very deeply struck, suggesting that it was struck over another maker's mark.

One other mid nineteenth-century adumbration of the colonial revival spirit was the making of colonial-style pieces such as slop bowls and teakettles to add to older and less complete sets. A newspaper account of a Gorham exhibit in the 1851 Rhode Island State Fair in Providence noted: "Among the larger pieces are a plain octagonal kettle, designed to match the tea service of a lady of this city, by whose order it was made."[3]

The prevailing styles of American silver in the 1850s and 1860s were rococo revival and an eclectic mixture of styles which may be dubbed high Victorian. These fashionable, highly decorated new styles accelerated the obsolescence of the plain styles of the past. Style changes are never completely monolithic, but in the late 1860s the taste for the new fancier forms had made the older wares almost completely passé. An 1868 article about Gorham Company in *Harper's New Monthly Magazine* expresses the prevailing disdain for old silver:

> In the manufacture of silver-ware the first operation is, of course, to buy the silver. Wall Street is the usual source of supply. Occasionally, however, a long-hoarded treasure will find its way to the melting-pot from remote and unexpected quarters. The vicissitudes of life sometimes consign to the crucible a quantity of the clumsy "old plate" which people used to cherish with so much pride; and many persons now deliberately exchange their ancient implements and vessels for the elegant creations of modern taste.[4]

The first hint that the tide of fashion would start to turn appeared in 1870, in flatware. In this year both Tiffany and Gorham introduced flatware patterns that were adaptations of older patterns with names that evoke the colonial past. Tiffany's Antique and Queen Anne are variations of plain eighteenth-century patterns. Gorham came out at about the same time with two almost identical patterns, calling them Antique and Mother's. In the 1870s Gorham also reissued its 1840s coin-silver

---

[3] *Providence Journal* (September 13, 1851), p. 2.
[4] "Silver and Silver Plate," *Harper's New Monthly* 37, no. 220 (September 1868): 438–39.

patterns, naming them Tipt and Fiddle. (In the 1840s the Fiddle pattern was called French Tipt.) These old patterns were now made in sterling on steam-powered drop presses, whereas in the 1840s they had been made in "common" 800/1000ths fine silver by hand with the simplest of hand tools.

One can speculate that the emergence of these plain patterns in the early 1870s answered a demand for familiar forms of the past. They certainly did not represent any revolt against the prevailing high Victorian taste. If anything, they were the result of marketing decisions to satisfy conservative tastes.

Besides flatware, a few hollowware pieces in the colonial style were also made in the 1870s. The Tiffany coffeepot or chocolate pot in figure 3, made about 1878, derives from early nineteenth-century classical pieces. It could possibly have been made to match an old tea set, since it is quite atypical of Tiffany silver of the period.

The elegantly simple coffeepot in figure 4, made by Gorham in 1875, is based on earlier American and English forms and can be classified as colonial revival. However, its total look is actually away from the past and toward the future. It could almost be a mid twentieth-century pot with a Bakelite handle. It has a sleek, machine-made appearance that completely belies its age. Such objects had no effect on twentieth-century design. It is not likely that the designers would have known of them. They have come to be viewed as precursors only because we know of similar objects designed in the twentieth century.

More colonial revival hollowware was made in the 1880s. The Gorham coffeepot in figure 5, made in 1889, is also beginning to show signs of the coming art nouveau movement, with fluting that undulates on the base and curls on the top. Every era tends to interpret the old colonial styles in a way that also reflects the style of its own time.

Souvenir spoons were another manifestation of the colonial revival mentality at the turn of the century. Their manufacture started about 1890, and the Salem Witch spoons in figure 6, made by Gorham and retailed by Samuel Low of Salem, set off one of the great collecting booms. Between 1890 and 1905 thousands of designs issued from dozens of makers. Gorham Company, because of its substantial manufacturing and design capabilities, dominated the business almost from the beginning, producing over a thousand different designs. Tiffany made fifty or so.

Fig. 3. Coffeepot or chocolate pot, Tiffany and Company. New York, ca. 1878. Engraved with coat of arms of the Ridgely family of Baltimore. Reeded body and spout; ebony handle and finial. H. 8½". Mark: TIFFANY & Co. / 5232 MAKERS 8919 / STERLING-SILVER / 925-1000 / M. (Photo, Winterthur.)

Souvenir spoons celebrated the people and places of American history. The spoon on the left in figure 7 depicts in its bowl the Boston Tea Party; the one on the right shows Boston's Old South Meeting-house. Indians were also a popular motif, the 1880s and 1890s seeing a great popularization of American Indians, who were treated romantically and sentimentally after we had killed off many of them and backed

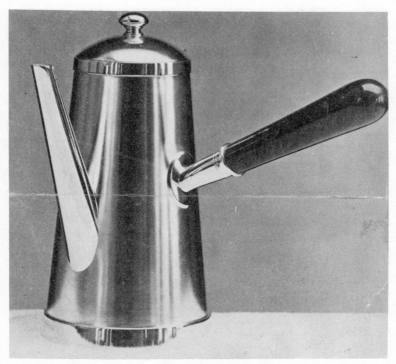

Fig. 4. Coffeepot, Gorham Company. Providence, 1875. Ebony handle. (Photo, Gorham Company.)

onto reservations those who remained. The souvenir spoon craze lasted about fifteen years, petering out after 1905, but never entirely ending.

The end of the nineteenth century and the beginning of the twentieth saw the real triumph of the colonial revival. It became the dominant style in American silver and has remained so throughout the twentieth century. The silver catalogues of Gorham and others at the turn of the century show clearly that the relatively plain colonial revival silver quickly replaced the more ornamental styles of the past, although some of the most expensive tea and coffee services continued to be made in a variety of academic Beaux-Arts styles.

The coffee set in figure 8, made by Gorham about 1920, was named

Fig. 5. Coffeepot, Gorham Company. Providence, 1888. Ebony handle and finial. (Photo, Gorham Company.)

Colonial. Embodying art deco influences, it is another example of how the colonial revival updated late eighteenth-century styles.

John S. Holbrook, a Gorham vice-president, described colonial revival in a 1910 address before the School of Applied Design for Women in New York:

We take up now our Colonial style and show in a few examples its relationship to the period of George III. The same beauty of line is evident, the same restraint of decoration, and in the revival of taste today the demand for Colonial examples and Colonial reproductions is one of the most hopeful signs we see, in my opinion, for the development of a sincere, pure, and true style of American art. . . .

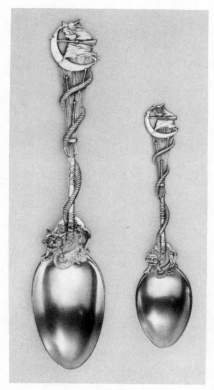

Fig. 6. Souvenir spoons, Gorham Company. Providence, 1890. *Left:* teaspoon; L. 5⅞". On front of handle: SALEM 1692. Mark: lion-anchor-G / STERLING. *Right:* coffee spoon; L. 4⅛". On front of handle: SALEM 1692. Mark: lion-anchor-G / STERLING / DANIEL LOW. (Gorham Company Collection.)

Fig. 7. Souvenir spoons, Gorham Company. Providence, ca. 1890. *Left:* Boston Tea Party; L. 5". Mark: lion-anchor-G. *Right:* Old South Meetinghouse; L. 5". (Gorham Company Collection.)

The chief characteristics of the Colonial style, as evidenced by the examples, are a careful study of form, and the shapes showing classical tendencies and a marked repression of ornament. The ornament used is largely engraved or flat chased, or if any relief, it is extremely low. Simple forms of saw-piercing were used as in porringers but as a rule articles of this style depend but little upon decoration for their effect, and indeed many of them are severely plain.[5]

[5] John S. Holbrook, *The Art of the Silversmith and Its Development* (New York: Privately printed for Gorham Co., n.d.), pp. 16–18.

Fig. 8. Coffee service, Gorham Company. Providence, ca. 1920. (Photo, Gorham Company.)

The colonial revival did not look only to American models for its inspiration. A piece of Gorham promotional literature advertising their Louis XVI silver (about 1912) reveals that French silver was a significant source for the colonial revival:

With the accession of Louis and Marie Antoinette, came a complete revolution in the world of art.

The marked characteristic of the style is a well defined return to more symmetrical and more classical forms. Another point of interest for us in America in the Louis XVI period is the fact that this style, transmitted through England in the time of the Georges, gave rise to our own Colonial, than which no style better adapted to our own home needs has been developed. One of its main elements of strength lies in the fact that it is in such exquisite taste, when executed, one never tires of it, as one often does of the more elaborately ornamented or over-ornamented style.

Fig. 9. Coffeepot, Gorham Company. Providence, ca. 1908. (Photo, Gorham Company.)

It is good to live with in everyday homes, and its refined beauty is beyond reproach.[6]

The French influence appears directly in simplified and modified versions of the Beaux-Arts styles such as the coffeepot in figure 9, made by Gorham about 1910.

The silversmiths of the arts and crafts movement embraced both the making procedures *and* the styles of the eighteenth century. The service in figure 10 was designed and made by George Gebelein of Boston about 1905. He was a well-trained silversmith who had worked as a

[6] Gorham Company files, Providence, R.I.

Fig. 10. Tea and coffee service, George C. Gebelein. Boston, 1931. H. (coffeepot) 7¼". (Photo, Gebelein Silversmiths.)

journeyman at the Tiffany and Company plant in Newark, New Jersey, Sheibler Company in New York, and Durgin Company in Concord, New Hampshire, before joining the Handicraft Shop of Boston—a small group of independent craftsmen—in 1903.

The Gebelein service was advertised in *American Collector* with the caption:

A REFLECTION OF THE 18TH CENTURY

Both practical and beautiful is the engraved oval type of the George III period which is interpreted in this XX century creation by Gebelein—panelled and fluted version entirely hand-made in the original manner of craftsmanship—the complete service comprising teapot and stand, coffee pot, sugar bowl, cream pitcher, waste bowl, and water kettle.

The trend in home furnishings to the 18th century English (and contemporaneous American) treatments is a natural return to what might be called the "good design standard," and a conscious appreciation of the contribution of that period of great artistic development in decoration is inevitable to educated taste. Designs preserved in art museums entered again their function of gracious service in the home because they are found to meet best the requirements of enduring beauty, liveableness, and practicality, while also peculiarly suited to harmonize in existing schemes drawn from Georgian or Colonial sources or channels of inspiration.[7]

Although Gebelein prided himself on using the age-old techniques of silversmithing, he did not at the beginning try to copy earlier work. Margaretha Gebelein Leighton, in her biography of George Gebelein, noted:

With regard to designing and creating new and original forms, it should be recorded that the styles exemplified most characteristically in the work of the silversmiths in The Handcraft Shop were simple in form and detail with the exception of fluting. Pieces were designed directly from basic concepts with the aim of obtaining pleasing shapes for practical purposes; consequently, they sometimes took a form which appeared related to Colonial models.[8]

After about 1920 most of Gebelein's work was in the colonial revival style, which is what his customers wanted:

While some of his work continued to exemplify the original, free-designing motivation of his earlier years, the trend in design at Seventy Nine Chestnut Street was led by the demands of his clientele into the reinterpretation of the designs of the early American silversmiths and their British contemporaries of the Georgian Period. The influence of the late Colonial craftsmen and those of the early Federal Period were also reflected in his work.

Gebelein's versions of these designs were generally "adaptions" rather than copies[,] although several "replica" projects were made on special order. Treatment of the classic themes, associated with Paul Revere, included matching components of confirming designs, especially in the case of tea sets, few of which were handed down intact from the eighteenth century. Then, too, twentieth-century tastes often dictated variations in sizes; yet the Gebelein adaptations as well as his "replicas" followed the same techniques in re-presentation as those created by the craftsmen of Paul Revere's day.[9]

[7] Advertising flyer from *American Collector* 17, no. 1 (February 1948).
[8] Margaretha Gebelein Leighton, *George Christian Gebelein, Boston Silversmith, 1878–1945: A Biographical Sketch* (Boston: Privately printed, 1976), p. 47.
[9] Leighton, *Gebelein*, p. 73.

Fig. 11. Soup tureen and ladle, Arthur J. Stone. Gardner, Mass., 1915. (Photo, Winterthur.)

Arthur Stone and his associates in Gardner, Massachusetts, made silver by hand in a number of styles, but colonial revival dominated the later years of the shop. The covered tureen in figure 11, made in 1915, is a handsome example of how a good silversmith can take a relatively hackneyed design and transform it with taste and fine silversmithing.

In the early years of the twentieth century there was a heightening interest and increasing knowledge of objects made by the great craftsmen of the past, which created a demand for good reproductions. Starting about 1912 both Tiffany and Gorham made copies of eighteenth-century American and English silver. In the second and third decades of this century Tiffany and Company helped Judge A. T. Clearwater form his collections of American silver which he willed to the Metropolitan Museum of Art in New York in 1933. Many of the colonial objects were studied by the Tiffany silversmiths, and a number were copied. These ranged from a Paul Revere tea set, a small bowl by Ephraim

Brasher, eighteenth-century flatware, and a chocolate pot by Edward Winslow. Such objects as the Brasher bowl reproduction have little of the feel of the original. The modern copy was spun on a lathe, which gave it a more perfect surface than that of the hand-raised original. Nevertheless, such pieces as the Winslow chocolate pot (fig. 12) are remarkably close to the original, although the fluting of the copy is a bit more mechanically regular. The original has Edward Winslow's mark conspicuously stamped in the middle of the body between the handle and the spout and on the plain part of the lid directly above,[10] while Tiffany marked its copy on the bottom.

The working drawings for the Paul Revere reproduction cream pot in figure 13 indicate how thoroughly the Tiffany silversmiths had studied the original pieces. In the case of the cream pot they made detailed, full-scale drawings of the original from the side, the front, and the top. There were drawings of the foot, the handle, and the engraving on the piece. Plaster casts of the original were made, together with photographs from all angles and two electrotypes. The gauges of the metal of the body, the foot, the handle, and the top edge were carefully noted.

The making of reproductions by such commercial firms as Tiffany and Gorham ended by the 1930s. Silver reproductions made in this country since World War II have almost all been sponsored by museums. When Williamsburg needed flatware for food services in the Raleigh Tavern complex, reproductions were purchased. Later, in 1954, Williamsburg set up a working silversmith shop where William de Matteo and his assistants made, in full public view, reproductions of eighteenth-century silver. De Matteo's wares found a ready market. Like other American museums, Williamsburg also sells reproductions of early silver wares made for them by commercial firms. The proliferation of museum shops has led to a proliferation of silver and silver-plate reproductions of the works of such silversmiths as John Burt, Jacob Hurd, Joseph Richardson, Jr., Ebenezer Moulton, and Paul Revere. Gorham Company made the reproduction of the Paul Revere spoon in figure 14 for New York's Metropolitan Museum of Art. This spoon has a machine-made look as a result of die stamping, while the original clearly had been hand chased. The marks on the Revere reproduction spoon (on the back of the handle) are made very deep to discourage faking.

[10] Graham Hood, *American Silver: A History of Style, 1650–1900*, American Decorative Arts Series, ed. James Biddle (New York: Praeger Publishers, 1971), p. 67.

Fig. 12. Reproduction of Edward Winslow chocolate pot, Tiffany and Company. New York, ca. 1920. H. 9¼". (Photo, Christie, Manson & Woods International, New York.)

The colonial revival style has dominated commercial silver wares of the twentieth century, and the trend continues unabated. Since World War II the modern movement has had only a peripheral effect on the decorative arts in America. The vibrant upheavals in American painting of the postwar years—when abstract expressionism, pop art, and minimalism gave international fame to such artists as Jackson Pollock, Mark Rothko, Andy Warhol, and Ad Reinhardt—have had little influence

Fig. 13. Reproduction of Paul Revere cream pitcher, Tiffany and Company. New York, ca. 1918. H. 6¾". (Gebelein Silversmiths: Photo, Winterthur.)

on the decorative arts of this country. The colonial revival movement has had the support of many antiques collectors, scholars, and curators throughout this century. There is a direct correlation between the scholarship in the field of American silver of the late nineteenth and early twentieth centuries and popular taste. The first books on American silver by John Buck (1880 and 1903)[11] and pioneering exhibitions

[11] J. H. Buck, *Old Plate, Ecclesiastical, Decorative, and Domestic: Its Makers and Marks* (New York: Gorham Manufacturing Co., 1888); and J. H. Buck, *Old Plate: Its Makers and Marks* (New York: Gorham Manufacturing Co., 1903).

Fig. 14. Reproduction of Paul Revere spoon, Gorham and Company. Providence, 1954 or later. (Photo, Gorham Company.)

such as Washington's Inaugural Centennial in New York (1889) and exhibitions in Boston (1906), at the Metropolitan Museum of Art (1909), and in Worcester (1913) all focused on silver made before 1815. The silver of the 1825–1900 period was dismissed as an aberration. There was widespread agreement that design went downhill after 1825 and that the whole Victorian era was a time of decadence in the decorative arts. It was felt that we should go back to earlier, simpler styles. Hollis

French, in his introduction to Hermann Frederick Clarke's *John Coney, Silversmith* (1932), summed up the academic bias in favor of the colonial revival:

Appreciation of the artistic value of our early silver has certainly increased greatly. When we compare the designs of the silver made in this country, say, fifty or sixty years ago, it is very evident that great improvement has been made. This is partly due, no doubt, to the general improvement in public taste after the low point of the Victorian Era, but it is possible to trace directly the influence of the silver of colonial times in many of the new designs now being used.[12]

The tradition of the old has led to a continuing conservatism in the decorative arts in America that is quite at odds with the technological achievements of the twentieth century. It is obvious that today's silver manufacturers think of colonial revival as a safe, tried-and-true style. Market research shows that people buy it. Museums, newspapers, magazines give their approval. The style seems fated to be with us for a long time, although it has stultified American design for much of the twentieth century. I would hope that perhaps by the twenty-first century the colonial revival style will have lost its stranglehold on the American decorative arts. Let it be an alternate style for those who want it, but we need not make everything in it. John Marshall Phillips's statement in his 1949 book, *American Silver*, is still valid today:

The revival of craftsmanship in silver during the past thirty years, largely conditioned by patronage, has been restricted mainly to copies of, or designs based on, early styles. One of the great charms of the silver of the seventeenth and eighteenth centuries, in addition to the necessary attributes of appropriateness of form, lies in its expression of contemporary life. It is still to be hoped that an era in which such progress has been made in science, medicine, architecture, the machine, moving picture and radio [to Mr. Phillips's list we may add television, computers, and space exploration] can evolve a style in silver that two hundred years hence will be as expressive of our own time as John Hull's silver is of his.[13]

[12] Hermann Frederick Clarke, *John Coney, Silversmith, 1655–1722* (Boston: Houghton Mifflin Co., 1932), pp. xiv–xv.
[13] John Marshall Phillips, *American Silver* (New York: Chanticleer Press, 1949), p. 126.

The New England, or "Olde Tyme," Kitchen Exhibit at Nineteenth-Century Fairs
Rodris Roth

The New England kitchen was intended as a reproduction of a "colonial," or "olde tyme," kitchen. It was an exhibit, a restaurant, and, to some extent, a variety show. One of the many attractions at fairs and expositions during the second half of the nineteenth century, the New England kitchen was, depending on the sponsor, a fund raiser for charity or a commercial venture. In either case, the purpose, according to contemporary accounts, was to show how people lived a hundred years earlier by exhibiting furnishings, food, decor, and costumes, and by staging planned activities. As a self-conscious use of the American past to amuse and educate the public, the New England kitchen deserves examination for its role in the colonial revival.

Perhaps the best-known kitchen exhibit was the New England Farmer's Home and Modern Kitchen at the International Centennial Exposition in Philadelphia. It was described at the time as "a representation of the New England farmer's home of a century ago, and a kitchen fitted up in modern style, thus comparing the 1776 and the 1876."[1] It

[1] Samuel J. Burr, *Memorial of the International Exhibition* (Hartford: L. Stebbins, 1877), p. 681; Dianne H. Pilgrim, "Inherited from the Past: The American Period Room," *American Art Journal* 10, no. 1 (May 1978): 6. See also Martin Filler, "Rooms without People: Notes on the Development of the Model Room," *Design Quarterly* 109 (1979): 6; Elizabeth Stillinger, *The Antiquers* (New York: Alfred A. Knopf, 1980), pp. 3–16.

is no surprise that the best-known kitchen would appear during the Centennial, an appropriate time to look back. But, while many "olde tyme" kitchens followed it, the 1876 exhibit was not actually the first. In 1864 there were at least six independent kitchen exhibits in as many cities: Brooklyn, Poughkeepsie, New York City, Saint Louis, Philadelphia, and Indianapolis.

During the Civil War, fairs were held in many Northern cities to raise funds for the United States Sanitary Commission, forerunner of the Red Cross and a great central relief organization, which labored to improve the sanitary conditions of the Union army. The kitchens were attractions at these charity bazaars, or "Sanitary Fairs," as they were called. Conceived, organized, and run in large measure by women's committees, the Sanitary Commission Fairs began in 1863 (the first in Chicago) and continued through the remainder of the war. Most lasted two or three weeks, were open from ten in the morning to ten in the evening, and charged admission. They received a good deal of publicity, attracted large crowds, and, according to a recent assessment, "proved the most fertile instrument of fund raising for the Commission."[2]

The first of the 1864 kitchens was featured at the Brooklyn and Long Island Sanitary Fair, which opened on George Washington's birthday, February 22, and ran for nearly three weeks at the Academy of Music. The kitchen itself was housed across the street from the academy with the Department of Manufactures. A covered bridge connected it with the main part of the fair. Like the five colonial kitchens that followed it during 1864, Brooklyn's was hailed as the "most novel and curious feature" of the Sanitary Fair. The Brooklyn fair ran until March 11 and was followed by the Dutchess County and Poughkeepsie Sanitary Fair held in Poughkeepsie, New York, March 15–19, featuring the Old Dutchess County Room. The Knickerbocker Kitchen was part of the Metropolitan Fair in Aid of the United States Sanitary Commission held in New York City April 4 to 23. From May 17 to June 18 a New England kitchen was operated at the Mississippi Valley Sanitary Fair in Saint Louis. In Philadelphia, at the Great Central Fair in Aid of the

[2] William Y. Thompson, "The U. S. Sanitary Commission," *Civil War History* 2 (June 1956): 57. See also William Y. Thompson, "Sanitary Fairs of the Civil War," *Civil War History* 4 (March 1958): 51–67. For another view of the commission, see George M. Fredrickson, *The Inner Civil War* (New York: Harper & Row, 1965), pp. 98–112. I am grateful to Sally McMurry for bringing this book to my attention.

United States Sanitary Commission, June 7–28, there was a Pennsylvania kitchen. Finally, during October 4–8, a Yankee kitchen was set up at the Sanitary Fair in Indianapolis.[3]

Where the idea for the colonial kitchens came from is not entirely clear. It is unlikely that the kitchens appeared fully developed and without antecedents. That each kitchen was appropriately furnished and carefully thought out suggests the existence of some precedent, possibly a literary one. As we shall see, the kitchen at the New York City fair had very explicit literary associations. And there were traditional regional origins as well. Native New Englanders dominated the committee responsible for the kitchen at the Brooklyn fair. One witty Brooklynite wrote of the fair: "We also have a New England Kitchen, in deference to the powerful and respectable element in our midst, which hails from New England, and naturally divides itself into the saints, the sinners and the Beecher family—the first moving the churches, the second the purses, and the third a little of both." The history of the Brooklyn and Long Island fair attests to the role Brooklyn's New England contingent played in the creation of the kitchen and provides a more precise clue to the genesis of this kind of exhibit. "The plan of a New England Kitchen was broached, by Mrs. Ray Potter, President of the Sanitary Aid Society." The society, however, abandoned its plans for a charity bazaar when the Sanitary Fair was proposed. A "Special Committee was selected to take charge of the 'New England Kitchen,' comprising among its members the ladies and gentlemen who originated the plan. This committee took hold of the work *con amore*, their New England blood fired with the determination to make the 'Kitchen' a grand success."[4]

---

[3] "The Fair Movement in the Loyal States. No. 6. The Brooklyn and Long Island Fair," *Our Daily Fare* (Philadelphia) (June 14, 1864); the New York City kitchen was "one of the most interesting and attractive features" ("The Knickerbocker Kitchen," *New York Daily Tribune* [April 5, 1864]); the St. Louis kitchen was "the most popular and one of the most interesting attractions" ("New England Kitchen," *Daily Missouri Democrat* [St. Louis] [May 19, 1864]); the Indianapolis kitchen was "the novelty of the Fair" (*Indianapolis Journal* [October 6, 1864]).

[4] E. C., "A Letter from Brooklyn—The Brooklyn Fair. Brooklyn, Feb. 25, 1864," *Canteen* (Albany) (March 1, 1864); *History of the Brooklyn and Long Island Fair* (illus. ed.; Brooklyn: The Unicorn, Steam Presses, 1864), pp. 72–73. For another reference to Brooklyn's New England "settlers" and kitchen, see *A Record of the Metropolitan Fair in Aid of the United States Sanitary Commission* (New York: Hurd and Houghton, 1867), p. 182. No information has been found about Mrs. Potter. Ray W. Potter, merchant, is listed in the Brooklyn city directory for 1864. The names of committee members for the kitchens are known, but I have not been able to identify any as collectors or antiquaries.

The kitchens at the various fairs were pretty much alike, especially in what they contained. But there were differences, the most pronounced of which were regional. Brooklyn drew upon the New England background of some of its inhabitants, as did Saint Louis and Indianapolis. New York emphasized its Dutch forebears, and Philadelphia recalled its German heritage.

We shall look first at the Brooklyn kitchen as an illustration of the features common to all of the kitchen exhibits. This New England kitchen was the subject of one of four large colored lithographs in the deluxe edition of *The History of the Brooklyn and Long Island Fair* (fig. 1). It is the only picture in the book of a specific display, which suggests how highly regarded the kitchen was at the time. During the planning of the fair, the committee for the kitchen issued a circular outlining the project:

The idea is to present a faithful picture of New-England farm-house life of the last century. The grand old fire-place shall glow again—the spinning wheel shall whirl as of old—the walls shall be garnished with the products of the forest and the field—the quilting, the donation, and the wedding party shall assemble once more, while the apple-paring shall not be forgotten—and the dinner table, always set, shall be loaded with substantial New England cheer. We shall try to reproduce the manners, customs, dress, and, if possible, the idiom of the time; in short, to illustrate the domestic life and habits of the people, to whose determined courage, sustained by their faith in God, we owe that government, so dear to every loyal heart. The period fixed upon is just prior to the throwing overboard of the tea in Boston Harbor.

Interestingly, the objectives of the 1864 exhibit were similar to those of today's period rooms and historical restorations.[5]

The physical arrangement of the various kitchens generally followed

---

A few were listed in the *National Cyclopaedia of American Biography* but none in the *Dictionary of American Biography* or *Notable American Women*. Local histories remain to be examined. City directories show that many members were merchants, lawyers, clerks, salesmen, teachers, and grocers; a few were doctors, ministers, and judges, or, more often, their wives, sisters, daughters, or mothers. I am indebted to Olive Graffam for helping to search city directories.

[5] "Brooklyn & Long Island Fair in Aid of the Sanitary Commission. 'New-England Kitchen,' " circular dated January 18, 1864, War Fund Committee Records, 1841–71, box 3, Long Island Historical Society, Brooklyn. See *History News* 35, no. 1 (June 1981), for articles describing current examples of role playing in period settings; see also Shomer Zwelling, "Social History Hits the Streets: Williamsburg Characters Come to Life," *History News* 35, no. 1 (January 1981): 10–12.

Fig. 1. New England Kitchen, Brooklyn and Long Island Sanitary Fair, 1864. From *History of the Brooklyn and Long Island Fair* (illus. ed.; Brooklyn: Unicorn, Steam Presses, 1864). (Smithsonian Institution.)

one of two plans. Either the exhibit and a restaurant shared a room, as in the Brooklyn and other Sanitary Fair kitchens, or they were in different rooms or buildings, as at the Philadelphia International Centennial and Chicago Columbian expositions. If exhibit and restaurant occupied the same room, the two activities associated with each were nevertheless separated. Eating was confined to tables in the center portion of the room. In Brooklyn's kitchen "long tables were laid in the centre of the room, for repasts in the New England style." The "genuinely old objects" were displayed around the edge of the room or limited to a specific area, sometimes marked off by a barrier. The size of the kitchens—the combined restaurant and exhibit—averaged about 3,000 square feet. An admission fee was charged—usually ten cents—and the restaurant charges were separate.[6]

[6] Discussions about the similarities of the kitchens as to plan, furnishings, food, clothing, activities, and so forth are based mainly on the descriptions of the exhibits cited here:

Meals were served by costumed waitresses at midday and in the evening (if the fair was open at night). A horn might announce mealtime: at five o'clock in the Brooklyn kitchen "the country dinner horn was blown and the company sat down to dinner." Like the costumes, furnishings, and entertainment, the menu was meant to be colonial, too. "On the tables [at Brooklyn] were bountiful supplies of toothsome viands— pork and beans, cider apple-sauce, Boston brown bread, pitchers of cider, pumpkin, mince, and apple pies, doughnuts, and all the savory and delicate wealth of the New England larder."[7]

So much for the typical meal. The surroundings in which it was consumed included many common features. Most important was the fireplace, the centerpiece of the kitchen exhibits. Whether the cooking was actually done in the kitchen or in a separate restaurant, the fireplace was essential as a symbol of the previous century. It contrasted strikingly with the range or cookstove of the modern kitchen. The fireplace in Brooklyn's kitchen was described as "strictly after the old New England type."[8]

Brooklyn: *Drum Beat* (February 22, 24, 25, 26, 1864); *History of Brooklyn Fair*, pp. 72– 78; Bloodgood H. Cutter, *A Poem on the New England Kitchen* (n.p., 1864). Indianapolis: *Sanitary Fair Bulletin* (October 4, 8, 1864). New York: "The Knickerbocker Department," *New York Herald* (April 4, 1864); "The Knickerbocker Kitchen," *New York Daily Tribune* (April 5, 1864); *Record of Metropolitan Fair*, pp. 182–86. Philadelphia: "The Great Central Fair," *Daily Evening Bulletin* (June 9, 1864); Thomas Izod, ed., *Philadelphia Sanitary Fair Catalogue and Guide* (Philadelphia: Magee Stationer, 1864), pp. 11, 28–29; "The Pennsylvania Kitchen," *Our Daily Fare* (June 14, 1864); Charles J. Stille, *Memorial of the Great Central Fair for the U. S. Sanitary Commission, Held at Philadelphia* (Philadelphia: U. S. Sanitary Commission, 1864), pp. 100–104. Poughkeepsie: *Report of the Dutchess County and Poughkeepsie Sanitary Fair* (Poughkeepsie: Platt and Schram, 1864), pp. 11, 221–23. St. Louis: "New England Kitchen," *Daily Missouri Democrat* (May 17, 19, 31, 1864); "A Visit to the Yankee Kitchen," *Daily Countersign* (May 27, 1864). International Centennial Exhibition: *Catalogue of New England Farmers' Home of 1776* (Philadelphia, 1876); J. S. Ingram, *The Centennial Exhibition Described and Illustrated* (Philadelphia: Hubbard Bros., 1876), pp. 706–8; James Dabney McCabe, *The Illustrated History of the Centennial Exhibition* (Philadelphia: National Publishing Co., 1877), pp. 722–23; "The New England Kitchen," *Leslie's Illustrated* (June 17, 1876), p. 238; Frank Henry Norton, *Illustrated Historical Register of the Centennial Exhibition . . . and of the Exposition Universelle* (New York: American News Co., 1879), pp. 87, 312–13. Permanent Exhibition: *Official Catalogue of the International Exhibition . . . 1877* (Philadelphia: J. B. Lippincott, 1877), p. 14. World's Columbian Exposition: Hubert Howe Bancroft, *The Book of the Fair*, vol. 2 (Chicago: Bancroft Co., 1895), p. 840.

[7] *Drum Beat* (February 24, 1864); *History of Brooklyn Fair*, p. 75.

[8] *History of Brooklyn Fair*, p. 74.

Every kitchen also had its strings of dried apples draped across the mantel or hung from the rafters or, as in Brooklyn, from racks suspended from the ceiling. In most kitchens there were candlesticks on the mantel, and, in many, there was also a gun hung over the mantel. Usually there was a "tall clock sedately ticking in the corner," like the one to the left of the fireplace in Brooklyn. Other "old-fashioned" furnishings common to most of the kitchens were a Bible, a teapot, a cupboard or, perhaps, a dresser—or both—with pewter and china, a table, and some chairs. It was reported that in Brooklyn's kitchen "[of] the chairs on which the guests sat while eating, almost all had a history." Certainly, the ladder- and banister-back chairs seen at the tables are eighteenth-century forms.[9]

Furnishings were lent by committee members, or offered by families, or solicited from individuals and families. Collecting expeditions also were organized, which is how the Brooklynites gathered together their exhibit in 1864. This is noteworthy as an early instance of collecting deliberately for public display and with an eye toward regionalism. A reporter for *Drum Beat*, the newspaper published at the Brooklyn fair, suggested the sources of the kitchen's furnishings. "These articles have been loaned for the occasion from all parts of the East, several gentlemen interested in the Fair having taken extensive tours through the New England States, expressly to collect such specimens."[10]

In every kitchen there was a spinning wheel, that quintessential symbol of colonial times.[11] Often there were two wheels, a large one for wool and a small one for flax. Spinning was demonstrated as well as knitting, which was usually practiced near the fireplace. Spinsters and knitters, like servers and attendants, were dressed in an old-fashioned manner. References to "quaint attire" are common. The one article of clothing that seemed most to signify life in the eighteenth century was the mobcap, mentioned in the accounts of just about every kitchen exhibit.

To the untrained eye, the costumes worn by the women and men seen in the pictures of the kitchens look sufficiently colonial. However,

[9] *History of Brooklyn Fair*, pp. 75, 74. See also " 'New-England Kitchen' " circular, War Fund Committee Records, which includes a list of articles wanted, such as "100 old-fashioned Chairs, most of them for use at tables."

[10] *Drum Beat* (February 26, 1864).

[11] Christopher Monkhouse, "The Spinning Wheel as Artifact, Symbol, and Source of Design," in *Victorian Furniture: Essays from a Victorian Society Autumn Symposium*, ed. Kenneth L. Ames (Philadelphia: Victorian Society in America, 1982), pp. 153–72.

the costume historian readily recognizes them for what they are, theatrical outfits (or, as one young clothing specialist put it, "phony colonie"). In the few instances where genuine period clothing was used, it generally dated from the early 1800s rather than the 1700s.[12]

Photographers as well as artists recorded the Sanitary Fairs, including (as we have seen) the kitchen exhibits. The popularity of Brooklyn's exhibit as a pictorial subject is further indicated by the official history of the fair, which notes that a "series of twelve stereoscopic pictures of scenes in the Kitchen, was taken by Mr. W. E. James." So many views of a single exhibit suggest that there was a large audience for the stereographs. The titles included *New England Cooks, Paring Bee, New England Spinners, Old Costumes, New England Belles, Quilting Bee,* and *The Wedding Party.*[13]

Reviewing "the Entertainments in the Kitchen," the historian of the Brooklyn fair wrote of the wedding: "this was the grand crowning effort of the managers of the New England Kitchen to reproduce the manners and customs of the past age." The minister officiated "in laced cocked hat and black knee-breeches." Following refreshments, "the festivities of the evening were closed with dancing in which all joined merrily." Among the other activities scheduled in the kitchen were a donation, or "giving visit to the Parson, in the olden time, being very humorously rendered," a quilting party, a series of old folks' concerts, "presented simply to give an idea of the method of rendering the music of a century ago," and an apple bee, "one of the best of the series of entertainments given in the Kitchen," where besides paring apples, "stories were narrated and riddles and conundrums propounded for the company to guess."[14]

The New York City fair opened April 4, 1864, and ran for nearly three weeks. Officially known as the Metropolitan Fair in Aid of the United States Sanitary Commission, it was located in two buildings

[12] I am especially grateful to my Smithsonian colleagues Carol Kregloh, for assistance with the subject of clothing, and Anne Golovin, for guidance in pursuing the subject of the New England kitchen.

[13] *History of Brooklyn Fair,* p. 77. Long Island Historical Society has thirteen card stereographs by James documenting the New England kitchen (War Fund Committee Records, boxes 3, 5), including, in addition to those cited, *Mrs. Partington and Ike,* spinning wheels, and kitchen fireplace. The stereograph *New England Cooks* is in the collection of Susan Myers, to whom I am indebted for sharing with me this and other stereographs of Sanitary Fairs.

[14] *History of Brooklyn Fair,* pp. 76–77.

near Union Square. The temporary building at the north end of the square housed the Knickerbocker Kitchen, New York's counterpart to Brooklyn's New England Kitchen. By its very name the Knickerbocker Kitchen proclaimed its New Amsterdam ancestry. A "Dutch revival," as one writer summed it up, the kitchen owed a debt to Washington Irving's 1809 *History of New York*, a mock heroic account of Dutch New Amsterdam, which purported to be the work of one Diedrich Knickerbocker. For many observers, the quaint pages of that book materialized in the form of the Knickerbocker Kitchen.[15]

An illustration of the exhibit provides a view from an angle adjacent to the fireplace, with the eating area nearby and an additional display area beyond the railing in the background (fig. 2). An observer of this scene wrote: "the centre of the room was filled with tables surrounded by high, broad-backed chairs, and set out with steel knives and forks and old-fashioned china, in expectation of the guests who were never wanting." Around the room's edge were "novel and interesting specimens of 'ye olden times,' " while "in the parlor, which was cut off from one end of the kitchen, were some of the more stately pieces of antique furniture and a collection of portraits." All the elements of the colonial kitchen were here. The fireplace, candlesticks on the mantel, a gun over the mantel, and strings of dried apples draped from the ceiling. The spinster and her wheel were next to the fireplace, the cupboard in the corner, and a dresser on the far wall.[16]

A more particularly Dutch flavor was imparted to the room by the jambless fireplace with a cloth valance attached to the mantel. In this instance the cloth may have been designed in imitation of tiles. After attending the fair on April 7, John Ward, a young New Yorker, wrote in his diary: "we went into the Knickerbocker Kitchen & saw Mrs. Roosevelt dressed up as a Dutch lady. . . . Colored women waited on tables.— We saw a cradle marked 1754, etc. Calico is stretched above the fireplace to look like Dutch tiles (blue)." Dutch inscriptions heightened the evocation of New Amsterdam days. They are seen over the window and the fireplace in a view of the room from another angle published in

[15] *Record of Metropolitan Fair*, pp. 182–83, 186; "The Knickerbocker Department," *New York Herald* (April 4, 1864), a three-column article, more than half of which is devoted to "A Kitchen and Parlor in the Time of Wouter Von Twiller—Something about Ancient Dutch Habits, Dresses, Fat Pork and Doughnuts, &c &c."

[16] *Record of Metropolitan Fair*, p. 184; *New York Herald* (April 5, 1864); *Record of Metropolitan Fair*, p. 184.

Fig. 2. *The Knickerbocker Kitchen, Union Square.* Metropolitan Sanitary Fair, New York City, 1864. From *Harper's Weekly* (April 23, 1864). (Library of Congress.)

New York Illustrated News and titled *The Knickerbocker Kitchen—A Special Object of Interest in the Metropolitan Sanitary Fair.*[17]

A special attraction of the Knickerbocker Kitchen was the fiddler. "In the chimney-corner sat Chloe and Caesar, respectable people of color, the one busy with knitting, the other 'on hospitable cares intent,' scraped his fiddle for the beguilement of visitors." The waitresses also were blacks, who, remarked one reporter, "it will be remembered, were the universal

[17] "Diaries of John Ward of New York City," vol. for April 1–20, 1864, Manuscript Room, New-York Historical Society, New York; "The Union Square Exhibition," *New York Herald* (April 6, 1864). The picture cited from *New York Illustrated News* is an undated clipping, Metropolitan Fair Papers, List of Contributors box, New-York Historical Society. Another view of the kitchen, in "Exterior and Interior Views of the Union Square Building" from the same newspaper and collection, is dated April 24, 1864. See also "Plan of the Fair Buildings," *Harper's Weekly* (April 16, 1864), p. 246.

'helps' in the old Dutch families."[18] Besides the fiddling, there were other entertainments in the Knickerbocker Kitchen, such as a quilting bee and fortune reading, "with tea leaves in the bottom of the cup." The women, dressed in "the robes of their great-grandmothers," noted a visitor, wore "high crowned Dutch caps." While we may question the authenticity of the clothing shown in a photograph reproduced in the published report of the Metropolitan Fair, the furniture, or certainly some of the chairs in the kitchen, may actually have dated from the 1700s. According to the *New York Herald*, the "large collection of antiquated china and furniture" was "got together from different parts of the State."[19]

The food, too, was supposed to be of an old-time sort. "Lunch, tea, caudle and coffee will be served up at all hours," it was reported in the *New York Times* of April 6. Tickets, brightly colored yellow, green, pink, and orange, printed with black lettering, were required for the different refreshments:

COFFEE
Fifteen Cts.

CAUDLE
50 Cts.
WITH BISCUIT OR CAKE.

DUTCH TEA
Seventy Five Cts.

The Dutch taste was also evident in such specialties as "the unctious olykoek, the crisp kroiler."[20] No Boston baked beans and brown bread were served in the Knickerbocker Kitchen.

Nor was Boston fare served in the Pennsylvania Kitchen. In Philadelphia, the Great Central Fair in Aid of the United States Sanitary

[18] *Record of Metropolitan Fair,* p. 183; "The Knickerbocker Department," *New York Herald* (April 4, 1864).

[19] *Record of Metropolitan Fair,* pp. 184–85; *New York Daily Tribune* (April 5, 1864); "Costumes of Ladies in Knickerbocker Kitchen," *Record of Metropolitan Fair,* facing p. 184; "The Knickerbocker Department," *New York Herald* (April 4, 1864).

[20] *New York Times* (April 6, 1864); "The Knickerbocker Kitchen," *New York Times* (April 4, 1864). Tickets are pasted in a scrapbook, "Metropolitan Fair in Aid of the United States Sanitary Commission, 1864, Mr. John Kensett, Chairman, Art Department," item 34.467.1, Prints and Manuscripts, Museum of the City of New York.

Fig. 3. Pennsylvania Kitchen, Great Central Sanitary Fair, Philadelphia, 1864. (Library Company of Philadelphia: Photo, attributed to Oliver
H. Willard, Philadelphia, 1864.)

Commission was held in June in an enormous structure built specially
for it on Logan Circle. The Pennsylvania Kitchen (fig. 3) was located
at the north end of "Union Avenue," the bazaar's grand thoroughfare.
Pennsylvania's German heritage was immediately evident in the food
served in the kitchen. "There is a bill of fare in sound Pennsylvania
Deutsch," announced a satisfied customer, which included the "good
things peculiar to the Kitchens of our State: Ofenbrod, Zwieback . . .
Pretzels . . . Noodles . . . Summer-wurst," and on and on to a total of
twenty different foods. There were also inscriptions in Pennsylvania
German: GRANT'S UP TO SCHNITZ crowned the fireplace, the letters appropriately formed of dried apples. A history of the fair translated:
"being literally interpreted, [this] means 'Grant's up to dried applies
[*sic*],' but which it may be as well to interpret 'Grant's up to snuff.' "

Other German characteristics in the kitchen included the "white washed walls spotted over with blue, in true Teutonic rural taste" and the "very old fashioned Lancaster or Berks county appearance."[21]

In Poughkeepsie, while the influence was also Dutch, the most striking feature of the exhibit was undoubtedly "the exterior of one side of a spacious house," which served as the entrance to the "Dutchess County Room of one hundred years ago." A circular described the setting: "Completely furnished as in that olden time, and the House-keeping carried on by Ladies in Costume, such as our great-grandmothers wore. Flax and Wool Spinning Wheels in operation. Admission 10 cents. No half price. Tea in the ancient style every evening from 5 to 10 o'clock. Price fifty cents." Besides its importance as a reconstruction of a colonial setting, inside and out, and as an enactment of life a century before, this room is worthy of attention because of one of its committee members, Benson J. Lossing (1813–91), author, editor, artist, engraver, best known for the *Pictorial Field Book of the American Revolution* (1850–52). Tremendously popular and successful in its day, this narrative sketchbook, as it has been called, "still commands respect." Lossing is the only historical specialist I have found in connection with the colonial kitchens. What his role was (if any) in old-time exhibits other than the Dutchess County Room remains to be explored.[22]

Two other Sanitary Fairs had kitchens. At Indianapolis, the Yankee Kitchen, as it was called, was reported to be "under the management of live yankees." Everything about it, "the red peppers strung from the rafters, the strings of pumpkins and dried apples, and above all the savory smell of pork and beans," rhapsodized a nostalgic correspondent, "carried the visitor away deown east to a New England farmhouse in the

---

[21] "The Pennsylvania Kitchen," *Our Daily Fare* (June 14, 1864); *Our Daily Fare* (June 11, 1864); Stille, *Memorial*, p. 101; "The Pennsylvania Kitchen," *Daily Evening Bulletin* (June 4, 1864); "The Great Central Fair," *Daily Evening Bulletin* (June 9, 1864).

[22] *Report of Poughkeepsie Fair*, p. 21; *Dictionary of American Biography*, s.v. "Benson John Lossing." Lossing's connection with other Sanitary Fairs is indicated by a letter and a Poughkeepsie circular quoted, "A Hundred Years Ago," inscribed "March, 1864 / Benson J. Lossing," located in a collection of Philadelphia Sanitary Fair papers. See the John A. McAllister Papers, Scrapbooks . . . Relating to U. S. Sanitary Commission, vol. 2, p. 136, Library Company of Philadelphia; Charles G. Leland to John Welsh, March 30, 1864, Horace H. Furness Papers, Sanitary Fair Correspondence, box 7, Historical Society of Pennsylvania. I am indebted to Martha Briggs, Huntington Library, San Marino, Calif., for checking their collection of Lossing papers. Nothing on other kitchens was found in this collection.

full tide of husking." As in other kitchens, "curiosities" were displayed and old-fashioned meals were served. "The hour for opening the larder," explained a devotee of the Indianapolis kitchen, "is announced by the blowing of a horn. Whenever you hear the toot, just know the Yankees want a quarter, and you want your dinner."[23]

Farther west, Saint Louis had seen their New England Kitchen some five months earlier. A photograph (fig. 4) shows the kitchen's full cast of characters—and characters they were: Grandma Brown, Jonathan Jones (he sold genuine nutmegs), Mr. Deacon Twitchell from Iowa, Miss Polly Bluestocking, sundry country cousins, Aunties Nabby, Sally and Polly from Cape Cod, Miss Prissy the village dressmaker, Miss Rogers the Yankee schoolmarm, and so on. Besides costumed attendants, there were planned activities and old-time meals featuring brown bread, mush, and pumpkin pies. A reporter for the *Daily Missouri Democrat* summed up the room in these words: "The reproduction of this relic of olden times is a success. The big fire place, the large oven, the antique furnishings, call to mind very vividly the descriptions of the New England Kitchens as they formerly existed." All the ingredients of an old-time kitchen were to be found on the banks of the Mississippi, even a *Mayflower* relic. "A pitcher supposed to have come over in the May Flower" was displayed in the Saint Louis kitchen, prompting a skeptic to remark: "it is suggested that that ship must have been about the size of the Great Eastern to have carried all the things reported to have come over in her cargo." The Saint Louis committee had reproduced as genuine a New England kitchen as any of their counterparts back East, and perhaps even more authentic. The East had come West.[24]

With the end of the Civil War, the Sanitary Fairs ended as well, and the New England, or colonial, kitchen seems mostly to have disappeared for a time. Further investigation may show that they were set up at local celebrations and bazaars. For example, about the fair held in

---

[23] *Sanitary Fair Bulletin* (October 4, 8, 1864).

[24] "The New England Kitchen," *Daily Missouri Democrat* (May 19, 18, 17, 1864). Characters at Brooklyn's kitchen included "Grand'ma Downing, Patience, her daughter, Grand'ma May Flower, Deborah, Aunt Tabitha," according to the written inscription on the back of the stereograph *New England Spinners*, War Fund Committee Records, box 3. For a picture of Jerusha, a young woman in colonial costume spinning, see "The Centennial Exhibition—Old Time New England Farm-House," *Harper's Weekly*, Supplement (July 15, 1876), p. 585; and for characters in the kitchen at the Permanent Exhibition of 1877, see fig. 7, below. No source has been located for these characters.

Fig. 4. New England Kitchen with costumed characters, Mississippi Valley Sanitary Fair, Saint Louis, 1864. (Missouri Historical Society.)

Georgetown to raise funds for the Aged Women's Home, the following was reported in the *Washington Evening Star* of February 17, 1868: "the New England kitchen forms quite an attraction, and so does the picture gallery."[25] Generally, however, there was a hiatus in the exhibition of New England kitchens between the Sanitary Fairs and the Philadelphia exposition of 1876.

The world's fair celebrating the centennial of the United States was held in Fairmount Park, Philadelphia, from May to November 1876. The New England log house and kitchen were located south of Agricultural Hall near the center of the grounds, "snugly nestled among the tall trees." There were two buildings, the old-time kitchen in a log structure and the modern kitchen, or restaurant, in the frame building

[25] Quoted in the Commission of Fine Arts and the Historic American Buildings Survey, *Georgetown Commercial Architecture—Wisconsin Avenue Northwest, Washington, District of Columbia. HABS Selections No. 3* (Washington, D.C.: By the commission, 1967), p. 59. The Aged Women's Home remains today in the same building at 1255 Wisconsin Ave.

Fig. 5. New England Farmer's Home and Modern Kitchen, International Centennial Exposition, Philadelphia, 1876. (Free Library of Philadelphia: Photo, Centennial Photographic Co., Philadelphia, 1876.)

(fig. 5). How the exhibit, a commercial venture, came into being was explained by one of the many reporters covering the fair: "The originator of the idea illustrated in this building was Miss Emma Southwick, of Boston, Mass. Miss Southwick visited the Vienna Exposition, and being greatly interested in the representation of peasant life in Hungary and Tyrol which she found there, conceived the idea of reproducing American pioneer life of a hundred years ago, at the Centennial Exposition. She accordingly procured the construction of this cabin."[26] Considering the popularity of the colonial kitchens during the Civil War, it is curious that no mention is made of them and that Emma Southwick is called the "originator" of an idea inspired by a foreign rather than an

[26] Norton, *Historical Register*, pp. 87, 312. The kitchen was not "an appendage of the Women's Pavillion," as stated in Edward C. Bruce, "The Century—Its Fruits and Its Festivals. XII—Detached Exhibits," *Lippincott's* 18 (December 1876): 664; nor was it in any way associated with the Women's Centennial Executive Committee, as far as can be determined.

American example. In any case, the International Exhibition in Vienna where Southwick got her idea had been held in 1873. Dwellings of various countries and regions, particularly Hungary and Austria, were set up in Exposition Park, some complete with fenced gardens. The houses were furnished, and men and women in ethnic costume engaged in activities such as weaving, sewing, and playing musical instruments. There also were a number of national restaurants with waiters and waitresses in regional dress.[27]

Erecting an entire New England house rather than just setting up a room was probably a new idea and may have been inspired by the 1873 Vienna fair. The layout of the New England Farmer's Home at the Centennial was described by a visitor: "[It] is a plain one-story log house, and is built and arranged in the style of the New England farm-houses of a century ago. It contains a parlor, or 'settin-room,' a kitchen, and bed-rooms, all of which are furnished with veritable heirlooms contributed by the people of New England." The building is a log cabin because in 1876 it was believed that New England settlers, like frontier pioneers, lived in log houses. The centennial house was both a product and a perpetuator of the log cabin myth.[28]

Intended to show life at the time of the American Revolution, the centennial exhibition kitchen (fig. 6) consisted of the same basic ingredients as the 1864 kitchens: "There is the wide chimney, with its high mantel, the latter decorated with candlesticks, and other articles in familiar use at that period. . . . An old-time spinning-wheel stands in one corner, and a small wheel for flax in another. There is a cradle which was in early use in the colonies [the Fuller cradle], and a diminutive desk

[27] For descriptions of dwellings in the "primitive woodland village" adjacent to the exhibition building, see H. W. Sweny, "Buildings in the Park," in Great Britain Royal Commission for the Vienna Universal Exhibition of 1873, *Reports on the Vienna Exhibition of 1873* (London: Her Majesty's Stationery Office, 1874), pp. 299–301. Presumably these were the buildings Southwick visited. One structure reminded Sweny of New England: "Roumanian log house with its quaint chimney, shingled roof and air of rough solidity, recalled the times of the 'Pilgrim Fathers.' 'Miles Standish,' 'the Pequots ringing whoop, the soldiers wild halloo' " (Sweny, "Buildings," p. 300). Pictures of the exterior and the interior of a Hungarian and a Tyrolian house, with brief descriptions, appeared in *L'Exposition Universelle de Vienne Illustrée Organe officiel de la Commission Royale de Hongre (Autriche)* (Paris: Administration, 1873), pp. 195–97. For information about and pictures of national restaurants, see Sweny, "Buildings in the Park," pp. 314–15; and *L'Exposition*, pp. 149, 381, 493, 593.

[28] McCabe, *History of the Centennial*, p. 645. See also Harold R. Shurtleff, *The Log Cabin Myth* (1939; reprint ed., Gloucester, Mass.: Peter Smith, 1967), pp. 186–208.

Fig. 6. New England kitchen interior, International Centennial Exposition, Philadelphia, 1876. From *Leslie's Illustrated* (June 10, 1876). (Smithsonian Institution.)

which John Alden brought over with him in the Mayflower."[29]

Drawings of the Centennial's kitchen were popular in such magazines as *Leslie's Illustrated* and *Harper's Weekly*, often carefully delineated, but sometimes crudely drawn, perhaps to suggest the roughness of cabin life. The photographers were at work, too. A few of the same objects shown in the sketches are seen in stereographs. Magazine illustrations were sometimes copied from photographs instead of being drawn directly from the room itself.[30]

[29] E. B. D. [Mrs. E. B. Duffey], "The Smaller Buildings of the Centennial Exhibition," *Arthur's Illustrated Home* 44, no. 9 (September 1876): 508.

[30] Other pictures include: *Exterior of the New England Kitchen*, in *Leslie's Illustrated* (June 17, 1876), p. 237; *Old Time New England Farm-House*, in *Harper's Weekly*, Sup-

The New England Farmer's Home had costumed guides. South-wick's "able corps of assistants" (appropriately from New England) were described as "ladies who are dressed in the quaint costumes of their great-grandmothers, and who conduct visitors through the house and explain to them the story and uses of its contents." Further guidance was provided by a seven-page catalogue enumerating the objects throughout the house. Number 71 reads: "Old Settle, always found in old-fashioned kitchens, home-spun garments hung on the back."[31] This can be seen to the left of the fireplace in *Harper's* illustration *Old Time New England Farm-House*.

Following the Centennial, the so-called Permanent Exhibition, also known as the International Exhibition, was set up in the Main Build-ing. An ill-fated venture, it was to close in a few years. But before this happened, many of the centennial exhibitors refurbished their displays and rented space in the Main Building, Southwick among them. The following announcement appeared in the *Official Bulletin of the Inter-national Exhibition:* "Miss Southwick has returned from California expressly to take charge of this log cabin, which, with the kitchen attached to it, proved so attractive a feature of the Centennial." The log house was photographed in its new setting (fig. 7), which can be identified by the hint of the "placid pool of water" in the front yard, a feature men-tioned in the 1877 *Official Catalogue of the International Exhibition.* The handwritten caption below the picture identifies the sitters as Pris-cilla, Mother (almost certainly Emma Southwick), Grandfather, Obe-diah, and Jerusha. The restaurant was moved, too. The menu, decorated with a picture of the log cabin, is clearly marked "Permanent Exhibi-tion" (fig. 8). Here are all the favorites from earlier New England kitch-

plement (July 15, 1876), p. 585; *Interior of the New England Kitchen* in Joseph Miller Wilson, "History, Mechanics, Science," in *The Masterpieces of the Centennial Interna-tional Exhibition*, vol. 3 (Philadelphia: Gebbie and Barrie, 1878), p. clviii; *The New England Log Cabin and Modern Kitchen (Exterior)*, in McCabe, *History of the Centen-nial*, p. 722; *Silk Weaving in Log Cabin*, in Norton, *Historical Register*, p. 265; and card stereographs by Centennial Photographic Company: *Log Cabin Studies: Cat's Cradle*, Free Library of Philadelphia; *Log Cabin in "Ye Olden Times"* (with costumed guides) and *Furniture of "Ye Log Cabin,"* Smithsonian Institution. Two photographs titled *New England Kitchen in "Ye Olden Time"* previously identified as centennial interiors in Rodris Roth, "The Colonial Revival and 'Centennial Furniture,' " *Art Quarterly* 27, no. 1 (1964): 65, fig. 5, prove on closer examination not to conform to the 1864, 1876, 1877, or 1893 kitchens. They are marked "McCormack, Photo. 22 Winter Street." Boston street direc-tories list John L. McCormack, photographer, at 22 Winter St. from 1882 to 1889.

[31] Wilson, "History, Mechanics, Science," 3:clxiv; McCabe, *History of the Centennial*, p. 723; *Catalogue of New England Farmers' Home of 1776*, p. 4.

Fig. 7. New England log house with costumed characters, Permanent
Exhibition, Philadelphia, 1877. (Smithsonian Institution.)

ens, including, of course, Boston baked beans and brown bread.[32]

In Chicago, at the World's Columbian Exposition of 1893, the menu
still had at the top of the list Boston baked beans and brown bread, as
can be seen on the board to the left of the restaurant entrance (fig. 9).
This world's fair was laid out along the shore of Lake Michigan, except
for the section known as the Midway Plaisance, which extended inland.
The Midway, billed as the "Highway through the Nations," contained
sideshows, entertainments, and restaurants of different nations, *the* original
Ferris wheel, and, not far from the entrance, "The New England Log
Cabin and Ye Olden Time Restaurant." Still a log house (indeed, there
were a number of log cabins at the Columbian exposition put up by
various groups), the New England kitchen of 1893 continued to feature
a rustic porch at the door and, as seen earlier in 1877 at the Permanent
Exhibition, dormer windows. If the arrangement sounds reminiscent of
the centennial exposition, that is to be expected, since the person in
charge was "Emma S. Brinton, Concessionaire":

[32]*Official Bulletin of the International Exhibition*, no. 4 (May 1877), p. 31; *Official
Catalogue of the International Exhibition*, p. 14. I am indebted to Barbara Carson for
bringing to my attention five views of the New England kitchen at the Permanent Exhibition in the collection of North Andover Historical Society.

PERMANENT EXHIBITION

Log Cabin Reſtaurant.

RIGHT OF MUSIC STAND.

Yᴱ Old Tyme Meals.

Yᴇ Baked Beans, prepared as in yᵉ faſhion of yᵉ Olden Tyme in yᵉ Ancient City of Boſton, Brown Bread, Coffee or Tea	25
Cold Ham, Bread and Butter, Coffee or Tea	25
Cold Tongue, " " " "	25
Roaſt Beef, " " " "	25
Corned Beef " " " " Tuesdays & Fridays	25
Potatoes, boiled	10
Boiled Eggs (2)	10
Fried Eggs	15
Sandwiches	10
Oat-Meal and Milk	15
Bread and Milk	15
Pie	10
Doughnuts	5
Molaſſes Gingerbread	5
Sponge and other Cakes	5
Iced Tea or Coffee	10
Bread and Butter	10
Ice Cream	10
Soups	20

Fig. 8. Menu of Log Cabin Restaurant, Permanent Exhibition, Philadelphia, 1877. (Historical
Society of Pennsylvania.)

A small frame building on which is the sign: "Old-Tyme Farmer's Dinner."
Here pork and beans, doughnuts, pies, and other viands are served by Vassar
and Wellesley girls, attired in costumes of the olden days, on little square tables
with horn-handled knives, two-pronged forks of steel, and the quaintest of antique
dishes. The idea of furnishing such meals originates with Mrs. Brinton, better
known as "Mother Southwick," the name which she bore at the Centennial
Exposition, where she presided over a similar place of entertainment. Nearby
she has reproduced another of its features in the model of a revolutionary log
cabin, with its two rooms and loft, the parlor extending across the building, and
with yawning fireplace, crane, and kettles, and all the other furnishings of a

Fig. 9. Restaurant and New England kitchen, World's Columbian Exposition, Chicago, 1893. (Smithsonian Institution Collection of Business Americana.)

century ago. Opposite the door is ranged upon a sideboard the family plate; and here are ancient hymn-books, candlesticks, and spinning wheels, and oldest of all, the cradle of Peregrine White, the so-called "babe of the Mayflower."[33]

The Miss Southwick of 1876 had married by 1893.

The attendants and waitresses in their old-style dresses and mobcaps were photographed for a publication titled *Midway Types* (fig. 10).

[33] "Isolated Exhibits, Midway Plaisance," in *World's Columbian Exposition Official Catalogue* (Chicago: W. B. Conkey Co., 1893), p. 11; Bancroft, *Book of the Fair*, 2:840. I am indebted to Susan Prendergast Schoelwer for identifying Mrs. Brinton as Miss Southwick and for sharing with me these and other references to the New England kitchen of 1893. No further information about Emma B. Southwick has been found. She is not mentioned in *Notable American Women* or in Boston city directories, 1875–1900. She did not attend either Wellesley or Vassar colleges (Leigh Maccini, Wellesley College Alumnae Association, to Rodris Roth, April 13, 1983; Polly M. Kuhn, Alumnae and Alumni of Vassar College, to Roth, April 5, 1983).

Fig. 10. *"Ye Olde Tyme" Restaurant.* World's Columbian Exposition, Chicago, 1893. From *World's Columbian Exposition Portfolio of Midway Types* (Chicago: American Engraving Co., 1893), pt. 3, n.p. (Smithsonian Institution.)

Depicting the different nationalities seen at the 1893 world's fair, the New England kitchen group, identified as "the manager and her assistants" (presumably Emma S. Brinton, or "Mother Southwick," is on the right), was selected to represent the United States. Like every other kitchen before it, the one at the Columbian exposition had a knitter with her needles and a spinner with her wheel.[34]

As we have seen, the New England, or "Olde Tyme," kitchen exhibits at nineteenth-century fairs follow a pattern. The 1876 kitchen closely approximates the Brooklyn kitchen of 1864, although there is no corroborating evidence that Southwick had the Brooklyn prototype in mind when she conceived the Philadelphia kitchen. But Miss Southwick—

[34]Other views of the kitchen include *New England Kitchen (Exterior)*, *Mrs. Preston [Spinning]*, *New England Kitchen, Midway*, and *New England Girls and Their Chaperon*, from the *New England Kitchen* in Hezekiah Butterworth, *Zigzag Journeys in the White City* (Boston: Estes and Lauriat, 1894), pp. 185, 187, 188; and *An Olden Time Quartette* in *World's Columbian Exposition Portfolio of Midway Types* (Chicago: American Engraving Co., 1893), pt. 7, n.p.

now Mrs. Brinton—was responsible for the New England kitchen at the World's Columbian Exposition of 1893 in Chicago. The aim of all the kitchens was to depict life as it was lived a hundred years earlier. Accordingly, the kitchens were filled with relics of bygone times, costumed guides interpreted the settings, costumed waitresses served the meals, and various activities of an old-time sort were conducted.

The relation of the New England kitchens to period rooms calls for further exploration. The full picture of "life in olden times" that was the purpose of the kitchens and which was executed with imagination and a sense of enjoyment warrants consideration as a valid and vivid way of interpreting the past. This approach is having something of a revival today.

The role of women in the 1864 New England kitchen exhibits deserves attention, too. Their organizational abilities and managerial talents were of major importance to the success of the kitchens. Additionally, they were features of the exhibits themselves: knitters, spinsters, waitresses, attendants, and character actors. There are ironies in this: here were women, working outside the home, but still in the kitchen. Furthermore, most of the women, well-to-do volunteers, had servants at home and so were seldom in any kitchen. They were playing at kitchen—a fact not lost on the historian of the 1864 Metropolitan Fair, who referred to the Knickerbocker Kitchen as a "play kitchen," but conceded that such play "entailed serious work upon those who insured its success."[35] The term *play kitchen* further conveys the sense of participation in a game or, even more, in a show, a play.

The objects in the kitchen varied in their age. For the generations of 1864, 1876, and 1893, the furnishings and clothing of their grandparents or great-grandparents were old-fashioned enough to be considered "colonial," a vague period two generations ago or more, an indiscriminate blend of the seventeenth, eighteenth, and nineteenth centuries. Regionalism was a factor in depicting the past, and there was an awareness of rural versus urban life. Kitchens were often meant to be those of the New England farm. In 1876 the exhibit was called a farmer's house, and in 1893 the meal served was a farmer's dinner. To city dwellers the ways of country folk must have seemed old time—as they

[35] *Record of Metropolitan Fair*, p. 186.

probably were to some extent. But, clearly, there was a farmer myth entangled with the log-cabin myth.

A reflection of interest in the American past, these rooms had a popular appeal. They reinforced colonial virtues as codes for the modern citizen to follow even as they showed how far the country had progressed since its founding. Change was especially well illustrated by objects, the "veritable antiques" gathered in the exhibits. The kitchens are early instances of the collecting and study of artifacts for private pleasure as well as public edification.

Curious Relics and Quaint Scenes: The Colonial Revival at Chicago's Great Fair
Susan Prendergast Schoelwer

The World's Columbian Exposition opened its gates on May 1, 1893, celebrating one year late the 400th anniversary of Christopher Columbus's discovery of America. Occupying a lakeshore site in Chicago's Jackson Park, the fair was most famous for its gleaming White City of Beaux-Arts exposition buildings created by Daniel Burnham and his team of architects. Beyond the grand Court of Honor, however, there was much more to see—650 acres of landscaped grounds set with statuary and laced with entrancing waterways, nineteen foreign and thirty-nine state buildings, an exotic Midway Plaisance, and, most of all, over 5 million square feet of exhibits.

Not least among the wonders of the fair were many "curious relics" and "quaint scenes" from the colonial past. Among the great competitive and commercial displays of modern technology, observant visitors found themselves face to face with innumerable expressions of colonial architecture, interior decoration, historical exhibitions, and commemorative activities. More examples of the colonial revival—both original and replicated—were gathered on the grounds of the World's Columbian Exposition than had ever been brought together anywhere else in the country. The extent of these colonial expressions, together with their diversity, location, date, and large audience, suggests that they played a major role in the development and popularization of the colonial revival movement as a national phenomenon. While previous studies of the colonial revival have mentioned specific elements of the World's Columbian Exposition, none has considered the total impact of its extensive colonial manifestations on the subsequent spread of colonial revival architectural and decorative styles or the collecting of American art and artifacts by both private antiquarians and public museums.[1]

The first and most evident manifestation of the colonial revival at the fair was the architecture of the state buildings, which comprised a small city of their own to the north of the White City itself. Of the thirty-nine state buildings, twenty-one were designed in what was loosely described as the "colonial style"—either modeled after specific structures or incorporating individual design motifs considered typical of colonial architecture.

Four colonial state buildings were immediately distinguishable by their close resemblance to historic structures: Virginia's replica of Mount Vernon, Pennsylvania's adaptation of Independence Hall, Massachusetts's recreation of the demolished John Hancock mansion, and New Jersey's version of the Morristown residence once used as General Washington's headquarters. Even these most literal of state buildings, however, were hardly authentic by present-day preservation standards. The state buildings functioned "primarily as headquarters for the commissioners . . . and as club rooms for reception and entertainment of visitors."[2] As such, they had to provide facilities for visitor registration, information desks, mail pickup and delivery, newspaper reading rooms, libraries, reception halls, dining rooms, separate ladies' and gentlemen's parlors, and staff quarters—a variety of functions for which a true colonial structure would have been inadequate. Consequently, with the exception of Virginia's Mount Vernon, the colonial replicas were adapted quite freely to suit current needs.

In his design for the New Jersey building, for example, architect Charles Alling Gifford made several significant alterations in the floor plan and scale of his model, the fairly simple white frame Ford mansion that

[1] The major modern works to consider the manifestations of the colonial revival at the World's Columbian Exposition are William B. Rhoads, *The Colonial Revival* (New York: Garland Publishing, 1977); and Rodris Roth, "The Colonial Revival and 'Centennial Furniture,' " *Art Quarterly* 27, no. 1 (1964): 57–81.

[2] John J. Flinn, *Official Guide to the World's Columbian Exposition* . . . (souvenir ed.; Chicago: Columbian Guide Co., 1893), p. 131.

George Washington had made his temporary headquarters. These changes only partially obscured the colonial features of the original in Morristown. One contemporary writer assured visitors: "While one or two [major] changes were made from the design of the original, such as the addition of a wing and the extension of the verandas, the minor details were faithfully copied. The small window panes, dormer windows, and outside chimneys of the original were not lacking, and weatherboarding, blinds, and shingled roof all contributed to the quaintness of the structure."[3]

Similar adaptation could be seen on the popular Massachusetts building, modeled after the demolished Beacon Hill residence of John Hancock (fig. 1). In announcing the architectural competition for this building, the Massachusetts Board of World's Fair Managers had requested a design in the spirit—if not an exact copy—of one of the state's many well-known historical buildings. From at least five plans submitted by local architects, the board in 1891 selected that of the noted Boston firm Peabody and Stearns. The architects later described their search for an appropriate historical reference: "In casting about for models that might fitly recall New England surroundings, the Old State House at the head of State Street, and the Hancock mansion, which once stood on Beacon Hill, seemed to offer the best possible types. This Hancock house, with its terraced gardens, was the most picturesque as well as the most architectural of these two buildings." Peabody and Stearns went on to explain that "the Massachusetts house was never intended to be, in absolute strictness, a copy of the old Hancock mansion," as "the old house would have seemed lost in the company of the large fair buildings" and certain changes were required to expand and adapt the structure to the specifications of the state board. Rather than an exact copy, the new building was an "enlarged and enriched version of the home of the bold signer of the Declaration of Independence," with three stories, gambrel roof, dormers, and imposing central pediment. Although constructed of staff (an inexpensive and easily worked mixture of straw and plaster), the surface was quoined and rusticated to resemble the original granite walls. "Old models" were followed for all elements not part of the original house, such as the entrance gable and columns, which followed those of the Lindens in Danvers, Massachusetts. The lantern, which was added to make the structure look less like

---

[3] Rossiter Johnson, A *History of the World's Columbian Exposition* . . . , 4 vols. (New York: D. Appleton, 1897), 2:471.

a private home and more like an official state building, also helped to identify the building to visitors arriving by water or elevated railway, to whom only the rooftops would be visible.[4]

Pennsylvania's state building deviated even further from its distinguished model, for only the tower and entrance door were reproduced from Independence Hall (fig. 1). In September 1891, the Executive Committee of the Pennsylvania Board of Managers had advertised a competition, limited to Pennsylvania architects, for a state building "to be completed with Pennsylvania materials so far as practicable." By the November 12 deadline, twenty-nine separate plans had been submitted; seven met the board's basic requirements. The first prize of $1,000 was awarded to Philadelphia architect Thomas P. Lonsdale, whose final design featured a fairly accurate replica of the Independence Hall clock tower set atop a cluster of spreading red-brick halls and white piazzas intended simply to provide a comfortable and commodious reception center.[5]

In selecting Lonsdale's design, the state Board of Managers was clearly attracted by its patriotic and historical symbolism: "Within [Pennsylvania's] borders stands the Hall of Independence, with all the sacred associations that cluster around it, and while she cannot transfer the building to Chicago, she can erect on the ground of the exposition a structure for the use of the citizens of the state that will be a *fac-simile* of this historic hall, so that millions of American citizens who may never visit Philadelphia, will be able to see a copy of the building so closely allied to the Declaration of Independence and the Federal Constitution." Most contemporary descriptions of the building recognized that only its tower and entrance were colonial replicas and apparently found no discrepancy in the juxtaposition of colonial and colonial revival elements. As the official state catalogue explained, "In architecture, it is colonial, and is new in design, except that the exterior of the tower is a *fac-simile* of the present tower of Independence Hall in Philadelphia."[6]

More recently, architectural historian John Maass has classified the

---

[4] *Report of the Massachusetts Board of World's Fair Managers* (Boston: Wright and Potter, 1894), pp. 12, 31–32; Rhoads, *Colonial Revival*, p. 127.

[5] A. B. Farquhar, comp., *Pennsylvania and the World's Columbian Exposition . . .* (Harrisburg: E. K. Meyers, n.d.), pp. 42–45.

[6] Farquhar, *Pennsylvania and the Exposition*, p. 29; *Catalogue of the Exhibits of the State of Pennsylvania and of Pennsylvanians at the World's Columbian Exposition . . . Prepared under the Direction of A. B. Farquhar, Executive Commissioner* (n.p.: Clarence M. Busch, 1893), p. 13.

Fig. 1. *Right to left:* State buildings of Massachusetts, New York, and Pennsylvania, World's Columbian Exposition, Chicago, 1893. From William Henry Jackson, *The White City (as It Was)* . . . (Chicago and Denver: White City Art Co., 1894), n.p. (Courtesy Chicago Public Library Special Collections Division.)

Pennsylvania State Building as the first of many replicas of Independence Hall, and as such it has frequently been criticized for its rather loose interpretation of the original. In his study of the colonial revival movement, William Rhoads called this building an "ostentatious parody" with "little in the jumble of balconies, balustrades, roof garden, indented curved walls, verandas and sculpture" to indicate that its architect had studied the original. These criticisms ignore the primary objective of the state board, which clearly was not to create an architecturally precise replica, but to fashion an easily recognizable, symbolic icon of Pennsylvania as "one of the most moral, intelligent, wealthy, patriotic and progressive members of the Union."[7]

[7]John Maass, "Architecture and Americanism or Pastiches of Independence Hall," *Historic Preservation* (April–June 1970): 18, as cited in Rhoads, *Colonial Revival*, p. 635;

Perhaps the single most popular colonial revival project on the fairgrounds was Virginia's Mount Vernon, a reasonably authentic reproduction of George Washington's home along the Potomac River. Designed by Richmond architect Edgerton Rogers, the building was one of the most accurate reconstructions at the exposition: "Not only is the edifice at Jackson Park an exact reproduction of the original, but many of its contents are also reproduced in fac-simile." Even the landscaping reflected Mount Vernon, for the land in front of the state building sloped down to the lakeshore as the original lawn slopes down to the Potomac. Modern reviewers have pointed to the addition of a porch and the omission of a Palladian window as the only deviations from the original structure.[8]

Virginia's decision to reproduce Mount Vernon reflected both state pride and economic compromise. The Virginia legislature had appropriated only $25,000 for all aspects of the state's participation in the fair, a paltry sum compared to the $150,000 spent by New York on its building alone, the $121,000 allotted by Pennsylvania, or even the $44,000 approved by Massachusetts. Although construction of any large edifice was clearly impossible, Mount Vernon, a "plain and roomy building with little of ornamentation, . . . could be reproduced at small expense, and[,] as the home of the father of his country[,] would be to American visitors as the Mecca of their pilgrimage, and to foreigners an object of surpassing interest." As state funds were inadequate for even this modest project, private funds had to be raised—a task assigned to the women of Virginia, who had earlier organized to save from destruction the original Mount Vernon. In May 1892, the Virginia Board of World's Fair Managers appointed a special ladies' committee charged with "the patriotic duty of raising a fund to duplicate at Chicago, Mount Vernon, the home of Washington, as the Virginia Building, and that an appeal be made to the women of Virginia to render every assistance to this laudable undertaking." Contributors to the fund (minimum, $1) were to receive a certificate of membership in the Mount Vernon Columbian Memorial Association of Virginia.[9]

The Virginia building was a great success, winning critical approval

Rhoads, *Colonial Revival*, pp. 128–29; Farquhar, *Pennsylvania and the Exposition*, p. 11.

[8] Hubert Howe Bancroft, *The Book of the Fair*, 3 vols. (Chicago: Bancroft Co., 1895), 3:787; Rhoads, *Colonial Revival*, p. 131.

[9] For appropriations, see Johnson, *History of the Exposition*, 2:460, 475, 479, 484. For the Virginia State Building, see Bancroft, *Book of the Fair*, 3:787; and *Organizations, By-*

for its accuracy as well as attracting large crowds. According to fair historian Rossiter Johnson, a nearby stop on the fair's shuttle (the "intramural railway") was called Mount Vernon, and "oftentimes the announcement of the name sufficed to empty the train." Despite this success, Virginians remained ambivalent about their state building. While clearly proud of its position as "the grandest of grand links in the chain of the Union," a fitting symbol of the "mother of states and statesmen," the state remained somewhat embarrassed that it had been unable to afford a more elaborate edifice, "a headquarters that would not suffer by comparison with the costly and ornate structures of her sister States."[10] While sentimentally appropriate, the colonial style was clearly not considered as impressive as the classical revival styles used in the large exposition buildings.

In addition to New Jersey, Massachusetts, Pennsylvania, and Virginia, six others of the thirteen original English colonies erected state buildings in Chicago. Georgia and South Carolina had no funds allotted by their legislatures, and North Carolina, after failing to raise enough private contributions, had to give up its plan to reproduce Governor Tyron's Palace at New Bern. Other states also considered, then rejected, the idea of replicating specific colonial structures. Instead of the Annapolis State House model originally contemplated, or the Carroll Mansion outside Baltimore suggested by architectural critic Montgomery Schuyler, Maryland built a more generic "manor house of generous proportions, such as might have stood on the shores of Chesapeake bay during the colonial period." Although contemporaries described the design as "free classic architecture" with a "colonial style" interior, it might have been more aptly called "steamboat colonial," resembling as it did a long, low ship's bridge decorated with Adamesque garlands.[11]

In early plans for the exposition, the New York state managers apparently considered reconstructing the Van Rensselaer manor house in Albany. Later, however, architect Charles McKim successfully pre-

---

Laws, Plan of Work, Local and General, of the Board of World's Fair Managers of Virginia . . . (n.p., 1892), p. 25.

[10] Johnson, *History of the Exposition*, 2:485; Rand, McNally & Company, *A Week at the Fair* . . . (Chicago: Rand, McNally, 1893), p. 224; Bancroft, *Book of the Fair*, 3:787; Johnson, *History of the Exposition*, 2:484.

[11] For Georgia and the Carolinas, see Rhoads, *Colonial Revival*, pp. 132, 637. For Maryland, see Bancroft, *Book of the Fair*, 3:791; Johnson, *History of the Exposition*, 2:458; and Rhoads, *Colonial Revival*, p. 638.

sented plans for an ornate Florentine palace based on the Villa Medici (fig. 1). In justifying this far more elaborate and non-American design, which departed drastically from the colonial motif of the neighboring buildings, the New York commissioners commented that

these had been affected entirely by local historical associations, and it was evident that if New York were to follow [Massachusetts's and Pennsylvania's] lead the result would be a kind of architectural conglomerate, in harmony neither with itself nor the carefully considered scheme of the great exposition structures. In point of fact, there were more failures than successes in Jackson Park in the attempted reproduction of historical buildings in unfamiliar surroundings, and in the opinion of all discriminating critics, New York did wisely in refusing to join in this competition.

At least one popular guidebook evidently missed the change in plan, however, as John J. Flinn blithely reported to unsuspecting visitors that the florid and expensive Renaissance revival summer palace was "a reproduction, slightly modified, of the old Van Rensselaer residence, for many years one of the historic landmarks of New York city. The quaint architecture recalls a most interesting period in our national history, when the great commercial and financial metropolis was but a straggling seaport town."[12]

Delaware and Connecticut both erected comfortable residential structures. The Delaware building, constructed of native woods, was a "plain, unpretentious structure; but not without elements of the picturesque." Although described as "mainly of the southern colonial" style, its many gables and its shingle covering suggested lingering traces of the shingle style. For its headquarters, Connecticut erected a spacious, two-story frame structure with broad double porches and a pedimented central portico extending the full height of the building (fig. 2). Painted yellow with white trim and green shutters, the Connecticut house prompted widely differing reactions. While one commentator called it "a typical Connecticut residence of a hundred years ago," another judged it more accurately as "such a mansion as anyone could wish his grandfather had lived in before the Revolution, and could be certain that he did not." Still another, evidently disappointed by its homelike charac-

[12] Rhoads, *Colonial Revival*, pp. 133–34; *Report of the Board of General Managers of the Exhibit of the State of New York at the World's Columbian Exposition* . . . (Albany: James B. Lyon, 1894), p. 94 (hereafter cited as *New York Report*); Flinn, *Official Guide*, p. 143.

Fig. 2. Connecticut State Building, World's Columbian Exposition, Chicago, 1893. From James W. Shepp, *Shepp's World's Fair Photographed* . . . (Chicago and Philadelphia: Globe Bible Publishing Co., 1893), p. 365. (Courtesy Chicago Public Library Special Collections Division.)

ter, lamented that "the Connecticut Building sacrificed everything to comfort. It was one of the structures which was most difficult to remember." Nonetheless, the Connecticut Board of Lady Managers, who furnished the building, was pleased to report that "one of Chicago's most successful architects felt that he had received more inspiration, more actual help for his future work from the Connecticut house than from any other house upon the grounds."[13]

[13] For Delaware, see Bancroft, *Book of the Fair*, 3:778; and Rhoads, *Colonial Revival*, p. 638. For Connecticut, see Johnson, *History of the Exposition*, 2:441; Kate Brannon Knight, *History of the Work of Connecticut Women at the World's Columbian Exposition* . . . (Hartford: Hartford Press, 1898), p. 15; *Halligan's Illustrated World. A Portfolio of Photographic Views of the World's Columbian Exposition* . . . , World's Fair Series, vol. 1, no. 11 (April 5, 1894): n.p.; and Knight, *Connecticut Women*, p. 16.

The second aspect of the colonial revival presented to fairgoers was that of interior decoration, including woodwork, wall and window treatments, and both authentic antiques and reproduction pieces intended to show "how homes were furnished more than a century ago." Except for original relics, most of the furniture was made especially for the state buildings "after designs of old furniture which was used in pre-Revolutionary times." Many furnishings were donated directly by manufacturers or retailers, but the exact sources of reproduction furniture were rarely identified. Some furniture was apparently made locally; as historian Hubert Bancroft noted, the furniture in the New Jersey building (possibly the "country Chippendale" chairs visible in surviving photographs), "which so aptly reproduces the early colonial pattern, was supplied by a Chicago firm."[14]

Unlike modern period rooms, the intent of the state building interiors was not to present an authentic reconstruction of colonial living quarters, but merely to suggest what their planners believed to be a pleasant old-fashioned setting. The Connecticut Board of Lady Managers hoped to make its state building "Colonial in character, as nearly as possible, or, failing that, to have it represent a house of a date not later than the time of the Revolution, collecting from Connecticut homes the necessary furniture." Despite consultation of colonial inventories in their quest for "historically suitable" furnishings that would balance "the earliest simplicity and the later luxury," the finished interior strongly reflected federal and late Chippendale tastes, with little to represent the earlier period (fig. 3). Nor was the Connecticut interior significantly different from other buildings that treated the colonial simply as a pleasant style. In the Massachusetts building, the architects designed a "commodious and simple interior, in keeping with the exterior" and "altogether the rooms were such as might have been, though no definite model was followed." Although the floor plan did not follow that of the old Hancock mansion, the Massachusetts building did incorporate many details of the "quaint old style": leaded glass, leather fire buckets, red-brick tiles artificially browned with oil and wax to suggest old age, and a Dutch kitchen with wainscoting, hewn ceiling beams, and blue-tiled fireplace, intended to recall "the old Dutch houses of New York and Pennsylvania, as well as western Massachusetts." The central staircase with twisted

[14] Bancroft, *Book of the Fair*, 3:782; *Report of Massachusetts*, p. 14; Bancroft, *Book of the Fair*, 3:778.

Fig. 3. Main hall, Connecticut State Building, World's Columbian Exposition, Chicago, 1893. From Kate Brannon Knight, *History of the Work of Connecticut Women at the World's Columbian Exposition . . .* (Hartford: Hartford Press, 1898), facing p. 58. (Courtesy Chicago Public Library Special Collections Division.)

balusters followed Portsmouth and Newport models, while the mahogany doors, white door frames, mantels, wainscots, fluted pilasters, and swan's-neck pediments were also based on "the old patterns."[15]

In addition to their colonial furnishings, many of the state buildings housed formal historical exhibits of rare and valuable colonial relics. The number and variety of these exhibits—like most things at the World's Columbian Exposition—defied easy classification and description. The Connecticut building, sometimes criticized as too sparsely furnished, contained at least 250 historical relics borrowed by the state Board of

[15] For Connecticut, see Knight, *Connecticut Women*, pp. 14, 58. For Massachusetts, see Johnson, *History of the Exposition*, 2:459–60, 462; Rand, McNally, *Week at the Fair*, p. 222; and *Report of Massachusetts*, pp. 32–33.

Lady Managers from old Connecticut families: a seventeenth-century oak chest; "rare old hautbois"; Windsor and English fiddle-back chairs; an acorn from the Charter Oak; needlework; a set of English Chippendale furniture; a "bridal chest," 250 to 300 years old, descended in the Brewster family; a 1742 Litchfield deed; "quaint old china"; and much more.[16]

Massachusetts's award-winning historical exhibit was even more extensive, featuring an entire room furnished by the Essex Institute of Salem (fig. 4), in which "there was not a piece of furniture less than a hundred years old." Citing "the desirability and importance of having at Chicago a characteristic exhibit from Salem, both from the historic fitness of things and from the standpoint of present business interests," the institute had gathered from its own and private collections a rich variety of "choice examples of the genuine colonial style . . . of interest from their connection with Massachusetts history." Included in the display were at least forty-one pieces of furniture and ten glass cases that must literally have been stuffed full of manuscripts, graphics, printed documents, and small artifacts, including much china, a rare 1650 pine-tree shilling, Paul Revere's engraving of the Boston massacre, the "Scarlet Letter" law of 1704, Anne Gower's pre-1628 sampler, painting on glass, early commercial, religious, and governmental manuscripts, a deposition and a table from the witchcraft trials, Elias Haskett Derby papers, and various articles of everyday life. And this was only the beginning of the Massachusetts exhibit—in another room, the ladies of Boston had assembled a second collection, including a Copley and other portraits, colonial costume and textiles, manuscripts and autographs. One upstairs chamber was furnished as a reproduction of John Hancock's bedroom; others held the Adams family cradle, the desk-and-bookcase used by George Washington at Cambridge, and Miles Standish's watch.[17]

The most famous of the state colonial exhibits was certainly Pennsylvania's Liberty Bell, which arrived in Chicago on the evening of April 28, 1893, accompanied by large newspaper headlines: "Cherished Relic

[16] Knight, *Connecticut Women*, pp. 64–71.

[17] Johnson, *History of the Exposition*, 2:460; *Salem at the World's Columbian Exposition . . . Report of Essex Institute Committee* (Salem: Essex Institute, 1893), pp. 2–3, 28–52; Johnson, *History of the Exposition*, 2:460–62; *Report of Massachusetts*, pp. 16–27; Johnson, *History of the Exposition*, 2:462–63; Bancroft, *Book of the Fair*, 3:782–83.

Fig. 4. Essex Institute parlor, Massachusetts State Building, World's Columbian Exposition, Chicago, 1893. From *Report of the Massachusetts Board of World's Fair Managers* (Boston: Wright and Potter, 1894), facing p. 14. (Courtesy Chicago Public Library Special Collections Division.)

of the Revolution to Get Here To-Night—Will Be Royally Received." The bell completed the state manager's grand but impossible plan that Chicagoans and their guests should not only see a copy of the building but also "hear the peals of the same old bell that rang out the sweet tones of liberty in 1776." Visitors could also see the original royal charter granting William Penn his colony, the Proprietor's portrait and his surveying tools, Benjamin Franklin's clock, Thomas Jefferson's chair, John Paul Jones's ale mug, a 1750 map of Philadelphia, and the table on which the Declaration of Independence was signed.[18]

Even New York's ostentatious Florentine palace included a very pop-

[18] *Chicago Post* (April 25, 1893) clipping in James W. Ellsworth, comp., "Newspaper Record of World's Columbian Exposition," scrapbooks, vol. 2, sec. 12, n.p., James W. Ellsworth Papers, Chicago Public Library Special Collections Division; Farquhar, *Pennsylvania and the Exposition*, p. 29; *Catalogue of Exhibits of Pennsylvania*, pp. 15–26; Johnson, *History of the Exposition*, 2:478–79. The plan to ring the Liberty Bell seems to have ignored the unfortunate fact that the badly cracked bell had not pealed since Chief Justice Marshall's funeral in 1835.

ular "relic room" furnished mainly with mementos of "home life of the past," especially the colony's early Dutch period: a cannon from the Van Rensselaer family; the original 1656 deed to the Bayard property in New Amsterdam; a life-size portrait of Deborah Glen, survivor of the Schenectady massacre; spinning wheels; silver tankards and candlesticks from old New York families. From a slightly later period came George Washington's complete pewter camp service, a Charles Willson Peale miniature of Alexander Hamilton, and a 1728 plan of New York.[19] Unlike Massachusetts and Connecticut, however, New York displayed few pieces of colonial furniture.

As befitted a shrine to the Father of His Country, the planners of the Virginia building paid closer attention to interior details than did many other furnishing committees. According to Hubert Howe Bancroft's history of the fair, the building's furniture was of an "antique, colonial pattern, as are the mantels, the carvings, mouldings, and trimmings; and in a word there is little that is modern about this building, except for the people who frequent it." As with so many descriptions of the colonial revival at the fair, it is difficult to tell how much of the furniture was actually antique and how much was simply "of antique pattern," newly made for the display. Other descriptions do identify a number of specific antiquities gathered for the Virginia building: bronze lions from Mount Vernon itself; a mahogany sideboard from Monticello; a Peale portrait of Washington; framed autograph letters from the first president; Thomas Jefferson's prayerbook, watch, and telescope; Martha Washington's chest of drawers; a chair used by General Cornwallis; a harpsichord played by Dolley Madison; the pistol that killed Alexander Hamilton; and other relics of the colonial and federal periods. The Washington chamber held an exact replica of the bed on which Washington died, complete to its reproduced coverlet. The sentimental value of these relics was obviously very high, and Rand, McNally's guide predicted that the visitor would leave "somewhat saddened by his visit to the home of the 'father of his country.' "[20]

Having completed the grand tour of state buildings, the visitor could receive yet another large dose of the colonial in the United States Government Building. In the domed rotunda, exhibition planners had allotted

[19]Johnson, *History of the Exposition*, 2:475; *New York Report*, pp. 177–78, 194–96.
[20]Bancroft, *Book of the Fair*, 3:787; Johnson, *History of the Exposition*, 2:485–86; Bancroft, *Book of the Fair*, 3:788; Rand, McNally, *Week at the Fair*, p. 225.

space for still more historical exhibits by the thirteen original colonies. These exhibits of "colonial and historical relics and curios" were organized by the various state Boards of Lady Managers and included both valuable original relics and photographic reproductions. The Woman's Columbian Exposition Committee of Massachusetts, for example, gathered nearly 150 relics for this exhibit—a drum beaten at the Battle of Bunker Hill, a green silk umbrella, silver and pewter plate, a piece of Plymouth Rock mounted in a silver casket, a copy of the Stamp Act, tea from the Boston Tea Party, bullet molds, and Miles Standish's pipe. Pennsylvania displayed here Benedict Arnold's journal, Benjamin Franklin's tea caddy, relics of William Penn's first house and the Treaty Elm, revolutionary war weapons, papers and regimental colors, and "many other articles not definitely classified." New York's display, its commissioners proudly reported, "was specially attractive in interesting relics owing to the broad and rich domain of early New York history and to the exertions and influence" of its organizers in "bringing many famous mementoes from their hiding places."[21]

Elsewhere in the Government Building, the federal Departments of War, State, Justice, and Treasury displayed early treaties and maps; relics and letters of George Washington, Thomas Jefferson, Benjamin Franklin, and other early leaders; a broadside printing of the Declaration of Independence; photographic facsimiles of the Declaration and the Constitution; colonial and Revolutionary uniforms, flags, and arms; a bronze cannon captured at Yorktown; early laws and currency; state documents; autographs and portraits of many of the Founding Fathers.[22]

Isolated specimens of the colonial could be found throughout the grounds, often in the most unexpected locations. The Woman's Building housed a variety of colonial items—early embroidery in the New York lace exhibit; antique furnishings (said to come from Salem County, New Jersey) in the office of Mrs. Potter Palmer, president of the Board of Lady Managers; and a "Brewster chair" in the colonial-style Kentucky room (fig. 5). Designed by Josephine Carter of Versailles, Ken-

[21] Bancroft, *Book of the Fair*, 1:101–2; *New York Report*, pp. 83, 164, 177–78; *World's Columbian Exposition, 1893; Official Catalogue, United States Government Building, Part XVI . . .* (Chicago: W. B. Conkey Co., 1893), pp. 166–77; *Catalogue of Exhibits of Pennsylvania*, pp. 171–73; *New York Report*, p. 83.

[22] *Official Catalogue, U.S. Government Building*, pp. 11–25, 51–52, 64–65, 79, 124–27, 133–34; Bancroft, *Book of the Fair*, 1:101–3; Johnson, *History of the Exposition*, 3:492–97.

Fig. 5. Kentucky Parlor, Woman's Building, World's Columbian
Exposition, Chicago, 1893. From James W. Shepp, *Shepp's World's
Fair Photographed* . . . (Chicago and Philadelphia: Globe Bible Pub-
lishing Co., 1893), p. 283. (Courtesy Chicago Public Library Special
Collections Division.)

tucky, after a statewide decorative competition, the Kentucky room
featured Ionic columns decorated with sprays of wild rose, an "old-
fashioned" mirrored fireplace, and Adamesque detailing set off in gold
and white. The nostalgic effect created by the room's "quaint construction and ornamentation" was further enhanced by antique silk curtains
"yellow with the stains of age," old mahogany furniture, oriental rug,
and, of course, the Brewster family chair, "kept with almost sacred care
. . . through these nearly 300 years."[23]

[23] *New York Report*, pp. 202–3; Bancroft, *Book of the Fair*, 1:264–67; Flinn, *Official
Guide*, pp. 213–14; Jeanne Madeline Weimann, *The Fair Women* (Chicago: Academy
Chicago, 1981), pp. 229–31, 238, 247; Flinn, *Official Guide*, pp. 213–14; Weimann,
Fair Women, p. 230.

In the Leather and Shoe Trades Building one could see eighteenth-century pocketbooks and several pairs of colonial shoes, while in the Agricultural Building a Minnesota milling company showed a replica of a mid eighteenth-century flour mill near Reading, Pennsylvania. In addition to many contemporary paintings with colonial themes, a special retrospective loan exhibit in the Art Palace featured works by Blackburn, Smibert, West, Copley, the Peales, Stuart, and other early American painters. The Manufactures and Liberal Arts Building housed colonial musical instruments from the Morris Steinert collection in New Haven, Connecticut, and the New York State Library's display of the great chain that American revolutionaries had stretched across the Hudson from West Point, together with King Charles's royal charter to the duke of York, Major André's letters, and "other relics and curios." In the anthropology department, Pennsylvania showed a model of the building occupied by the Continental Congress in York during 1777 and 1778.[24]

Even the commercial exhibits and private concessions contained colonial materials, either as furnishings or as exhibit items. The Scribner publishing exhibit in the Manufactures and Liberal Arts Building included several simple Chippendale-style colonial revival side chairs, while the Standard Oil Company pavilion in the Mines and Mining Building featured a white, two-story colonial facade, complete with garlands, pediment, and clock tower erected according to designs furnished by Beattie Manufacturing Company of Chicago.[25]

Foreign governments also contributed to the colonial theme, with France displaying numerous Lafayette relics and Holland sending a model of Henry Hudson's ship, the *Half Moon*. Even outdoors it seemed that one could not escape the colonial. Outside the Horticultural Building, New York planted a 2,400-square-foot "old-fashioned . . . garden" intended to portray "as nearly as possible, the beauties and peculiarities

[24] *Salem at the Exposition*, p. 20; *Halligan's Illustrated World's Fair: A Pictorial and Literary History of the World's Columbian Exposition* 5, pt. 29 (November 1893): 701; *World's Columbian Exposition, Revised Catalogue, Department of Fine Arts* . . . (Chicago: W. B. Conkey Co., 1893), pp. 32–38; Flinn, *Official Guide*, p. 48; *World's Columbian Exposition, 1893; Official Catalogue, Manufactures and Liberal Arts Building, Department L—Liberal Arts . . . Part XI . . .* (Chicago: W. B. Conkey Co., 1893), p. 46; Flinn, *Official Guide*, p. 156; Bancroft, *Book of the Fair*, 1:231–32; *New York Report*, pp. 464, 474–89; *Catalogue of Exhibits of Pennsylvania*, p. 163.

[25] Johnson, *History of the Exposition*, 3:349; *Halligan's World's Fair* 5, pt. 25 (July 1893): 592.

of one of those old gardens known on Manhattan Island many years ago. . . . Seldom, if ever, has there been such a collection of 'old-time' flowers seen together in so small a space": daisies, thyme, rosemary, lavender, cabbage and moss roses, mignonette and pot marigolds, hollyhocks and foxglove, monkshood and snapdragons, phlox, larkspur, Jacob's ladder, dusty millers, Joseph's coat, heartsease, fuchsias, verbenas, heliotropes, columbines and Canterbury bells, lilies, primroses, sunflowers, and honeysuckles. Another old-fashioned garden surrounded the Massachusetts State Building, fenced and terraced to recall the original Hancock mansion grounds. One observer commented that the garden "added more than any other feature to the look of dignified repose that characterized the building."[26]

Adjacent to the main fairgrounds, the Midway Plaisance hosted yet another colonial attraction. The New England log cabin, operated by Emma Southwick Brinton of Massachusetts, featured "Ye Olde Tyme New England dinners, served by handsome young ladies from New England States, in colonial dress." For twenty-five cents each visitor could feast on hearty old-fashioned meals of pork and beans, roasts, puddings, pumpkin pie, doughnuts and tea, flapjacks and molasses. The cabin itself was furnished with "colonial relics" intended to suggest "New England life of one hundred years ago." When not waiting on tables, the female attendants also demonstrated colonial domestic crafts such as wool and flax spinning.[27]

Finally, the visitor had to confront not one, but three, replicas of that preeminent patriotic icon, the Liberty Bell, the original of which was in the Pennsylvania building. In the Agricultural Building, Pennsylvania displayed a liberty bell made of native wheat, oats, and barley, with a cluster of electric lights forming the clapper. California sent to the Horticultural Building another constructed of citrus fruits. The last, called the Troy Bell, was (like almost everything at the World's Columbian Exposition) a larger-than-life replica, cast from metal melted down

[26] Johnson, *History of the Exposition*, 2:417; Flinn, *Official Guide*, p. 196; *New York Report*, pp. 287–88; Johnson, *History of the Exposition*, 2:459.

[27] *World's Columbian Exposition, 1893; Official Catalogue of Exhibits on the Midway Plaisance . . . Part XVII . . .* (Chicago: W. B. Conkey Co., 1893), p. 11; *The Chicago Times Portfolio of the Midway Types* (Chicago: American Engraving Co., 1893), pts. 3, 7; Rand, McNally, *Week at the Fair*, p. 243. For information on the development of New England kitchens at the nineteenth-century fairs, see Rodris Roth's contribution to this collection.

from over 200 authentic relics: a copper kettle from the Jefferson family, revolutionary war uniform buttons, swords and pistols, a surveyor's chain link and bronze tag formerly owned by George Washington, and eighteenth-century flatware.[28]

In addition to the architecture, the interior decoration, and the exhibits just described, the colonial revival found expression in a wide variety of ephemeral activities at the exposition—speeches, parades and pageants, fireworks, state-day celebrations, theatrical and musical performances. The calendar of state-day celebrations reads like a chronology of colonial and early republican history. Massachusetts Day, June 17, celebrated the anniversary of the Battle of Bunker Hill, "a day which the citizens of the bay state and especially those of Boston hold in religious veneration . . . for Bunker Hill created the republic, as Yorktown made sure and solid its foundations." On June 21, New Hampshire commemorated its ratification of the Constitution in 1788, while Virginia on August 9 honored the assembly of North America's first legislative body, the House of Burgesses, at James City in 1619. On August 18 North Carolina Day remembered the birth of Virginia Dare in the lost colony of Roanoke Island. New York's September 3 celebration of Henry Hudson's arrival in New York Bay was followed four days later by Pennsylvania Day, "in commemoration of an event with which all the world is familiar." Finally, on September 12, Maryland Day recalled the bombardment of Fort McHenry and the creation of the national anthem.[29]

These and many other occasions at the fair—building dedications, opening and closing ceremonies, acceptances of appointments, receptions for visiting dignitaries, formal parties sponsored by Chicago chapters of the Society of Sons of New York and similar fraternal organizations—provided ample opportunity for grandiose speeches recalling the colonial past: "Pennsylvania was the cradle of liberty—the first extended domain under God's earth where mankind was free; free to think and to speak their thoughts, and from the soil of Pennsylvania

[28] *Catalogue of Exhibits of Pennsylvania*, p. 28a; *Final Report of the California World's Fair Commission . . . Chicago, 1893* (Sacramento: State Office, 1894), p. 75; *Halligan's Illustrated World* 1, no. 18 (May 31, 1894): n.p.

[29] Bancroft, *Book of the Fair*, 3:783, 786, 790; Stuart C. Wade and Walter S. Wrenn, comps., *"The Nut Shell": The Ideal Pocket Guide to the World's Fair and What to See There . . .* (Chicago: Merchants' World's Fair Bureau of Information Co., 1893), p. 8; *New York Report*, p. 110; Bancroft, *Book of the Fair*, 3:776, 792.

emanated the immortal Declaration of Independence." On a more entertaining note, Imre Kiralfy's *Grand Historical Spectacle, America* presented in music, dance, costume, and scenery the story of the nation from Columbus to the Columbian. The seventeen scenes included "The Plymouth Plantation," "Washington Crossing the Delaware," "The Surrender of Yorktown," and "The Palace of Progress."[30]

The colonial revival at the World's Columbian Exposition incorporated several unique aspects. In comparison with individual public or private collections or structures usually discussed as colonial revival projects, it was very large, encompassing several thousand exhibited items and at least twenty-two separate buildings that in some way reflected a colonial ethos. Because of its size, it did not reflect the interpretation of any single architect, patron, or collector. Instead, the colonial revival at the exposition was created through the collaboration of many separate state boards of managers and lady managers working through innumerable subcommittees, advisors, collectors, decorators, architects, and sundry volunteers, answerable to their state legislatures for funding and only indirectly coordinated by the official exposition administration. As a result, the colonial revival at the World's Columbian Exposition found expression in a range of viewpoints, styles, and media so diverse as to defy classification.

This diversity, combined with the exposition's large attendance, its location, and its integration of colonial past with technological present, made the fair a turning point in the colonial revival movement. Whether expressed in architecture, art, interior decoration, costume, or literature, this movement was essentially a backward-looking phenomenon—a nostalgic flashback to America's early years. The great nineteenth-century expositions, of which Chicago's 1893 extravaganza was the largest, were generally forward-looking events. They were first and foremost commercial ventures, intended to show off the latest products of industry and technology, to the profit of both the host country and the other exhibitors. As reviewers of the 1876 exposition have noted, representation of the colonial past was by no means a major part of all American expositions. By 1893, however, colonial revival architects, designers, and antiquarians had available a reservoir of historic research and a

---

[30] Farquhar, *Pennsylvania and the Exposition*, p. 40; *Imre Kiralfy's Grand Historical Spectacle, America . . . Music by Angelo Venanzi*, program (Chicago: Imre Kiralfy, 1893), South Shore Historical Society Collection, South Shore Branch, Chicago Public Library.

stylistic vocabulary that had not been codified in 1876. At the time of the Columbian, the colonial revival was sufficiently established to allow its export west of the Appalachians.[31] In addition, the exposition's organizers apparently discovered that inclusion of historic architecture and exhibits served several useful functions. First, the selection of a historic theme—the centennial of American independence, the quadricentennial of its discovery, or the centennial of its greatest expansion (in the Louisiana Purchase)—provided both an excuse and a justification for a great national celebration. Such themes also served as unifying motifs around which decorations, invocations, publications, and souvenirs could be focused. Finally, if the purpose of the exposition was to show off the nation's progress, no better proof of that progress could be found than the juxtaposition of its modern conveniences with the crude relics of its early history.

The huge attendance and the location of the Columbian exposition were crucial factors in its significance to the colonial revival movement. The fair was seen and shared by over twenty million visitors, thus giving colonial revival architecture, decorative styles, and artifacts far more exposure than ever before. Even for individual state buildings, the attendance figures were impressive. The 800,000 tourists who visited the Massachusetts building that summer were no doubt many times the number which would have seen the Essex Institute's historical collection at home in Salem.[32]

Not only were there over twice as many visitors at the Columbian exposition as there had been at the Centennial, but those who came were far less likely to be familiar with colonial architecture and artifacts. Because Chicago and the Midwest were largely unaccustomed to the colonial, use of the style at this exposition attracted attention by its novelty; construction of the same buildings on the East Coast would probably have been less popular and more open to invidious comparison with the originals. According to Rhoads, only a few colonial revival structures had been built in the Midwest prior to the early 1890s, so the

---

[31] The Chicago fair's claim to supremacy in size was based on its total acreage and number of exhibits; only the Paris fair of 1889 exceeded it in total attendance. See Reid Badger, *The Great American Fair: The World's Columbian Exposition and American Culture* (Chicago: Nelson Hall, 1979), p. 131. For the remarks on the 1876 fair, see Rhoads, *Colonial Revival*, pp. 56–63, 637–41; and Roth, "Colonial Revival," pp. 57–81. For developments by 1893, see Rhoads, *Colonial Revival*, p. 125.

[32] *Report of Massachusetts*, pp. 28–29.

colonial buildings at the fair would have been unfamiliar sights to many of the visitors.[33]

Although a large number of easterners visited the World's Columbian Exposition and many midwesterners had certainly emigrated from eastern states or had at least traveled through them, an equally large, if not larger, number of fairgoers were native midwesterners or foreign immigrants who had never seen the historic shrines of the original thirteen colonies. The experience of these fairgoers is suggested in a popular novel of the time, *Uncle Jeremiah and Family at the Great Fair*. En route to Chicago from his farm in Iowa, Uncle Jeremiah explains his reason for the trip: "this is a great country; and, as I have lived in it nigh onto sixty year . . . without seeing much of it but what I tramped over with Sherman to the sea, I concluded to take the whole world in at once by spending a month or so at the Exposition."[34] For many thousands of visitors, a trip to the exposition was a once-in-a-lifetime chance to see the world and all its glories, both past and present.

Finally, the exposition's location, combined with its theme, allowed a much broader interpretation of the colonial than would have been possible had the fair been held on the East Coast—a catholicity of colonial styles flourished along the shores of Lake Michigan. Because the site had no inherent colonial heritage, little natural preference was felt toward the New England colonial over Southern colonial or the English colonial over other traditions. The theme, harking back to the very beginning of the colonial period, encouraged the appearance of the broadest possible range of colonial manifestations, commencing with a replica of Leif Ericsson's Viking ship. The Columbian period itself was heavily represented, with models of the explorer's three caravels, the *Nina*, the *Pinta*, and the *Santa Maria*, and a reconstruction of the convent at LaRabida, Spain, at which Columbus once lodged and which now held numerous important historical relics loaned to the exposition.[35]

The Spanish colonial tradition also influenced at least four state buildings and their exhibits. California erected one of the largest state

[33] Rhoads, *Colonial Revival*, pp. 314–28.
[34] Quondam [Charles McClellan Stevens], *The Adventures of Uncle Jeremiah and Family at the Great Fair: Their Observations and Triumphs* (Chicago: Laird & Lee, 1893), p. 8.
[35] Johnson, *History of the Exposition*, 1:3, 404–5, 2:370–81; William Eleroy Curtis, *The Relics of Columbus: Souvenir of LaRabida . . .* (Washington, D.C.: William H. Lowdermilk Co., 1893).

pavilions, designed by A. Page Brown of San Francisco in a composite "old mission" style with specific references to Santa Barbara, San Luis Rey, and San Diego. Florida selected for its headquarters a one-fifth–scale reproduction of one of the nation's oldest buildings, Saint Augustine's Fort Marion, or San Juan de Pinos, erected in 1620. The Texas building, funded by private donations raised by the Board of Lady Managers, reflected "early Spanish influences" with windows designed by San Antonio architect J. Riley Gordon after one of the local missions. The Spanish renaissance style selected by Colorado, while hardly colonial, was nonetheless intended to recall "Spanish-Moresque influences" on the state's early settlements. Similarly, Arkansas's fanciful French rococo building was meant to suggest the state's settlement by French colonists, while Louisiana's "Creole" mansion also evoked the French colonial tradition, with a double gallery and overhanging roof. Inside, Acadian women demonstrated "ancient spinning-wheels and looms," while "colored cooks and waiters brought directly from the plantatiions of the river country" served Creole food. Illinois also managed to display a few legitimate colonial icons, such as the first bell used in the Mississippi Valley, cast in France in 1741 and presented by Louis XV to the mission church at Kaskaskia.[36]

Even within the Anglo tradition there was much diversity, with Southern, Middle Atlantic, and New England forms all represented. State buildings erected after the "Southern colonial" taste included those of Maryland and Virginia (already described), as well as West Virginia and Kentucky. Designed by Chicago architect Lyman Silsbee, West Virginia's "wide-spreading house, with great hospitable piazzas," weatherboarding, central pediment, corner pilasters, and rooftop balustrade, was intended to recall in a general way Mount Vernon, Monticello, Harperly, Malvern, and other historic seats along the Potomac, Rappahannock, York, and James rivers. The Kentucky building, designed by Maury and Dodd of Louisville, featured Palladian windows, heavy entablature, and imposing central portico supported by two-story Ionic columns. This "great pillared porch" was generally considered typical

[36] For California, see Johnson, *History of the Exposition*, 2:435–36; and Bancroft, *Book of the Fair*, 3:819. For Florida, see Johnson, *History of the Exposition*, 2:442–43; and Bancroft, *Book of the Fair*, 3:797. For Texas, Colorado, and Arkansas, see Johnson, *History of the Exposition*, 2:481–82, 440, 433. For Louisiana, see Johnson, *History of the Exposition*, 2:456–57; and Bancroft, *Book of the Fair*, 3:798–800. For Illinois, see Bancroft, *Book of the Fair*, 3:805.

of both "the old Kentucky homestead" built in the early nineteenth century and the southern colonial style (as distinguished from that of New England).[37]

In addition to Pennsylvania's much maligned clock tower, the middle colonies were represented by Delaware's shingle-style house (described as southern colonial by most observers) and New Jersey's more authentic revival. New England forms could be found in Massachusetts's mansion, Connecticut's comfortable house, and Rhode Island's vaguely classical temple, for which architects Stone, Carpenter, and Wilton borrowed elements of both the Georgian and the later Greek revival styles—Ionic columns and pilasters, balustrade and urns, entablature, and semicircular bay with arched openings.[38]

A significant number of midwestern and western states also built in the colonial mode or at least included colonial features: Ohio, Wisconsin, Nebraska, North Dakota, South Dakota, Utah, and the Territories. Painted beige with white trim, the Ohio building designed by James McLaughlin of Cincinnati featured a semicircular portico over double Ionic columns, pilasters, balustrade, and decorative urns. Although several guides described it as colonial, one judged it Italian renaissance, "simple yet dignified," and another considered it "partly colonial and partly modern." Although Wisconsin's state house, like Delaware's, was primarily shingle style, swan's-neck pediments over the bay windows and other details suggested the colonial revival. Of the Central Plains states, Nebraska and both Dakotas incorporated colonial features, especially two-story columned porticos and modillioned cornices on what were otherwise quite undistinguished structures. Finally, from the Far West, both Utah and the Territories (Arizona, Oklahoma, and New Mexico) included academic colonial motifs in their buildings. The Territorial Building, set in a landscape of cactus, was aptly described as a "composite" style, with Georgian columns, urns, and balustrades perched incongruously on a long, low structure very reminiscent of early Spanish colonial forms (fig. 6).[39]

[37] For West Virginia, see Rand, McNally, *Week at the Fair*, p. 216; and Rhoads, *Colonial Revival*, p. 639. For Kentucky, see Bancroft, *Book of the Fair*, 3:792–93; Rand, McNally, *Week at the Fair*, p. 212; and Rhoads, *Colonial Revival*, p. 639.

[38] Bancroft, *Book of the Fair*, 3:779–80; Rand, McNally, *Week at the Fair*, pp. 222–23; Rhoads, *Colonial Revival*, pp. 131–32.

[39] For Ohio, see Johnson, *History of the Exposition*, 2:475–76; Bancroft, *Book of the Fair*, 3:805, 810–11; Rand, McNally, *Week at the Fair*, p. 205; Flinn, *Official Guide*,

Fig. 6. Arizona, Oklahoma, and New Mexico Territorial Building, World's Columbian Exposition, Chicago, 1893. From *The Dream City* . . . (St. Louis: N. D. Thompson Publishing Co., 1893), pt. 17, n.p. (Courtesy Chicago Public Library Special Collections Division.)

Still other states expressed themselves in a colonial mode, although not in any of the formal colonial styles. If we consider the term *colonial* not as a finite time period or specific constellation of aesthetic motifs, but rather as a state of mind or a condition of government defined as that of any "group of people who leave their native country to form in a new land a settlement subject to, or connected with the parent state," the list of colonial buildings and exhibits extends much further. Numerous midwestern and mountain-plains states displayed relics of their own "colonial" periods, often just a few years past. Chicago rebuilt on the fairgrounds a building from old Fort Dearborn, the most significant

p. 143; and Rhoads, *Colonial Revival*, p. 639. For Wisconsin, see Bancroft, *Book of the Fair*, 3:810–12; and Rhoads, *Colonial Revival*, p. 639. For Nebraska and the Dakotas, see Bancroft, *Book of the Fair*, 3:813–18; and Rhoads, *Colonial Revival*, p. 640. For Utah and the Territories, see Bancroft, *Book of the Fair*, 3:382; and Johnson, *History of the Exposition*, 2:480.

historical site of its own early days. California displayed John Sutter's lump of gold; Idaho, an early hunter's camp; and North Dakota, the cart used to bring home the bride of the state's first settler.[40]

Review of these widespread state exhibits makes clear that boosterism and state pride played major roles in establishing the colonial revival at the World's Columbian Exposition. The construction of individual state buildings in a group in one section of the grounds was a new idea introduced at this fair; for although several states had erected buildings at the centennial exhibition in Philadelphia, these had been scattered across the grounds. The idea of grouping them together no doubt emanated from the office of chief Columbian architect Daniel Burnham, who must also be credited with the original suggestion of the colonial style for the state buildings.[41] However, due to the complex administrative structure of the fair, Burnham as director of works for the World's Columbian Exposition corporation had no direct authority over the state managers, who had been appointed to the quasi-governmental World's Columbian Commission by a special act of Congress. That so many nevertheless chose to follow his advice testifies to both the strength and the appeal of the colonial revival movement.

The close juxtaposition of state buildings invited comparison and prompted competition. As historian Hubert Howe Bancroft noted: "no such cooperation between state and Exposition authorities [existed at the Centennial] as at the Columbian Fair. To this was largely due the excellence of the state displays collectively and individually. Each of the boards felt itself responsible for the good name of the community, stimulating rivalry among the intending exhibitors."[42]

Each state searched for a design that would expressively summarize and symbolize its past contributions and current progress: "a display of taste, genius, production and enterprise as will fill our people with increased love for the state." Several followed a geographic motif, others selected one of the many popular eclectic styles, but most chose something at least vaguely colonial:

Among the State buildings may be found exemplified all the various methods of solving the neat little problem of appropriate expression which might be supposed to present themselves. . . . The readiest, and, when possible, the

[40] *American College Dictionary*, 1960, s.v. "colonial"; Flinn, *Official Guide*, pp. 186–87, 219; Bancroft, *Book of the Fair*, 3:814, 828–29.

[41] Rhoads, *Colonial Revival*, pp. 125–26.

[42] Bancroft, *Book of the Fair*, 2:799–800.

safest, form of thus crystallizing in concrete architectural shape all that the State means,—in history, in commerce, in the eyes of its inhabitants,—is, naturally, to select the typical, natural architectural style of the commonwealth. . . . The second method . . . is, evidently, to undertake to strike out an architectural emblem, as it were some edifice that would express justly the place in civilization of the commonwealth it stood for. . . . Between these . . . distinct solutions of this knotty question there are, of course, innumerable shades of meaning and of no meaning,—for, as the painter, nowadays, seems to be emancipating himself more and more from the trammels of "literary art," the architect seems to be becoming involved in it. His edifice is now much more than a structure for shelter,—he has to be able to tell what it means. There are a great many meanings in the northwestern corner of Jackson Park, and many of them, it must be said, are very tolerably clear.[43]

As these comments reveal, the colonial revival at the World's Columbian Exposition operated on at least three levels: as an aesthetic style, as narrative history, and as patriotic symbols. As an aesthetic style, expressed in both exterior architectural design and interior decoration, the revival must be considered only a limited success at the World's Columbian Exposition. Although the colonial buildings and exhibits introduced to the Midwest new ways of designing and furnishing buildings, enthusiasm for the style exceeded clear understanding of colonial forms and their uses. Even the most "colonial" structures strongly reflected their Victorian heritages. The Pennsylvania building, for example, was considered by noted architect Charles McKim "a sufficiently recognizable caricature of Independence Hall to make good Pennsylvanians blush," while critic Montgomery Schuyler only reluctantly concluded that its historical interest outweighed its architectural disadvantages.[44]

Despite these aesthetic deficiencies, the Pennsylvania building and most other colonial revival projects at the World's Columbian Exposition did provide powerful ideological symbols and played significant educational roles as narrative history. For both immigrant and native-born visitors—many with only a limited education and few having visited the original settings of colonial history—the revival helped bridge the gap from 1492 to 1893 more personally, directly, and vividly than any history textbook could have done. In place of long-forgotten school

[43] Farquhar, *Pennsylvania and the Exposition*, p. 9; William Walton, *Art and Architecture, World's Columbian Exposition*, 1893, vol. 1 (Philadelphia: G. Barrie, 1893), p. lxii.
[44] Rhoads, *Colonial Revival*, pp. 128–29.

lessons, the Pennsylvania building and its relics retold in an immediate and memorable fashion the glorious story of the nation's past. As ideological symbol, the colonial revival at the Columbian exposition fostered state pride, national unity, Americanization, and a sense of historical accomplishment.

The Columbian guidebooks all recommended a full circuit of the state buildings in addition to visiting one's home-state headquarters. Certain colonial exhibits, such as the Liberty Bell and Mount Vernon, were also listed as "musts." Unfortunately, after completing the grand tour, the fairgoer was often left with considerable confusion about what he had actually seen. By modern standards, both the architectural adaptations and the exhibits seem cavalier, unsophisticated, and misleading, airily blending priceless originals with crude reproductions on the assumption that lively narrative and sentimental symbolism did, in fact, outweigh authenticity. Reading through the descriptions today, it is often difficult to tell what was authentic and what was a replica, and many of the fairgoers were equally confused. The fictional country visitor, Uncle Jeremiah, complained of this problem several times during his visit to the fair: "Now the only thing I've got to grumble about . . . is what's models and what's facts. . . . Over there in the Transportation building I seen what it said was the boat Columbus sailed in; but after all, Fanny said it was a model. . . . That's what I don't like about this White City. So much of it is so, and so much of it ain't so that I can never tell what is so." The guidebooks and official catalogues were of little help in sorting out this confusion of replicas and relics, since they provided only the barest listings and were often glaringly inaccurate. The colonial loan exhibit in the United States Government Building displayed only a printed copy of the Declaration of Independence and a photographic facsimile of the original manuscript. However, Flinn's very popular "official" guide not only told unsuspecting visitors that the original was there but also fabricated an elaborate story of its shipment in a steel trunk via special car to Chicago.[45]

Interpretation of the colonial exhibits was almost nonexistent, although the Essex Institute did publish descriptive notes based on Irving Lyon's pioneering study, *Colonial Furniture in New England*. Other catalogues and guides treated the colonial exhibit as simple accumulations

[45]Quondam, *Adventures of Uncle Jeremiah*, pp. 82–93; *Official Catalogue, U.S. Government Building*, p. 22; Flinn, *Official Guide*, p. 101.

of "curious relics," rarely giving any information beyond the simple statement of provenance or historical association necessary to justify the object's venerable status. As a result, it is hardly surprising that, as the Connecticut Board of Lady Managers lamented, "Except for the very few [visitors] who treated the sight-seeing as a moral obligation, there was no attempt to study things in detail," and no one except the organizing committees had time to realize fully the meaning of the historical exhibits.[46]

The size, diversity, and, above all, arrangement of the colonial buildings and exhibits almost defied popular understanding on any but the most superficial levels. The strong element of competition rather than cooperation among the states blocked the organization of any comprehensive and therefore more logical presentation of the *American* colonial rather than the Massachusetts colonial, the Pennsylvania colonial, or the Virginia colonial. During the early stages of planning for the fair, authorities suggested that the state boards combine their historical exhibits into a general display, each state having its particular section: "In this way much historical information could be given which would be of great educational value, as well as of interest for comparative study to all visitors to the Exposition; whereas, if these exhibits were made in the several state buildings, they would lose in their importance."[47] Unfortunately, this plan was not followed, and the states proceeded to mount their own exhibits in addition to those contributed to the central colonial display in the Government Building.

Since most exhibited items were distinguished primarily by their historical associations, the fact that they were usually displayed by the state in which their current owner happened to live greatly reduced their effectiveness as narrative history. John Hancock's dress sword was shown in the Pennsylvania building, for example, while Virginia showed the pistol used in the Hamilton–Burr duel.[48] Innumerable examples of similarly misplaced relics could be cited, but the competitive nature of the colonial exhibits (although they were not usually entered for official awards) was nowhere better evidenced than in the omnipresent memorials to the Father of His Country.

Every major eastern state, in addition to others, such as Louisiana,

[46] *Salem at the Exposition*, pp. 28–31; Knight, *Connecticut Women*, pp. 15–16.
[47] Farquhar, *Pennsylvania and the Exposition*, p. 165.
[48] Johnson, *History of the Exposition*, 2:479; Bancroft, *Book of the Fair*, 3:789.

displayed George Washington relics and, whenever possible, a reproduction of some room in which he had slept within the state boundaries. Connecticut presented two such rooms, one from the Governor
Ellsworth home at Windsor and the other from the Wells house at
Wethersfield, together with manuscripts and a chair from yet another
Washington chamber. Massachusetts showed the desk Washington used
while headquartered in Cambridge as well as numerous manuscripts
and medals. New Jersey reproduced the general's bedchamber from the
Morristown headquarters, while New York presented an extensive array
of Washington family relics: the general's pewter camp service, cane,
fish knife, and snuffbox, together with manuscripts and his wife's needle
book and a fragment of her wedding dress. Pennsylvania showed a
Masonic emblem, an apron, a punch bowl, a portrait, and a life mask.
Virginia, however, emerged the clear victor in the Washington stakes,
for it brought to the fair the general's very home, complete with manuscripts and portraits, Martha Washington's chest of drawers and tea
caddy, other furniture resembling the originals, and even a reproduction of Washington's death chamber—just one short step from the great
man himself.[49]

Despite its inaccuracies and inadequacies in presenting and interpreting the colonial, the World's Columbian Exposition touched the
lives of millions. From this alone we may suggest that it popularized
the colonial revival and helped transform it from a parochial eastern
phenomenon to a national leitmotiv with a common set of historical
icons capable of unifying a national psyche still fragmented by the Civil
War and now continually assaulted by waves of foreign immigration.
Although some Civil War items eventually appeared in the displays,
the initial plans specifically noted, "It is considered desirable that all
exhibits relating to the civil war should be excluded."[50]

The Columbian exposition introduced many Americans and foreigners to the colonial as another style option, as narrative history, and as
patriotic symbol. For architects, it meant the dissemination of an estab-

---

[49] For Connecticut, see Knight, *Connecticut Women*, pp. 63–71. For Massachusetts,
see Johnson, *History of the Exposition*, 2:462; and *Salem at the Exposition*, pp. 45–52.
For New Jersey, see Johnson, *History of the Exposition*, 2:471. For New York, see *New
York Report*, pp. 194–96. For Pennsylvania, see *Catalogue of Exhibits of Pennsylvania*,
pp. 15, 173. For Virginia, see Johnson, *History of the Exposition*, 2:485–86; and Bancroft, *Book of the Fair*, 3:788.

[50] Farquhar, *Pennsylvania and the Exposition*, p. 165.

lished but previously isolated vocabulary to a new national audience. The exposition's effect on museums, historical societies, period rooms, and private collectors of American art and antiques is less clear but equally suggestive. For the volunteer committees who organized the exhibits, the owners (largely family descendants) who loaned items, and the governments who sponsored the projects, the exposition fostered an increased appreciation of colonial objects.

The colonial exhibits were organized mainly by the various state Boards of Lady Managers, and without their efforts at fund raising and at locating and displaying historic items, there would have been far less of the colonial revival represented at the World's Columbian Exposition. Most of these exhibits were organized against very tight deadlines and with minimal funding, primarily by women with no formal experience in handling historical materials and at a time when documentation of colonial collections was just beginning. That these committees succeeded at all was in itself remarkable. The Connecticut furnishing committee, chaired by Mrs. P. H. Ingalls of Hartford, had a mere two months (February and March of 1893) to locate "historically suitable" items for the state building, while Mrs. Frederick Rhinelander Jones, chairwoman of New York's colonial exhibit, admitted frankly that at the outset of her duties she had "no definite idea of the cost of such an exhibit."[51]

Despite these initial uncertainties, most subsequent reports note successful records in insuring, packing, shipping, and installing the priceless colonial relics. Surely these skills would have been equally useful in building subsequent collections, public or private. Although largely overlooked today, the extensive colonial exhibits at the World's Columbian Exposition gathered an unprecedented amount of colonial materials in a protomuseum atmosphere at a time when few established museums collected American art and artifacts. The fair's colonial displays predated by over fifteen years the 1909 Metropolitan Museum of Art exhibition that has been called "the first nationally recognized exhibition to present American furnishings." And although the official class reserved for exhibits by museums saw no entries by American institutions, many exposition participants hoped to encourage American collections. For example, the Essex Institute, an established historical society,

---

[51] Knight, *Connecticut Women*, p. 58; *New York Report*, p. 177.

intended its exhibit to "show some of [its] historical work . . . and also to give the idea of the directions in which it was hoped its collections would be increased," while the Pennsylvania managers "expected that some of these rare relics will serve in days to come, as the basis of a state museum . . . to become the repository of many curiosities, now scattered throughout the state, whose preservation will thus be measurably insured against the ravages of time, and whose silent and patriotic teachings will thus be continued to latest generations." Furthermore, the recognition accorded the colonial relics must surely have sparked many searches like the one that had uncovered a mahogany sideboard displayed in the Virginia building. Originally used to furnish Monticello, the sideboard had been rescued from use as a hen coop in West Virginia, repaired, polished, and sent to the fair.[52] Items shown at the Columbian exposition, together with pieces rediscovered and saved as a result of it, are doubtless to be found in most major Americana collections today.

The colonial revival at the World's Columbian Exposition was an ephemeral event, flourishing for a brief span of less than six months. By January 1894, the "Dream City" lay in smoking ruins. Constructed largely of staff, the main exposition buildings had barely withstood the traffic of a single summer. By 1893, they had begun to crumble, and a major fire the following winter ended all hopes of preserving them. Of the famous World's Columbian Exposition, only the Art Palace, reconstructed later in stone, remains standing today. Most of the state buildings were also destroyed, although a few, constructed of permanent materials, were sold as private residences and moved to other sites or taken apart and rebuilt in their home states. The official historical exhibits were dispersed, and objects were returned to their original owners or, in a few cases, turned over to state libraries or museums.

The colonial revival on Chicago's lakefront was thus physically shortlived. However, its artistic, educational, and emotional impact has lasted much longer, foreshadowing major trends and manifestations of the colonial revival movement: architectural and decorative styles, artifact collecting, reproduction and revival-style furniture, costume, pageants

[52] Charles B. Hosmer, *Presence of the Past: A History of the Preservation Movement in the United States before Williamsburg* (New York: G. P. Putnam's Sons, 1965), p. 216; *Salem at the Exposition*, p. 21; Farquhar, *Pennsylvania and the Exposition*, p. 45; Bancroft, *Book of the Fair*, 3:787.

and celebrations, painting, theater, historical research, scholarly and popular literature, tourism, historic preservation, and museum building. The World's Columbian Exposition included all these and other aspects of the movement, making the fair a fragile but prophetic microcosm of the colonial revival and its role in American life down to the present day.

The Beginnings of the Period Room in American Museums: Charles P. Wilcomb's Colonial Kitchens, 1896, 1906, 1910
Melinda Young Frye

A particularly interesting museum device for presenting America's cultural past is the "period room." Several valuable commentaries have examined its historical beginnings, its conceptual variety, and its dra-

When initially prepared for presentation at the colonial revival conference at Winterthur, this paper was entitled "The First Period Room in an American Museum: The Case for Charles P. Wilcomb." I suspected that the claim would be disputed, and I sincerely hoped the conference would reveal other period rooms that might rightfully challenge the title. In fact, information that had escaped my notice was conveyed to me there about the early kitchen setting at Deerfield's Memorial Hall.

From the beginning of this study, however, I have been concerned not so much with establishing *who* was responsible for the first period room in an American museum, but rather with recognizing the pioneers who preceded George Francis Dow's so-called first period rooms at the Essex Institute. I believe the growing interest in Charles Wilcomb's contributions to American museology and the reminder of George Sheldon's work at Deerfield expands the field to show the early development of the period room as a museum technique. It is enough to recognize that the methodology did not emerge full-blown with Dow. Still, some will seek a label of "first." It is my belief, after attempting to define the true period room, that if *any* American curator deserves to be called "first" it is Charles P. Wilcomb.

My gratitude goes to C. Malcolm Watkins, who recognized more than a decade ago the potential importance of Charles Wilcomb's work.

matic impact.[1] As early collectors and antiquarians gathered objects, the question of how to store and display them arose. Interior groupings began to appear in the mid nineteenth century, and by the early twentieth such groupings had become widely known, if not common. Most general studies of the early preservation and museum movement have understandably but incorrectly credited George Francis Dow of Salem's Essex Institute with setting up the first period room in an American museum.[2] These studies have not adequately acknowledged the earlier contributions of others to the development and public success of the period room.

One pioneering collector and curator created what may well be the first serious museum period room as early as 1896 in San Francisco. Charles Presby Wilcomb opened his Colonial Kitchen exhibition to the public in that year at the Golden Gate Park Museum, the forerunner of today's M. H. de Young Memorial Museum of the Fine Arts Museums of San Francisco. Wilcomb followed up his first work in the West with a museum setting in a Connecticut private home (1906) and another public museum setting at Oakland, California (1910).

Before the Oakland Museum's research, exhibition, and publication project examining Wilcomb's life and collections, his work had been largely overlooked.[3] This is understandable, since, unlike Dow, Wilcomb left no published writings to speak for him. Primary sources for Wilcomb's work include his artifact collections themselves, glass-plate negative photographs, manuscripts, correspondence, collection records, and public records of the institutions in which he worked. Following a general account of Wilcomb's professional accomplishments, we will briefly chronicle the development of period room exhibits in this country, examine the place of Wilcomb's contributions to that development, analyze several rooms, and consider the influence of the colo-

[1] Edward Alexander, "Artistic and Historical Period Rooms," *Curator* 7, no. 4 (1964): 263; James Deetz, "A Sense of Another World: History Museums and Cultural Change," *Museum News* (May / June 1980): 40; E. McClung Fleming, "The Period Room as a Curatorial Publication," *Museum News* (June 1972): 39; A. E. Parr, "Mood and Message," *Curator* 6, no. 3 (1963): 204.

[2] Charles B. Hosmer, *Presence of the Past: A History of the Preservation Movement in the United States before Williamsburg* (New York: G. P. Putnam's Sons, 1965), p. 212; Alexander, "Period Rooms," p. 264.

[3] Melinda Young Frye, ed., *Natives and Settlers: Indian and Yankee Culture in Early California (the Collections of Charles P. Wilcomb)* (Oakland, Calif.: Oakland Museum, 1979).

nial revival movement on the appearance and popularity of such rooms.

Third son of a farmer turned railroad man, Charles Wilcomb (fig. 1) was born in 1868 on the shores of Lake Winnipesaukee in the little town of Weirs, New Hampshire, moving as a child to Lake Village (now part of the town of Laconia). The family was strongly influenced by the remote setting of the lake region. Legends of local history were alive among the people, legends about their own ancestors who had come from Massachusetts during the revolutionary war and about the native populations who had preceded them.

In the 1920s Charles Wilcomb's elder brother recalled the beginnings of their joint interest in collecting antiquities:

Half a century ago . . . at the age of 16, I developed propensities which my folks called queer notions—the collection of articles of antiquity and historical data concerning the Winnipesaukee lake region. Then I got a little handpress and thereafter the printing hobby occupied so much of my time that I had to let up on the other. The collection of curios I turned over to my brother, Charles, who made it a lifework, resulting in his becoming curator of the Golden Gate Park Museum in San Francisco, which he was chiefly instrumental in establishing.[4]

According to family accounts, Charles Wilcomb came by his collecting pursuits naturally. There is no record of family interests being greatly influenced from outside. Laconia was off the beaten track, although the nearby lake did attract summer tourists, outsiders who may have brought with them news of domestic styles. But in that fairly isolated location, local residents retained much of the pride and history of their forebears who had settled the region just a hundred years earlier. By the 1870s family objects from generations before probably filled attics and barns. Nevertheless, although Charles was only eleven years old at the time of the Philadelphia International Centennial Exhibition, with its displays of colonial relics, we can be fairly sure that word of the fair and its patriotic message reached his family and affected him, even in far-off New Hampshire. Many people believe that this national event did more than any other occasion to set off a mania for articles of the "olden time," and one can imagine that the Wilcomb neighbors, perhaps even the Wilcombs themselves, looked among stored possessions for items of

[4] Edgar Harlan Wilcomb, *Winnipesaukee Lake Country Gleanings* (Worcester, Mass.: By the author, 1923), n.p.

Fig. 1. Charles Presby Wilcomb, 1896. (Oakland Museum Archives.)

"antique charm" that could be brought down from the attic to decorate the parlor. We do, in fact, know that Charles's mother and aunt both owned extensive collections which he inherited in the early 1890s.

The adolescent Wilcomb, growing up in a rural area where only a few families sent boys to college, moved from secondary school directly into the typical Yankee pursuit of trade. Enamored of bicycles, he became a salesman's agent for Rudge and other cycle companies, combining athletic trips on his big wheel with the search for and sale of antiquities. The Wilcomb collections at this time consisted primarily of coins, Indian relics, and natural-history specimens; his shop in Lake Village advertised a wide selection of rare stone aboriginal implements and stuffed birds.

When so-called California fever struck New England's youth in 1888, Wilcomb and two friends headed for the coast. Settling in the San Joaquin Valley, to which an older brother had preceded him, he pursued the druggist's trade while increasing his Indian collections. The New England Yankee had an important revelation in California, as traditions of his Eastern heritage surfaced in bold relief. Malcolm Watkins has observed:

> Although Wilcomb was perhaps less than conscious of the profound effects of America's industrial revolution so long as he remained in the rural environment of Lakeport, he was probably struck nostalgically by them after his arrival in California. The traditions and products of the handcraft era were still commonplace in New Hampshire, but they were scarcely so in California, where attention was centered more excitingly on the present and the future. Even rural Visalia had little of the ambience of antiquity that had been part of Wilcomb's daily experience as a youth. The absence of this quality in his new setting could only have made him feel sharply the separation in both space and time between the East of his upbringing and the West of his future. It is certain that he sensed that a gap in continuity was alienating a whole new generation of Californians from their roots. Without understanding the handcraft society which lay behind them, without being able to see the cumulative richness and variety of things people made and used, either out of necessity or for their own enjoyment, and without knowledge of what it meant to survive by hand labor and individual skills, upcoming generations of Californians were in danger of losing their sense of origins and connections with their colonial past.[5]

Over the next five years, young Wilcomb divided his time between East and West, returning home by train each summer to work at the lakeside resorts. These treks gave him an even greater opportunity to compare and contrast regions of the country and cultural environments. The museum curator–educator–cultural ethnographer in him was beginning to emerge. But meanwhile, it was the collector who gained speed.

Ever since the days of the curio shop in Lake Village, Wilcomb had dreamed of establishing a proper museum setting in which to display and interpret collections. His eye was on San Francisco, especially when plans were announced for a major exposition to be held in 1894. Called the Midwinter Fair, it was actually a replay of the 1893 World's Colum-

[5] C. Malcolm Watkins, " 'Colonial' Traditions Come West," in Frye, *Natives and Settlers*, pp. 40–41.

bian Exposition; city officials persuaded a number of exhibitors to stop off in San Francisco on their way home from Chicago. The fair became San Francisco's opportunity to establish a museum. As had happened in other cities, when the fair closed, many exhibits were consolidated into one building reopened as a more-or-less permanent museum (fig. 2). Apparently, Wilcomb was highly convincing in his contacts with the fair's managers—although his having donated to the city several years earlier a natural-history collection to "form the nucleus for a museum" must also have helped. At any rate, in 1895, he was named the new museum's first curator. Local newspapers reported: "The Park Commissioners have had him in mind for some time. Mr. Wilcomb has been a natural history student and collector since he was a boy and will probably make the study his life work. If he is not stinted, the museum in the Park will contain in a few years one of the best collections of natural curiosities outside of the Smithsonian in Washington."[6]

While newspapers featured the natural-history collections, and Midwinter Fair officials praised European paintings and sculpture in the new museum, two other collection areas were the personal contributions of curator Wilcomb: the American Indian galleries and a narrow corridor of four large wall cases called the New England Hall. Wilcomb's museum guidebook describes these objects as "an interesting collection of ancient articles made and used in New England in the early days. The collection was formed many years ago by a native-'downeaster' who enjoyed unusual facilities for gathering the most desirable examples of these old-time relics."[7] The listing of objects that followed in the guidebook included every variety of spinning and weaving equipment, lighting devices, fireplace and cooking utensils, pewterware and crockery, farm tools, and firearms. The exhibit reflected everyday domestic life in the preindustrial past, rather than the sophisticated elegance of decorative goods created in cities for the drawing rooms of the wealthy.

Within a few months of the museum's opening, Wilcomb was off on a collecting and museum fact-finding trip to the East Coast. Visiting over thirty-three museums (including the Smithsonian) and private collections from Chicago to New England, he gathered museum manage-

    [6]"A Fine Position: C. P. Wilcomb Appointed Curator of the Golden Gate Museum," *Daily Morning Delta* (Visalia, Calif.) (August 19, 1894).
    [7][C. P. Wilcomb], *Guide to the Halls and Galleries of the Memorial Museum* (San Francisco: H. S. Crocker, 1895), p. 116.

Fig. 2. Golden Gate Park Memorial Museum, ca. 1900. (Fine Arts Museums of San Francisco: Photo, W. C. Billington.)

ment tips while building up the colonial collection. In reports to the Golden Gate Park Commissioners, Wilcomb wrote:

> During my brief stay in New England I drove my teams in the oldest settled regions among the isolated farms, where I searched the forsaken corners of attics, cellars, and barns, with gratifying results. From an aunt I inherited a valuable and famous collection of colonial and revolutionary relics, which has been forwarded to the museum. . . .
>
> If installed in a room of sufficient capacity, finished in Colonial Style, the collection will form a most impressive and instructive exhibit. Our Colonial department will be the most complete and, from an educational standpoint, the most valuable in the United States.

Later that year Wilcomb stated:

> The collection is quite complete and will make a very instructive and interesting feature. With it I propose to illustrate in a simple but effective manner the modes of life of our forefathers and ancestors. To accomplish this successfully

the interior of the exhibition room should be made to harmonize with the exhibits. All I require is a low ceiling with rafters; ceiling and walls covered with plain pine boards; two or three windows, and an imitation fireplace.[8]

Upon his return to San Francisco, the plan was carried out. Charles Wilcomb's colonial kitchen (fig. 3) and bedroom exhibits opened to public acclaim in November 1896. John Bennett, writing for *New England Magazine* about the Yankee influence in California, described it: "Most [of the objects in the collection] are of domestic utility, but there are a few gathered under the head of Arms, and some sustaining the caption of Fine Arts. The dresser of pewter ware shows a complete set of pieces of that metal, and the blue china cupboard contains a display which would inspire covetousness in the breast of any ancient New England lady." Bennett went on to list in detail the tall clock, the spinning and weaving equipment, cooking and lighting devices, and so on. "These objects," he wrote, "Mr. Wilcomb has arranged in rooms fitting for their appropriate display. One is a low-ceilinged, rough-raftered, smoke-stained and small-paned New England kitchen, with its great fireplace and characteristic settings; another is a bedroom in which a chair made in 1680 consorts with a colonial bedstead of English importation while a shaving stand and a worn Puritan Bible reflect the cleanly and pious habits of those to whom those articles were common in that necessary room."[9]

Although Wilcomb envisioned the fledgling San Francisco museum as potentially *the* cultural headquarters of the West, his hope and work were not understood or appreciated by those in charge. He resigned in 1905, following several years of difficulties with the park commissioners (who sat as the museum's board of directors) over the fate of hundreds of artifacts which the curator had personally collected for the institution. The city had no budget for the active collection of exhibits, which depended entirely on gifts from the public. And San Francisco did have reason to expect that wealthy patrons like M. H. de Young would continue to donate "sufficient" materials. De Young had helped to found the museum, and his paintings and European antiquities swelled the galleries. Wilcomb, however, was concerned that the museum present

[8]C. P. Wilcomb, typescripts, February 17, 1896, pp. 2–3; August 7, 1896, p. 1, Archives, M. H. de Young Memorial Museum, San Francisco, Calif.

[9]John Bennett, "New England Influences in California," *New England* 17, no. 6 (February 1898): 705–6.

Fig. 3. Colonial Kitchen, Golden Gate Park Memorial Museum, 1896. Installed by C. P. Wilcomb. (Photo from an early postcard view in the Fine Arts Museums of San Francisco.)

the story of America's experience and that it play a leading role in preserving the heritage of the California Indian through the active field collection of artifacts. It could not depend solely on occasional private donations, especially donations of European materials. Using his own salary of $100 a month, Wilcomb had made numerous forays into Indian encampments in California during his ten years in San Francisco, building up collections that he believed would be an important resource for California's public. In addition, the colonial material he collected and brought by train from New England to create period kitchens and bedrooms were his personal property. The museum had never formally acquired them, although he had long hoped they would do so. He offered the collection to the museum in 1902, asking $1,500 for more than 500 colonial artifacts, including mammoth furniture pieces. The commissioners countered with $500. Wilcomb, ever the Yankee trader, retorted with an offer of $900, explaining that the collection could not be recreated for $2,000 and calling it "an almost complete representation of the household articles of that period, in fact one of the most complete in existence." Reminding them of the pleasure and instruction the colonial exhibits had afforded the millions who had seen them over the past eight years, he concluded that, having spent more than half of his own income on completing the collection, he could not now part with it unless he realized his basic investment. The commissioners accepted the final offer, and the exhibit was secured for San Francisco.[10]

The San Francisco colonial rooms remained on exhibit until 1924 when the old museum building was demolished and the new M. H. de Young Museum, erected next door, restricted its focus to the fine arts. Over the next several decades the de Young Museum disposed of the bulk of the Wilcomb colonial collection at auction and in the 1960s loaned the remainder to California's Department of Parks and Recreation for exhibition at pre–gold rush and gold rush historical sites. Ironically, in 1976, the de Young Museum created a new American period room in conjunction with a recently acquired collection of American paintings. A number of decorative objects were borrowed from other museums because of de Young's shortage of such materials. Of course, the new period rooms are primarily artistic rather than historical in orientation—high styled—whereas the old Wilcomb rooms had portrayed everyday, middle-class rural life.

In resigning, Wilcomb sold his Indian collection to a private collector, Robert C. Hall of Pittsburgh, and accompanied the material East, where he installed it in the second-floor galleries of the Hall home, rechristened the Hall Museum of Anthropology. Between 1905 and 1908, Wilcomb acted as Hall's private curator, the two men becoming charter members of the American Association of Museums in 1906. In addition to managing the Hall ethnographic collection at Pittsburgh, Wilcomb created a "colonial" interior for the Halls' eighteenth-century farmhouse in Lyme, Connecticut, a project involving the acquisition and arrangement of antique furnishings. Although the home was a vacation retreat for the Hall family, clearly Wilcomb had been asked to

[10]C. P. Wilcomb to Golden Gate Park Commissioners, December 26, 1902, Oakland Museum Archives, Oakland, Calif.

create a museum atmosphere and to give particular attention to authenticity. Photographs confirm that he did just this. The Lyme rooms reveal as much staged historical informality as any museum period room of the time. The "colonial kitchen" in this house was clearly a museum setting. Replete with crane and cast-iron cooking pots, it surely was not intended for Mrs. Hall actually to use.

Upon the death of Robert Hall in 1915, the collections were dispersed.[11] The colonial material is believed to have been distributed by sale and gift to family acquaintances, including the Connecticut chapter of the Colonial Dames. Tradition states that much was transferred to Florence Griswold, whose home housed an artists' colony and is now headquarters for the Old Lyme Historical Society.

Charles Wilcomb returned to public museum work and the West Coast in 1908, creating for the Oakland Public Museum his third and most enduring colonial collection. The building opened as a general museum in 1910 (fig. 4), with Wilcomb's colonial department, especially the period kitchen and bedroom, as centerpiece (figs. 5, 6). Oakland supported Wilcomb's work as San Francisco never had. There was money for acquisition of objects, and the colonial collection belonged to the city from the start. Wilcomb kept meticulous records on the sources and prices of nearly 2,000 pieces, records which remain in the History Department collections of the Oakland Museum, successor to the Oakland Public Museum. The museum has organized all manuscript and illustrative material pertaining to Wilcomb's work as the foundation of an Oakland Museum archive.[12]

In order to understand the role and importance of Wilcomb's three colonial kitchens in the development of the period room as a successful museum exhibition and interpretation device, it is necessary to review briefly the history of the earlier period rooms and their prototypes. As Edward Alexander has pointed out, the period room idea probably had its inspiration with the French *monument historique* movement about 1830, which promoted a recognition of the value of older buildings from historical, architectural, and associational perspectives. The early

---

[11] For decades the Wilcomb–Hall Indian collections were on loan to the Carnegie Institute. During the 1950s, the collections returned to California with Hall family descendants and are now the property of the state of California. Plans call for their eventual display in a new state Indian museum.

[12] See also Melinda Young Frye, "Pioneers in American Museums: Charles P. Wilcomb," *Museum News* 55, no. 5 (May / June 1977): 55.

Fig. 4. Oakland Public Museum, 1910. (Oakland Museum Archives.)

preservation of certain American properties occurred soon thereafter when Washington's headquarters at Newburgh, New York (Hasbrouck House), opened to the public in 1850 and when Mount Vernon opened nearly ten years later. During the Civil War, the so-called Sanitary Fairs, minor expositions organized to raise funds for widows, orphans, and other war-related charity work, adopted "colonial mood" rooms as participatory spaces in which refreshments were sold by ladies dressed in Martha Washington mobcaps and pseudo-eighteenth-century costumes. As Elizabeth Stillinger has so interestingly shown, these vaguely colonial kitchens were more like today's "theme parks," providing entertainment and refreshment, but making little serious attempt at authentic recreation of early American interiors.[13] Of course, the fairs themselves did not exist for the purposes of preservation and education, as museums later did.

[13] Alexander, "Period Rooms," p. 263; Elizabeth Stillinger, *The Antiquers* (New York: Alfred A. Knopf, 1980), p. 15.

Fig. 5. Colonial Kitchen, Oakland Public Museum, 1910. Installed by C. P. Wilcomb. (Oakland Museum Archives.)

Continuing the pattern of the Sanitary Fair kitchens, the best-known of the nineteenth-century colonial kitchens appeared at the Philadelphia International Centennial Exhibition. Located in the New England Farmer's Home, the Modern Kitchen was "furnished in that miscellaneous manner characteristic of the nineteenth, rather than the eighteenth, century. Bedroom, parlor, and true kitchen accessories were combined with heedless abandon. The purpose was not to give a correct impression of past life, but to gather objects around which stories could be built."[14]

Meanwhile, in Europe, the leading exponent of the historical or ethnographic setting, Artur Hazelius, created in 1872 Stockholm's Nordiska Museet, which included several three-dimensional recreations of important moments in Norway's past. In 1878, Hazelius caused a sensation in Paris at the world's fair with a carefully arranged panoramic family scene depicting the little-known lifeways of remote Lapplanders.

[14] Stillinger, *Antiquers*, p. 16.

Fig. 6. Colonial Bedroom, Oakland Public Museum, 1910. Installed by C. P. Wilcomb. (Oakland Museum Archives.)

Earlier European precedents for the American period room include animal habitat group exhibits—an 1867 Paris exposition camel caravan under lion attack—and the development of Madame Tussaud's wax museum.[15]

American antiquarians had begun to preserve aspects of historic interiors within domestic settings. The prime example of this practice was Ben: Perley Poore, who developed his house at West Newbury, Massachusetts, beginning about 1850. His Indian Hill contained paneling and fragments from many historic buildings, including Boston's John Hancock mansion.[16] This pattern was a valuable prelude to the museum rooms that developed later.

[15] Alexander, "Period Rooms," p. 269.
[16] Hosmer, *Presence of the Past*, p. 211.

In seeking the beginning of museum period room development in America, one must recognize the important work of George Sheldon and others of the Pocumtuck Valley Memorial Association in Deerfield, Massachusetts. The Deerfield Academy building, constructed in 1798 and doubled in size in 1809, was taken over by the association when the academy vacated it in 1878. The association set about adapting the structure for use as a museum: "The Committee thought it well to set apart one room . . . in which to exhibit an old family kitchen; one for an old-time parlor; one for an ancient bedroom."[17]

These proto–period rooms opened in 1880. The kitchen (fig. 7) was located in the former Boy's Room on the ground floor of the museum and featured a "huge fireplace made up of building fragments taken from a number of houses in and around Deerfield. The wooden lintel came from the residence of George Sheldon (founder and first president of the association), the iron crane from a house long owned by the prominent Williams family of Deerfield, and the hearthstone from a house in the neighboring town of Greenfield." As an article in the 1896 *Worcester Telegram* explained: "The collection in the rooms is not a scientific collection, nor an ordinary museum, but the direct memorial of the inhabitants, both Indian and Puritan, of the Pocumtuck Valley."[18] It seems evident that the exhibit's intention was not to achieve an authentic recreation of the colonial kitchen, but rather to create a useful exhibit for displaying bereft fireplace fragments.

Period rooms were developing rapidly now in Europe. By 1888, the Germanic Museum at Nuremburg contained many rooms with period decoration and furnishings. Three years later Hazelius opened his outdoor folk-life museum, Skansen, inaugurating the idea of an "ethnographic park," in which the typical buildings of a nation or a region are moved together to show the development of an area.[19] By 1900 the Swiss National Museum contained some sixty-two period rooms, while the Bavarian National Museum at Munich housed seventy-six along the same lines.

At America's next major fair, the 1893 World's Columbian Exposi-

[17]J. P. Spang III, "Preservation Project: Deerfield's Memorial Hall," *Antiques* 94, no. 2 (August 1968): 206.
[18]Spang, "Preservation Project," p. 208; C. P. Wilcomb, Colonial Scrapbook, p. 21, Oakland Museum Archives.
[19]Alexander, "Period Rooms," p. 263.

Fig. 7. Old Kitchen, Memorial Hall, ca. 1900. Installed by George Sheldon. (Pocumtuck Valley Memorial Association, Deerfield, Mass.: Photo, Mary and Frances Allen.)

tion in Chicago, at least four state buildings incorporated the colonial theme, either through architecture or in portions of interior exhibits. The time-honored tradition of the Sanitary Fair—refreshment stands done up in patriotic colonial trappings—continued.

During the last decades of the nineteenth century, period rooms were moving out of temporary fairs and into permanent museums. Once again, America followed Europe's lead. The 1851 Crystal Palace Exposition in London resulted in a permanent collection first called the South Kensington and later the Victoria and Albert Museum. Likewise, America's centennial fair shipped many carloads of dismantled exhibits to the Smithsonian, where they reappeared as the new United States National Museum in 1881. Chicago's exposition found a final resting place as the Field Columbian Museum. As popular exhibitions moved into institutional halls, they took on an aura of importance and permanence lacking earlier. Their educational value began to be felt. As museum historian Germain Bazin put it: "Museums suddenly proliferated; even the smallest cities boasted them. Public service became the *raison d'etre* of the museological institution; this was particularly the case in America where the pedagogical habit inherited from England metamorphosed into a veritable obsession."[20]

The German and Scandinavian museums which were so thoroughly developing the strong educational direction had by then begun to abandon the traditional taxonomic classification method of arranging ceramics, glass, metals, furniture, and other categories according to their separate materials, functions, or chronology. Instead, they began to adopt a cultural history theory of arrangement, setting up collections mainly as a series of period rooms showing the development of human civilization.[21]

San Francisco's museum development reenters the story here, following as it did the Midwinter Fair of 1894/95. Wilcomb's earliest museum period rooms opened the following year. It was not until 1907 that George Francis Dow, generally credited with having begun period room exhibition in America, set up the colonial period rooms at the Essex Institute. Finally, Charles Wilcomb's third set of colonial rooms opened in Oakland in 1910.

There is little agreement on what constitutes a true period room. In his excellent study of artistic and historical period rooms, Edward Alexander avoided a definition and did not identify the point at which such settings became acceptable to museum scholars.[22] Perhaps step one was the moment at which they moved from the fair midway into the museum. Step two is harder to pinpoint. Relocation of old woodwork indoors (whether to private home or museum) and the placing of a few antiques at random within the space do not constitute a true period room. Questions of authenticity and originality also arise. Do original woodwork or window and door frames imported from a previous building make a period room authentic, even if the room is poorly conceived? Or does a room that includes much modern reproduction in the interior shell, but carefully selected antique furnishings which do present a meaningful ethnographic totality, deserve to be called true?

There is also the question of the artistic as opposed to the historical

[20] Germain Bazin, *The Museum Age* (New York: Universe Books, 1967), p. 267.
[21] Alexander, "Period Rooms," p. 270.
[22] Alexander, "Period Rooms," pp. 263–81.

room. As Alexander stated, most existing museum period rooms are a blend of the two—attempting to present pieces of exceptional aesthetic merit while simultaneously conveying a historically accurate collection of typical objects arranged in functionally appropriate relationships— frying pan by the fire, chair with the table, and so forth. So it would seem that artistic and historical labels alone do not define the true period room. A room may stress aesthetics or history or both. Alexander did suggest that in period rooms "the elements . . . are usually authentic and, whenever possible, original." He referred to paneling, fireplaces, windows, doors, furniture, and accessories; but wallpaper, curtains, lighting fixtures, and floor coverings may of necessity be reproductions. He stated that both artistic and historical period rooms seek to convey some sense of having been lived in, while the strict historical room seeks to recreate "the actual historical milieu with its anthropological or eth- nographic overtones."[23]

A true period room, in my view, should be judged on (1) the educa- tional purpose of the finished room, which may be dictated by its loca- tion (a museum or historic building as opposed to fairgrounds), (2) its success as a believable whole expressing a historical or artistic concept, and (3) the degree of authenticity or originality in its interior shell and furnishings. A room composed entirely of reproductions based on extensive research—the buildings and furnishings at the highly success- ful outdoor teaching museum, Plimoth Plantation, for instance—must be judged differently from rooms set with original pieces. Such exten- sive use of reproductions may point the trend in the twentieth-century evolution of the essentially nineteenth-century concept of the museum period room.

A final aspect of the early rooms that deserves discussion is the man- ner in which they were spatially experienced. This occurred in two ways: by walking into rooms themselves, experiencing the spaces directly as original occupants might have done, or by viewing the room from one side—"looking in at the window," as it were, usually from an open- air or glass-walled fourth side of the room, so that the viewer is not really a participant in the space. The window view probably afforded a more realistic experience—one not interrupted by labels, ropes, or lat- ter-day humans.

[23] Alexander, "Period Rooms," p. 273.

The earliest period rooms in American museums may now be discussed in detail for their place in this development. We must first ask of each whether it constitutes a true period room. In this group we shall not include the 1906 Wilcomb kitchen, which, although created to museum standards, was erected in a house, probably using an original in situ fireplace.

George Sheldon's 1880 colonial kitchen was created in a museum setting with the high-minded purpose of preservation. It stops short, however, of attempting the artistic, ethnographic, educational goals of the true period room. It is unsuccessful as an integrated whole—as an examination of a photograph of the room, probably taken about 1900, proves (fig. 7). Plain plastered walls, original schoolroom windows, and a series of incongruous plain board shelves flank the open brick fireplace. These hold miscellaneous tableware related to the kitchen, inaccurately arranged. The room receives fairly high marks for authenticity, as the fireplace and all of the objects in the room are antique. The remainder of the room, however, does not maintain the colonial mood, being simply as plain and unobtrusive as possible. The Deerfield room, then, qualifies as a proto–period room, rather than a true one.

San Francisco's 1896 kitchen was created in a museum setting with the clearly stated purpose of education. That the room was convincingly colonial is adequately attested to by contemporary descriptions of it (quoted above). Its authenticity was complete insofar as moveables were concerned. The interior shell, reproduced to scale, although not according to a particular model, was created to provide a background for the objects. A published sketch confirms that the Wilcomb kitchen was designed for visitors to enter and experience directly.[24] Labels were affixed to furniture and objects.

George Francis Dow's Essex Institute kitchen (fig. 8) was created in a museum and certainly with the aim of education and preservation and to evoke a sense of everyday life in the past. As a total concept, the room is very successful. The packed dirt floor, the nine-over-nine windows, the box-beamed ceiling, the wall paneling, the careful arrangement of articles for use near and in the open fireplace all convey a sense of reality. No tags or labels on individual objects disrupt the overall effect. Dow wrote that he had "taken pains to embody in the trim of

[24] Bennett, "New England Influences," p. 694.

Fig. 8. Colonial Kitchen, Essex Institute, Salem, Mass., 1907. Installed by George Francis Dow. (Oakland Museum Archives.)

these rooms original wood finish taken from a building about to be dismantled or to reproduce carefully architectural details from existing houses . . . the timbered ceiling of this room reproduced in effect the unplastered ceilings of hundreds of houses existing in New England."[25]

All three rooms contained similar artifacts—the long pole from which gourds and dried herbs hung, the rifle mounted above the mantel, one or more lighting devices on the mantel, bellows hanging to one side, iron crane and cooking pots, fire tools, collections of pewter plates, chairs, tables, textile equipment, and so on.

[25] George Francis Dow, "Museums and the Preservation of Houses," *Bulletin of the Metropolitan Museum of Art* 17, no. 11, pt. 2 (November 1922): 17–18, as quoted in Hosmer, *Presence of the Past*, p. 214.

This analysis suggests that the Sheldon kitchen of 1880 served as a precursor of the period room in America, while Wilcomb's 1896 kitchen in San Francisco stands as the first true period room. Dow made several refinements in the exhibit device by 1907, presenting in his Essex Institute kitchen a setting more sophisticated than either of the two earlier examples. Wilcomb's Oakland kitchen of 1910 followed or paralleled many of the Dow refinements, including fourth-side viewing, the absence of intrusive labels within the room, and careful selection of artifacts to illustrate documentable activities in the typical colonial kitchen. Furthermore, the number of such objects was realistic in relationship to the tasks suggested.[26] Neither of Wilcomb's kitchens in California included original woodwork, but this is perhaps excusable when one considers his distance from the East Coast colonial states.

Wilcomb's architectural inspiration may have come from such late nineteenth-century illustrated books as Edwin Whitefield's *Homes of Our Forefathers in Massachusetts* or Arthur Little's *Early New England Interiors*. It was surely encouraged by artists' depictions of "colonial" fireplaces reproduced in popular magazines, although the bulk of such clippings in Wilcomb's resource scrapbook date from after 1896. Most likely, his primary architectural source was, as Malcolm Watkins has suggested, the well-remembered New Hampshire houses of his youth.[27] He reproduced the typicality of colonial rooms rather than slavishly recreating a particular room. This practice Dow was later to make law by 1924 in the very popular period rooms of the Metropolitan Museum of Art's American Wing.

The possible influence of Alice Morse Earle's writings on Wilcomb's work is of considerable interest. Her 1892 *China Collecting in America* may have encouraged his appreciation for transferware ceramics. His first colonial collection of everyday objects, however, was made *before* the 1898 appearance of her classic *Home Life in Colonial Days*.[28] The

[26] Dow and Wilcomb were acquainted, as evidenced by correspondence in the Oakland Museum Archives. Wilcomb must have studied the Essex Institute rooms when he was East in 1906–8.

[27] Edwin Whitefield, *Homes of Our Forefathers in Massachusetts* (Boston: By the author, 1892); Arthur Little, *Early New England Interiors* (Boston: Williams, 1878); Watkins, " 'Colonial' Traditions," p. 47.

[28] Watkins, " 'Colonial' Traditions," p. 43; Alice Morse Earle, *China Collecting in America* (New York: Scribner's, 1892); Alice Morse Earle, *Home Life in Colonial Days* (New York: Macmillan Publishing Co., 1898).

collection uncannily approximates, object for object, the artifacts pictured and described in that book. There is the wooden calico stamp, the leaf-shaped pickle dish, as well as the more-expected clock reel and wooden tankard. So nearly did Earle's writings correspond to Wilcomb's own view of the important messages of the objects that he frequently cut out pictures and bits of text from *Home Life* and, with due credit, mounted them as labels for case material in the Oakland Public Museum's colonial department.

Although it was not assembled in a museum, Wilcomb's 1906 colonial kitchen for Hall's Lyme house (fig. 9) is worth examining. As mentioned, the kitchen was likely created around an existing fireplace. The stonework and lintel were apparently original, although the wooden mantel surface and braces seem to be replacements, so similar are they in design to those of the earlier San Francisco kitchen. The artifact collection and the placement of the cooking pots are quite similar to both of his California kitchens. Therefore, although located in a historic dwelling, the Hall–Wilcomb kitchen was created with the museum period room approach and, considering its early date, deserves attention as a visual document valuable to this study.

It is worth noting that from the earliest public displays, hearthside scenes were often accompanied by bedrooms. George Sheldon had his "primitive Bedchamber" at Deerfield in 1880, and Wilcomb had his "bedstead of English importation" in a compatible period room at San Francisco in 1896[29] and a more formal—almost federal—"colonial bedroom" at Oakland in 1910. Dow's colonial bedroom at Salem in 1907 (again usually credited as "the first") completes the early picture.

Charles Wilcomb's period rooms blend the artistic and the historical objectives outlined by Edward Alexander. While attempting to convey an actual room as it might once have appeared, Wilcomb did not copy an existing room, but combined sources to create a composite, what he thought of as the colonial kitchen.

While their goals were primarily historical, functional, and ethnographic, Wilcomb's rooms also achieved a kind of artistic success as what E. McClung Fleming called "curatorial publications." Wilcomb's collected artifacts have been called "inherently beautiful in their forms and textures," and the rooms certainly deserve an artistic recognition to

[29] Bedchamber illustrated in Spang, "Preservation Project," p. 208; Bennett, "New England Influences," p. 706.

Fig. 9. Colonial kitchen in the country home of Robert C. Hall, Lyme, Conn., 1906. (Oakland Museum Archives.)

which the protorooms at Deerfield could scarcely lay claim.[30]

As this paper was prepared for a Winterthur conference, its purpose was to explore an aspect of colonial revivalism in America at the turn of the twentieth century. The Wilcomb story unfolds both within and without that movement. It is probable that this curator would have pursued the collection and exhibition of early American artifacts even without a colonial revival movement. Family background and innate curiosity about cultural patterns (those of the Indian as well as the white settler) suggest that Wilcomb operated independently of the movement. Nevertheless, the growing mass of source material concerning the function and design of the artifacts he collected must have helped. Articles in *Country Life* and the *Saturday Evening Post* provided data before the

[30] See Fleming, "Period Room," pp. 39–43. Watkins, " 'Colonial' Traditions," p. 56.

standard books on colonial furniture appeared, or the later popular collector's books by the Shackletons, Walter Dyer, and others.

The growing popularity of the colonial period encouraged him to use the collections in a way that would appeal to the public. The colonial revival movement aided him in the self-imposed task of reminding Californians of their Yankee roots.

I submit that Charles P. Wilcomb's work of gathering thousands of authentic historical objects dating from preindustrial America (and called colonial by turn-of-the-century revivalists) was actually atypical of the colonial revival movement. His impact as an educator and a preservationist went considerably beyond the dilettantish interest in "olden times" that characterized many collectors and decorators of the era. Using carefully observed lessons from the built environment of New Hampshire, Wilcomb created a revivalist setting as a background for his carefully chosen authentic objects. The scientific approach of the anthropologist and the cultural historian in collecting and exhibiting artifacts, together with the climate of appreciation created by the colonial revival movement, made possible the development of the first serious museum exhibitions of early American living styles. Charles Wilcomb deserves belated recognition as one of the pioneers in the field.

Inside the Past: The Interior and the Colonial Revival in American Art and Literature, 1860–1914
Celia Betsky

The late nineteenth-century vogue for American antiques that became the colonial revival involved both people and objects. The interior brought them together in one place and, as a single overarching metaphor, identified them with each other. The frequently symbolic space that was the inside of the colonial revival mixed people and things, blended disparate bits of American history and historical styles. After all, as Clarence Cook instructed a new generation of aesthetically inclined Americans in his influential 1878 *The House Beautiful*, the beauty and meaning of the past would be revived not through antiquarian exactitude but by capturing the "spirit" of the past.[1] Even as American interest in a national past grew increasingly knowledgeable during the decades preceding the First World War, art, literature, connoisseurship, and collecting retained the poetic, the imaginative, the emotionally charged aspects of that spirit.

The colonial revival came to be considered an emotional, spiritual, and intellectual heritage, something that was carried inside. It was a

[1] Clarence Cook, *The House Beautiful: Essays on Beds and Tables, Stools and Candlesticks* (New York: Scribner, Armstrong, 1878), p. 190. This book originally appeared as a series of articles in *Scribner's Monthly* in 1877.

question of character. As interiors from the past or containing reminders of the past became the symbol and setting for certain types of people and pastimes, these were in turn viewed as embodiments of old-fashioned qualities and internal characteristics that connected them to historical time. Architectural order, the pride of the colonial interior, implied moral order. The rediscovery of the American past through the colonial revival meant the furnishing of mental interiors as well as of architectural ones. These were to change over time, emotional and moral connotations shifting subtly to more social implications, and a once ingenuous enthusiasm about the interior entering the more precarious and challenging recesses of the inner self.

The architectural interior has traditionally been a symbol of permanence, stability, shelter, and enduring values, or, as Henry James's Rowland Mallett thinks to himself in the novel *Roderick Hudson* (1875), gazing at "the clear white houses" of an old New England village: "Here were kindness, comfort, safety, the warning voice of duty, the perfect absence of temptation." But the interior was pervasively called upon as such in this country for the first time really only during the second half of the nineteenth century, when, as one critic commenting nostalgically on the colonial scenes depicted by Francis D. Millet wrote, "great cities poison the air for millions, and great worldly successes poison content in unsuccessful more." Urbanization, with its physical and human squalor, and industrialization and its discontents caused much of American culture to move inside and turn inward. The great raw expansionist frontier nation, having suffered through a tragic civil war, withdrew to the interior to find the stuff of romance in a more distant past—the romance Nathaniel Hawthorne had declared extinct only a few years earlier in *The Marble Faun* (1859), when he bemoaned "the difficulty of writing a romance about a country where there is no shadow, no antiquity, no mystery, no picturesque and gloomy wrong." As one genteel professor commented in a William Dean Howells novel, Americans cultivated the self-image of being an inherently "indoors people."[2]

[2] Henry James, *Roderick Hudson* (1875; reprint ed., Boston: Houghton Mifflin Co., 1977), p. 67; Charles M. Skinner, "The Domestic Pictures of Frank D. Millet," *International Studio* 32, no. 128 (October 1907): 120; Nathaniel Hawthorne, *The Marble Faun* (1859; reprint ed., New York: New American Library, 1961), p. vi; William Dean Howells, *April Hopes* (New York: Harper & Bros., 1887), p. 33. I use the word *extinct* to describe Hawthorne's assessment of the American romance because, in such earlier works as *The Scarlet Letter* (1850) and in many of his stories, Hawthorne did not conceive of his native country as quite so unromantic a place.

A primarily rural population, historians and demographers tell us, became an increasingly urban one, leaving the security of old village ways for the challenges and dangers of the city.[3] This movement was reenacted in Thomas Hovenden's *Breaking Home Ties*, the most popular American painting at the 1893 World's Columbian Exposition in Chicago. Americans wanted to revive, mentally and somehow also physically to go back to and even go beyond, the old-fashioned interior depicted there, with old folks and the home hearth, maternal affection, family togetherness, and rustic old country furnishings. This they accomplished in the way they furnished their houses, by the objects they collected, the paintings they painted, and the novels they wrote. They used the interior as a means of entering history, of bringing the country into the city and grafting an idealized agrarian past, a bucolic colonial way of life, onto an alienating and impersonal urban present. They tried to dispel the anonymity of metropolitan life by seeking after the "personal" and "individual," feelings of identity they associated with the internal accoutrements of the past.[4]

Many Americans simply excluded the outdoor realities of the city by enthusiastically hanging on their walls reproductions of such colonial genre scenes as Frank Millet's *Cosy Corner* (1884; fig. 1). This particular scene was popular for decades after he painted it: "His pictures tell a story with so pure and appealing a touch. . . . Those [reproductions] that have the widest sale are scenes of old-time life—white-washed rooms, peopled by men and maids in seventeenth and eighteenth-century costume, and quiet corners that invite one to muse upon the charm of bygone days."[5]

Americans also read novels and art books that specialized in such illustrations as those by Percy Moran depicting an eighteenth-century

---

[3] See, for instance, Gunther Barth, *City People* (New York: Oxford University Press, 1980); Stephan Thernstrom, "Urbanization, Migration and Social Mobility in Late 19th Century America," in *Towards a New Past*, ed. Barton J. Bernstein (New York: Pantheon Books, 1968); and Arthur Schlesinger, *The Rise of the City, 1878–1898* (New York: Macmillan Publishing Co., 1933).

[4] Lorinda Munson Bryant, "Painters of American Home Life," *Mentor* 8, no. 18 (December 1920): 18; Elizabeth Stillinger, *The Antiquers* (New York: Alfred A. Knopf, 1980), p. 7. Both *personal* and *individual* were used frequently in late nineteenth-century American interior decorating manuals, such as the particularly influential *Principles of Home Decoration* (New York: Doubleday, Page, 1903) by Candace Wheeler. See also William Seale, *The Tasteful Interlude: American Interiors through the Camera's Eye, 1860 to 1917* (New York: Praeger Books, 1975), pp. 10–27.

[5] Bryant, "Home Life," p. 16.

Fig. 1. Francis Davis Millet, *A Cosy Corner*. New York, 1884. Oil on canvas; H. 36¼″, W. 24¼″. (Metropolitan Museum of Art, gift of George I. Seney.)

squirearchy. Typical pictures, like *Knights of Old*, featured women who were themselves reading about the nobles "in one of those decorative old interiors dear to the artist's heart . . . of a delicate and poetic suggestiveness." Or in the painting *Gossip*, ladies were shown engaged in that activity amid surroundings and in poses so authentic that "they do not suggest the model, but seem to have come down from a beautiful civilization."[6]

[6]George W. Sheldon, *Recent Ideals of American Art* (New York: D. Appleton, 1890),

Americans flocked to exhibitions featuring Thomas Wilmer Dewing's paintings of elegant interiors (which he discovered were more popular than his ethereal outdoor scenes) furnished with aristocratically attenuated American antiques, dispelling any sense of mundane actualities with an air of reverie and secluded mystery (fig. 2). They inspired the psychological realism of Thomas Eakins, who, in a painting like *William Rush Carving His Allegorical Figure of the Schuylkill River* (1877), carefully researched vignettes of public as well as personal history in the middle of Victorian Philadelphia.[7] They lapped up the rural renovations and revival styles championed by architects McKim, Mead, and White, who, in the words Clarence Cook used to describe the *House Beautiful* illustration *Things New and Old*, showed "an uncommon sort of skill in finding out what was left of [an] old house to build upon for modern comfort and elegance." William Mead's novelist brother-in-law, William Dean Howells, was doubtless thinking of him when he had an architect in *The Rise of Silas Lapham* (1885) advise some nouveau riche city dwellers to decorate their parlor "like those pretty old country houses."[8]

The idea art and literature shared of the interior as past was bolstered, then, by many real contacts. Common stylistic traits and subject matter were absorbed from interiorization as well—intimacy, a sense of craft, a moral outlook, a taste for the personal and the romantically authentic, a well-furbished subjectivity, and a host of character types regarded as embodiments of colonial interiors and interiority. Often the figures portrayed were women. Not only was interior decoration in female hands by the 1870s and the indoors increasingly considered woman's sphere, but womanhood supposedly possessed certain enduring inner qualities—not the least of which was expressed in a favorite phrase, "the

---

p. 114; Alfred Trumble, *Representative Works of Contemporary American Artists* (New York: Scribner's, 1887), n.p.; Sheldon, *Recent Ideals*, p. 8.

[7] Thomas Wilmer Dewing to Charles Lang Freer, February 16, 1901, Charles Lang Freer Correspondence, Archives of American Art, Washington, D.C. (hereafter cited as AAA). Eakins's *William Rush Carving His Allegorical Figure* is, despite its historical subject, full of autobiographical references to Eakins's life and his ideas about art, especially in view of the controversy in which he was embroiled at the Pennsylvania Academy of the Fine Arts, where, as an instructor, he wished both male and female students to be able to study the human body from live models rather than from classical casts. Autobiography rather than historical accuracy seems to be responsible for the nude model depicted in the painting. Rush's actual model probably did not pose nude.

[8] Cook, *House Beautiful*, p. 189; William Dean Howells, *The Rise of Silas Lapham* (1885; reprint ed., New York: Holt, Rinehart and Winston, 1949), p. 43.

Fig. 2. Thomas Wilmer Dewing, *Yellow Tulips*. New York, 1908. Oil on wood panel; H. 20″, W. 15⅞″. (Courtesy Freer Gallery of Art, Smithsonian Institution.)

eternal feminine"—which connected them to the past.[9]

The many old people we find in historical interiors were viewed in similar ways (fig. 3). Articles like Mrs. M. E. W. Sherwood's 1881 "The Influence of Aged People" declared that "No genre picture is so

[9] Seale, *Tasteful Interlude*, p. 19. Howells invoked "eternal feminine" in an essay attacking what he considered the American national habit of keeping antique furniture in storage so that it could never grow old naturally (William Dean Howells, "The Standard Household-Effect Company," in *Literature and Life* [1902; reprint ed., Port Washington, N.Y.: Kennikat Press, 1968], p. 291).

Fig. 3. Edward Lamson Henry, *The Old Clock on the Stairs*. Philadelphia, 1868. Oil on canvas; H. 20¾", W. 16½". (Shelburne Museum, Shelburne, Vt.)

ornamental to the fireside as an old lady with gray curls." Social commentators often reflected on the wisdom and goodness of old age. The combination of femininity and old age stressed in Sherwood's article was in fact highly typical and took on increasingly symbolic dimensions. The figure of the grandmother and the concept of "the generation of our grandmothers" came to stand more and more for the American past, helping to link the meaning of history to a feminization of American culture. Henry James knowingly presented the figure of Columbia herself, ensconced under the Capitol dome, "motherly, chatty, clear-spectacled . . . who reads all the newspapers . . . and is fenced off, at worst, but by concentric circles of rocking-chairs." Americans were in less and less danger of having to be warned, as Jennie June Croly had done in 1864: "Don't Be Ashamed of Grandmother." Quite the opposite. Louisa May Alcott was only one of the first to populate her stories with exemplary old ladies, and by the time James came to write his complex international romance, *The Golden Bowl* (1904), he tenderly endowed his heroine, Maggie Verver, with a "small still passion for order and symmetry, for objects with their backs to the walls" that "spoke even of some probable references, in her American blood, to dusting and polishing New England grandmothers."[10]

A further attraction of the colonial revival interior in art and literature was that it allowed for a masculine presence at a time when the absence of men from the domestic scene had increasingly become the frequently regretted norm.[11] The communal togetherness of the family was felt to be in peril during the late nineteenth century. The historical interior helped alleviate such fears. During a period when men seemed to be turning into mere cogs in an industrial machine, into rapacious businessmen, or affected aesthetes, any rustic interior worth its salt included a gun over the mantel, like the one watching over Millet's *Cosy Corner*, to signify, even in the absence of a male figure, the presiding masculine qualities of bravery, concerned courage, and aggressive caring, harking back to the days when pioneering souls had carved a civilized colony out of the wilderness.

If a single object, like a gun over the mantel, could evoke such powerful associations, the multiplicity of styles brought together under the roof of the colonial revival—objects from the sixteenth century to the 1830s—were endowed with even more meaning. Decorating manuals

[10] Mrs. M. E. W. Sherwood, "The Influence of Aged People," in *Amenities of Home* (New York: D. Appleton, 1881), p. 79; Henry James, *The American Scene* (1907; reprint ed., Bloomington: Indiana University Press, 1968), p. 362; Jennie June Croly, *Jennie Juneiana: Talks on Women's Topics* (Boston: Lee & Shepard, 1864), p. 136; Henry James, *The Golden Bowl* (1904; reprint ed., Baltimore: Penguin Books, 1966), p. 403. A helpful summary of the numerous references to "grandmother's generation" during this period is David P. Handlin, *The American Home: Architecture and Society, 1815–1915* (Boston: Little, Brown, 1979), pp. 412–13.

[11] See, for instance, Mrs. S. W. Oakey, *From Attic to Cellar: A Book for Young Housekeepers* (New York: G. P. Putnam's Sons, 1879). Mrs. Oakey was Thomas Dewing's mother-in-law.

and social histories, fiction and art discussed styles and objects as the products of historical periods, assigning each epoch certain human traits— traits that late nineteenth-century America suspected it had lost. The inclusion of an English Restoration revival chair in William H. Lippincott's *Punch and Judy Show* (1896), for instance, infused a touch of robust class and educated strenuousness into the midst of the mass-produced Grand Rapids furnishings surrounding the children in a formal scene of stuffy affluence. The Queen Anne style evident in so many paintings offered—perhaps in the form of a Queen Anne-ish chair— memories of the chairs brought over on the *Mayflower* and made a statement about a gracious mode of existence that recalled the "unostentatious people of gentle manners and culture" modern-day revivalists hoped they were imitating properly.[12]

The prevalent Chippendale style was a form of shorthand in fiction for a durably patrician personality; there was hardly an interior in the historical novels or society romances of that would-be Philadelphia aristocrat, S. Weir Mitchell, that did not boast "Antique furniture of Chippendale patterns" or "a small, round Chippendale table of dark mahogany." It graced the visual arts with similar implications. Mitchell, an avid collector, lent Eakins the chair used in *William Rush.*[13] The Chippendale revival table at the center of William McGregor Paxton's personal favorite, *A Girl Sweeping* (1911; fig. 4), and many of Paxton's other paintings, indicates a way of life kept tidy and genteel with the help of servants.

Old Dutch New York had an equally solid appeal. Novelists from Harriet Beecher Stowe to Edith Wharton and Henry James were readily understood when they created high-class characters with "Van" as part of their names.[14] A defeated South sought to recover its certainties and

[12] William H. Lippincott, *Punch and Judy Show*, Vassar College Art Gallery, Poughkeepsie, N.Y.; Christopher Monkhouse, "The Spinning Wheel as Artifact, Symbol, and Source of Design," in *Victorian Furniture: Essays from a Victorian Society Autumn Symposium*, ed. Kenneth L. Ames (Philadelphia: Victorian Society in America, 1982), p. 155; Harriet Prescott Spofford, *Art Decoration Applied to Furniture* (New York: Harper & Bros., 1878), p. 157. For comments on the meaning of the Elizabethan style in furniture, see Spofford, *Art Decoration*, p. 107.

[13] S. Weir Mitchell, *Roland Blake* (1886; reprint ed., New York: Century Co., 1909), p. 59; S. Weir Mitchell, *Characteristics* (1891; reprint ed., New York: Century Co., 1909), p. 92; Lloyd Goodrich, *Thomas Eakins: His Life and Work* (New York: Whitney Museum of American Art, 1933), p. 61.

[14] Harriet Beecher Stowe's *My Wife and I* (1871) featured the Van Arsdel family; Edith

Fig. 4. William McGregor Paxton, A *Girl Sweeping*. Boston, 1911; copyrighted 1912. Oil on canvas; H. 40¼", W. 30¼". (Courtesy Pennsylvania Academy of the Fine Arts.)

serenities in images of colonial plantation life and drawling chivalry, which were commemorated in countless historical novels and in many paintings of tranquil interiors.

After the Civil War, however, a desire to reconcile and forget boosted the popularity of colonial New England over all other regions and styles.

Wharton's *The House of Mirth* (1905), the Van Osburghs and the Van Alstynes; and Henry James created aristocratic heroines descended from old New York Dutch families in *The Portrait of a Lady* (1881) and *The Wings of the Dove* (1902).

Puritanism was touted as the cradle of all that was best about colonial America. New England's descendants were automatically endowed by novelists with an admirable sense of "right and wrong" or with "high intentions." Life in Puritan New England stood for unity and morality. It stood for the kind of stern and just religiosity and "inconceivable austerity and solemnity with which Puritanism invested this moral life," for courage and structure, and for an Anglo-Saxon covenant with God.[15]

It offered a welcome contrast, in other words, to the sense of displacement, doubt, loss of faith, and crises of confidence Americans felt "in a world without traditions, without reverence, without stability," as Edith Wharton characterized the modern wasteland beyond a sequestered New England college town in her tale of love and loss, "The Pretext" (1908). Urban crowding, class conflicts, and intrusive foreign elements were declared among the further ills of the age. Charlotte Perkins Gilman, heroically atypical as a radical feminist and socialist, was sounding a very typical note when, in her autobiography, she described moving back to the Connecticut of her forebears: "it is true that two-thirds of the population are aliens, but they are not so overwhelmingly in evidence as in the great city. The people we meet . . . are of native stock."[16]

New England and its heritage became the heart and soul of the nation into which novelists delved ever deeper, both psychologically and geographically. Howells's "Pursuit of the Piano" (1900) takes the protagonist into increasingly remote reaches of the old Northeast and into increasingly refined old homes where he finds the wife of his dreams. From the folksy locales of Eastman Johnson's Nantucket (fig. 5) to Edmund Tarbell's turn-of-the-century Boston (fig. 6), artists illustrated the inward journey with what were often simply entitled "New England interiors." To "see New Englandly," as poet Emily Dickinson had so beautifully phrased it, was the essence of the colonial revival vision.[17]

[15] William Dean Howells, *Dr. Breen's Practice* (Boston: Ticknor, 1881), p. 25; William Dean Howells, *Annie Kilburn* (1888; reprint ed., New York: Harper & Bros., 1919), p. 6; Harriet Beecher Stowe, *The Chimney-Corner* (Boston: Ticknor & Fields, 1868), p. 261.

[16] Edith Wharton, *The Collected Short Stories*, vol. 1 (New York: Charles Scribner's Sons, 1968), p. 636; Charlotte Perkins Gilman, *The Living of Charlotte Perkins Gilman* (1935; reprint ed., New York: Harper & Row, 1963), p. 324.

[17] William Dean Howells, "The Pursuit of the Piano," in *A Pair of Patient Lovers* (1900; reprint ed., Freeport, N.Y.: Books for Libraries Press, 1970); Frederick W. Coburn, "Edmund C. Tarbell," *International Studio* 32, no. 127 (September 1907): 82; Emily Dickinson, *The Complete Poems of Emily Dickinson*, ed. Thomas H. Johnson (Boston: Little, Brown, 1960), p. 132.

Fig. 5. Eastman Johnson, *The New Bonnet*. Nantucket, 1876. Oil on cardboard; H. 20¾", W. 27". (Metropolitan Museum of Art.)

Through these historical interiors the American past was domesti-cated and history personalized.[18] The writing of history ran increasingly to the anecdotal. Historical fiction was built on a human, domestic, and often sentimental scale. History painting became a form of genre, with Johnson's homey and earnest *Boyhood of Lincoln* (1868) leading the way. Genre and enlarged still life, in a sense, illustrated history. As Cook announced to his readers, *Old Colony Days* in *The House Beau-tiful* had originally been drawn by Frank Lathrop as an illustration for Bryant and Gay's *History of the United States*, and the engraving *Why*,

[18] For examples of this, see Alice Morse Earle, *Home Life in Colonial Days* (New York: Macmillan Publishing Co., 1898); Alice Morse Earle, *Colonial Dames and Good Wives* (Boston: Houghton Mifflin Co., 1895); and Esther Singleton, *Social New York under the Georges, 1714–1776* (1902; reprint ed., Port Washington, N.Y.: Ira J. Friedman, 1969).

Fig. 6. Edmund C. Tarbell, *A Rehearsal in the Studio.* Boston, ca. 1904. Oil on canvas; H. 25″, W. 30″. (Worcester Art Museum.)

This is Spode! was actually from E. L. Henry's *Lover of Old China* (1889; fig. 7).[19]

Attics—than which there was "no nobler forage-ground for a romantic, venturesome, mischievous boy"—were found to contain forgotten treasures, and lessons galore. "Old garrets are really factories of History, Poetry, and the Drama," Sherwood told the readers of *Home Amusements* (1881). "The taste for old furniture has rather emptied the garret of its time-honored chairs and old clocks, but still in its ghost-haunted corners there is quite enough goblin-tapestry for the fancy of a growing

[19] Cook, *House Beautiful,* p. 256.

Fig. 7. Edward Lamson Henry, A *Lover of Old China*.
New York, 1889. Oil on academy board; H. 14″, W. 12″.
(Shelburne Museum, Shelburne, Vt.)

child." Frequently describing themselves as digging through such attics
or as braving the homes of poor folk where old objects had long been
lying neglected (Clarence Cook divulged that he had found a precious
old sideboard being used as a chicken coop), Americans dusted off the
facts and artifacts of their history and overlaid them with a new coat of
fantasy. They proudly displayed the objects in their homes, and placed
the inner qualities ascribed to people of the past in the foreground of
their emotional and moral value systems. They depended on the past
to initiate them into the mysteries of what one critic, remarking on the

Artists and writers were led to comment both favorably and disapprovingly on colonial revival collecting and design, which were, it was felt, important indications of morality and taste. E. L. Henry, himself an energetic antiquarian, suffused his canvases with happy connoisseurship, taking pride in his relationship to A *Lover of Old China* (fig. 7), in which his aunt, Mrs. Livingston Murray, is pictured. He was apparently so pleased by his friendship with William Loring Andrews, an antiquarian and bibliophile who wrote books on American history, that he put himself into an 1875 portrait of Andrews's famous library, dressed as an eighteenth-century gentleman. Art critics liked to point out that Childe Hassam's pictures benefited from his father's having collected domestic Americana, and one critic declared Eastman Johnson's "unmistakable New England interior[s],—the bare white walls, the old-fashioned mirror and sideboard, the chest of flasks, the Chinese porcelains on top of the corner closet, telling of former days of prosperity in the East India trade . . . sufficient to turn to livid green the envious visage of the bric-a-brac hunter" (fig. 5).[25]

It was this very envy that got people into trouble and served, according to many, as an all too revealing reflection of character. Echoing the social critics and interior design writers of the day, novelists scolded their characters for the incongruity of putting old pieces in new houses, for buying sham antiques, or for organizing extravagant scavenger hunts through the countryside. They used such behavior in their fiction to expose falseness and immorality. Mrs. Farrell, an unthinking flirt who is the title character of an 1875 Howells novel, uses old objects as theatrical props to ensnare a man she does not love; they are objects she has "wheedled" out of local country residents. Annie Kilburn, an aristocratic and highly moral American heiress in Howell's eponymous 1888

Wheeler, *Yesterdays in a Busy Life* (New York: Harper & Bros., 1918), pp. 39–48; see also Wheeler, Home Decoration. Dewing to Freer, February 15, 1892, Freer Correspondence, AAA. See Clarence Cook, "Casts and Tapestry in Room-Decoration," *Monthly Illustrator* 4 (June 1895): 327; Dewing to Freer, May 28, 1892, Freer Correspondence, AAA; Cook, *House Beautiful*, p. 260; Elizabeth Bartol Dewing, *Other People's Houses* (New York: Macmillan Publishing Co., 1909).

[25] Elizabeth McClausand, "The Life and Work of Edward Lamson Henry, N.A., 1841–1919," *New York State Museum Bulletin* 339 (1945); *The Library of William Loring Andrews* (New York: Century Association, 1875); Adeline Adams, *Childe Hassam* (New York: Academy of Arts and Letters, 1938), p. 10; S. R. Koehler, *American Art* (New York: Cassell, 1886), p. 55.

novel, most fully realizes the discriminatory pretentiousness and men-
dacious snobbery of a bourgeois lady by the name of Mrs. Brandreth
when she enters the Brandreth home—a mixture of "imitation" medieval pieces, Oriental knickknacks, newly acquired colonial furnishings,
and a recreated New England kitchen. The only kind of new wealth
that passed novelistic muster belonged to those who managed to remain
true to their humble roots. In Harriet Beecher Stowe's *My Wife and I*
(1871), a self-made millionaire maintains, in the midst of his lavish
New York mansion, a room out of the "old New England farmhouse"
of his impoverished youth.[26]

Literary social arbiters could do little more than criticize, however.
Colonial antiques and reproductions—"travesties," Edith Wharton called
them—became a part of everyday life and the most casual observations
of it. Playing a game of metaphor with the profession of writing itself,
Howells had a canny businesswoman in his parable "The Critical Bookstore" (1913) furnish an establishment with colonial reproductions in
order to attract customers. In painting, the resuscitated old and the mass-
manufactured "antique" mirrored moods and created an "atmosphere"
for the lowliest housemaid sweeping around a Chippendale revival table
(fig. 4) or artistic spirits engaged in a rehearsal in the studio (fig. 6).
They could, in fact, act as the saving grace, the one redeemable feature
of a canvas—Henry James commended the Hepplewhite "buffet" in
Eastman Johnson's *Earring* (1873), a picture he otherwise cordially
despised.[27] Such critical indictments were no small matter in the larger
scheme of late nineteenth-century aesthetics. The moral nature of old-
time subjects was taken into account when passing judgment on the
character and creative abilities of those who painted them.

Such attitudes were encouraged, too, as more and more painters of
the interior illustrated scenes and figures from the nostalgic and often
moralizing literature that had first stimulated the colonial revival. E. L.

[26] Spofford, *Art Decoration*, 158; William Dean Howells, *Mrs. Farrell* (New York:
Harper & Bros., 1921), pp. 77, 186. Originally published serially in *Atlantic Monthly*
under the title "Private Theatricals," this story did not appear as the novel *Mrs. Farrell*
until 1921, after Howells's death. Howells, *Annie Kilburn*, pp. 107–8; Harriet Beecher
Stowe, *My Wife and I* (1871; reprint ed., New York: J. B. Ford, 1871), p. 194.

[27] Edith Wharton and Ogden Codman, Jr., *The Decoration of Houses* (1897; reprint
ed., New York: W. W. Norton, 1978), p. 26; William Dean Howells, "The Critical
Bookstore," in *The Daughter of the Storage and Other Things in Prose and Verse* (New
York: Harper & Bros., 1916), pp. 185–224; Henry James, "On Some Pictures Lately
Exhibited," *Galaxy* 20, no. 1 (July 1875): 93.

Henry's *Old Clock on the Stairs* (1869; fig. 3), for instance, set in the house of Philadelphia collector and preservationist William Kulp, was based on one of Longfellow's best-known poems, as was a painting by Thomas Eakins's wife, Susan Macdowell Eakins. The authors of decorating guides and social and political historians used the work of these same older poets and novelists to embellish their texts. The centennial exposition of 1876 in Philadelphia—where Henry's *Old Clock*, Millet's *Portrait of a Lady in a Costume of 1740*, and Eakins's *William Rush* were on display—showcased perhaps the most popular literary subject adopted by the colonial revival, the love affair between John Alden and Priscilla Mullins from Longfellow's *Courtship of Miles Standish*. Both lovers were commemorated by objects placed in the New England kitchen at the fair, itself an appropriate symbol of a poem which, its author wrote, "aims to reconstruct the interior household life, as well as to record the more public events, of New England."[28]

Sanctified by her colonial context, her sweet intelligence, and her natural goodness, Longfellow's Priscilla made her way into innumerable paintings and engravings. The text accompanying a photogravure of Elizabeth Gardner's *Priscilla* (ca. 1888; fig. 10) announced that the expatriate artist had been the only American woman to win a medal at the Paris Salon. Priscilla charmed Thomas Dewing into an early attempt at narrative painting, furnished the copy for an advertisement selling a whimsy called "Old Flax Spinning Wheel Chair" (recommended as a wedding gift), and was updated in Thomas Eakins's *Courtship* (1878), as well as in Harriet Beecher Stowe's novel *The Minister's Wooing* (1859). If Childe Hassam could claim kin to the ancient Hawthorne clan, contemporaries were even more impressed that Frank Millet had John Alden and Priscilla up his family tree.[29]

[28] Stillinger, *Antiquers*, p. 37; Seymour Adelman, *Susan Macdowell Eakins* (Philadelphia: Pennsylvania Academy of the Fine Arts, 1973), p. 21; United States Centennial Commission, *International Exhibition: 1876, Official Catalogue* (Philadelphia: John R. Nagle, 1876); Monkhouse, "Spinning Wheel," n.p.; Henry Wadsworth Longfellow, *The Courtship of Miles Standish and Other Poems* (1858; reprint ed., Boston: Houghton Mifflin Co., 1896), p. 7. See Earle, *Home Life*, for the reference to older American poets and novelists.
[29] Sheldon, *Recent Ideals*, p. 131; Thomas Dewing, *Portrait of Priscilla at the Spinning Wheel* (1880), Art Gallery, Brigham Young University, Provo, Utah; Edgar deN. Mayhew and Minor Myers, Jr., *A Documentary History of American Interiors: From the Colonial Era to 1915* (New York: Charles Scribner's Sons, 1980), p. 262; Thomas Eakins, *Courtship*, M. H. De Young Memorial Museum, San Francisco; Harriet Beecher Stowe,

Fig. 10. Elizabeth Gardner, *Priscilla*. Paris, ca. 1888.
Oil on canvas; H. 32¼″, W. 25″. (Private collection:
Photo, Mastercraft Gallery, Fort Worth, Tex.)

An apotheosis of sorts for the colonial revival interior, the figure and
story of Priscilla emphasize the inner space that dominated the inward
movement of revived history—the home. The term *homespun*—as in
the cloth Priscilla manufactured—acquired a patriotic ring, and as
Americans made retrospection a national habit, they endowed certain
elements of the home with symbolic dimensions. Many household advice

The Minister's Wooing (New York: Hurst, [1859]), p. 27; Adams, *Childe Hassam*, p. 10;
Bryant, "Home Life," p. 16.

books featured elderly females who acted as mentors to the younger generation and proved their wisdom by instilling the customs of old-time housekeeping. Their base of operations was the kitchen, the "throne-room" and "pride" of the New England matron, "the most cheerful, homelike, and picturesque room in the house," the memory of which was enough to make any modern soul "homesick" for the past.[30]

In the age of the despised furnace, the old-fashioned hearth, especially the great kitchen fire, was worshipped as the "warm and glowing heart" and ritual center of homelife and domesticity. To even the most scientifically modern medical writers it represented hospitality, familial bonding, and human warmth, teaching the lesson, as a popular painting by Thomas Hicks would have it, that *There's No Place Like Home*. It told histories and fairy tales by the dozen, sometimes by way of old pictorial tiles, such as those in Enoch Wood Perry's *Fireside Stories* (ca. 1889), a vignette of a mother interpreting the fireside decorations for her inquisitive little son, or in the Lawrence house in Louisa May Alcott's *Little Women* (1869), with its "Sleepy Hollow chairs, queer tables and . . . best of all, a great open fireplace with quaint tiles all around it."[31] In Johnson's *New Bonnet* (1876; fig. 5), the hearth acts as a display shelf for the past while offering a welcome distraction from the present.

Next to the hearth, literally and figuratively, were handicrafts. Quilting recorded "secret memories, and incidents and stories and associations"; sewing and knitting were synonymous with female virtue. Scenes like Johnson's *Corn Shelling* (1864) showed an elderly man in front of a blocked-off hearth hoping to teach young hands old skills. Above all, there was spinning, Priscilla's characteristic activity. According to late nineteenth-century history books, it had also been turned into a patriotic act by Revolutionary ladies who made home products in protest against British rule. Viewed as the most old-fashioned or timeless of objects,

---

[30] Stowe, *Wooing*, p. 18; Earle, *Home Life*, p. 52; Fanny Fern, *Folly as It Flies, Hit at by Fanny Fern* (New York: Carleton, 1868), p. 167.

[31] Earle, *Home Life*, p. 52; Edward B. Foote, *Plain Home Talk—About the Human System* (New York: Murray Hill Publishing Co., 1896), p. 109; Thomas Hicks, *There's No Place Like Home* (1877), Schweitzer Gallery, New York (this painting was also widely engraved); "Fireside Stories, from an Engraving by E. Wood Perry," in *American Art and American Art Collections*, ed. Walter Montgomery, vol. 2 (Boston: E. W. Walker, 1889), p. 571; Louisa May Alcott, *Little Women* (1869; reprint ed., New York: Macmillan Publishing Co., 1962), p. 65.

the spinning wheel became a symbol of domestic romance and even—
as implied by the "electrical thrills" John Alden feels when he holds a
skein for Priscilla—of sexuality.[32]

On a more elevated—or at least aesthetic—plane, spinning was an
integral part of the arts and crafts movement that flourished at the time,
with nostalgic emphasis on handwork and usefulness and its penchant
for the concept of sincerity. *Sincere* was a key term for the colonial
revival, whether appearing frequently in decorating guides or in a critic's valiant attempts to explain Thomas Eakins's disturbing realism to
his contemporaries. It was taken so seriously that it provoked parody;
looking back on the 1860s, an 1882 *Harper's* article recalled: "It was
about this time that the word 'sincere' came into the furnishing world.
The old mahogany square and straight-legged tables of our grandfathers, finely finished old bureaus with their 'sincere' brass handles, plain
papers, plain carpets began to crowd out our floriated patterns. The
classification of pottery became a study. Not every cracked tea-pot from
the kitchen shelf was a treasure, only every other tea-pot."[33] In the
aesthetic terminology of the arts and crafts movement, sincerity meant
a lack of ornament; it meant honesty, strength, and integrity, and the
functionalism it promoted took the nineteenth century well on its way
to modernism. More generally, the idea of sincerity helped supplement
the Puritan doctrine of good works with an invigorated belief in hard
work, handwork, and holy domesticity, in material and moral
authenticity.

Thus the colonial revival interior helped turn the American past into

[32] Croly, *Juneiana*, p. 53. See also Lois Dinnerstein, "The Industrious Housewife:
Some Images of Labor in American Art," *Arts* 55, no. 8 (1981): 109–19; Eastman Johnson, *Corn Shelling*, Toledo Museum of Art, Toledo, Ohio; Earle, *Home Life*, pp. 183–
84; Earle, *Colonial Dames*; and Longfellow, *Courtship*, p. 120. There is a similar scene
in Howells's *Mrs. Farrell*. Johnson's *Winding Yarn* (Cleveland Museum of Art) also depicts
a rustic flirtation.

[33] See Anthea Callen, *Women Artists of the Arts and Crafts Movement*, 1870–1914
(New York: Pantheon Books, 1979); Johathan L. Fairbanks and Elizabeth Bidwell Bates,
American Furniture: 1620 to the Present (New York: Richard Marek, 1981); David M.
Cathers, *Furniture of the American Arts and Crafts Movement* (New York: New Ameri-
can Library, 1981); and Robert Judson Clark, ed., *The Arts and Crafts Movement in
America* (Princeton: Princeton University Press, 1972). For examples of the term *sincer-
ity*, see Ella Rodman Church, *How to Furnish a Home* (New York: D. Appleton, 1881).
Like Mrs. Sherwood's books, this was a volume in Appleton's Home Books series. See
Cortissoz, *American Artists*, p. 81, for the comments on Eakins. "Certain New York
Houses," *Harper's New Monthly* 65 (October 1882): 681.

an ideal. *Puritan* came to stand for pureness, for social, moral, and sexual purity. Paradoxically reversing—even rebelling against—modern theories of progress, novelists, medical writers, social commentators, and household advisors insisted that physical, mental, and moral health had been superior in old colony times. S. Weir Mitchell, both a historical novelist and a psychiatrist, compared his unhealthy and neurasthenic patients unfavorably to the strapping colonial dames encountered in Hawthorne's *Scarlet Letter*. Millet's *Grandpa's Visit* (1885), in which a healthy-looking old man comes to pay a sick call on a young lady invalid languishing in a quaint rural interior, may have been making a similar point. The most ordinary social customs were sentimentalized and idealized. The friendliness of teatime or the ready companionship provided by an eighteenth-century village inn contrasted (as one critic wrote of Millet's *At the Inn* [1884]) with the snobbish French restaurants and rude lunch counters of modern times.[34]

The most powerful idealism of all, religion, was transformed into a nostaglic act as well, with Priscilla reading her prayer book at her spinning wheel, threadbare old folks perusing the Bible, or families sharing Sunday morning devotions in a pious atmosphere that made the humblest home a chapel.[35] By making scenes of domestic poverty religious allegories through a historical context, nineteenth-century American culture softened harsh realities and placed social inequities at a safe historical and psychological distance.

The art of Lilian Westcott Hale, too, it was suggested over the years, owed its refined quality to the generations of clergymen from whom she was descended, and her interior scenes, such as *L'Edition de Luxe* (1910), were considered blessed by the transcendent atmosphere of the "two century old New England house" she had inherited from those divines.[36] The tone of such comments also hints at something very different from religious idealism, however. Increasingly prevalent from the late 1880s

[34] S. Weir Mitchell, *Wear and Tear; or, Hints for the Overworked,* 1871 (Philadelphia: J. B. Lippincott Co., 1887), p. 34; Francis Davis Millet, *Grandpa's Visit* (sold April 1, 1981, at William Doyle Galleries, New York, N.Y.; this painting was reproduced in the *Woman's Home Companion* in December 1912); Trumble, *Representative Works,* n.p.

[35] A typical example is J. G. Brown's *Consolation* (ca. 1905), Maurice Sternberg Galleries, Chicago. Johnson's family picture *Sunday Morning* (New-York Historical Society) was often the subject of such pious critiques.

[36] *L'Edition de Luxe,* Museum of Fine Arts, Boston; Rose V. S. Berry, "Lilian Westcott Hale—Her Art," *American Magazine of Art* 18, no. 2 (February 1927): 60. Another Hale relative was Charlotte Perkins Gilman.

onward were evocations of the colonial revival interior as an enclave of social aspirations, as a symbol of elitist sentiments. Puritan? By the end of the century the term mostly meant pure stock. Conservationism snuggled up to conservatism. The colonial revival interior came to represent physical and social exclusivity.

In perceptions of the past, the shift was from the spinning wheel to the spinet, as it were, from a focus on the more democratic connotations of colonial life to emblems of wealth and aristocracy. The spinet was a favorite subject in the high-toned art of Thomas Dewing, for example. If the New England kitchen had been the artifactual metaphor for the American past at the 1876 Philadelphia exhibition, at the 1893 Chicago exposition genteel reception rooms in historical private houses took over that role. When Esther Singleton published her book *Social New York under the Georges, 1714–1776* in 1905, she was quick to point out that the "picture so often drawn of the goodwife spinning in the kitchen" needed to be supplemented—if not replaced—by that of the "high-heeled aristocratic and wealthy woman" who was "accustomed to pedal the harpsichord, but had slight acquaintance with the spinning-wheel."[37]

The new religion was "ancestor worship." The domestic interior was supposed to house genealogical prestige. The colonial revival had been primarily an upper-middle-class phenomenon all along, a glorification of past simplicities, as Thorstein Veblen noted, by people who could "conspicuously" afford to downplay their wealth.[38] But with the proliferation of a "shabby genteel" caste of Americans, birth increasingly gained cachet over money among those whose dwindling wealth made the idea of old families more valuable than economic and material status. The issue of colonial survival as opposed to colonial revival became a more and more pressing one. An inherited lineage was deemed superior to freshly made millions. Family background was an heirloom that no recently purchased antiques could surpass. A kind of nobility of native origins evolved as the fear of foreign immigration grew.

Novels and paintings now moved into ancestral mansions in droves,

[37] See, for example, Thomas Dewing's *The Spinet* (1902), National Museum of American Art, Washington, D.C. Stillinger, *Antiquers*, p. 55; Singleton, *Social New York*, pp. 55, 336.
[38] Gilman, *Living*, p. 325; Thorstein Veblen, *The Theory of the Leisure Class* (1899; reprint ed., New York: New American Library, 1953), p. 100.

while authors and painters disparaged revival interiors that could only pretend to be genuinely hallowed halls. Fabricated patricians were held up to ridicule and moral contempt. In the Brandreth house that Annie Kilburn visits, "everything, nearly . . . was an heirloom, although Annie could not remember afterwards any object that had been an heirloom in the . . . family." Critical writing began to use terms such as *good taste, pedigree,* and *breeding.*[39] Genealogy seemed to become the new form of aesthetics.

While Thomas Dewing painted aristocratic versions of the American past, his wife, Maria, a Boston blueblood whose mother had written books on Boston society, named their country house Doveridge after her family's ancestral home in England.[40] Art critics discussed Frank Weston Benson's distinguished background in terms of the old houses in his native Salem, and the women in his portraits and interiors were likened to the Puritan and eighteenth-century mistresses of these stately mansions (fig. 11). Such women were "like ancestral mahogany, not to be found in every fashionable drawing-room. Their breeding and simplicity [were] . . . patent." According to articles illustrated with such works as Childe Hassam's *In the Old House* (1914; fig. 12), Hassam structured his interiors with an eye for clarity and rationality inherited from his Puritan forebears. His own social geography was an exclusive one: writing about the role of art, he decided that "As the artist practices his peaceful profession he can hold himself aloof from the rabble without the least danger of damage to his work."[41] J. Alden Weir's art appeared to critics to "fix the survival of the older American, Anglo-Saxon American founders of our old families"; in *The Miniature* (1888) he portrayed his wife holding the kind of eighteenth-century miniature that had been kept in hers. Even pieces of ancient orientalia were pounced on as signs

[39] Howells, *Annie Kilburn,* p. 108; for examples of critical vocabulary, see Minna C. Smith, "The Work of Frank W. Benson," *International Studio* 35, no. 140 (October 1908): 100.
[40] Thomas Wilmer Dewing Papers, AAA. See also Jennifer A. Martin, "The Rediscovery of Maria Oakey Dewing," *Feminist Art Journal* 5, no. 2 (Summer 1976): 24–44; and Susan Hobbs, "Thomas Wilmer Dewing: The Early Years, 1851–1885," *American Art Journal* 13 (Spring 1981): 4–35. I am grateful to both Jennifer Martin Bienenstock and Susan Hobbs for providing me with valuable information about the Dewings.
[41] Smith, "Work of Benson," p. 100; Israel L. White, "Childe Hassam—A Puritan," *International Studio* 45, no. 178 (December 1911): 29–33. Hassam quotation on a scrap of paper included with the Childe Hassam Papers and Correspondence, American Academy of Arts and Letters, New York.

Fig. 11. Frank W. Benson, *Girl Playing Solitaire*. Boston, 1909. Oil on canvas; H. 50″, W. 40″. (Worcester Art Museum.)

of a family history in the China trade and the "romance of the old India trade." About 1909 one reviewer of a painting by William McGregor Paxton interpreted a blue jar in the composition as "a symbol of euthenics" and the young woman in the painting as a symbol of "eugenics."[42]

[42] Duncan Phillips, "Julian Alden Weir," in *Julian Alden Weir: An Appreciation of His Life and Works* (New York: E. P. Dutton, 1922), p. 6; William Dean Howells, *A Woman's Reason* (Boston: Houghton Mifflin Co., 1882), p. 45; Henry James, *The Europeans* (1878; reprint ed., Baltimore: Penguin Books, 1975); clipping from William McGregor Paxton file, Fine Arts Division, Boston Public Library, Boston. I would like to thank Doreen Bolger Burke for telling me about the miniatures handed down in Anna Baker Weir's family, which are still in possession of the Weir descendants.

Fig. 12. Childe Hassam, *In the Old House*. East Hampton, 1914. Oil on linen support; H. 31⅜″, W. 48⅜″. (IBM Corporation, Armonk, N.Y.)

With growing frequency, the ancestor portrait came to oversee these intentional and unintentional snobberies. In fiction John Singleton Copley, Charles Willson Peale, and Gilbert Stuart were invariably invoked as the household gods of familial longevity. Visual references made similar claims in such paintings as E. L. Henry's *Lover of Old China* (fig. 7) or Childe Hassam's genteel portrayal of a woman playing piano in *Improvisation* (1899). Judgment is passed from another angle in Eastman Johnson's *Not at Home* (1872–80), in which a stern ancestral figure and other inherited furnishings seem to express displeasure at a woman's bid for freedom from timeworn social obligations.[43]

It would seem, however, that at its more sensitive moments this tra-

[43] Portraits by Copley, Peale, and Stuart appear frequently in both S. Weir Mitchell's historical novels and his more contemporary society romances; three Stuarts also hang in a Boston parlor in Howells's *Woman's Reason*. Childe Hassam, *Improvisation*, National Museum of American Art, Washington, D.C.; Eastman Johnson, *Not at Home*, Brooklyn Museum, New York.

ditionalizing of gentility came out of the genteel tradition, which had at its ethereal core a worship of the intellect, a theology of intelligence. Americans were discovering that, in the words of Santayana, "by the mind only do we exist." Maria Oakey Dewing, who taught her husband to love Emerson and other philosophers, felt that "the artist who has the most mind will go farthest." The indwelling spirit of the colonial revival stemmed ultimately from the cult of the mind, which profoundly occupied the period. "Because the old Puritan days were not the childhood of our race but the first episode in our history," Van Wyck Brooks theorized in 1908, "we are the most purely intelligent people in the world."[44] The colonial revival as ideal could claim as its root the word *idea*. Its interiors were lit by the glow of cerebral pastimes, its quaint rooms were conducive to such labels as *Meditation*. Its subjects suggested a contemplative atmosphere that was, according to the title of a Thomas Anshutz painting of a woman reading, A *Bit of the Last Century*, and the importance it gave to pure idea filled the empty inner spaces dreamed up by Thomas Dewing, an artist who said that all he wanted were models with "brains."[45]

American culture as a whole, in fact, was regarded as a colony of the Italian Renaissance, of Holland's Golden Age, of Elizabethan, Queen Anne, and Georgian England—all periods, it was stressed, characterized by "thought." These ages had produced great styles of furniture and artifacts—"the best product[s] of a thoughtful time"—even as they planted a mature civilization on the shores of the New World. Dewing's women were readily classified as "the type of the Quattrocento," who manifested "the survival of the intense mysticism of the middle ages, vivified by the keen intellectuality and social freedom of their own day."[46]

[44] George Santayana, "The Genteel Tradition in American Philosophy" (1911), in Cleanth Brooks, R. W. B. Lewis, and Robert Penn Warren, *American Literature: The Makers and the Making*, Book C (New York: St. Martin's Press, 1974), p. 1551; Abbott Handerson Thayer to Maria Oakey Dewing, April 22, 1906, Abbott H. Thayer Papers, AAA; Van Wyck Brooks, *The Wine of the Puritans: A Study of Present-Day Americans* (New York: M. Kennerley, 1908), p. 19.

[45] A charming example of this common subject is George Newell Bowers, *Meditation* (1889), Museum of Fine Arts, Springfield, Mass. Although the owner of the Anshutz painting, Pennsylvania Academy of the Fine Arts, calls it A *Studio Study* (1891), it appears in a contemporary source under the title A *Bit of the Last Century*. Dewing Papers, AAA.

[46] Spofford, *Art Decoration*, p. 89; Wheeler, *Home Decoration*, p. 169; Charles H. Caffin, "The Art of Thomas Dewing," *Harper's Monthly* 116, no. 695 (April 1908): 723. See also Richard Guy Wilson, "The Great Civilization," in *The American Renaissance, 1876–1917* (New York: Pantheon Books, 1980), pp. 9–55.

A further influence on Dewing and others was Vermeer, rediscovered during this period as the great and mysterious genius of the Dutch seventeenth century, an epoch known for its triumphs in art, science, philosophy, and exploration.

Animated—made animate—by such assumptions about the American past, the colonial revival interior often fervently expressed the anti-materialistic, "suggestive" mood that marked much avant-garde art and literature.[47] In doing so, it was able to colonize the spirit and forms of ancient Japan and China. The analogies between Puritan asceticism and Oriental metaphysics were not hard to draw. Nor were the Chinese origins of the ball-and-claw foot and the cabriole leg of the Queen Anne style forgotten, along with other connections fully exploited in the colonial revival interior, where heirloom Oriental ceramics seemed to grow more valuable by the minute. In paintings, the shapes of Eastern fans and porcelains were picked up by those of Windsor chairs and spinning wheels, ornate screens enfolded a sheltered existence, and every act was a study in reflection.

Such acts of introversion seemed reflections on time itself, the colonial revival as intellectual process stating more and more clearly that it was an exercise in memory. Its interiors epitomized both personal remembrance (Emily Dickinson compared memory to a house) and national nostalgia, with the very old and very young playing the roles of internal commemoration or the lost innocence of youth.[48] As Enoch Wood Perry's old clock doctor (fig. 13) might have been explaining to the young companion seated across from him in a rustic rural interior, the symbol for time in the literary and artistic prop rooms of the colonial revival was the clock. It was perhaps first popularized by Longfellow's poetic musings on time, history, and evanescence, "The Old Clock on the Stairs" (fig. 3). Expatriate painter Walter Gay remembered his own New England youth and that of his country with a picture of the ancient grandfather clock in New Hampshire's Wentworth house, for instance,

---

[47] *Suggestive* and *decorative* were both used to describe what were essentially abstract formal qualities in the work of a painter like Dewing and that of Tonalist artists in general.

[48] W. L. Kimberly, *How to Know Period Styles in Furniture* (Grand Rapids, Mich.: Periodical Publishing Co., 1912), p. 83; Dickinson, *Complete Poems*, p. 524. For an enlightening discussion of the intentional juxtaposition of Oriental and Western objects in the colonial revival interior, see Monkhouse, "Spinning Wheel." See also Siegfried Wichmann, *Japonisme: The Japanese Influence on Western Art in the Nineteenth and Twentieth Centuries* (New York: Harmony Books, 1981).

Fig. 13. Enoch Wood Perry, *The Clock Doctor*. New York, 1871. Oil on canvas; H. 21¾″, W. 26⅛″. (Courtesy Richard York Gallery, New York.)

and Jefferson Chalfant portrayed the dying art of the old clockmaker.[49]

Timepieces were a favorite device in fiction as well. Henry James, whose American stories were usually set well in the past, rewarded a Boston lady in "A New England Winter" (1884) for sticking to old ways by having her inherit all the clocks from her family's fine collection of antiques. Alongside the ticking of an old tall clock, in S. Weir Mitchell's novel *Roland Blake* (1886) is the "clock-like" clicking of knitting

[49] Walter Gay, *Grandfathers Clock, Wentworth House, New Hampshire* (n.d.), private collection; Jefferson Chalfant, *The Old Clockmaker* (1899), Fine Arts Museums of San Francisco.

needles wielded by a grandmother whose "eighty-five years of accumulated memories appeared to have supplied her with sufficient food for
thought." This was the kind of temporal music colonial revivalists liked
to hear; knitting, sewing, and spinning not only recalled the past, they
made time audible and as visible as Thomas Waterman Wood's portrait
of old Miss Mary Caldwell at work in "the interior of . . . one of the
most spacious of Montpelier's Colonial homes," which he called A Stitch
in Time (1894). In the cultured backwaters of Salem and Concord,
Henry James discovered New England and its spirit personified as "Some
grave, refined New England matron of 'the old school.' . . . From her
position, her high-backed chair by the window . . . she looks up intel-
ligently, over her knitting . . . with . . . a hint of that loss of temporal
perspective in which we recognize the mental effect of a great weight of
years."[50]

Such metaphorical scenes and settings were surpassed in import only
by images of unadulterated retrospection itself. Along with "Memory"
or "Memories," "Retrospection" became the title of many paintings,
including Worthington Whittredge's depiction of an old man seated by
the window in an interior, surrounded by objects even older than himself, gazing inward to what contemporaries were fond of calling "the
chambers of memory." Retrospection was the historically minded interior stripped to its essence, distilled to Dewing's figures dressed in antique
gowns meditating on the past's survival into the present, or to Thomas
Eakins's Retrospection (1880), in which a pensive young woman in an
old-fashioned dress is seated in an old chair, becoming both the subject
and the object of memory. It was also Eastman Johnson's old Nantuck-
eteers stationed by the fireside in Embers (ca. 1880) and The New Bonnet (fig. 5), reliving their lives while awaiting their deaths.[51]

In letters written to his old friend Jervis McEntee in 1879 and 1881,
Johnson described his sojourns on Nantucket and the scenes he painted

[50] Henry James, "A New England Winter," in The Complete Tales of Henry James, ed.
Leon Edel, vol. 6 (Philadelphia: J. B. Lippincott Co., 1963), p. 93; Mitchell, Roland
Blake, p. 59; A Stitch in Time, reproduced in Catalogue of the Pictures in the Art Gallery
in Montpelier—The Thomas W. Wood Collection (Montpelier, Vt.: Capital City Press,
1913), n.p.; James, American Scene, p. 259.

[51] Retrospection, Yale University Art Gallery, New Haven, Conn.; Sherwood, Amusements, p. 8; Eastman Johnson, Embers, private collection. See also Kenneth Ames,
"Eastman Johnson: The Failure of a Successful Artist," Art Journal 29, no. 2 (Winter
1969/70): 174–83.

there as a relief from the urban art world, as an escape from the present into the past. Yet it is evident from *The New Bonnet, Embers,* and others that, like so many of his contemporaries in art and letters, Johnson had made his way into the deepest and most somber regions of the colonial revival. Here was no mindless escape.

For, in the end, the colonial revival found in the interior did not represent uncomplicated bliss. Artists and writers realized that the legacies of colonial days were often psychological strains, the enervation of Puritanism, and the bankruptcy of other once-proud relics of the American past. "The old life of Puritan New England was indeed hard upon the young," one author wrote about the youth of Harriet Beecher Stowe, "a time of storm and stress, mainly for mental and religious conflicts." And in his psychological novel, *Dr. North and His Friends* (1900), S. Weir Mitchell created the symbolic figure of the neurotic Sybil Maywood, the offshoot of an ancient line that had come down in the world, a woman with a beautiful head on a deformed body. George Santayana, of course, made intellectual history by symbolizing all that was progressive and alive about American culture as a skyscraper and everything that was retrogressive, hidebound, weak, and hypocritical as a "Colonial mansion."[52]

The physical and psychological interiors of the colonial revival came to be experienced as inhibition and restriction. Charlotte Perkins Gilman's novel about female entrapment and madness, *The Yellow Wallpaper* (1892 and 1899), used the image of a colonial house as a symbol of blind conservatism and repression. New England, some felt, had left its female descendants in particular with an inherited conscience that crippled their emotions "as the Chinese do . . . their children's feet." The region had instilled in all its descendants a heritage of guilt and a consciousness of sin that had hardened into a modern-day Puritanism of narrow-minded social proprieties. No longer the "great Puritan . . . whip for conscience and nerves," this heritage had turned into a prim "conscientiousness" that was "kept for state occasions, like . . . great-grandmother's Crown Derby." Such psychological heirlooms entailed

---

[52] Eastman Johnson to Jervis McEntee, November 17, 1879, and September 22, 1881, Letters of Artists, Charles E. Feinberg Collection, AAA; Hattie Tyng Griswold, *Personal Sketches of Recent Authors* (Chicago: A. C. McClurg, 1898), p. 168; S. Weir Mitchell, *Dr. North and His Friends* (New York: Century Co., 1900), p. 35; Santayana, "Genteel Tradition," p. 1545.

prejudice—like some nineteenth-century Hester Prynne, Emily Dickinson was reputed in her village to be a witch—sterility, and a sense of decay. The only vital signs that appeared in the cold New England houses, which observers liked to view as symbols of lonely gloom, were morbidity and the neuroses and sickliness encountered in Edith Wharton's *Ethan Frome* (1911). In this short novel, existence in a world and a house of stiff resentments leads to unhealthy acts and cruel insanities.[53]

Having used the interior and interiorization to revive its colonial past, a backward-looking culture ultimately seemed to discover introspective sadness, loneliness, a withdrawal into the self. To be a Puritan was to be not happy. There was a recognition of things that never were what the modern searchers had wanted them to be. The mood expressed in words and paint is a reflection on time passing and passed, an elegiac tone created by the lonesomeness of introversion in such paintings as Frank Benson's *Girl Playing Solitaire* (1909; fig. 11). It is a sense of loss—a loss of faith, of security, of hope. "They must be Puritans to their finger-tips," a foreign visitor says of his American relatives in Henry James's *Europeans* (1878). "They are sober, even severe. They . . . take things hard . . . they have some melancholy memory or some depressing expectation."[54] Contained in these psychic legacies, however, were bequests that seemed to contemporaries to make all the suffering and sadness worthwhile. A fin de siècle culture that put an increasing premium on psychological awareness began to perceive the Puritan trait of introspection as its most significant inheritance, as a welcome means of self-knowledge, and as a tool for getting at the essence of people and things. Frank Benson was viewed as a portraitist of this finely tuned, nervous subjectivity. So was Thomas Dewing, whose women betrayed "an inherited trait of seriousness. . . . They [were] still the daughters of Puritanism. . . . Generations of repressed emotion have made them

[53] Charlotte Perkins Gilman, *The Yellow Wallpaper* (1892 and 1899; reprint ed., Old Westbury, N.Y.: Feminist Press, 1973); S. Weir Mitchell, *In War Time* (New York: Century Co., 1884), p. 158; James, *American Scene*, p. 232; Howells, "Household-Effect," p. 289; Edith Wharton, "The Mission of Jane" (1904), in *The Descent of Man* (1904; reprint ed., Freeport, N.Y.: Books for Libraries Press, 1970), p. 39; Van Wyck Brooks, *New England Indian Summer* (1904; reprint ed., New York: E. P. Dutton, 1965), p. 330; Edith Wharton, *Ethan Frome* (1911; reprint ed., New York: Scribner's, 1960). Walter Gay, a friend of Wharton, painted the interior of the old Fairbanks House in Dedham, Mass., a structure Wharton later christened "the Ethan Frome house."

[54] James, *Europeans*, p. 33.

Fig. 14. Thomas Eakins, *The Old-Fashioned Dress—Portrait of Miss Helen Parker*. Philadelphia, 1908. Oil on canvas; H. 60⅜", W. 40¼". (Philadelphia Museum of Art, gift of Mrs. Thomas Eakins and Miss Mary A. Williams.)

incapable of passion; strenuousness survives only in their supersensitive nerves." Thomas Eakins aged his sitters—like the young girl in *The Old-Fashioned Dress* (1908; fig. 14)—to get at their emotional centers; his historical subjects formed a bridge between his earlier physical realism and the psychological realism of his later years. Introversion, memory, psychology itself were hailed as modern forms of Puritan self-examination, and the "sincerity" of old colony days was praised as intensity of feeling, an authenticity of experience. History as interiorization led to the inside as insight. Antimodernism evolved into a modernist sense of self. In the interior not only renovation but innovation took place.[55]

[55]Charles H. Caffin, "The Art of Frank W. Benson," *Harper's Monthly* 119, no. 709 (June 1909): 105–14; Charles H. Caffin, *The Story of American Painting* (New York: Stokes, 1907), p. 189. For psychological awareness, see Henri Ellenberger, *The Discovery of the Unconscious* (New York: Basic Books, 1970); and George M. Beard, *American Nervousness: Its Causes and Consequences* (New York: G. P. Putnam's Sons, 1881). The theme of psychological awareness is articulated throughout late nineteenth-century American art and literature. For a recent and stimulating discussion of antimodernism, see T. J. Jackson Lears, *No Place of Grace: Antimodernism and the Transformation of American Culture, 1880–1920* (New York: Pantheon Books, 1981).

A Pedigree for a New Century: The Colonial Experience in Popular Historical Novels, 1890–1910
Beverly Seaton

Between 1890 and 1910, historical novels about the colonial period were very popular with American middle-class readers. During this time, six appeared on the best-seller lists: *Hugh Wynne, Free Quaker* by S. Weir Mitchell, *Richard Carvel* by Winston Churchill, *Janice Meredith* by Paul Leicester Ford, *To Have and to Hold* and *Audrey* by Mary Johnston, and *Alice of Old Vincennes* by Maurice Thompson. In addition, many other popular novelists published colonial historical novels during this period, notably Robert W. Chambers, Maud Wilder Goodwin, Sarah Orne Jewett, Robert Neilson Stephens, and Mary Hartwell Catherwood. For juvenile readers, there were Amanda Douglas's Little Girl series (*A Little Girl in Old New York*, and so on), adventure novels for boys by Everett Tomlinson, Mary Wells Smith's Boy Captive and Young Puritans series, and the fictionalized biographies of Jefferson, Franklin, William Penn, and Lafayette by Hezekiah Butterworth (the editor of *Youth's Companion*). Readers interested in the colonial period also made a successful author of Alice Morse Earle, whose twelve books, published between 1891 and 1903, cover various aspects of colonial life. Publishers capitalized on the current interest in American history by reissuing such colonial historical novels of the past as Henry Peterson's *Pemberton* and *Dulcibel*, Daniel Thompson's *Green Mountain Boys*, and J. G. Holland's *Bay Path*, a novel about the Puritans which in its 1899 Homewood edition is indiscriminately illustrated with hundreds of stereotyped images of the American colonial experience, many not at all related to the period of the story.

In *A Season of Youth*, Michael Kammen pointed out the popularity of historical novels about the American Revolution at the turn of our century and said that this period, like others when such novels were popular, was a time of "cultural indirection" when "national values needed to be defined or redefined."[1] Certainly we will all agree that at the beginning of the twentieth century all sorts of social and economic changes were apparent. My analysis of these popular books about American colonial life shows that their authors were shaping their perspective on history to answer new questions and meet new challenges. These books have many elements in common, which suggest what the American colonial experience must have meant to their readers.

Of course, some of the elements of these books are shared with popular fiction in general. Before focusing on significant aspects of the colonial theme, therefore, we need to clear the ground of these more general features. One of them is the extensive use of young heroes and heroines, who typically marry at the end of the story. In using young men and women as the main characters, "colonial" writers followed the pattern of most popular novels. Likewise, the hero is often unusually sympathetic to women, interested in their costumes, fond of reading and flowers (of course, he is also an excellent swordsman and a courageous fighter). In popular fiction, the reader identifies with the main character, and if the novelist expects to attract readers of both sexes (and most novelists did at the turn of the century), he must create characters with whom both sexes can identify. Melodramatic elements have been a constant component of popular fiction since its beginnings, and there is no more stereotyped melodramatic plot element than mysterious parentage, which is very common in these historical novels. Also, dastardly villains and cruel, selfish parents are common melodramatic characters. Colonial historical novels also share two significant stylistic conventions with the general run of popular historical novels: the use of the

[1] Michael Kammen, *A Season of Youth: The American Revolution and the Historical Imagination* (New York: Alfred A. Knopf, 1978), pp. 175–76.

first person to give an element of authenticity and cameo appearances by major historical figures.

While not all the popular historical novels about American colonial life focused on the Revolutionary period, most did. Of the biggest best-sellers, for example, only the two by Mary Johnston—*To Have and to Hold* and *Audrey*—are not set during the Revolution. And these two novels, as well as the historical novels of Maud Wilder Goodwin, are set in the swashbuckling Old South. Mary Catherwood's novels concern the French in the Midwest. Conspicuously missing are novels about the Puritans, who had had their chroniclers among earlier historical novelists J. G. Holland, Catharine Maria Sedgwick, Henry Peterson, and Lydia Maria Child.

The absence of novels about the Puritans may be associated with a significant aspect of the fiction I am discussing, the unsympathetic treatment of strict, old-fashioned religion. In *Janice Meredith*, Janice's mother, once pleasant and cheerful, becomes depressed by the loss of her other children and turns to hellfire religion. She wants the fifteen-year-old Janice to marry a Presbyterian clergyman, a widower with five children. In a Victorian romance, the motherly warnings she gives Janice about her behavior and the state of her soul would have been an expression of the novel's major point of view, but Paul Leicester Ford made them the vehicle of fanaticism and depression—one more sign of the victory of Henry Ward Beecher over his father, Lyman. Hugh Wynne's stern Quaker father lapses into religious fanaticism also, albeit the Quaker version rather than the Presbyterian. Hugh's father objects to his son's fighting in the Revolution and to his participation in worldly activities generally. He is dismissed from meeting on July 4, 1776. Similarly, Douw Mauverensen, the Dutch hero of Harold Frederic's *In the Valley*, renounces the strict Calvinism of his clergyman father.

Even in those novels in which religion is not made an issue, its very absence is a sign that the novelist is not looking at our history as the work of God's providential hand. In several of the novels, the only visible representative of religion is a corrupt clergyman—Reverend Allen, Richard Carvel's tutor, for example. Plainly, readers at the turn of the century were not looking for reassurance that God was at work in American history; rather, they were looking for a version of our past that accorded better with contemporary views of religion.

By the turn of the century, the victory of liberal Protestantism as represented by Henry Ward Beecher over the strict religion of old New England was an acknowledged aspect of our cultural life. Religion had its place, of course, but the strongly morbid tone of Calvinistic theology was unpopular and considered misguided. In *Child Life in Colonial Days*, Alice Morse Earle referred to Puritan children pictured in the books of those times as "short-lived and morbid young Christians" and called Isaac Watts "a bigoted old bachelor" and Richard Coddington, author of *For the Instructing of the Younger Sorts of Maids and Boarders at Schools*, a "tiresome old bore." When writing of the books written for Puritan children, she said, "I will not give any of the accounts in full, for the expression of religious thought shown therein is so contrary to the sentiment of today that it would not be pleasing to modern readers."[2] Earlier novelists such as Henry Peterson and Catharine Maria Sedgwick had shown the harsher aspects of Puritan culture, notably the witchcraft trials and related issues, but only as the darker side of a generally positive culture.

The novelists of 1890–1910 ask us to look toward the non-Puritan colonists for our heritage. Their view of Puritan thinking is expressed in an outburst of Gideon Darden, the drunken Church of England clergyman in Mary Johnston's *Audrey*. Darden attacks Mr. Eliot, a minister from New England who dares to preach a sermon directed at Audrey, an innocent with a damaged reputation: " 'Ye beggarly Scot!' [Darden] exclaimed thickly. 'Ye evil-thinking saint from Salem way, that know the very lining of the Lord's mind, and yet, walking through his earth, see but a poisonous weed in his every harmless flower! Shame on you to beat down the flower that never did you harm!' "[3]

That the author's sympathy here is with a drunken clergyman reflects another aspect of these novels, one related to the issue of nineteenth-century religion. The authors make very clear that back in colonial days men swore and drank a lot and that perhaps loose women were prominent in good circles; they always explain in some way that times were different then, and we must be understanding. Instead of showing a past age of sinless men and women, they hasten to display our ancestors as people of the world in every sense. While turn-of-the-century readers might have had more refined manners, they were plainly expected to

[2] Alice Morse Earle, *Child Life in Colonial Days* (New York: Macmillan, 1899), p. 250.

[3] Mary Johnston, *Audrey* (Boston: Houghton Mifflin Co., 1902), p. 294.

be worldly as well, to accept such an explanation as this typical one in *Hugh Wynne*. Wynne recalls the merrymaking of his fellow apprentices: "I liked it well, and, with my aunt's warning in mind, drank but little, and listened to the talk, which was too free at times, as was the bad custom of that day."[4] Hugh was warned by his aunt, incidentally, because he had been drinking too much, a fault which later gets him into much trouble. Many of the young heroes of these novels get drunk, and almost all of them indulge in duels. Readers of the time were very fond of the kind of romantic and exciting action characterized by the duel, and some of the other popular historical novels of the period that were not about American history also featured such high-tempered behavior—Charles Major's *When Knighthood Was in Flower*, for instance, or Henryk Sienkiewicz's *Quo Vadis*.

In characterizing the heroes as young men of liberal habits and quick tempers, our novelists were distancing them from the tamer heroes of Victorian romances. The dashing hero, whether in costume of the Continental army officer or the Virginia Cavalier of the seventeenth century, served as a historical model for a new man, less the Victorian gentleman, more the twentieth-century man-about-town. Our novelists used historical models to justify those changes in manners that were beginning to appear in their own time. Their interest in the hero as a "new man" was less intense, however, than their concern with the heroine.

One of the most striking features of these novels is the uniformity of the characterization of the heroines. Almost without exception, they could be called minxes, a term actually used in most of the books. When we first meet Janice Meredith, for instance, she is being scolded for reading novels, and we see that she is far from repentant after her mother's remarks. We have the same introduction to Alice Roussillon, of *Alice of Old Vincennes*. She, too, is reading romances and reacts to an old priest's chastising by arguing with him. These "new women" are argumentative, willful, courageous, and, above all, flirtatious. As young girls they are tomboys—running races, for example, as do the heroines of *Audrey* and *Cardigan*; besting the hero at throwing the tomahawk, as does the heroine of *The Maid-at-Arms*; or even winning a dueling match with the hero, as Alice does. But when they become women,

[4] S. Weir Mitchell, *Hugh Wynne, Free Quaker*, vol. 1 (New York: Century, 1897), p. 103.

they are most marked by their impatient willfulness. Some of them are willful to the point of arrogance, as Stephens's heroines Elizabeth Phillipse *(The Continental Dragoon)* or Margaret Winwood *(Philip Winwood)*; the same can certainly be said of the younger Janice Meredith. Margaret Winwood goes so far as to engage in spying against the army of Washington, in which her husband serves. Perhaps the two women who love Richard Carvel, Patty Swain and Dolly Manners, best illustrate the old and the new in style of heroine. Patty is the apotheosis of the Victorian heroine—quiet, domestic, fair-minded—while Dolly is the proud and clever woman of the world. Naturally, Richard loves Dolly, although Patty is so much more worthy of his devotion. Worth, in fact, is a very much outmoded concept in feminine attractions when these novelists work out their plots. Beauty, wit, and spirit are the major qualities looked for in the heroines.

I was much struck with a recurring scene in these novels, which might be called the young woman's rite of passage—her first social appearances dressed in the clothes of a grown woman. The heroine is often a childhood companion of the young hero who fails to realize that the girl has become a woman until he sees her descending the stairs in full regalia. The astonishment of the hero and the triumph of the girl is a set piece in most of these novels. When fourteen-year-old Dolly Manners appears dressed for the Christmas party at Carvel Hall, for instance, Richard's grandfather says, " 'Richard, she has outstripped you, fair and square. You are only an awkward lad, and she—why i'faith, in two years she'll be beyond my protection.' "[5] Michael Cardigan is so upset when he first sees Silver Heels (Felicity Warren) dressed up that he engages in a disastrous flirtation with another girl. When Dorothy Varick of *The Maid-at-Arms* appears in her best outfit, the hero does not even recognize her. Alice Roussillon wears her only fancy gown to a ball in order to impress Fitzhugh Beverley, the Virginia gentleman who later marries her and takes her back to a big white house in Virginia (where she belongs, by the way—her real name is Tarleton).

A tragic version of the great scene appears in *Audrey*, when the hero, drunk and angry, causes his young ward Audrey to be dressed up to dance with him at the governor's ball at Williamsburg. Since the town has been speculating that she is his mistress, she is treated with extreme

[5] Winston Churchill, *Richard Carvel* (New York: Macmillan, 1899), p. 47.

rudeness. Meanwhile he suddenly realizes that she has become a woman and falls in love with her. Clothes do indeed make the woman. Our novelists dwell on the details of clothing and hairstyles, even when the first-person narrator is a male. Hugh Wynne, for instance, explains his unusual interest in women's dress: "If you should wonder how, at this distant day, I can recall her dress, I may say that one of my aunt's lessons was that a man should notice how a woman dressed, and not fail at times to compliment a gown, or a pretty fashion of hair."[6]

The heroines are of course all extremely beautiful, Janice Meredith and Dolly Manners so much so as to test the reader's belief. All of fashionable London is at Dolly's feet; and Janice is loved by every man she meets, perhaps even George Washington (although nothing scandalous is intended). Such prodigious sex appeal annoyed one reader at least, who wrote on the flyleaf of a copy of *Janice Meredith* owned by Frederick Dickson, "The heroine, Janice, is an insufferable piece of baggage, that every man apparently, for some unknown reason, wants to marry, and she at times is evidently ready to marry any or all of them."[7] Our heroines are not stupid girls; wit naturally demands intelligence. But looks, rather than their minds, are their fortunes. Whether they were in agreement with the hero's politics from the first or had to be won over, they all find happiness in a romantic love scene far from the setting of ordinary domestic life. Janice Meredith, after all the trials to which she is subjected as she is pulled from one Revolutionary battle to another, speaks this testimonial to her maturity: " 'O mommy—isn't it a relief to be told what to do, and not to have to worry one's self. He didn't make us think once.' "[8]

Whereas the Victorian gentlewoman found a historic pattern for behavior in the Puritan maiden, the young woman of the turn of the century could find a model of worldliness and sprightly behavior in these colonial dames outside the Puritan tradition. While some young women of the time were only momentarily touched by the "Janice Meredith hairdo" and danced briefly to the "Janice Meredith Waltz," others were more enduringly influenced by the model of feminine behavior

[6] Mitchell, *Hugh Wynne*, 1:165.

[7] Quoted in Frederick Stoever Dickson [Almon Dexter], *And the Wilderness Blossomed* (Philadelphia: Fisher, 1901), pp. 79–80. Dickson kept a small library of popular novels at his summer home, in which this autobiographical work is set, and quotes many of the comments readers made on the flyleaves of the novels.

[8] Paul Leicester Ford, *Janice Meredith* (New York: Dodd, Mead, 1899), p. 386.

described in the book. Many novelists were interested in the question of the "new woman," who wanted to ride a bicycle, vote, and work in business offices. In the face of such challenges, some popular novelists, such as Harold Bell Wright, labored to show that the old-fashioned Victorian pattern of womanhood was best. Yet, plainly, America's concepts of proper womanly behavior were changing, and the colonial minxes gave historic sanction to some of the aspects of the change.

An interesting contrast to the minx is the version of the colonial woman given in the work of Alice Morse Earle. This author tried to support changes in women's behavior differently, concentrating more on responsibility, maturity, and intelligence than on beauty and "spirit," in such books as *Colonial Dames and Goodwives, Margaret Winthrop*, and *Home Life in Colonial Days*. Her work shows a tendency to look for historic precedents for the roles taken by her contemporaries, with an emphasis on the serious. The more popular novelists, in contrast, allow women new frivolities but little else.

Changes in religious attitudes and the roles of women were alterations within the middle classes, but the tides of southern European immigration transformed American society from the outside. While the cultural and ethnic demography of America was altered by the new immigrants, Americans of the dominant "native" culture were finding many ways to fortify their own sense of nationality. Kammen has pointed out that the Revolutionary historical novels of the turn of the century emphasize elitism and stress our ties with England in response to America's perception of a threat to its "racial purity." There is abundant evidence that the idea of "racial purity," which perhaps reached its peak during the presidency of Theodore Roosevelt, was a popular concept. I will examine some of the dimensions of the elitism shown in these novels.

Most obvious is the upper-class status of many of the heroes and heroines. Once in a while, it is true, the hero is a lower-class individual who rises in the world, succeeding as well in working out his role in the politics of the time or winning the heroine. Douw Mauverensen of *In the Valley* is one of those with the greatest social mobility, some of which he owes to his upbringing by his foster father, a peer of Sir John Johnson. The hero of *Janice Meredith* is John Brereton, whom we first meet as an indentured servant just off the boat; of course he turns out to be a youth of good English family and ends the war as an American general. (The unhappy reader of Frederick Dickson's copy caviled at the plausibility of this: "A man might resign from the British army and emigrate to distant lands because he did not approve of his mother's conduct, but with plenty of money at his command, he would *not* sell himself as a slave.")[9] The hero of Mary Johnston's *Prisoners of Hope* is also first met just off the boat, an indentured servant of the heroine's father. Although he turns out to be a gentleman, he fails to get the girl because of his politics. (But she will always love him.)

The more typical hero, however, is a youth of the upper classes, and the successful heroine (the one who gets to marry the hero) is also almost always of such a family. The most notable exception is Audrey, whose beauty wins the heart of one of colonial Virginia's finest young gentleman, one loved by Col. William Byrd's own daughter; yet she is killed in the final scene, the novelist thus preventing a most unsuitable marriage. Readers are expected to sympathize with the upper classes, and the advice given to Richard Carvel is followed by most of the heroes: " 'Seek no company . . . beyond that circle in which you were born.' " Paul Leicester Ford apologizes for a scene in his *Janice Meredith* which shows the blue-blooded Janice working alongside the servants—in those days people were much more familiar with their servants than we should think of being. Likewise, the "tall, blond, stalwart, blue-eyed" Lt. John Seymour Seymour, "of an old and distinguished Philadelphia family, so proud of its name that in his instance they had doubled it," who is the hero in Cyrus T. Brady's truly awful novel *For Love of Country*, verges on caricature for us—but was taken seriously by readers of that time.[10]

Many of the novels have scenes in London, allowing the novelist to provide cameo appearances of famous eighteenth-century Englishmen and to emphasize the English origin of our national heritage. Wrote Winston Churchill, "Ah, London town, by what subtleties are you tied to the hearts of those born across the sea? That is one of the mysteries of race." As Kammen has shown, many of the novels promote the idea that the Revolution did not really pit America against England, but Englishmen against other Englishmen. In keeping with the general tone of Anglophilia, there are many English officers and colonial aristocrats

[9] Quoted in Dickson, *Wilderness Blossomed*, p. 79.
[10] Churchill, *Richard Carvel*, p. 25; Cyrus T. Brady, *For Love of Country* (New York: Scribners, 1899), p. 5.

of old Virginia who do not favor the forces of democracy, yet are treated favorably by the novelists. Of course there are the evil ones, too—exaggerated portraits, many of them. Robert W. Chambers's portrayal of Walter Butler makes him a truly black-hearted villain. In *Cardigan*, Chambers described Lord Dunmore (who is pictured as a degenerate fop lusting after the beautiful Silver Heels) as "for all the world like a white cat dancing through hell fire."[11] My own favorite among the foppish villains is Lord Carnal, of *To Have and to Hold*, who came to Virginia after Jocelyn Leigh, the heroine, to force her to marry him. He dresses in red and black and is accompanied by an Italian doctor who specializes in subtle poisons.

There are plenty of villains among the ordinary citizens, and in general the populace is depicted as cowardly and mean-minded. Paradoxically, the novels that have the rise of democracy as a theme (whether set during the Revolution or in some early Southern rebellion) usually present aristocratic leaders among common folk who, in contrast to the altruistic leaders, foment rebellion only in their own selfish interests without regard for the general good. *Janice Meredith* is most vehement in this, picturing the ordinary Jerseymen of the day in the worst possible light. Many of the historical characters such as Washington and Major André (to cite the most popular) are shown as exemplars of their class, while John Paul Jones's troubles are related to his low origins in *Richard Carvel* and *The Tory Lover*.

Racism is so obvious in these novels that it needs little commentary. Blacks are nowhere considered of any importance, except as a threat in some of the Southern novels, and Indians are seldom treated favorably. In *Alice*, for instance, Thompson said of Indians, "Their innate repulsiveness is so great that, like the snake's charm, it may fascinate; yet an indescribable, haunting disgust goes with it. And, after all, if Alice had been asked to tell just how she felt toward the Indian she had labored so hard to save, she would promptly have said, 'I loathe him as I do a toad.' " Anti-Semitism is especially marked in *Richard Carvel*. One of Richard's new friends in London, a charming but dissipated gambler, asks Richard, " 'Do you have Jews in America?' " The gambler has set aside a special waiting room in his quarters which he calls "the Jerusalem Chamber, where I keep my Israelites"—that is, money lenders trying

---

[11] Churchill, *Richard Carvel*, p. 284; Robert W. Chambers, *Cardigan* (New York: Harper, 1901), p. 97.

to collect on loans.[12] Irish, Poles, Italians, and Greeks are conspicuous by their absence (excepting Lord Carnal's Italian physician), while the French are treated with suspicion, and Germans are most often represented one-dimensionally as the Hessian troops. The cheerful mixture of American immigrants described in James Fenimore Cooper's *Pioneers* is quite unlike what we find in these later novels.

A further aspect of the elitism of these novels can be seen in their descriptions of homes and gardens. The use of colonial artifacts as adjuncts to gracious living is one of the most familiar facts about the colonial revival, and these historical novels fully participate in this popular movement, tying the objects to persons of culture and refinement. In some of her books, Earle related some personal experiences of collecting china; perhaps more familiar are the stories Robert and Elizabeth Shackleton told in their popular tales of collecting colonial materials. They would ride around the countryside in a horse-drawn buggy, stopping at farmhouses where they would try to buy Washington pitchers and mahogany mirrors for dimes and quarters, often succeeding. One striking aspect of their narratives of such ventures is the tone of ridicule adopted to describe the farm homes and farm people. While their rural hosts had a genuine connection with the past, it was not one to elicit any sympathy; rather, these collectors wanted to rescue the old china or furniture from these modern peasants and give it an honored place in their own magnificent homes. Although Earle lovingly described the household cares of the colonial wife in many books, she had little good to say about the contemporary version of such a woman.

When we look back at the Puritans or the early settlers on any of our frontiers, we do not find a high standard of living. But the colonial aristocrats, either of the Old South or of eighteenth-century Philadelphia or New York, provided a historical precedent and sanction for living on an opulent scale. The idealized life-styles mirrored in the pages of *Country Life in America* had their genealogy traced in these works of fiction. Not much attention was given to the nineteenth-century state of the old homes or the area that surrounded them. *Alice of Old Vincennes* sometimes compares the scenes of the past with contemporary Vincennes, using the Roussillon cherry tree as a significant landmark. In the fictional foreword to *Richard Carvel*, Daniel Clapsaddle

[12] Maurice Thompson, *Alice of Old Vincennes* (Indianapolis: Bowen-Merrill, 1900), p. 48; Churchill, *Richard Carvel*, pp. 293–94.

Carvel of Pennsylvania says that Mr. Carvel's town house in Annapolis "stands to-day, with its neighbours, a mournful relic of a glory that is past," while the interior furnishings of these homes have "gone to decorate Mr. Centennial's home in New York or lie with a tag in the window of some curio shop." Anthony Gresham of Groton, Connecticut, hero of Chauncey Hotchkiss's *In Defiance of the King*, provides a footnote to architectural history: "In the days of my greatest activity our house was considered somewhat pretentious, but at this writing (1830) it is looked upon as a fair type of the style known as Colonial, and has fallen from its former prestige."[13] But as in most genealogy, greatest attention is given to the past rather than the present state of the "family." To call attention to the decay of mansions or neighborhoods would introduce a theme of change and development which had no part in these historical romances.

Most of the descriptions of homes and gardens simply revel in the magnificence of it all, many writers romanticizing even the homely details of colonial housekeeping. Lionel Carvel's estate on the Eastern Shore is a central presence in *Richard Carvel*, and the early chapters give a detailed account of the life of young Richard, spent between the estate and the Annapolis town house. *Hugh Wynne* describes gracious living in Old Philadelphia, both in the Wynne home and in that of his aunt Gainor Wynne, who is not a Quaker and thus lives a more worldly life. Central to the plot of *Janice Meredith* is Greenwood, the title character's home near New Brunswick, New Jersey. Phillipse Manor is of similar importance as the principal setting of Robert Neilson Stephens's *Continental Dragoon*.

Humbler homes were described in Amelia E. Barr's two novels of early New York, *A Maid of Old New York* and *The House on Cherry Street*, which show the homes of well-to-do Dutch burghers, whose wives did their own work. The writers presented standard house and room description, giving such details as the contents of the bookshelves and the kind of furniture and pictures found in the rooms, and tended to show happy family scenes related to the decor. In *Hugh Wynne*, for example, Mrs. Wynne takes young Hugh to see the patterns she had traced in the sand of her dining room:

---

[13] Churchill, *Richard Carvel*, p. vii; Chauncey C. Hotchkiss, *In Defiance of the King* (New York: Appleton, 1895), p. 27.

The great room where we took our meals is still clear in my mind. The floor was two inches deep in white sand, in which were carefully traced zigzag lines, with odd patterns in the corners. A bare table of well-rubbed mahogany stood in the middle, with a thin board or two laid on the sand that the table might be set without disturbing the patterns. In the corners were glass-covered buffets, full of silver and Delft ware; and a punch-bowl of Chelsea was on the broad window-ledge, with a silver-mounted cocoanut ladle.[14]

Perhaps no book has more feeling in its descriptions of colonial homes and gardens, though, than *Audrey.* The hero and heroine spend much time in the garden of the hero's estate, Fair View, in tidewater Virginia, and sundials, roses, paved walks, and box hedges are prominent images. *Audrey* was published in 1902, two years after the great success of *To Have and to Hold,* the profits from which Mary Johnston spent building herself a palatial country home in Warm Springs, Virginia. The profits from some other historical romances went into the creation of fine homes, too. Paul Leicester Ford bought a fine city home; Robert Chambers furnished an old home at Broadalbin, New York, with antiques; and Winston Churchill built Harlakenden House at Cornish, New Hampshire. Using the proceeds from the sales of their books, authors built the homes they had described, the homes they had made America's increasingly affluent middle class dream of.

The popular historical novels written for children during this period reflect some of the same ideas that we find in the adult novels and teach lessons in patriotism and good behavior. While Mary Wells Smith published several books about young Puritans, which emphasize the adventures of their lives and show little sympathy for the conservative elders in the stories, most of the popular books for children concern life around the time of the Revolution or slightly after it. None of Amanda Douglas's Little Girl books is set in Puritan New England—not even *A Little Girl in Old Salem*—and Douglas showed scant respect for the old-time religious characters in her stories. In *A Little Girl in Old Boston,* she mildly ridicules old Puritan ways, especially in the character of Mrs. Leverett, writing, "The intangible change to liberalness puzzled her." Mary Smith wrote patronizingly that, "Despite their grimness, there was plenty of human nature in the Puritans" (whatever that means).[15]

[14] Mitchell, *Hugh Wynne,* 1:24–25.
[15] Amanda Douglas, *A Little Girl in Old Boston* (New York: Dodd, Mead, 1898), p. 80; Mary Prudence Wells Smith, *The Young Puritans of Old Hadley* (Boston: Roberts, 1897), p. viii.

The prevailing sentiment in the stories is that bright, cheerful, *worldly* people are the best and the most attractive to the children who are characters in the stories. Religion is little discussed, except to comment on its grimness.

Young heroes are the juvenile images of the heroes of the adult romances, especially the swashbuckling Noah Dare, hero of several of Everett Tomlinson's works. The young heroines are similar to the minxes of the adult works, much given to pretty clothes, spirited skirmishes with other children, and flirtations with grim old uncles. All of the Little Girls, for instance, are similar to one another in character, despite their different backgrounds and locations. The Little Girl books tend to trace the heroine from her arrival in the city—often as an orphan come to live with relatives—until the time of her marriage. And dressing up is important to them. In *A Little Girl in Old Washington*, one of the girls warns a young admirer, " 'Wait until you see me in the gorgeous-ness of a train and top-knot. You will wonder at my dignity. Perhaps you will not even recognize me.' "[16]

Certainly the children's books share the racism and bigotry of the adult novels. Indians are the villains in Mary Smith's stories of the Deerfield massacre and the siege of Hadley. Catholics are unfavorably treated in *A Little Girl in Old Detroit*, in which the mother of our heroine is a religious fanatic who has entered a convent. The church tries to entrap the bright and vibrant young girl, but she is rescued by her father. Unlike the characters in the adult stories, however, those in the children's books are often middle class rather than aristocrats. The life of the past is often described in more detail than in the adult novels, with more emphasis on the way people used to do things rather than on fashion and manners.

Hezekiah Butterworth emphasized historical facts and persons more than the other writers did, while Amanda Douglas often frankly com-pared past ways with those of the present, usually to the detriment of the past. "When people sigh for the good old times they forget the hardships and the inconveniences," she wrote of bathing in the kitchen. Douglas usually ended her books with praise of the modern city, as in this typical passage:

Old Pittsburg did not vanish with the little girl, however. But she went on her way steadily, industriously. The new century came in with great acclaim.

[16]Amanda Douglas, *A Little Girl in Old Washington* (New York: Dodd, Mead, 1900), p. 75.

Shipbuilding prospered. Iron foundries sprang up. The glass works went from the eight pots and the capacity of three boxes at a blowing to double that number, then doubled it again. The primitive structure erected by George Anshuts before the century ended was the progenitor of many others sending their smoke defiantly up in the clear sky. And all along the Monongahela valley as well as in other places the earth gave up its stores of coal as it had given up its stores of iron.

And in 1816 Pittsburg was incorporated as a city and had a mayor and aldermen and her own bank. It was a new Pittsburg then, a hive of human industry, where one business after another gathered and where fortunes were evolved from real work, and labor reaps a rich reward.[17]

This mixture of pleasure in thinking of old ways even as we recognize the superiority of modern American life is generally the same as what we find in the adult novels. "Sitting in the liberal geniality of the nineteenth century's sunset glow," wrote Maurice Thompson, "we insist upon having our grumble at the times and the manners of our generation; but if we had to exchange places, periods and experiences with the people who lived in America through the last quarter of the eighteenth century, there would be good ground for despairing ululations."[18]

In his study of the Revolution as cultural icon, Kammen concluded that Americans have generally regarded the War of Independence as a rite of passage. Traditionally, the rite of passage marks the transition from youth to adulthood; using this model, we can say that the popular novels of 1890–1910 treated the colonial period as the childhood of the successful, productive adult America of the nineteenth century. Childhood is normally romanticized, yet few adults want to return to it. This state of affairs adequately represents the novelists' perspective on the period they were portraying. They looked back on it with pride and pleasure from the superiority of the adult considering the child he has been.

The source of their pride is revealed in their continual emphasis on the social quality of our colonial ancestors. Rather than searching the family tree for the workmanly traits of ambition, initiative, or independence, the novelists demonstrate that America had her colonial aristocracy. An almost direct contrast can be found in the popular twentieth-century

[17] Douglas, _Little Girl in Boston_, p. 80; Amanda Douglas, _A Little Girl in Old Pittsburg_ (New York: Dodd, Mead, 1909), pp. 333–34.
[18] Thompson, _Alice of Old Vincennes_, p. 183.

novels about the frontier experience—mostly the western frontier of the nineteenth century—which emphasize the concepts and person- alities that created modern America. The colonial period as seen in turn-of-the-century novels, however, does not show action so much as situation: our significant colonial ancestors were significant for their social and economic situation, not for character or deeds.

This reading of the colonial experience served its purpose in its time. In the pages of these novels, readers found a spiritual ancestry for liberal religion, patterns for social behavior, comforting reminders of our "racial purity," and delightful glimpses of a sumptuous style of life. The readers of these novels were the same persons who made that "retired" Congre- gational minister Wallace Nutting a rich man by buying his platinum prints of women in colonial costume pouring tea or doing needlework while seated in authentic Windsor chairs in authentic colonial drawing rooms. Devotees of colonial revival fiction hung these pictures on the walls of their little suburban homes where they lived through the chal- lenges of a new century.

Of Cherry Trees and Ladies' Teas: Grant Wood Looks at Colonial America
Karal Ann Marling

The Great Depression should have been a singularly auspicious moment for another colonial revival. This was, after all, an embattled decade in search of the security of a "usable past." "Driven by a pressing need to find answers to the riddles of today," wrote novelist John Dos Passos, "we need to know what kind of firm ground other men, belonging to generations before us, have found to stand on."[1] And so the National Archives rose on Federal Triangle, and the thirties set out to find answers, models, and reassurances in history. FDR reviewed his second inaugural parade from a scale replica of the Hermitage perched on the White House lawn. Lincoln loved and lost Ann Rutledge on Broadway and on the silver screens of Main Street. Jackson and Lincoln were common men writ larger than life in the heyday of the common man; they reminded America that greatness often comes in plain wrappers and prevails against great odds. The New Deal put Monticello on the nickel and built the Jefferson Memorial temple on the Tidal Basin. The Sage of Monticello bore more than a passing resemblance to the Squire of

---

[1] Van Wyck Brooks, "On Creating a Usable Past," *Dial* 64, no. 13 (April 11, 1918): 339; John Dos Passos, *The Ground We Stand On: Some Examples from the History of a Political Creed* (New York: Harcourt, Brace, Jovanovich, 1941), p. 3. The seminal discussion of the "usable past" concept is Alfred Haworth Jones, "The Search for a Usable Past in the New Deal Era," *American Quarterly* 23, no. 4 (December 1971): 710–24.

Hyde Park. Clever men, who could turn "From buying empires / To planting 'taters, / From Declarations / To Trick dumb-waiters," were the national stock-in-trade. The plain folk and the witty had seen America through other crises. The native genius could do no less in the face of this latest calamity.[2]

Desperate reverence for the past contrasts sharply with the attitude of the palmier Republican twenties, when drubbing the Puritans had amounted to a mark of cultural maturity. Van Wyck Brooks introduced the sport of retrospective debunking; William Carlos Williams became its most savage adept. But "where the generation of the twenties wanted to revenge themselves on their fathers, the generation of the thirties needed the comfort of their grandfathers." Discredited Puritanism notwithstanding, the historical origins of America assumed particular importance. Federal muralists, dispatched to hundreds of little post offices from Maine to California, gave local citizens their own slice of the usable past in the form of American genesis icons. Treasury artists painted pictures of the historic moment when a town was planted and its future secured by energetic, capable pioneers who were the very image of their modern-day descendants—folks who could surely lick a depression.[3]

[2] The Archives Building was dedicated in 1937. For the Roosevelt inaugural, see Douglass Adair, "The New Thomas Jefferson" (1946), in Douglass Adair, *Fame and the Founding Fathers*, ed. H. Trevor Colbourn (New York: W. W. Norton, 1974), p. 239. The love story of Lincoln in New Salem dominated three important dramatic manifestations of the Lincoln legend in the thirties. In 1938, the Works Progress Administration's Federal Theater Project (FTP) opened *Prologue to Glory* on Broadway. Later that same year, Raymond Massey brought Robert Sherwood's version of the story—*Abe Lincoln in Illinois*—to Broadway, too. Massey also starred in a film version of the Sherwood play, produced by RKO in the summer of 1939. John Ford's evocative film *Young Mr. Lincoln*, with Henry Fonda in the title role and Pauline Moore as Ann Rutledge, opened that same year. See John O'Connor and Lorraine Brown, eds., *Free, Adult, Uncensored: The Living History of the Federal Theatre Project* (Washington, D.C.: New Republic Books, 1978), esp. pp. 15–16; Alfred Haworth Jones, *Roosevelt's Image Brokers: Poets, Playwrights, and the Use of the Lincoln Symbol*, National University Publications (Port Washington, N.Y.: Kennikat Press, 1974), pp. 35–41, 51; and Peter Bogdanovich, *John Ford* (rev. ed., Berkeley: University of California Press, 1978), pp. 72–73, 134. The FTP's *Prologue to Glory* also played at the New York World's Fair during the summer of 1939. For Jefferson iconography during the New Deal period, see Merrill D. Peterson, *The Jefferson Image in the American Mind* (New York: Oxford University Press, 1960), esp. pp. 420–32. For the quotation, see Rosemary and Stephen Vincent Benét, "Thomas Jefferson," in *A Book of Americans* (New York: Rinehart, 1933), pp. 39–41.

[3] See, for example, William Carlos Williams, *In the American Grain* (1925; reprint ed., New York: New Directions Publishing Co., 1956), esp. p. 142, which mentions "the obscene anecdote [George Washington] told that night in the boat crossing the Dela-

Warren Susman argues that the gala opening of the Williamsburg restoration in 1935 expanded to the national arena what had been a local search for sturdy roots. The tangibility of colonial America guaranteed the survival of an entrepreneurial culture still flourishing on the spot under the auspices of John D. Rockefeller, Jr. Similarly, the mechanized commercial World of Tomorrow that bedazzled visitors to the New York World's Fair of 1939 lay at the feet of a glistening white 65-foot effigy of the greatest colonial leader, the *Pater Patriae*, George Washington (fig. 1). The sight of that colossal Washington of 1939 gave historian James Truslow Adams renewed confidence in the future. "After a century and a half of achievement," he declared, "we need not believe in the prophets of doom."[4]

That the thirties revived the past and used it vigorously in the realms of politics, scholarship, state ceremonial, the fine arts, and popular culture is beyond question. But analysis falls short of revealing why some eras and figures were deemed more usable than others or even that such preferences were expressed at all. We have failed to pin down what, exactly, the thirties wanted and needed from history. Simple reassurance seems too vague a concept to account for such diverse phenomena as John Ford's *Young Mr. Lincoln* and the National Archives and the world's fair effigy of George Washington. Nor does "comfort" fully explain the cultural choice of Williamsburg tract housing over pseudo log cabins in the suburbs, nor does it suggest why the Trylon and Perisphere salt shakers of 1939 were outsold during the 1940 season at the fair by a Toby jug with a streamlined profile that lent George Washington the rakish air of a neocolonial hood ornament (figs. 2, 3).[5]

---

ware," a story considered below. For Williams's view of American history, see Karal Ann Marling, "*My Egypt*: The Irony of the American Dream," *Winterthur Portfolio* 15, no. 1 (Spring 1980): esp. 32–33. For the quotation, see Alfred Kazin, "What Have the 30s Done to Our Literature?" *New York Herald Tribune* (December 31, 1939), Books section, p. 1. For Treasury Department murals of the period, see Edward Bruce and Forbes Watson, *Art in Federal Buildings*, vol. 1 (Washington, D.C.: Art in Federal Buildings, 1939). For "genesis" icons in murals, see Karal Ann Marling, "A Note on New Deal Iconography: Futurology and the Historical Myth," *Prospects* 4 (1979): 420–40.

[4] Warren Susman, Introduction to *Culture and Commitment, 1929–1945*, ed. Warren Susman (New York: George Braziller, 1973), p. 6. The monumental statue on Constitution Mall at the 1939 fair was the work of James Earle Fraser. See James Truslow Adams, "1789–1939: A Nation Rises," *New York Times* (March 5, 1939), sec. 8, p. 7.

[5] These Washington souvenirs were produced and copyrighted by the American Potter in 1940. The trademark on the base of the vessel is, interestingly, superimposed on a relief likeness of the Trylon and Perisphere shakers.

Fig. 1. Cover, *New York Times* (March 5, 1939),
sec. 8. (Collection of the author.)

The solution may lie in artifacts like the various "moderne" Washingtons of the New York World's Fair. As publicity ballyhoo about James Earle Fraser's giant statue mounted, Grant Wood of Iowa began work on his own painted version of Washington in a small downpour of press leaks hinting at a lampoon of the hero of Flushing Meadow (fig. 4). It is not wholly coincidental that Wood unveiled his controversial *Parson Weems's Fable* in New York at the height of the Washington revival of 1939.[6] Nor were Washington and colonial America new themes for

[6]For the dated evolution of the painting over a span of months, see Darrell Garwood, *Artist in Iowa: A Life of Grant Wood* (New York: W. W. Norton, 1944), p. 222; and "Grant Wood Presents Parson Weems," *Art Digest* 14, no. 8 (January 15, 1940): 7.

Fig. 2. Salt shaker set, Trylon and Perisphere, 1939. Plastic; H.
3½″. Inscribed: New York World's Fair. (Collection of the author.)

Wood, albeit his rare canvases treating historical myth and legend occur
at two distinct and widely separate points in a short working life. The
Midnight Ride of Paul Revere (fig. 5) and *Daughters of Revolution* (fig.
6) were painted as Franklin Delano Roosevelt did battle with Herbert
Hoover at the ballot box and as the New Deal took shape in the enclaves
of the Roosevelt brain trust. The *Fable* marks the beginning of World
War II in Europe. Together, then, Wood's history paintings bracket the
life span of the usable past, when national concern turned inward to
focus exclusively upon the economic and spiritual salvation of America.

Fig. 3. George Washington Toby jug, 1940. Earthenware with ivory glaze; H. 4½". Inscribed on bottom (over relief of Trylon and Perisphere): The American Potter, N.Y. World Fair, 1940. (Collection of the author.)

Although Wood is labeled a regionalist, these works abandon pigs-and-chickens chauvinism to address more broadly national topics. Indeed, his topics might legitimately be called contemporary issues, for the canvases enjoyed enormous popularity in their day. As a theorist, Wood believed that "a work which does not make contact with the public is lost."[7] A mass public (excluding the critical establishment, which had little interest in corn-fed aesthetics) either liked these pictures hugely or hated them passionately. People who liked them responded with belly

[7] Grant Wood, as quoted in Joan Liffring-Zug and John Zug, eds., in cooperation with Nan Wood Graham, *This is Grant Wood Country* (Davenport, Iowa: Davenport Municipal Art Gallery, 1977), p. 1.

Fig. 4. Grant Wood, *Parson Weems's Fable*, 1939. Oil on canvas; H.
38⅜", W. 50⅛". (Amon Carter Museum, Fort Worth.)

laughs, eruptions of mirth lost on the audience of today to whom they
seem wry or mildly funny in ways that elude precise definition. In contrast, Wood's enemies at one time foamed when his titles were mentioned, whereas nowadays even the Daughters of the American Revolution
(DAR) themselves might use his backhanded tribute in an advertising
campaign.

Time has robbed the paintings of the snappy contemporaneity characteristic of all very good jokes. Because Wood grounded his art in
popular culture—because he succeeded in making electric contact with
the public of 1931, 1932, and 1939—his usable and much-used past
has become puzzling, even opaque. For this reason, close scrutiny of a
handful of paintings by Grant Wood provides an excellent starting point

Fig. 5. Grant Wood, *Midnight Ride of Paul Revere*, 1931. Oil on composition board; H. 30″, W. 40″. (Metropolitan Museum of Art.)

for cracking the cultural code of the thirties and for recapturing an evanescent moment when George Washington and colonial America were, in fact, pressing and deeply meaningful issues to the artist and to the bygone society he delighted and enraged.

Art historians have routinely connected the 1932 *Daughters of Revolution* to Wood's personal squabble with the local chapter of the DAR, which had objected to his plan to execute in Germany, homeland of the enemy, a World War I memorial window for the Veterans' Memorial Building in Cedar Rapids. With this incident as his proximate inspiration, Wood did not fail to capitalize on the wrath of patriotic societies when he discussed the painting in retrospect. "They could ladle it out," he chortled. "I thought I'd see if they could take it." What passed unno-

Fig. 6. Grant Wood, *Daughters of Revolution*, 1932. Oil on masonite panel; H. 20″, W. 40″. (Cincinnati Art Museum, Edwin and Virginia Irwin Memorial Fund.)

ticed is the contemporary significance of the steel engraving in the background of the scene. It is, of course, a print after Emanuel Leutze's *Washington Crossing the Delaware*, "mottled grey with age." This American holy card seems to suggest both the textbook traditions the Daughters guard and the authentic Revolutionary spirit they have put firmly behind them. But the specific choice of this image of Washington to make the point was anchored in events of 1932—in a government-sponsored celebration of Washington's birth so extravagant and ubiquitous that viewers with little stake in the DAR or Wood's problems with it could grasp the notion of an impertinent parody afoot. The work was funny in 1932 because Wood was satirizing a Washington revival run amok.[8]

[8] Matthew Baigell is typical of art historians who cite the DAR squabble; see Matthew Baigell, "Grant Wood Revisited," *Art Journal* 26, no. 2 (Winter 1967): 119–20. Wood quoted in Garwood, *Artist in Iowa*, p. 138. James Dennis notes that the work was painted "in the election year of 1932" but detects no further contemporary resonance in the use of the Leutze Washington imagery (James M. Dennis, *Grant Wood: A Study in American Art and Culture* [New York: Viking Press, 1975], p. 110). Louis Untermeyer offered this interpretation: "That picture—*Daughters of Revolution*—is a complete Sinclair Lewis novel. Why the very words 'communism' or 'revolution' make the D.A.R.'s froth at the

Created under Calvin Coolidge in 1926 and retired in a mad cre-
scendo of activity under Hoover between February 22 and Thanksgiving
Day of 1932, the United States George Washington Bicentennial Commission was the brainchild and passion of Rep. Sol Bloom of New York,
a renegade Tammany Democrat whose fistfights on the House floor
were almost as legendary as his devotion to George Washington. A former "hootchy-kootchy inventor . . . and backer of the first ferris wheel,"
Bloom achieved awesome results as director of these Republican revels:
a modest selection of the pageants, poems, sermons, speeches, atlases,
and stray pamphlets he generated fill four massive volumes belatedly
issued (with a noteworthy absence of fanfare) under the new Roosevelt
administration. Bloom set a radio antenna atop the Washington Monument for official commission broadcasts. He cajoled foreign nations
into naming various things after the first president. By proclamation of
the Reichstag, a grim byway in Hamburg became Washingtonstrasse
and a desolate concrete overpass near Turin carried the Via Washington. Using costume-pattern books supplied by Bloom, the embassy staff
in Tokyo mounted a George-and-Martha playlet; since there were not
enough meaty roles to go around, several young military attachés were
forced to impersonate the Mount Vernon house slaves in blackface. In
Saigon, children attired as Marianne—the symbol of France—and George
Washington consecrated an authorized bronze replica of the Houdon
bust at Mount Vernon, made by Gorham Manufacturing Company
(fig. 7).[9]

---

mouth. And there they are, praising Washington—Washington, the revolutionist" (quoted
in Garwood, *Artist in Iowa*, p. 137). Barbara Groseclose suggests that the painting of
1851 may have been intended to stir up American support for the waning 1848 revolution
in Leutze's German homeland (Barbara S. Groseclose, *Emanuel Leutze, 1816–1868:
Freedom Is the Only King* [Washington, D.C.: Smithsonian Institution Press, 1975], p.
40). It is probable that Wood was making a deliberate double joke: on the "Martha Washington Teas" that figured in DAR ceremonial, and on the German origin of the Leutze
icon, since his own problems with the stained-glass window and the DAR involved his
use of German artisans.
   [9]For Sol Bloom, see Marshall W. Fishwick, *American Heroes, Myth and Reality*
(Washington, D.C.: Public Affairs Press, 1954), pp. 49–50. See also *The History of the
George Washington Bicentennial Celebration*, 4 vols. (Washington, D.C.: United States
George Washington Bicentennial Commission, 1932). For some of the odder foreign
tributes to Washington, see *History of the Celebration*, 4:33, 93–94, 102–3, 155, 168,
209, 331, 533. Four-inch-tall cast-iron unauthorized miniature imitations of Gorham
Manufacturing Company's "official" bronze bust were issued by Almar Metal Arts of

The children and the official commission bust define the thrust of the 1932 celebration. The success of the program hinged on public education, on reestablishing the primacy of fact. "To do this," Bloom declared, "Washington and his generation must be stripped of all the myth and legend which have been accumulated for nearly two centuries and their sterling human qualities allowed to appear." Hence the national search by a panel of commission experts for a pure image of Washington settled on the Houdon bust as the official effigy because, "modelled from the living figure of Washington, it has every guarantee of absolute accuracy."[10]

Bloom was determined to put an accurate likeness of the Father of His Country in a million American schoolrooms. But, if he insisted on the Houdon statue, the salutary influence of which was demonstrated in a commission poster by Norman Rockwell, his $338,000 Congressional appropriation could never be stretched far enough to accomplish that mission (fig. 8). The necessary two-dimensional alternative was chosen by popular demand. By November 24, 1932, a full-color poster-size reproduction of Gilbert Stuart's Athenaeum portrait, duly framed in fumed oak, blinked down upon every schoolchild in the continental United States, its territories and possessions. Adults got the message with their mail: the green one-cent bicentennial stamp showed the Houdon bust, and the popular red two-cent stamp featured the Stuart. The nation, like the little boy in the best-known of the bicentennial posters, was about to confront a demythologized Washington directly (fig. 9). Enough of cardboard hatchet drills at school assemblies. Enough of the cherry-tree Washington of Parson Weems's perfidious "yarn," against which Bloom and his minions fulminated loudly. Bloom's "Questions and Answers Pertaining to the Life and Times of George Washington" asked, "Who originated the Washington cherry tree story?" and answered: "It was originated by the Reverend Mason Locke Weems, in his 'Life of George Washington.' It is interesting to note that this

---

Point Marion, Pa. Below the bust proper is the legend: George Washington, 1732, 1932. For the selection of the Gorham edition of the Houdon bust, see "Houdon Bust Official Washington Portrait," in *Special News Releases Relating to the Life and Time of George Washington, as Prepared and Issued by the United States George Washington Bicentennial Commission*, vol. 1 (Washington, D.C.: Government Printing Office, 1932), p. 72.

[10] *Special News Releases*, 1:50, 72.

Fig. 7. Children costumed as the French national symbol, Marianne, and as George Washington dedicating bronze bust of George Washington (made by Gorham Manufacturing Co.). Saigon, French Indochina, 1932. (Photo, United States George Washington Bicentennial Commission.)

yarn did not appear in the first few editions, but was added in a later edition (5th edition, printed in 1806). No evidence to prove this story has been found. In writing this work, Weems gave full play to his imagination without very much regard for historical facts, even acknowledging that he did this for moral purposes." It was time for the nation to meet the real George Washington, distinguished from the generation

Fig. 8. Norman Rockwell, United States George
Washington Bicentennial Commission poster, 1932.
Lithograph in color. (Collection of the author.)

of present-day exemplars of American commercial culture only by his
having been cast in bronze.[11]

The drive to suppress myth and humanize a Washington grown "rigid
with congealed virtue" coincided with the establishment of the com-

[11] *Special News Releases*, 1:5, 14. Congress authorized 750,000 reproductions of the
Stuart portrait, but it is likely that the indefatigable Bloom indeed printed the million he
wanted. For the projected classroom use of a plaster copy of the Houdon bust, see *Hand-
book of the George Washington Appreciation Course for Teachers and Students for the
Two Hundredth Anniversary Celebration, 1732–1932* (Washington, D.C.: United States

mission in 1926. It took two wildly divergent courses. On one side were ranged such popular hard-boiled biographers as Rupert Hughes and W. E. Woodward (the man who coined the verb *to debunk*) along with a smattering of intellectuals, like William Carlos Williams. The updated Washington they portrayed told "obscene anecdote[s]" while crossing the Delaware. He kept a string of Loyalist mistresses stashed in Jersey and lusted after washerwomen. He was, in fact, a sheikh, a male flapper, the heartthrob of colonial America. Passionately in love with his best friend's wife—the piquant Sally Fairfax—he pursued her in secret, wrote her steamy letters until the day he died, having married Martha only for her money. This he did because, in the final analysis, George Washington was an embryonic George Babbitt, "a typical financial magnate" cursed with a modern "business mind."[12]

George Washington Bicentennial Commission, 1931), p. v. For the significance of special postal issues, with emphasis on depictions of the Revolutionary period, see David Curtis Skaggs, "Postage Stamps as Icons," in *Icons of America*, ed. Ray B. Browne and Marshall Fishwick (Bowling Green, Ohio: Popular Press, Bowling Green State University, 1978), pp. 198–208. Skaggs correctly notes that the Washington bicentennial stamps can be examined in any recent edition of the *Scott Standard Postage Stamp Catalogue*. The poster illustrated in figure 9, a color lithograph after a design by Henry Hintermeister, who provided the commission with many illustrations, was copyrighted by Bloom and seems to have been supplied to many institutions in an oak frame, protected by glass. See Rebecca Keim and Anedith Nash, *Contact: American Art and Culture, 1919–1939* (Minneapolis: University Gallery, University of Minnesota, 1981), p. 43. For a typical school assembly program using cardboard hatchets, see Joseph C. Sindelar, ed., *Washington Day Entertainments, Recitations, Plays, Dialogues, Drills, Tableaux, Pantomimes, Quotations, Songs, Tributes, Stories, Facts* (Chicago: Teachers' Supply Bureau, 1910), pp. 113–16, a precommission volume. A "Colonial Dames' Tea Party," with a costumed "Martha Washington" as hostess, is recommended "for eight girls of the intermediate grades" (Sindelar, *Washington Day*, p. 117). For debunking of the cherry-tree fable, see Sol Bloom, "Questions and Answers Pertaining to the Life and Times of George Washington," in *History of the Celebration*, 3:687.

[12] The phrase "rigid with congealed virtue" was used in Owen Wister, *The Seven Ages of Washington: A Biography* (New York: Macmillan Co., 1907), p. 3. A thumbnail biography of Woodward is provided in Dixon Wecter, *The Hero in America: A Chronicle of Hero-Worship* (Ann Arbor: University of Michigan Press, 1963), p. 438. For Williams, see note 3. For sexual exploits, see John C. Fitzgerald, *The George Washington Scandals* (Alexandria, Va.: Washington Society of Alexandria, 1929), esp. p. 2. Fitzgerald wrote his book with the pious intention of refuting scurrilous Tory pamphlets and plays about the rebel commander in chief. For Sally Fairfax, see W. E. Woodward, *George Washington: The Image and the Man* (1926; reprint ed., Garden City, N.Y.: Garden City Publishing Co., 1942), pp. 99–101. Woodward's speculations about Washington's purported romance with Fairfax and about the attraction of Martha's wealth come verbatim from Eugene E. Prussing, *George Washington in Love and Otherwise* (Chicago: Pascal

Fig. 9. Henry Hintermeister, United States George
Washington Bicentennial Commission poster, 1932.
Lithograph in color. (Collection of the author.)

Questioned about the mania for Washington debunkery, Calvin
Coolidge glanced out the window of the Oval Office and muttered,
"Well, I see the Monument is still there." Yet the normally silent Cal
revived the custom of Washington's Birthday oratory to present a coun-

Covici, 1925), esp. pp. 15–33. See also Rupert Hughes, *George Washington: The Human
Being and the Hero, 1732–1762,* vol. 1 (New York: William Morrow, 1926), esp. pp.
176–203, 402–17. For Washington as "a typical financial magnate," see Woodward,
George Washington, p. 90. The high-water mark of this characterization is Halsted L.
Ritter, *Washington as a Business Man* (New York: Sears Publishing Co., 1931), with
Introduction by Albert Bushnell Hart, Bloom's chief factotum and "official" historian of
the commission. The book, says Hart, is an attempt to counter the romantic image of
"the boy who chopped down the cherry tree."

tervailing history lesson to Congress and used the commission as an instrument to combat heresy. The Washington manufactured by successive Republican presidents was also humanized in a 1920s fashion as a modern businessman-hero associated with exceedingly positive values. Coolidge called him "the first commercial American" and enumerated his greatest achievements thus: Washington managed his estate "in a thoroughly businesslike manner," kept "a very careful set of books," and ever stayed "on the lookout for sound investments."[13]

Hoover attacked unseemly "humanizing" of Washington in his 1932 Washington's Birthday address, perhaps recalling in horror that Bernie Babcock's torrid romance of 1932, *The Heart of George Washington, a Simple Story of Great Love,* had been dedicated to himself. Both Hoover and Washington, Babcock gushed, "each in his own way, had to learn that in affairs of love and labor . . . Human Nature must give way to Destiny." In that same address, however, Hoover waxed poetic about Washington's business acumen in establishing "the nonexistent credit of an insolvent infant nation" and lauded his practical accomplishments as an administrator and surveyor. Bertrand H. Snell, the keynote speaker at the 1932 Republican convention, caught Hoover's sly innuendo and expatiated on Washington the businessman-engineer, who "solved stupendous and vexatious problems for the benefit of mankind," as would, of course, "Herbert Hoover, the engineer President of the United States," if reelected by a beneficent Destiny.[14]

The implicit equation between Hoover—the Great Engineer—and the bicentennial Washington ultimately garnered few votes, but may have some bearing on a strange Grant Wood painting. *The Birthplace of Herbert Hoover* (fig. 10) was executed in 1931 at the behest of local businessmen who intended to present it to the president during his campaign swing through his hometown of West Branch, Iowa. The debunkers had extended their rude remarks to cover Wakefield, Washington's birthplace on Pope's Creek in Virginia. Described by one wit as a "crazy

---

[13] Calvin Coolidge quoted in Wecter, *Hero in America,* p. 144; the Washington's Birthday speech is quoted at length as a bona fide historical source in Sol Bloom, "Washington the Business Man," Honor to Washington pamphlet series, no. 12, in *History of the Celebration,* 1:144.

[14] Bernie Babcock, *The Heart of George Washington: A Simple Story of Great Love* (Philadelphia: J. B. Lippincott Co., 1932), p. 7; "Address of Herbert Hoover, President of the United States, Delivered at a Joint Session of Congress, February 22, 1932," in *History of the Celebration,* 2:12; Bertrand H. Snell quoted in Charles A. Beard and Mary R. Beard, *America in Midpassage,* vol. 3 (New York: Macmillan Co., 1939), p. 125.

Fig. 10. Grant Wood, *The Birthplace of Herbert Hoover*, 1931. Oil on composition board; H. 29⅝″, W. 39¾″. (Minneapolis Institute of Arts and Des Moines Art Center.)

structure of undressed boards," the house had long since burned down, and another wag took malicious pleasure in noting that an obelisk erected to mark the spot had mistakenly been placed over the plantation outhouse. Fanciful illustrations of Wakefield, showing a fairy-tale cottage, punctuated the Washington bicentennial literature: Bloom commissioned an official pageant entitled *Wakefield, a Folk Masque of America*, starring a symbolic genius loci. With the assistance of technicians from Colonial Williamsburg and a $50,000 gift from the federal government, a red-brick Wakefield was built de novo in 1931 at a discreet distance from the obelisk.[15]

[15] For the genesis of *The Birthplace of Herbert Hoover*, see Garwood, *Artist in Iowa*, p. 130; and Dennis, *Grant Wood*, pp. 114–16. For the debunkers, see Woodward, *George*

Some commentators feel that Wood's painting mocks the log-cabin legend and the obligatory humble origins of political figures.[16] There is some support for this view in the preliminary cartoon (fig. 11). At the lower left, Wood inserted a vignette showing the original Hoover cabin, an unprepossessing shack foiled off against the ample dwelling which had swallowed it whole. The finished painting has another point to make, however. A gesticulating tour guide—the prototype for the neo-colonial Parson Weems in Wood's 1939 Washington picture—directs attention to a preternaturally tidy and prosperous complex. This is an Iowa Williamsburg, the bicentennial Wakefield—a manufactured, modernized birthplace mythos. The synthetic history cranked out by the bicentennial commission, laundered and cosmetized for popular consumption, is Wood's target, even as the title of the painting evokes longing for the rude legends so rudely displaced by official fiat.

Wood, for his part, never warmed to Hoover and went on to become a fervent New Dealer. Nevertheless, he liked his jibe at tailor-made history well enough to revive it in *Parson Weems's Fable*. The spanking-new star-spangled Washington manse in that painting is Wood's own 1858 house at 1142 East Court Street in Iowa City, the new town show-place, which he had just rebuilt down to the last green shutter on the basis of his idea of how Iowa's pioneer past ought to have looked but of course never really did (fig. 12). Herbert Hoover proved less than high-minded about myths concerning himself: he rejected Wood's picture because the Great Engineer's lowly cabin—obligatory in an election year—was obscured from public view.[17]

Washington, p. 21; and Hughes, *George Washington*, 1:17. The official pageant: Percy MacKaye, *Wakefield, a Folk-Masque of America, Being a Midwinter Night's Dream of the Birth of Washington, Designed and Written for the United States Commission for the Celebration of the Two-Hundredth Anniversary of the Birth of George Washington* (Washington, D.C.: United States George Washington Bicentennial Commission, 1932). For MacKaye's commission, see *Special News Releases*, 1:57. For the restoration of Wakefield, see *Special News Releases*, 1:5, and esp. 1:85–87.

[16] See, for example, Dennis, *Grant Wood*, p. 114.

[17] The restoration of the Iowa City house, with its frieze of stars, is described in Garwood, *Artist in Iowa*, pp. 193, 200, and is illustrated in Liffring-Zug and Zug, *Grant Wood Country*, p. 56. See also Park Rinard, "Grant Wood Restores an Heritage of Charm," *Our Home*, no. 2 (1939): 16–17. The comments of the *Cedar Rapids Gazette* on the restoration work are quoted in Hazel E. Brown, *Grant Wood and Marvin Cone: Artists of an Era* (Ames: Iowa State University Press, 1972), p. 82. The artist's sister, Nan Wood, explained the Hoover rejection in a 1975 interview quoted in Dennis, *Grant Wood*, p. 115.

Fig. 11. Grant Wood, sketch for *The Birthplace of Herbert Hoover*, 1931. Chalk and pencil on paper; H. 39⅜", W. 29⅜". From James M. Dennis, *Grant Wood: A Study in American Art and Culture* (New York: Viking Press, 1975), p. 115.

Legend, reality, and the usable intermingling of past and present in the popular culture of the early thirties dominate the *Midnight Ride of Paul Revere* of 1931, a painting that serves as a reprise of *The Birthplace of Herbert Hoover* and a prelude to *Daughters of Revolution*. As the humor of *Daughters of Revolution* would depend on the jolt of recognizing the Leutze icon, a picture and a legend everybody knew, so *Midnight Ride* seized upon Longfellow's poem—"The Landlord's Tale" from *Tales of a Wayside Inn*—a ditty that clip-clopped through the memory of anyone who had survived the third grade. "Hardly a man is now alive / Who remembers that famous day and year" became, to the

Fig. 12. Grant Wood house, 1142 East Court Street, Iowa City, Iowa. From Joan Liffring-Zug and John Zug, eds., *This is Grant Wood Country* (Davenport, Iowa: Davenport Municipal Art Gallery, 1977), p. 56.

schoolchildren of several generations, an ironic untruth. And it is precisely the geography of the schoolchild's imagination that unfolds in the painting: in the singsong rhythms of a hilly roadway swaying past Medford, in the rocking horse Wood substituted for Revere's steed "flying fearless and fleet," in the Christmas window setting, miniaturized to toy-town scale by the angle of vision.[18]

Himself a modern-day Parson Weems, Wood recreated the historical sensibility of a dreamy child playing with lead soldiers on a pillowed quilt. Wood's national lullaby presented itself wreathed in the tender smiles of the nursery; he gave the viewer access to a sweet legendary realm which the modern adult could still remember and his modern child might still be able to inhabit—if the Sol Blooms of America went down to defeat. The legend is a contemporary psychic phenomenon.

[18] Thomas Byrom, Introduction to *Longfellow Poems* (New York: E. P. Dutton, 1970), pp. 393–95. A 1971 interview with Arnold Pyle is cited as Dennis's authority for the statement that Wood based the Revere image on a borrowed rocking horse (Dennis, *Grant Wood*, p. 109). Garwood says that Wood borrowed it from a Cedar Rapids family (Garwood, *Artist in Iowa*, p. 130).

Yet insofar as Grant Wood's New England landscape is factual, it is not the world of Paul Revere. The dollhouses are flooded with electric lights. The road is a seamless ribbon of concrete. The time is 1931. The scene is a pageant, a masque, a dream—pure make-believe. Behind the smiling mask of childhood Wood wears so lightly leers Peck's Bad Boy or the village atheist, who brings his audience face to face with the compelling truth of a lovely lie, daring the viewer to choose the hard adult realities of a modern present over the potent childlike fantasies slumbering in his heart. This is the choice Wood was to offer once more in 1939—the choice between the realism of Washington-the-businessman, embalmed in the bicentennial commission Stuart posters and then resuscitated for the world's fair, and the charming Washington of children's legends, a "St. George . . . moving through an orchard of ever-blooming cherry trees."[19] The artist preferred the legend spun for the schoolchild, who was already being indoctrinated into clear-eyed orthodoxy by the relentless Sol Bloom. Hence Wood could not resist challenging a grown-up America to suspend the disbelief he invited, defying the nation to make a guilty retreat into the sentimental morass of legend and magic.

Excepting perhaps the cherry-tree fable, no legend was more thoroughly trounced in 1932 than Leutze's rendition of Christmas night 1776. It led the list of damnable errors dismissed in the corrective catechism of "Questions and Answers Pertaining to the Life and Times of George Washington":

Q. Is the Leutze picture of George Washington Crossing the Delaware in the Metropolitan Museum of Art in New York, authentic?
A. This picture is not authentic because it shows the American flag which was not adopted until the following year. Also, it shows Washington standing in the boat. While there is no evidence available to prove that Washington did not stand in the boat, it is much more likely that he was seated.[20]

Even if the Leutze scene had not automatically raised the specter of "the obscene anecdote he told that night in the boat" and a related body of stories of Washington's immorality still "being bandied about in clubs," endorsed by "a well-known clergyman" and "given further currency"

---

[19] Henry Van Dyck, *The Americanism of Washington* (New York: Harper & Bros., 1906), p. 2; the comment was not meant as a compliment to Weems.

[20] Bloom, "Questions and Answers," p. 660. See also Wecter, *Hero in America*, p. 108.

by a United States senator "claiming special knowledge on the subject," the tableau would have failed to meet modern standards of authenticity. Captains of industry did not stand up in rowboats; nor did smart Kiwanians—and Bloom had just assured a group of them that Washington was "our kind of man. If George Washington were alive today . . . he would be a proud member of such a splendid group."[21]

Sol Bloom's attack on the authenticity of the cherished Leutze icon— an attack made in the name of *true* reverence—provided as fertile a field for satire as those smutty George Washington stories. Grant Wood painted *Daughters of Revolution* in parody of that combative spirit of truth-telling, although his immediate target was the institutions that guarded America's symbolic past. It is important to realize that Wood selected this particular icon—a beloved image of the hero, under heavy fire in 1932 from George Washington's bureaucratic custodians—in preference to a wide range of other pictorial symbols which could have served him well had his goal been a straightforward contrast between the glorious heritage of the nation and Iowa's perverters of that "democratic birthright."[22] As Wood organized his painting, much of the Leutze composition is hidden from view. The top of the image is radically cropped. The flanks are neatly covered by the heads of two of the women. Thus Washington's reckless marine posturing is spotlighted with some care; the error Bloom abhorred is exalted.

And by bringing his head to the very top of the canvas, Wood makes the hero and his renowned-in-history pose the axis about which the picture revolves both spatially and spiritually. In effect, Wood makes

[21] Paul Leicester Ford, *The True George Washington* (Philadelphia: J. B. Lippincott Co., 1896), p. 105—a book frequently cited in the bicentennial literature; Sol Bloom, "Washington the Every Day Man" (Address delivered before the Kiwanis Club and other civic groups, at Wilkes-Barre, Pa., June 30, 1932), as quoted in "Selected George Washington Bicentennial Addresses Delivered by Hon. Sol Bloom," in *History of the Celebration*, 2:153–55. Statements like Bloom's reflect popular adoration of the business leader in the twenties through successive Republican administrations. Bruce Barton's biography of Christ, *The Man Nobody Knows: A Discovery of Jesus* (Indianapolis: Bobbs-Merrill, 1925), was the nonfiction best-seller of 1925 and 1926: if Jesus could be worshipped as a successful businessman and a club joiner, why not George Washington? See Charles R. Hearn, *The American Dream in the Great Depression* (Westport, Conn.: Greenwood Press, 1977), p. 27. Barton's book was published in 1924, and Eugene Prussing took the same approach in several studies of George Washington as a "captain of industry," published in magazine and book form between 1921 and 1925. See, for example, Prussing, Preface to *Washington in Love*, listing Prussing's contributions to *Scribner's*.

[22] Baigell, "Grant Wood Revisited," p. 120.

popular legend dominate reality, neatly reversing the drive of the bicentennial crusade. Authentic facts—the carefully delineated, full-color figures in the foreground—are tested against enduring myth and found wanting in 1932, in the midst of a lavishly publicized debate over the very issue of fact versus myth.

It is also tempting to believe that Grant Wood, like William Carlos Williams, had heard a story or two about Washington's smutty remarks on the Delaware. Isolating the standing hero meant zeroing in on Washington's splayed legs. He is not, therefore, the foggy old gentleman of the canonical Stuart portrait, of whom Gertrude Stein could remark with some justice in 1931, "She is very sleepy, George Washington."[23] The Stuart portrait embedded in *Parson Weems's Fable* of 1939 shows that, in the world of legend, the child is the tardy offspring of the man he would become. Sol Bloom's schoolroom Stuart, the official and accurate 1932 poster, also figures here, apparently, but as the prototype for the white-haired Daughter on the far left, with the letter-box mouth and the puffy pink face. The Washington Wood enshrines at the center of the painting is a vigorous, virile man, a plausible Father of His Country, rendered all the more masculine by the polite tea party he is forced to attend. In his prime, Washington may well have been, as Bloom insisted, the sort of fellow to relish a 1932 Kiwanis Club meeting. He is decidedly out of place, however, in the modern-day company Wood provides for him.

Indeed, Wood's emphasis on the lavender-and-old-lace domesticity of the Daughters, with their tatted collars, print frocks, and blue-willow china, ultimately makes the painting a good deal funnier than it would seem at first glance. Wood's George Washington is a macho bull in a feminine china shop. As the men's club legends of Washington's "obscene anecdote" filter through the dainty, ladies-only atmosphere of genteel rectitude, one laugh—an early guffaw—is on the ladies. But the bigger laugh is on the supposedly authentic bicentennial Washington of 1932, tricked out in a flowered housedress and planted smugly before his truer, mythic self.

Because he was a popular painter, drawing upon popular and topical themes, Wood expected people to be able to laugh at his paintings. Once the shock had worn off, both New Yorkers and Wood's stolid

[23] Gertrude Stein, *Four in America* (New Haven: Yale University Press, 1947), p. 163.

Midwest neighbors found themselves chuckling at the smug little Geor-
gie of 1939, poised on a velvety lawn in an ideal Iowa City, turning his
authentic schoolroom face to his father and chirping, "Pa, you know I
can't tell a lie. I did cut it with my hatchet."[24] Yet, like the smiling
Parson Weems in the foreground, Wood also expected people to recognize a distinction between their world and the mythic background
behind the curtain and to laugh with him as he pondered the moral of
the story—the virtues of honesty and truth-telling.

Wood's colonial series offers an extended dialogue with—and argu-

[24] *Daughters of Revolution* was an extremely popular attraction when it was displayed
at the Chicago Century of Progress exposition of 1933; postcard reproductions sold briskly.
See Garwood, *Artist in Iowa*, p. 138. For the quotation from the fable, see Mason Weems,
A History of the Life and Death, Virtues and Exploits of General George Washington, ed.
Mark Van Doren (New York: Macy-Masius Publishers, 1927), p. 24.
  Wood readily enough admitted that "one of the things about the old Colonial portraits
that has always amused me is the device of having a person in the foreground holding
back a curtain from, or pointing at, a scene within a scene. This, it seemed to me, was a
very appropriate way to get Parson Weems into this particular painting" ("Wood Presents
Weems," p. 7). A likely specific prototype is Charles Willson Peale's self-portrait of 1822,
The Artist in His Museum (Pennsylvania Academy of the Fine Arts, Philadelphia), in
which Peale, like Wood, presents a pageant or a public show behind a curtain. Dennis
insists that Wood used a friend, Prof. John E. Briggs of the University of Iowa, as the
model for the parson's face (Dennis, *Grant Wood*, p. 113). Virginia Parks Morton, in a
statement made in 1977, also cites Briggs and adds that her nine-year-old son, James
Parks Morton, and her husband, Prof. Vance Morton, posed for George and Augustine
Washington (Liffring-Zug and Zug, *Grant Wood Country*, p. 56). While it is clear that
his friends and neighbors served as anatomical models for the bodies, there is a striking
likeness between the face of Weems, as Wood painted it, and the portrait of the parson
that served as the frontispiece for two biographies; see Lawrence C. Wroth, *Parson Weems,
a Biographical and Critical Study* (Baltimore: Eichelberger Book Co., 1911); and Harold
Kellock, *Parson Weems of the Cherry Tree, Being a Short Account of the Eventful Life of
the Reverend M. L. Weems, Author of Many Books and Tracts, Itinerant Pedlar of Divers
Volumes of Merit: Preacher of Vigour and Much Renown and First Biographer of G.
Washington* (New York: Century Co., 1928).
  Garwood, *Artist in Iowa*, pp. 223–26, traces but does not explain an evolution in
Wood's attitude toward his theme. At the outset, the work was to be an attack on Washington and his "smug" behavior, but Weems, the storyteller, had become the focus by
the time the picture was finished. Indeed, Wood planned to use the picture as the starting
point for a series recording "historic bits of American folklore" ("Wood Presents Weems,"
p. 7). It is, therefore, highly plausible to assume that Wood read Kellock's *Parson Weems*
while researching his topic and used the illustration in the book as the model for Weems's
head and face. Kellock was the only popular writer of the period (indeed, the *only* writer
of the period) to give the poor parson his due, treating him as a major folklorist and
appraising his contribution to American myth favorably in those terms. In other words,
Kellock resisted the bicentennial practice of judging tales and stories against supposed
"facts."

ment against—a species of usable history which predates the New Deal, a factual past that the twenties and not the thirties fashioned to meet a specific set of needs. The usable past constructed under Coolidge and Hoover was obsessed with honesty: legends were not good enough for a mature nation, a hard-nosed commercial race. Myths were children's tales, but they were bad for modern children, the businessmen of tomorrow. Authentic portraits and debunkery were allied expressions of a drive to iron the mythical wrinkles out of history and embroider a seamless tapestry of time in which 1932 and 1738 were very much the same. In this realm of pragmatic normalcy Washington was a meticulous accountant. He attended Kiwanis meetings and stood about in Iowa front yards. The *exemplum virtutis* descended from the heights of Mount Rushmore to become a mirror image of the facts and events and values of modern-day America. The world's fair statue, which prompted Wood to take up the Washington theme again after a long hiatus, was an anachronism, a pallid plaster ghost of the Practical Businessman Washington of the regime of the Great Engineer Herbert Hoover. As commercial America revived in the exposition at Flushing, so the commercial Washington rose to serve as the guardian angel of the postdepression business of tomorrow.

From the outset, Wood's history paintings quibbled with a past purged of the charm of distance, the veil of myth that hung between Weems and his fable. Legend possessed a compelling truth fact could neither approximate nor deny. Thus Wood's legendary paintings define a new realism. They define a kind of New Deal history tinged with a poignant awareness that the present and the past are *not* identical. The boy Washington and the hero of the Delaware are not blighted by modern values proved fallacious by the depression. Theirs is a different world; and if long-ago seems funny to modern eyes, it is because the world of legend is closed to those who lack the courage to become children again. It is closed to those who cannot become naive believers in the lovely dreams that soften a brutal present and beckon toward a smiling future.

The child within the grown-up Grant Wood chooses to take his seat at the front of the classroom, just beneath Sol Bloom's "authentic" Washington in its oaken frame. But, seated there, he recites this poem with a rueful grin when his turn is called:

George Washington, though great was he,
Was once a little boy like me.
And when a little lad like me,
They say, he chopped a cherry tree.
But when his father came to see,
He stood erect and brave, like—me!
And told the truth about that tree;
He wasn't a coward—oh, no, not he!
Now I've met folks and so have you
Who say this story is not true.
It makes no difference what they claim
The moral of it is the same.
And we boys know this teaching well
To follow it we plan.
If you've done wrong, don't fear to tell.
Own up like a man![25]

---

[25] "The Hatchet," in *Complete George Washington Anniversary Programs, for Every School Grade: New Ways to Honor the Father of Our Country*, comp. and ed. Alma Laird (New York: Noble and Noble, 1931), p. 19. Directions for performing "The Hatchet" call for recitation of the first seven couplets by "seven little boys," each carrying a hatchet. ("The hatchets may be made out of pasteboard.") The final two lines were to be spoken in unison. This poem is one of the few cherry-tree activities for children to survive Bloom's great purge of legends.

Arthurdale: A Social Experiment in the 1930s
Jeanne S. Rymer

Out of a miserable and depressed coal-mining community in Monongalia County, West Virginia, evolved a finely crafted line of furniture which has become known as Arthurdale. Its design origins were colonial, hill country, and Quaker; its political origins were the social programs of the first Roosevelt administration of the early 1930s.

It was in the autumn of 1932, during the worst of the Great Depression and just after Franklin Delano Roosevelt's inauguration, that First Lady Eleanor Roosevelt visited Scott's Run near Morgantown, West Virginia. The depression had hit this coal-rich region hard, closing mines and forcing men who depended on company stores, houses, and paychecks onto the dole. Hopelessness had been bred by the miners' exclusive ties to one way of life; they lacked alternative skills. Conditions of unrest, brawling, and lawlessness among the unemployed miners resulted in frequent murders, earning this embittered mine community the name of Bloody Run. Families living in abandoned mining camps were so destitute and conditions were so deplorable that an outbreak of typhoid fever was usual each spring. Outdoor privies were close to the run, at the bottom of which was the only water supply, a community spigot. Few children went to school regularly: for a family owned perhaps one pair of shoes for all the children, or no shoes at all. Usually the older children slept on rags on the floor, and the youngest child slept with the parents on the family's only bed, which might or might not have a mattress.[1]

[1] Anna Eleanor Roosevelt, *This I Remember* (New York: Harper & Bros., 1949), pp. 126, 129.

Eleanor Roosevelt was so deeply affected by this state of human suffering that she dedicated her efforts for many years to alleviating the horrible conditions of mine families, some of whom had not had steady incomes for seven years. The first lady shared this picture of misery with her husband after her August 1932 visit, warning him that the situation was explosive and that the administration must act quickly.[2]

The president agreed, accepting a loosely structured proposal offered by members of the American Friends' Service Committee and other social-service agencies working in the area. The basic plan was that the workers would be resettled in decent housing in a place they could farm and that they would supplement their farming incomes with some other work. It was a revolutionary idea: to take miners away from the pits—a way of life for generations—and turn them into farmers; to train them and their families in furniture making, household crafts, and metalwork; and to create a totally new self-sufficient community in almost complete isolation from the rest of society.[3]

And so the first New Deal subsistence homestead farm project was begun as a noble venture presided over by Eleanor Roosevelt aided by Louis Howe, Franklin Roosevelt's longtime friend and right-hand man. Plans for the Arthurdale experiment were implemented under the National Industrial Recovery Act of 1933, which provided $25 million for the development of subsistence homesteads for the relocation of stranded rural and industrial workers. There were to be fifty such subsistence homestead projects, of which this was the first. The proposed magnitude of the undertaking put it in the national and international limelight. Although Mrs. Roosevelt's position in the project was never made official, the experiment became known as Eleanor's "baby" and was the focus of her attention for many years. It contributed greatly to the rapidly developing image of Franklin Roosevelt as a savior of the downtrodden and depressed.[4]

Howe learned of the Arthur farm, a tract of land in Preston County, West Virginia, which had been used by West Virginia University at one time as an experimental farm. It belonged to a Pittsburgh hotel owner named Richard Arthur and had once been the plantation of Col. John

[2] Roosevelt, *This I Remember*, p. 120.
[3] William E. Brooks, "Arthurdale, a New Chance," *Atlantic Monthly* 155, no. 2 (February 1935): 196–204.
[4] "First Lady: Press Conferences Help Pet Projects and F.D.R.," *Newsweek* 9, no. 15 (April 17, 1937): 24.

Fairfax, one of George Washington's officers. The original 1,017 acres consisted of a woodlot and cropland near Reedsville. A 1940 *Harper's* article described the negotiations for the purchase of the farm, which began in the family quarters of the White House:

we catch glimpses of . . . Colonel Louis Howe dickering by long-distance telephone, through one of the Morgantown welfare workers, with Richard M. Arthur for the purchase of his farm, and holding firmly to a price of not more than $35,000 for the mansion house and 1,200 acres of land in the farm. We see him pointing a long bony finger . . . saying, "I'll buy the houses, [Secretary of the Interior Harold] Ickes, you'll buy the land. And Eleanor, you'll put the families in the houses." We see him ordering, again by long-distance telephone, fifty prefabricated summer cottages from a New England factory, to be rushed to the Arthur farm at once, at a cost just under $50,000.

The Washington atmosphere was charged with "haste, excitement, experiments and money."[5] Here was to be "planned economy"—but there was no plan, only some roughly conceived ideas. Architects, engineers, draftsmen, accountants, and other personnel simply materialized at Arthurdale, sent out from that mysterious place called Washington.

The first idea was to group the houses on high ground, reserving lower, more fertile land for one large community garden. But Washington rejected this because someone there dreamed of each household's having its own cow, barn, poultry house, corncrib, outbuildings, and root cellar for smoking meats and storing canned goods. So plans were drawn during one weekend to conform with this new concept, and Arthurdale developed in a haphazard fashion at dizzying speed because someone in Washington always had an ideal solution and the authority to implement it.

There were many snafus. Although the farm had been purchased only in October, the rush was on to get homesteaders in by Thanksgiving. When the prefabricated houses arrived they did not fit the foundations prepared for them. And they were too flimsy for the harsh Preston County winters. Architects and draftsmen from New York were hired to redo them, resulting in costs two or three times the original estimate. As the *Saturday Evening Post* reported, "they moved too fast."[6]

[5] Writers' Program of the Works Project Administration in the State of West Virginia, comp., *West Virginia, a Guide to the Mountain State*, American Guild Series (New York: Oxford University Press, 1941), p. 501; Millard Milburn Rice, "Footnote on Arthurdale," *Harper's* 180 (March 1940): 413.

[6] "The New Homesteaders," *Saturday Evening Post* 27, no. 5 (August 4, 1934): 5.

There was no heat, except for cookstoves and fireplaces; furnaces would be added later. Each house had its own well, pump, and septic system. (Within two years many of the wells in the lower part of the project would become contaminated, and homesteaders had to be advised to boil their drinking water.)[7] National publicity focused on Arthurdale, putting great pressure on the new administration to make a good showing with this social experiment. But Thanksgiving came and went without the installation of the first homesteaders. So the goal became Christmas dinner in the new homes. Then March 1934 was to be housewarming; then April, then May. Some of the more desperate families were moved into the mansion to await completion of their own homes (fig. 1).

It was not until August 1934 that families were moved into the first 50 homes. "Wild grapevines [were] brought in from the mountains, and trained over the trellis so that the pictures for the rotogravure section might have a finished look." Eventually two other groups of houses were built, making a grand total of 165.[8] The second group was better planned, of sounder frame construction with parquet floors in the living rooms. The 40 houses of the third and last group were begun in the summer of 1936 and were yet larger, more elaborate, better built—their most appealing feature a native-stone veneer.

An abandoned Presbyterian church several miles from Arthurdale was purchased, moved, and rebuilt as the community center by adding a pillared portico and changing the structure's ecclesiastical lines to colonial. Within two years wings were built to house a cooperative barber shop, a general-store sales room for the Mountaineer Craftsmen's Cooperative Association, and a weaving room. A gas station was added to the quadrangle, and later, near the site of the old mansion, the colonial-style Arthurdale Inn was built. A forge, too, was included, at which were made the door hinges and hardware for the Arthurdale homes, as well as iron, copper, and hand-spun pewter objects.

This was to be a self-sufficient community with its own schools. Bernard Baruch contributed generously—as did Roosevelt herself—to the establishment of a progressive system based on John Dewey's educational theories. Elsie Clapp was Roosevelt's hand-picked director of the

---

[7] Rice, "Footnote on Arthurdale," p. 414.

[8] Stephen Haid, "Arthurdale: An Experiment in Community Planning, 1933–1937" (Ph.D. diss., West Virginia University, 1975), p. 116; Rice, "Footnote on Arthurdale," p. 414.

Fig. 1. Arthurdale mansion and grounds with homesteader children, autumn 1933. From Elsie Ripley Clapp, *Community Schools in Action* (New York: Viking Press, 1939), p. 111.

school, which was to be the hub of the new community. She organized square dances, plays, and music festivals to bring neighbors together to fulfill their social needs as well as to aid in shaping a community spirit. Her philosophy of education was made explicit in the "Plan for the School at Arthurdale," drafted by the West Virginia Advisory Council Committee:

1. Faith in democracy and confidence in the ability of an enlightened people to govern themselves in economic and political affairs will be an accepted doctrine [of education].
2. This school should emphasize the fact that democracy and freedom are challenges to a self-realization, and that real progress with any people results from their own initiative and resourcefulness.
3. The child is to be regarded as an individual with unlimited possibilities, ever capable of learning [which is to be] understood as acquisition of moral and spiritual values rather than those usually associated with schools . . . that have bookish and academic [goals].
4. . . . the school should cultivate a toleration of, and an appreciation for, individual differences in intellect, emotions, and personal habits.
5. . . . the pupils should be living completely and happily . . . through extensive opportunities for creative expression by individuals. . . . It will follow

that children and adults will be to a large extent engaged in doing those things that they desire to do.

Facilities for students from two years old through high school were housed in six new buildings. Subjects not usually taught in a 1930s curriculum—electric shops, weaving, and meal planning—were included, and parents were encouraged to take part, even to the point of growing and preserving foods for the school lunch program.[9] Health care was provided through the Arthurdale Health Center.

Employment was needed for the relocated miners, since family farming itself was not expected to produce sufficient income. During the initial stage of development, homesteaders earned money by working on construction of the project itself, but one of the most urgent problems in the minds of subsistence homestead officials was providing permanent employment for the men. The very first plan called for the United States Post Office Department to establish a factory in Preston County for the manufacture of post-office furniture. However, this aroused so much opposition from the furniture lobby, which claimed that government was competing with private industry, that the plan had to be abandoned.[10] At this point the decision was made to draw upon a craft of specific West Virginia lineage as the basis for development of industry and jobs.

During several years before the project had begun, some unemployed miners in Monongalia County had been organized, with help from the Quaker-sponsored American Friends' Service Committee, into self-service clubs. Out of this grew what came to be called the Mountaineer Craftsmen's Cooperative Association (MCCA). It is difficult to trace exactly when the association was organized, and even its name changed during the course of the Arthurdale project. It was called Mountaineer Craftsmen in 1935, Arthurdale Association in 1936 (not yet a bona fide cooperative), and Mountaineer Craftsmen's Cooperative Association in 1937, when it received a government loan "to make temporary improvements and repairs to the craft shop facility." A 1937 portfolio

[9] Roosevelt, *This I Remember*, p. 130; Elsie Ripley Clapp, *Community Schools in Action* (New York: Viking Press, 1939), pp. 71–75.

[10] Haid, "Arthurdale," p. 120; "Mrs. Roosevelt Inspecting Site of Her Colony of Miners at Reedsville, West Virginia, Where 50 Homes Have Been Built," *Newsweek* 3, no. 2 (March 3, 1934): 10; "Hull House in the Hills," *New Republic* 79, no. 4 (August 1, 1934): 312.

of catalogue sheets identified the business as "Arthurdale Association, Inc., Mountaineer Craftsmen's Unit," with a return on the mailing cover, "Sales and Display Rooms Arthurdale, West Va.; 1506 Race St., Philadelphia." But yet another appellation, "The Arthurdale Handicraft Club," appears on a 1941 letter quoting availability and prices to a prospective furniture buyer. Many people in the area referred to it simply as "the craft shop."[11]

One of the first items the MCCA produced was the Godlove chair (fig. 2). The design and construction of this sturdy chair, a 200-year-old family secret, resided with Samuel Isaac Godlove, a skilled chairmaker from Hardy County. At the invitation of the Quakers, Godlove had come to Monongalia County to teach miners how to make his chair. Wooden, with a rush seat, made with simple hand tools, and rather small, the chair was very comfortable. It sold in 1934 for five dollars. Its secret was in the joining of kiln-dried rungs and slats to green uprights, which made inseparable joints when the uprights dried and tightened on the rungs and slats.[12]

Another early influence on MCCA furniture making was Daniel Houghton, a Philadelphia Quaker and a graduate mechanical engineer who had taught four years at Hull House in Chicago. Dedicated to helping in the resettlement of unfortunate Monongalia County families, he moved to Arthurdale to teach woodworking at the MCCA. His wife, Anne Houghton, acted as manager of the cooperative sales room and taught weaving to the women. The weaving room was located in the left wing of the community center, where the women made coverlets, aprons, towels, place mats, napkins, draperies, belts, handbags, pillows, neckties, scarves, baby blankets, bedspreads, and rugs for sale. Some even wove fabric for their own children's clothing. They worked with linen, cotton, and wool. The weavers formed a guild, filling orders from many states and several different countries.[13]

Looms for the young girls and women to weave on were made by the MCCA but were never offered for public sale. Eleanor Roosevelt donated

[11] "New Homesteaders," p. 5; Haid, "Arthurdale," p. 243; Arthurdale Association, Inc., catalogue (Arthurdale, W. Va., 1937), collection of author; Anne Houghton to Mrs. C. E. Stockdale, September 30, 1941, collection of author; Stockdale, interview with author, Morgantown, W. Va., February 1972.

[12] Arthurdale catalogue, sheet 9; Colleen Anderson, "Arthurdale Craftspeople, 1974," *Goldenseal* 7, no. 2 (April–June 1981): 22; Arthurdale catalogue, sheet 9.

[13] "New Homesteaders," p. 5; Houghton to Stockdale, September 30, 1941.

Fig. 2. Godlove chair, Mountaineer Craftsmen's Cooperative Association, Arthurdale, W.
Va., ca. 1937. Maple uprights, hickory rungs,
hand-woven splint seat; H. (seat) 17″. (Collection of the author.)

nine large looms to the weaving workshop, and Ruth Hallen was hired
as an instructor. Lova McNair—who was a member of the first high-
school graduating class at Arthurdale and who recalls President and
Mrs. Roosevelt's attendance at the 1938 commencement—reports that
many of the women became very skillful weavers. Still a resident of
Arthurdale in 1976, McNair has kept a loose-leaf notebook containing
colored samples of the patterns she learned from Hallen. The popularity
of this training was so great that some women had looms made for
themselves. Six were made by Hungarian-born Steve Deak, who was

one of the original fourteen-member Mountaineer Craftsmen's Cooperative Association chairmakers. Deak, with a home and a family in Morgantown, had declined an invitation to become a homesteader. However, he "used to go to Arthurdale and help out" and continued to sell his chairs through the cooperative salesroom. He also worked as a blacksmith and considered himself "first and last a craftsman."[14]

Pottery classes were organized by the Eleanor Roosevelt Women's Club, which also sponsored arts and crafts fairs at which ceramics were exhibited and sold.[15] Thirty or so men and women were guild members, and most of the potter's wheels as well as the kiln in the pottery workshop were made by Arthurdale settlers.

Training in metalwork was conducted by James Londus Fullmer, known to his friends as Lon, who had been a blacksmith for more than sixty years. He had a reputation as a good metalworker when he went to Arthurdale in 1934 and was soon gaining recognition as a creator of fancy ironwork, especially replicas of antique metal intruments. One of these, a copy of a sixteenth-century astronomy instrument, was exhibited at the Seattle World's Fair and was later transferred to the Smithsonian Institution. Fullmer did much of his work at the Arthurdale forge, where members of the MCCA produced a large selection of pewter, copper, and brass items, including plates, pepper shakers, spoons, mugs, pitchers, bowls, candlesticks, finger bowls, and teapots. Fullmer was an expert pewter spinner. His designs were authentic copies of colonial pieces or, occasionally, were original creations (fig. 3).[16]

Of all its crafts, Arthurdale became best known for furniture. Roosevelt had financial interests in a furniture factory at Val-Kill, Hyde Park, New York, when Arthurdale was being established. She and Nancy Cook, who directed the Val-Kill business, consulted with the Metropolitan Museum of Art and the Hartford Museum on questions of design, studying museum furniture and procuring working drawings for many pieces. As Roosevelt related in *This I Remember*, Cook preferred to use only methods employed "by our ancestors," but she compromised by allowing the first roughing-out stages of production at Val-Kill to be

---

[14] Anderson, "Arthurdale Craftspeople," pp. 21, 23.

[15] Anderson, "Arthurdale Craftspeople," p. 24.

[16] Fullmer had other talents as well: he played a lively fiddle, frequently doing so at Arthurdale square dances. One of his fondest memories was of dancing once with Eleanor Roosevelt (Anderson, "Arthurdale Craftspeople," pp. 24–25).

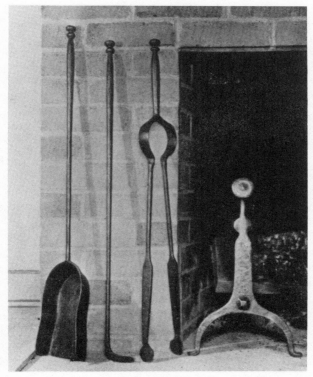

Fig. 3. Hand-forged-iron shovel, poker, tongs, and and-iron, Mountaineer Craftsmen's Cooperative Association. From Arthurdale Association, Inc., catalogue (Arthurdale, W. Va., 1937), sheet 16. (Winterthur Museum Library, gift of Jeanne S. Rymer.)

done on machines. However, the subsequent steps were all done by hand, and "therefore expensive . . . the wood looked and felt as though it had been used and polished for years."[17] It was this influence and background that Roosevelt brought to the production of Arthurdale furniture. First steps were done by machine, but the rest, including as

[17] Roosevelt, *This I Remember*, pp. 32–33.

many as seven hand-rubbed finish coats of lacquer, were done by hand.

The Isaac Godlove chair, original inspiration for subsequent MCCA furnishings, was offered in a 1937 catalogue with cherry or maple uprights and hickory rungs held together with pegs and with the joinery technique of green uprights tightened inseparably onto kiln-dried crosspieces. All stock used in production was indigenous to the Arthurdale area. On this original chair, as with all subsequent chairs and stools, the splint- or splat-bottom or woven-fiber seats were crafted by the women of the community.

In addition to the Godlove chair, the 1937 catalogue listed maple settles of 5-, 6-, and 7-foot lengths. In stick style, straight and clean lined, these pieces were obviously influenced by Daniel Houghton's Quaker heritage. A penciled note lists a price of $57.50, although it does not specify to which length of settle this price applied (fig. 4). The catalogue also offered a three-legged peg stool in walnut, maple, or cherry, and other stools—8½ by 15 inches—of the same woods. A 15-by-15-inch style with a rattan seat was also available. In addition to a 14-inch-high Godlove slipper chair, various children's chairs were available: 9- and 12-inch Godlove chairs (fig. 5), a 6-inch-high doll's chair, and two children's rocking chairs, 8 and 10 inches high. A ribbon-back armchair and a side chair, both in "Black Walnut with hand-woven rush seats," appeared in the catalogue as well (fig. 6). The ribbon-back design was a direct copy of one produced at Val-Kill and pictured in Roosevelt's *This I Remember*, with ribbonwork "perfectly chiseled out by hand" (fig. 7).[18]

The frontispiece of the catalogue pictures a sophisticated curved four-rung ladder-back chair with ball feet on straight, turned legs and with a rush seat. But this is not described within the catalogue. In addition, in my collection is an Arthurdale sewing rocking chair with a rush seat, which is not in the 1937 catalogue, but which was likely produced at this time (fig. 8). The catalogue was probably not a complete and accurate reflection of the total MCCA production.

The catalogue also pictures a wide range of beds, chests, desks, mirrors, tables, and accessory pieces of solid native woods as well as pewter, copper, tin, and wrought-iron accessory items of colonial design. One line of tables has straight, turned legs with many convolutions; one line

[18] Roosevelt, *This I Remember*, p. 68.

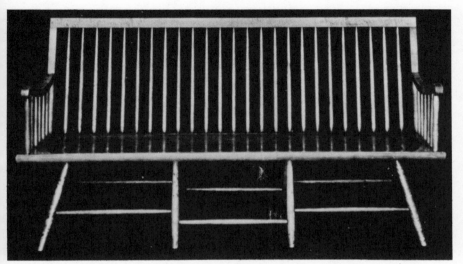

Fig. 4. Settle, Mountaineer Craftsmen's Cooperative Association. Maple; L. 5', 6', or 7'. From Arthurdale Association, Inc., catalogue (Arthurdale, W. Va., 1937), sheet 6, no. 475. (Winterthur Museum Library, gift of Jeanne S. Rymer.)

has heavier legs with no turnings; and another line shows legs of a more sophisticated design (perhaps influenced by Daniel Houghton), gently tapered and very graceful (fig. 9). Almost all of the case pieces are marked with a distinctive seared logo depicting a drawknife and a spokeshave, with the MCCA mark between these (fig. 10).

Solid wood is used throughout the 1937 line, some pieces revealing interesting combinations of woods. For example, one chest of drawers has hard-maple drawer fronts, curly-maple sides, and a cherry top. It is finely crafted with free-running drawers of four different heights, hardwood dust panels within, and colonial revival brasses that locals call upside-down-bat hardware from the community forge. Chests were offered with many options "to order": ball or bracket feet and various drawer arrangements, woods, and pulls.

A kneehole desk is of very reddish cherry with a finished back, bracket feet, and, oddly enough, a very narrow kneehole, hardly wide enough

Fig. 5. Godlove chairs, Mountaineer Craftsmen's Cooperative Association. *Left to right:* children's chair, H. (seat) 9″; children's chair, H. (seat) 12″; slipper chair, H. (seat) 14″. From Arthurdale Association, Inc., catalogue (Arthurdale, W. Va., 1937), sheet 10, nos. 210, 209, 181. (Winterthur Museum Library, gift of Jeanne S. Rymer.)

for a chair. The original finish consisted of many coats of lacquer, resulting in a rich, mellow patina. Another desk is of very golden hard maple in a student style with fine proportions. (It would appear that wood stains were not used on any of these pieces originally. When original finish is stripped, no color change is apparent.) The two side-by-side drawers just beneath the 1-inch plank top exhibit an expert butting of fronts and are extremely smooth-running, indicating, again, fine cabinetmaking skills.

There are thirty-three photographs in the loose-sheet 1937 catalogue. However, with the to-order options, the range of pieces actually produced no doubt greatly exceeded this number. Free shipping to points within the United States was provided from the neighboring village of Reedsville, West Virginia.

The styles offered in 1937 were probably produced through 1938 or

Fig. 6. Ribbon-back armchair and side chair, Mountaineer Craftsmen's Cooperative Association. Black walnut with hand-woven rush seats. From Arthurdale Association, Inc., catalogue (Arthurdale, W. Va., 1937), sheet 11, nos. 290, 291. (Winterthur Museum Library, gift of Jeanne S. Rymer.)

1939. However, new sales approaches and styles in 1939 or 1940 were meant to attract the "city trade," which might visit the cooperative's Philadelphia, New York, or Columbus, Ohio, showrooms. It is probable that the new sales approach and the new designs were fairly desperate efforts to broaden the appeal of the line and increase sales. An undated mailer, probably from 1939 or 1940, announces a "higher grade line of reproductions of fine early American furniture than made in the past," available through better furniture and department stores. It solicits the names of dealers who might serve interested purchasers. Orders could be shipped directly from the factory to any place in the United States. The flier illustrates a "number 700" bedroom group with thirteen pieces available in solid rock maple or solid cherry with hand-rubbed lacquer

Fig. 7. Eleanor Roosevelt and unidentified craftsman at Val-Kill furniture factory, Hyde Park, N.Y. From Anna Eleanor Roosevelt, *This I Remember* (New York: Harper & Bros., 1949), p. 68.

finish (fig. 11). Special colors and finishes were also available "to order." Specifications list mitered and doweled frames, mortise-and-tenon construction in case assemblies, drawer interiors of dovetailed oak, with framed-in bottoms, center-drawer guides, and full dust proofing throughout. The mailer further solicits inquiries for furniture built to order "in early American or other designs in accordance with your specifications." And, as a final sales appeal, the mailer suggests a "finishing touch to your Early American Rooms by adding some authentic reproduction in pewter" from the craft shop.[19]

From its inception the MCCA maintained an independent status at

[19] Advertising mailer for the mountaineer craftsmen's shop of Arthurdale Association (Arthurdale, W. Va., n.d.), collection of author. A reference to a mountaineer craftsmen's shop exhibit in the West Virginia building at the New York World's Fair suggests that the mailer was used in 1939 or 1940.

Fig. 8. Sewing rocking chair, Mountaineer Craftsmen's Cooperative Association, Arthurdale, W. Va.,
ca. 1937. Maple uprights, hickory rungs, hand-woven
rush seat; H. (seat) 15″. (Collection of the author.)

Arthurdale under many organizational structures. Because most work
was done by hand, the volume of production was very limited, and the
operation never realized a profit. Numerous attempts from 1935 to 1941
failed to get the operation on a financially sound basis or to improve
efficiency.

In 1937, for example, the outlook *seemed* to brighten. A new, more
efficient factory was built. In addition to regular business, orders were

Fig. 9. Bedside table, Mountaineer Craftsmen's Cooperative Association, Arthurdale, W. Va., ca. 1937. Cherry; H. 28″, W. 18½″, D. 15″. Logo seared on drawer bottom. (Collection of the author.)

in hand to furnish the Arthurdale Inn and to provide furniture under various government contracts. Twenty-eight homesteaders were employed, and increased demand led to overtime work and even refusal of orders. Increased production did not reverse the financial decline, however. At the end of 1937 losses were estimated at $25,000.[20]

[20] Haid, "Arthurdale," p. 249.

Fig. 10. Logo, Mountaineer Craftsmen's Cooperative Association. From Arthurdale Association, Inc., catalogue (Arthurdale, W. Va., 1937), sheet 12. (Winterthur Museum Library, gift of Jeanne S. Rymer.)

By 1939, even with the new factory, an expensive dry kiln, other improved equipment, and Roosevelt's donation of tools and equipment from the Val-Kill factory, the furniture operation lost $19,032. Losses were $25,116 in 1940. A request made by cooperative manager J. O. Walker for a $25,000 government loan included this statement: "We are informed by the community manager that unless the proposed loan is granted, this activity will have to be closed down or operated on a greatly reduced basis which will seriously handicap any future possibility of successful operation as well as present a serious employment problem."[21]

According to the acting director, Clarence Pickett, despite reorganization, new product lines, and increased sales, losses resulted because of excessive labor costs. His figures indicated that during the last half of 1940 the cost of production was approximately $1.29 for each $1.00 of sales. Although he argued that "it should be kept in mind that the Furniture Factory is employing 40 men who otherwise would be on Work Relief at $58.00 per month," the ax fell in early 1941 when the Farm Security Administration refused another loan and recommended liquidation of the cooperative and leasing to a private manufacturer. By the fall of 1941, Radio and Television Corporation leased the factory for the manufacture of radio cabinets, and a complete assembly-line operation was quickly effected. Thus ended the most expensive of all coop-

[21] Haid, "Arthurdale," p. 250.

No. 706 — 4 ft. 6 in.
No. 707 — 3 ft. 3 in.
Headboard Posts—54-3/4 in.

Fig. 11. Bedstead, Mountaineer Craftsmen's Cooperative Association. Offered in rock maple or cherry in two sizes. From advertising mailer for the mountaineer craftsmen's shop of Arthurdale Association (Arthurdale, W. Va., n.d.). (Collection of the author.)

erative failures. As Pickett later wrote: "One does not begrudge the greater income [offered by Radio and Television Corporation]; in fact, the men had almost no choice but to take it when it became available. But to see men who found great joy in producing beautiful handmade furniture abandon it for routine jobs that pay better causes one to ask questions about our civilization."[22]

[22] Haid, "Arthurdale," pp. 251, 252.

The leasing of the cooperative to the radio-cabinet manufacturer marked the end of handcrafted furniture production in Arthurdale, and the entry of the United States into World War II, in 1941, contributed to the decline of the other community cooperatives and activities there. Many Arthurdale men were called to military service or were enticed by higher wages to work at war plants. The federal government withdrew its support in 1942. The Arthurdale school was incorporated into the county system, and eventually the community property was sold to private interests.

Arthurdale today presents a picture of strong contrasts. The community building is falling down, despite frequent efforts to initiate a restoration project. Its portico is no longer pillared, but hangs unsupported, creating the bizarre impression of suspension in time and space. The forge has long since fallen into ruins. The salesroom is boarded up and overgrown with weeds—almost lost in them.

Most of the homes have been maintained by private owners, however, who made modern additions that are strange juxtapositions to the 1930s mounded root cellars. Even a few of the original homesteaders have remained in Arthurdale; they cherish the artifacts and skills of their unique heritage.

Today there is an air of remote peacefulness about this rural hamlet of 800 citizens, many of the third generation. Arthurdale is still distinctive among Preston County villages, although it is now primarily a commuter suburb of Morgantown. The original division of the properties into two- to five-acre plots has created a spacious, sylvan effect, with winding roadways connecting widely separated neighbors.

According to original resident Glenna Williams, who was a high-school student when her parents were moved to the homestead, "We were on the brink of catastrophe . . . the verge of disaster . . . the despair is hard to imagine." The social experiment failed in certain respects, but it did succeed in meeting needs for food, shelter, health, and employment for 165 families.[23] There was no clear-cut plan for the "planned economy," however, and this fact was at the root of much of the mismanagement. The social and economic isolation from other communities, coupled with administration by absentee managers in Washington, did little to encourage individual initiative in the home-

[23] Kathleen Cullinan and Beth Spence, "The New Deal Comes to Preston County," *Goldenseal* 7, no. 2 (April–June 1981): 7–20; Rice, "Footnote on Arthurdale," p. 419.

steaders. Families had little part in the development of their own environment, a condition of bureaucratic anonymity that alienated residents, who felt that Washington simply did not hear them.

But Arthurdale did succeed in perpetuating colonial cabinetmaking, forging, and weaving skills through such fine craftsmen as Godlove, Fullmer, Deak, Houghton, and Hallen. The experiment also contributed to the perpetuation of certain colonial styles and decorative arts as well as early joinery techniques which otherwise might have been lost. A limited amount of Arthurdale furniture that is currently valued for its fine design, craftsmanship, and beauty can be found in private collections in the East.

In addition to the aesthetic value of the Arthurdale experiment, its social and economic impact on those involved, and its political value to the new Roosevelt administration, there is another aspect of the project worth noting. It ran contrary to the usual theme of the colonial revival movement as an effort to preserve an old and elite order threatened by the laboring classes. In Arthurdale the social-class theme was reversed as working-class people devoted themselves to colonial revival arts not only as a revival of mountain folk craft traditions but, more important, as a means of survival in a worldwide depression that threatened upper and lower classes alike.

The Colonial Revival and the Americanization of Immigrants
William B. Rhoads

Between 1880 and 1930 the foreign-born population of the United States more than doubled from 6.7 to 14.2 million, the immigrants bringing their own speech, culture, and politics. Americans whose ancestors had arrived earlier were often fearful that their traditions would be swept away by the flood of foreign ideas and practices. From the 1890s until strict limitations were imposed on further immigration in 1924, many native-born Americans reacted to the threatened destruction of the American way of life by actively engaging in Americanization, the instilling of traditional WASP "American" values in the minds of the foreign-born.[1]

Most often Americanization simply took the form of English-language classes and instruction in American government and history. The great events of the nation's past might, it was felt, also be made more vivid if portrayed in murals within public buildings. Edwin Howland Blashfield, one of the best-known muralists of the early 1900s, testified that art in public buildings was "good . . . for the uneducated Irishman, German, Swede, Italian, who may stroll into some new city hall in our

---

This paper develops ideas first presented in William B. Rhoads, *The Colonial Revival* (New York: Garland Publishing, 1977), chap. 28.

[1] Bureau of the Census, *Historical Statistics of the United States, Colonial Times to 1970*, pt. 1 (Washington, D.C.: Government Printing Office, 1975), p. 117; Edward George Hartmann, *The Movement to Americanize the Immigrant* (New York: Columbia University Press, 1948); John Higham, *Strangers in the Land: Patterns of American Nativism, 1860–1925* (New York: Atheneum Publishers, 1969), pp. 234–63.

own country." This public art, he wrote, should serve as a "public . . . educator," teaching "patriotism" by presenting major events in American history. His own murals of 1903 in the Baltimore Court House included both historical and symbolic characters in *The Edict of Toleration by Lord Baltimore* and *Washington Laying His Commission at the Feet of Columbia.*[2]

The fledgling American might also be taken on a tour of surviving patriotic landmarks. Thomas Jefferson himself had observed in 1825 that even "small things [including the house where he had written the Declaration of Independence] may, perhaps, like the relics of saints, help to nourish our devotion to this holy bond of our Union." By 1883 attempts were being made to Americanize Irish and Italian youths in Boston by teaching them the historical significance of such places as Old North Church.[3]

In New York, the City History Club was founded by blue bloods in 1896 as a "kindergarten of citizenship." The club's brochure pictures that excellent old inhabitant "Father Knickerbocker making good Americans of the children of all nationalities" who found themselves in New York (fig. 1). Actually, the club tried to fill children with "local pride and patriotic sentiment" through classes on local history which used prints of New Amsterdam and old New York. Hundreds of immigrant children were taken to such landmarks as the Dyckman House. The very walls of the old Dutch house were said to present "our young citizens . . . [with a] living history of honest and upright life." Although children of older American stock could join its programs, the club found its most eager students among immigrant children, led by the Jews, with "the Germans, Italians, and Irish in hot pursuit."[4]

[2] Edwin Howland Blashfield, *Mural Painting in America* (New York: C. Scribner's Sons, 1913), pp. 8, 24, 199; William Walton, "Recent Mural Decorations by Mr. E. H. Blashfield," *Scribner's* 37, no. 3 (March 1905): 382.

[3] Thomas Jefferson to Dr. James Mease, September 26, 1825, as quoted in Andrew A. Lipscomb, ed., *The Writings of Thomas Jefferson*, vol. 16 (Washington, D.C.: Thomas Jefferson Memorial Association, 1905), p. 123; Barbara Miller Solomon, *Ancestors and Immigrants* (Cambridge, Mass.: Harvard University Press, 1956), p. 85.

[4] Michael Kammen, "The Rediscovery of New York's History: Phase One," *New York History* 60, no. 4 (October 1979): 380–83; A. Shaw, "Local History and the 'Civic Renaissance' in New York," *Review of Reviews* 16, no. 4 (October 1897): 446–49; Reginald Pelham Bolton, "The Dyckman House Park and Museum," *Beaver* 4, no. 2 (February 22, 1917): 3; Frank Bergen Kelley, "The Teaching of Civic Patriotism: The Work of the New York City History Club," *Municipal Affairs* 3, no. 1 (March 1899): 68.

THE CITY HISTORY CLUB

·1664·
SIGILLVM·CIVITATIS·NOVI·EBORACI

FATHER KNICKERBOCKER MAKING GOOD AMERICANS OF THE
CHILDREN OF ALL NATIONALITIES

Fig. 1. Orson Lowell, cover illustration, City History
Club, *Annual Report* (New York, 1897/98). (Vassar
College Library.)

Several social settlements in New York cooperated with the club's
educational efforts: one City History class met at the University Settlement in the Lower East Side. Founded in 1886, the University Settlement moved in 1898 into new quarters, which the *New York Times*
described as a "six-story building of Colonial style that stands as a sen-
tinel over the clustering tenements." The University Settlement's resident workers—college graduates "of refinement"—sought to mix social
work and friendship as they labored among their impoverished immigrant neighbors, ultimately attempting to Americanize them. Theo-

dore Roosevelt visited the newly opened building and denounced radical reformers while endorsing the activities of the University Settlement, which he considered "along the lines of true democracy and true Americanism."[5]

Genteel architect I. N. Phelps Stokes designed the building to be "architecturally modest, in general conformity with the neighborhood," but necessarily larger than the surrounding tenements in order to serve a variety of functions. Stokes was a collector of prints of old New York and urged that historical prints should be displayed in public art galleries and libraries, as they would "stimulate patriotism and civic pride." He may well have hoped that his own "colonial" architectural design would similarly influence the settlement's neighbors.[6]

Another supporter of the City History Club was the Henry Street Settlement, which provided nursing and social services to Lower East Side immigrants. Established in 1895 by Lillian Wald (who came from a middle-class, midwestern, German Jewish family), the Henry Street Settlement, in the person of Wald, came to advocate the development of a tolerant "Americanism" that would join Old and New World cultures and traditions. She was optimistic that the visibly patriotic young Jewish immigrant would "shoulder our hopes of a finer, more democratic America." Wald chose to house her settlement in a part of Henry Street which, as she wrote later, "bore evidences of its bygone social glory" (fig. 2). Number 265 in particular was "a house which readily

[5] Allen F. Davis, *Spearheads for Reform: The Social Settlements and the Progressive Movement, 1890–1914* (New York: Oxford University Press, 1967); Ronald Sanders, *The Lower East Side: A Guide to Its Jewish Past* (New York: Dover Publications, 1979), p. 39; *New York Times* (October 25, 1896, January 29, 1899, November 25, 1900). Seth Low, president of Columbia University (1890–1901) and reform mayor of New York (1902–3), was a sponsor of City History Club and University Settlement. The monumental, vaguely Georgian forms of the new Columbia campus were echoed in University Settlement.

[6] *New York Times* (December 13, 1896); I. N. Phelps Stokes, *The Iconography of Manhattan Island*, vol. 1 (New York: R. H. Dodd, 1915), p. xxiii. Mardges Bacon in her essay in this volume indicates that Stokes mixed American and European classicism in his designs: University Settlement does certainly have some of the monumentality of Beaux-Arts classicism. Moreover, Stokes presented to the settlement an "old carved marble mantel" from Florence for placement in the Common Room. See Stokes to Low, December 22, 1898, I. N. Phelps Stokes Papers, New-York Historical Society. For a discussion of the widespread understanding of the colonial revival as America's national style, see William B. Rhoads, "The Colonial Revival and American Nationalism," *Journal of the Society of Architectural Historians* 35, no. 4 (December 1976): 239–54.

Fig. 2. Abraham Phillips, "The House on Henry Street." From Lillian D. Wald, *The House on Henry Street* (1915) (New York: Henry Holt, 1935), frontispiece.

lent itself to the restorer's touch." She was intrigued that her house and those adjoining it were "built [in the 1830s] by cabinetmakers who came over from England during the War of 1812 and remained here as citizens." Wald viewed her house as an example of good American taste, particularly because upstanding citizens had already been created there. Moreover, as Fiske Kimball was to point out, settlements often occupied old buildings in an effort to become accepted as a part of the neighborhood rather than intrude themselves as grandiose impositions of wealthy outsiders. Nor, it seems, did Wald want her building to resemble those hybrid classical—and distinctly un-American—structures which had been erected recently in the Lower East Side by organizations of Jewish immigrants like Kletzker Brotherly Aid Association (1892).[7]

The Neighborhood Playhouse was an offshoot of the Henry Street Settlement. Financed by Irene and Alice Lewisohn, German Jewish philanthropists, the playhouse opened in February 1915 for the settlement's amateur productions. Ingalls and Hoffman designed the exterior to resemble the earliest extant buildings of the district, while the interior's "early Republican detail" was said to give it the "intimacy of a distinguished dwelling." Alice Lewisohn may have viewed the American style of the playhouse as a lesson in American culture for the immigrant playgoers. Lewisohn, who with her sister insisted on presenting most plays in English (much to the displeasure of the local Yiddish press), was frankly upset by her introduction to Henry Street when she and her father were jeered and their taxi pelted with pebbles by children who resented "the intrusion of rank uptowners." Wald's house, once reached, seemed a sanctuary, a "reposeful colonial setting," surrounded by noisy children, pushcarts, and garbage. The playhouse, wrote Lewisohn, had a good influence on the behavior of the once rude and boisterous children: "the very repose and beauty of the building commanded their respect"—they were learning American standards of conduct.[8]

Mary Kingsbury Simkhovitch, founder in 1901 and head of another important settlement, Greenwich House in Greenwich Village, took a

---

[7] Lillian D. Wald, *The House on Henry Street* (New York: Henry Holt, 1935); Fiske Kimball, "The Social Center, Philanthropic Enterprises," *Architectural Record* 45, no. 6 (June 1919): 526–27; Sanders, *Lower East Side*, p. 70 and fig. 85. One journalist wrote approvingly of Wald's choice of an "old family residence" and suggested, in the case of the similar, nearby quarters of College Settlement, that "the architecture of the house adds dignity to the work" and provides the immigrant a model of an "orderly, refined" home (Lillian W. Betts, "New York's Social Settlements," *Outlook* 51, no. 17 [April 27, 1895]: 684; no. 19 [May 11, 1895]: 787).

[8] G. H. Edgell, *The American Architecture of To-day* (New York: Charles Scribner's Sons, 1928), p. 328; Stephen Birmingham, *"Our Crowd": The Great Jewish Families of New York* (New York: Harper & Row, 1967), p. 346; Alice Lewisohn Crowley, *The Neighborhood Playhouse* (New York: Theatre Art Books, 1959), pp. 5, 47. Neighborhood Playhouse belonged to the "little theater" movement, which often used the colonial revival, apparently as an expression of its rejection of the commercialism of the big, opulent, syndicate-controlled houses. Ingalls and Hoffman had in 1912 completed the best-known example of the movement, Little Theatre (*New York Times* [February 13, 1915]; Rhoads, *Colonial Revival*, p. 406).

more liberal stand on Americanization. A woman of colonial ancestry who had studied social economics in Berlin and married a Russian-born professor of economics, Simkhovitch could not conceive of a "formal or mechanical method of Americanizing people." Civics classes and even English classes she thought of dubious value. For Simkhovitch, "Americanization" was best effected by "bring[ing] our foreign friends to meet Americans at our parties, entertainments, bazaars. . . . There must be constant, cordial, personal feeling on the part of Americans for foreign groups in order that there be a mutual understanding and building up of American life." Moreover, she advocated freedom in political forums for all viewpoints except those that proposed the violent overthrow of the government. This apparent support of "radical and revolutionary" ideas in 1920 won Simkhovitch and Greenwich House the condemnation of the New York State Joint Legislative Committee Investigating Seditious Activities.[9]

Architecturally, Greenwich House (built 1916) is surely not radical (fig. 3). It was designed by Delano and Aldrich to "reproduce the atmosphere" of the early nineteenth-century brick houses of Greenwich Village, which Simkhovitch found "picturesque" and "attractive." She was determined that the new house should look in no way institutional: its seven stories were to be "camouflaged by its colonial facade," and it was to be "homelike." She told the architects, "Make the entrance hospitable. . . . Plenty of fireplaces, the dining room and drawing room . . . easily accessible to all. . . . And of course a roof garden."[10]

William Dean Howells, of mixed and unremarkable ancestry, found Greenwich Village in the 1890s a strange melange of "quaintness" and "surly . . . even savage" Italians. Simkhovitch's warm welcome to her Italian and Irish neighbors was an outgrowth of her own firmly established American roots: she was proud that her ancestor Samuel Shaw had been with Washington at Valley Forge, and she remembered fondly family excursions to Plymouth where her mother's forebears had landed

[9] Mary Kingsbury Simkhovitch, *Neighborhood: My Story of Greenwich House* (New York: W. W. Norton, 1938); M. K. Simkhovitch, *The Settlement Primer* (Boston: National Federation of Settlements, 1926), pp. 9, 21; Joint Legislative Committee Investigating Seditious Activities, *Revolutionary Radicalism*, vol. 6 (Albany, N.Y.: J. B. Lyon, 1920), pp. 2955–58, 2967–68, 3000–3001.

[10] *New York Times* (August 13, 1916); Anne O'Hagan Shinn, "Where Barrow Street and Bleecker Meet," *Survey* 39, no. 9 (December 1, 1917): 245–46; Simkhovitch, *Neighborhood*, pp. 110, 179–80, 184.

Fig. 3. Delano and Aldrich, perspective, Greenwich House, New York, 1916. From *Survey* 39, no. 9 (December 1, 1917): 244.

in the seventeenth century. Happy, too, were her memories of her grandfather's farm with its open fires and its ancient clock ticking in the corner.[11] No civics classes and no settlement house modeled after Independence Hall for Simkhovitch. Rather, her Americanization was to be achieved through friendly social contact, in a big old-fashioned American home.

R. T. H. Halsey, the first curator of the American Wing of the Metropolitan Museum of Art, believed his wing represented "a visual personification of home life in this country" during its heroic formative

[11] William Dean Howells, *Letters of an Altrurian Traveller* (1894; reprint ed., Gainesville, Fla.: Scholars' Facsimiles and Reprints, 1961), p. 74; Simkhovitch, *Neighborhood*, p. 11.

years. He feared that "the influx of foreign ideas utterly at variance with those held by the men who gave us the Republic, threaten, and unless checked, may shake the foundations" of American life. The exhibition of early American architectural fragments and furniture could help shore up the Republic's structure: the objects would instruct the untutored foreigner in the "traditions so dear to us and so invaluable in the Americanization of many of our people, to whom much of our history is little known." It was noted when the wing opened in 1924 that the major donor, Robert W. de Forest, had been chairman of the state commission which secured a reform of the tenement house law in 1901. Now he had won recognition for his belief "that beauty as well as open air and cheap rents are essentials of the American home." Among the wing's early visitors were fifty mothers from Lower East Side tenements on an educational tour sponsored by settlement houses.[12]

While New York attracted more immigrants that any other American city and consequently was also the focus of settlement and Americanization efforts, colonial revival settlement houses were erected elsewhere. Philadelphia had its University House, dedicated in 1907. In Boston, New Englanders of Puritan stock established South End House and worked toward "instilling into the minds of the newcomers and their children American political ideas and American national loyalties." South End House commissioned R. Clipston Sturgis to design the South Bay Union. The Bulfinch-style building functioned as a "neighborhood town hall, designed to help the district achieve civic unity."[13]

Unlike the settlements discussed thus far, which resembled contemporary YMCAs in combining red brick and white classical details in a mildly cheerful way, the House of Seven Gables Settlement in Salem, Massachusetts, occupied the darkly picturesque house associated with

[12] R. T. H. Halsey and Elizabeth Tower, *The Homes of Our Ancestors as Shown in the American Wing of the Metropolitan Museum of Art* (Garden City, N.Y.: Garden City Publishing Co., 1937), pp. xxi–xxii (Introduction dated September 1, 1925). Avi Y. Decter, "The Colonial Revival: Ideological and Historiographic Assumptions" (Paper presented at the 24th Winterthur conference, November 13–14, 1981), drew my attention to Halsey. *New York Times* (January 9, 1925); "A Shrine of American Fireplaces," *Survey* 53, no. 5 (December 1, 1924): 267.

[13] F. D. Watson, "The New University House, Philadelphia," *Charities and Commons* 17, no. 23 (March 9, 1907): 1041; Robert A. Woods, *The Neighborhood in Nation-Building: The Running Comment of Thirty Years at the South End House* (Boston: Houghton Mifflin Co., 1923), p. 58; Kimball, "Social Center," p. 531.

Hawthorne's dreary tale of seventeenth-century Puritanism. By 1908, when Caroline Emmerton acquired the building for settlement purposes, Salem's population was polyglot rather than Puritan. Henry James, on his 1904 American tour, was shocked to find himself asking an Italian for directions to the House of Seven Gables and found the encounter distinctly unpleasant: "the way they *become* crude over here!" These surely were candidates for Americanization.[14]

Emmerton had the house restored in 1909 by Joseph Everett Chandler and soon enlarged the facilities by creating a quadrangle of new buildings as well as seventeenth-century structures that had been moved. In 1925 a visiting journalist found there "a neighborhood center to interpret America to the foreign-descended factory peoples of Salem"— about half of them Poles, a quarter Irish, and the rest diversely European. "Could anything be more fitting . . . ? There's probably not a more American house on the continent than this. . . . Its very beams are of the soil."[15]

Nor was the Americanization movement confined to the Northeast. In Chicago, George William Cardinal Mundelein believed in Americanization and was perhaps more conscious of architecture's role in the process than anyone else of his time. Mundelein knew well the immigrant world of New York's Lower East Side where he grew up in the 1870s and learned to speak the German of his grandparents. In later years, however, he would stress the long-standing contributions his family had made in America: a great-great-grandfather had helped build the first German Catholic church in the United States; a grandfather had been killed defending the Union at Fort Sumter. Installed as archbishop of Chicago in February 1916, Mundelein one month later organized his first new parish, Saint Thomas of Canterbury, and directed his architect, Joseph W. McCarthy, to design a colonial-style church. At its dedication, the archbishop told the parishioners that the new church was "pure colonial, which is the only distinctive American architecture.

[14] Caroline O. Emmerton, *The Chronicles of Three Old Houses* (Boston: Thomas Todd, 1935), pp. 29–31; Henry James, *The American Scene* (1907; New York: Horizon Press, 1967), pp. 265–70.
[15] Leon Whipple, "Hawthorne Gives Alms," *Survey* 55, no. 1 (October 1, 1925): 45–46; *New York Times* (October 19, 1924). Anne Farnam brought this settlement to my attention in "Historical Consciousness in Salem, Massachusetts: Colonial Revival or Survival?" (Paper presented at the 24th Winterthur conference, November 13–14, 1981), and subsequently provided me additional information.

Fig. 4. Joseph W. McCarthy, Saint Thomas of Canterbury, Chicago, 1916–17. (Photo, William B. Rhoads.)

There are many beautiful Yankee meeting-houses, but this is the only Catholic church, in this diocese at least, built in this style" (fig. 4).[16]

While we may not agree that the design was "pure colonial," the important question is why Mundelein thought a Yankee meetinghouse a good source for a Catholic church. Two months earlier, President Wilson had proclaimed a state of war with Germany; the need to assimilate hyphenated Americans seemed more critical and urgent than ever before. Mundelein proposed that "at this time when our country calls for every particle of our loyalty, [the building] is almost symbolic of the twin devotions of your heart, love of God and love of country." America was at war with Germany and allied with England: the archbishop of German descent wanted to make perfectly clear his own loyalty and that of his largely Irish parish. Moreover, he hoped to pacify antagonistic national groups within the archdiocese by bringing them together under the banner of Americanism.[17]

[16] For Mundelein's life, see Paul R. Martin, *The First Cardinal of the West* (n.p.: New World Publishing, 1934); and *Dictionary of American Biography*, s.v. "George William Mundelein." George William Mundelein, *Two Crowded Years* (Chicago: Extension Press, 1918), p. 58.

[17] Harry C. Koenig, *A History of the Parishes of the Archdiocese of Chicago* (Chicago: Archdiocese, 1980), pp. 939–41.

After the war, Mundelein began the project that he eventually regarded as his supreme achievement—the creation of a new major seminary, Saint Mary of the Lake (popularly called Mundelein Seminary), forty-five miles northwest of Chicago. The *American Architect* reported in 1920 that the seminary would be designed "entirely in our early Colonial style and consist largely of replicas of buildings which have emphatic historic interest." Why was the architecture to be "purely American"? The seminary students would be of recent foreign extraction, and the new colonial buildings would "teach a better Americanism, . . . imbue a veneration for our historical traditions and result in the development of better ideas of citizenship." Speaking in 1924, Mundelein expressed the fervent conviction that *his* seminarians would be "the real leaders of Americanization in this city, youths in whose veins run the blood of many lands, but in whose hearts burn ardently, and undyingly, the love of . . . the land of the Star Spangled Flag."[18]

The archbishop worked closely with McCarthy, checking each sketch and working drawing. It was Mundelein who selected the early nineteenth-century meetinghouse at Old Lyme, Connecticut, as the model for the chapel (fig. 5). Both the administration building and the library were intended as towerless adaptations of Independence Hall. (Mundelein presented to the library a collection of autographs of signers of the Declaration of Independence.) On the seminary grounds Mundelein erected his own villa (1932; fig. 6), not in the style of a Roman cardinal's retreat, but instead reminiscent of Mount Vernon. In 1916 he had praised Washington as "the noble and generous father of our country" and friend of Catholicism: "none more than we [Catholics] will strive to preserve his memory."[19]

While Mundelein was planning his grand seminary in Illinois, a modest Catholic church in the colonial style was rising at Great Kills, Staten Island. The Church of Saint Clare, by Eggers and Higgins, was praised

[18]*American Architect* 117, no. 2308 (March 17, 1920): 340; "Cardinal Mundelein Souvenir Number," *Illinois Catholic Historical Review* 7, no. 1 (July 1924): 72–73; Donald Drew Egbert, "Religious Expression in American Architecture," in *Religion in American Life*, ed. James Ward Smith and A. Leland Jamison (Princeton: Princeton University Press, 1961), p. 394.

[19]Reverend C. F. Donovan, *The Story of the Twenty-eighth International Eucharistic Congress* (Chicago: Eucharistic Congress Committee, 1927), pp. 112–15; Federal Writers' Project, *Illinois: A Descriptive and Historical Guide* (Chicago: A. C. McClurg, 1939), p. 419; Martin, *First Cardinal*, p. 103; Mundelein, *Two Crowded Years*, pp. 180–81.

Fig. 5. Joseph W. McCarthy, Chapel of Saint
Mary of the Lake Seminary, Mundelein, Ill.,
1925. (Courtesy Archdiocese of Chicago.)

by the *American Architect* for its use of "a style . . . purely American"—evidence that the church knew its "duty" to promote "every
patriotic impulse" within its membership, predominantly Irish in the
case of Saint Clare's parish. A tablet in the church proclaims that the
edifice was erected "for God and country." Moreover, at the May 1920
cornerstone ceremony the splendor of Patrick Cardinal Hayes's ecclesiastical garb was outshone by a plethora of Star Spangled Banners.[20]

[20] *American Architect* 119, no. 2351 (January 12, 1921): 41; cornerstone ceremony
photos, Saint Clare's parish files.

Fig. 6. Joseph W. McCarthy, cardinal's residence, Saint Mary of the Lake Seminary, completed 1932. (Courtesy Archdiocese of Chicago.)

In Springfield, Massachusetts, the American International College had as its mission the Americanization of young foreigners—largely Greeks, Italians, Poles, and Armenians in the early 1920s. Described as "this crucible for the making of wide-awake, aggressive American citizens," American International College emphasized the teaching of the English language, business, and American government. Such documents as the Declaration of Independence and Washington's Farewell Address played important parts in the curriculum. Two major additions were made to the small campus in 1924/25: a library and a women's dormitory designed by Kirkham and Parlett "in the general style of the earliest American college building." The dormitory was constructed with $60,000 from the Massachusetts Daughters of the American Revolution. Since the 1890s the DAR had been an important sponsor of Americanization, but here was its first significant building project for the cause, and consequently both state and national DAR officers assembled for the dedication (fig. 7). The regent of the Mercy Warren Chapter was confident that "this building . . . will be the means by which "young women from all parts of the world . . . will have instilled in them the spirit of patriotism and loyalty to America."[21]

[21] Charles G. Fairman, "College-Trained Immigrants: A Study of Americans in the Making," *New England* 42, no. 5 (July 1910): 577; Henry M. Bowden, "The American International College for Immigrants," in *Immigration and Americanization*, ed. Philip

Fig. 7. DAR officers at the dedication of the Massachusetts DAR Girls Dormitory (designed by Kirkham and Parlett), American International College, Springfield, Mass., June 23, 1925.

Brooklyn College was established in 1930 to serve the needs of that borough, a third of whose residents were foreign-born. (As late as 1955 the majority of Brooklyn College students were from immigrant homes.) At the ground-breaking ceremony in 1935, college president William Boylan warned his faculty not to allow radicalism—"half-digested ideas about the economic order"—to conflict with the principles of democratic education. Boylan shared the hope Franklin Roosevelt expressed as he laid the gymnasium's cornerstone in 1936: that the college would "build up a better American citizenship." Boylan was determined that his new campus should "conform to the traditional spirit of the American college." Thus he insisted that its forty-three acres be as "country-

Davis (Boston: Ginn, 1920), pp. 607–10; *Springfield Daily Republican* (April 2, 1924); pamphlets concerning the Massachusetts DAR dormitory furnished to me by Mrs. Donald J. Morton, state regent, November 6, 1981; *Springfield Union* (November 23, 1924).

Fig. 8. Randolph Evans with Corbett, Harrison, and MacMurray, perspective, Brooklyn College Library, 1935–37. From *Pencil Points* 18, no. 11 (November 1937): 16.

like" as possible and its Georgian revival buildings (fig. 8) should not relate to the surrounding metropolis, but to the University of Virginia and the new colonial revival buildings of Yale Divinity School and Dartmouth College.[22] The library, designed by Randolph Evans, specifically derives from the Dartmouth Library, but surely the resemblance to Independence Hall was also intentional.

In 1921 John D. Rockefeller, Jr., provided a million dollars to construct a splendid new building for International House near the Columbia University campus. Established to "promote friendly relations between foreign and American students and to bring foreign students in contact with American home life," International House had as residents men

[22] Thomas Evans Coulton, A *City College in Action: Struggle and Achievement at Brooklyn College, 1930–1955* (New York: Harper, 1955); *New York Times* (October 3, 1935, October 29, 1936, December 8, 1935).

and women from around the world who had come to New York to study at Columbia or other schools in the city before returning to their homelands. The goals of Rockefeller and the administrators of International House were not overtly Americanizing: Rockefeller had THAT BROTHERHOOD MAY PREVAIL carved over the front door (although under a vigilant American eagle), and students were encouraged to remain proud of their individual national cultures. Nevertheless there was a thousand-seat assembly hall where "American problems and ideals may be presented and discussed, and the voice of American leaders may reach the rising generation of all the world." Rockefeller's wife, Abby, saw to it that architect Louis Jallade modeled the assembly hall at least in part after "the old Beneficent Street Church which she had attended as a girl in Providence." She also ruled that furnishings throughout the house should be colonial (fig. 9). Abby Rockefeller was known as an advocate of the Americanization of immigrants, and while the foreign students at International House were not to be completely Americanized, they were, from exposure to Americans and to colonial design, to "experience . . . American life" and carry back a sympathetic impression to their native lands.[23]

Henry Ford, the son of an Irish immigrant, began a vigorous campaign to Americanize thousands of his foreign-born workers in 1914. A Ford publicist went so far as to write (only half in jest) that Ford was not really in the automobile business: "Mr. Ford shoots about fifteen hundred cars out of the backdoor of his factory every day just to get rid of them. They are but the by-products of his real business, which is the making of men." Ford himself told an interviewer that his employees, "these men of many nations, must be taught American ways, the English language, the right way to live . . . under conditions that make for . . . good citizenship." Therefore he created compulsory English classes at his Highland Park factory and incidentally also had his men learn American table manners and etiquette. Most remarkable, however, was the "Ford English School Melting Pot" pageant, where immigrants in native costumes descended into a great pot, while "new Americans" emerged wearing business suits and carrying American flags. Contem-

[23] Raymond B. Fosdick, *John D. Rockefeller, Jr., a Portrait* (New York: Harper, 1956), pp. 388–94; *New York Times* (July 10, 1921, December 17, 1922); *Time* 37, no. 3 (January 20, 1941): 60; *New York Times* (September 14, 1924); Mary Ellen Chase, *Abby Aldrich Rockefeller* (New York: Macmillan Publishing Co., 1950), pp. 77, 114–18.

Fig. 9. Louis Jallade, Great Hall, International House, New York, 1921–24. (International House.)

porary observers concluded that Ford's factories were "really . . . universities of citizenship."[24]

In the early 1920s Ford simultaneously collected old American artifacts and undertook a campaign of strident anti-Semitism. Depressed by his company's economic problems and the international political situation, Ford blamed powerful Jews for both. Furthermore, he believed that radical immigrant Jews were flooding American cities and trying to subvert traditional principles in American government and business. Ford's proposed solutions included immigration restriction and a return to the past. The study of history might be useful—but not the history to be found in books, which surveyed kings and wars. That kind of history was "bunk." What young Americans should learn was American life as lived, the everyday existence of ordinary people. Ford thought the best

[24] Samuel S. Marquis, "The Ford Idea in Education," *National Education Association, Addresses and Proceedings* 54 (1916): 910–17; *New York Times* (April 19, 1914); Philip Gleason, "The Melting Pot: Symbol of Fusion or Confusion?" *American Quarterly* 16, no. 1 (Spring 1964): 37; *Outlook* 109, no. 14 (April 7, 1915): 801–2; Stephen Meyer, "Adapting the Immigrant to the Line: Americanization in the Ford Factory, 1914–1921," *Journal of Social History* 14, no. 1 (Fall 1980): 67–82.

way to study American life was not through books but by looking at the objects he was collecting.[25]

In 1923 he bought the Wayside Inn, the old colonial tavern at South Sudbury, Massachusetts, immortalized in Longfellow's *Tales*. He opened it to the public as an inn and museum with furnishings from the seventeenth through the nineteenth centuries. (In the second-floor ballroom he could indulge in his favorite pastimes, fiddling and old-fashioned dancing.) The inn served his purpose of providing "foreigners who come to us . . . [with a] way of finding out what is the real [pioneer] spirit of this country." The DAR sent groups of Italian immigrant children from the Americanization departments of local schools. The inn's staff reported that they were "our most interested visitors. Their dark eyes sparkle and shine when we tell them of the things here that typify early American life."[26]

Ford opened the Wayside Inn Boys School in 1928 for some thirty teenagers—hyphenated Americans who were former inmates of state schools. The boys (who included Jews—Ford having dropped his anti-Semitic campaign in 1927) lived in a remodeled eighteenth-century house near the inn, where they studied no language but English, and little history other than that of industry. Civics was taught "with an eye to the demands of democracy upon the voting citizen." Meals were served at the inn, the boys remaining after Thursday dinner to dance in the ballroom, the fiddling furnished by a phonograph.[27]

The Wayside Inn Boys School was essentially a trade school whose top graduates could expect employment with Ford in Detroit. The boys learned various trades (including the repair and maintenance of Fords) in a new building called the laboratory (fig. 10) designed to resemble an old New England shop rather than Albert Kahn's technologically advanced Ford assembly-line factories. The *New York Times* was happy to observe that boys of "different national and racial stocks" were able

[25] *Ford Ideals; Being Selections from "Mr. Ford's Page" in the Dearborn Independent* (Dearborn: Dearborn Publishing, 1922), pp. 260–61, 276–77, 308–11; Keith Sward, *The Legend of Henry Ford* (New York: Rinehart, 1948), p. 146; *New York Times* (October 29, 1921, February 12, 1924); Samuel Crowther, "Henry Ford's Village of Yesterday," *Ladies' Home Journal* 45, no. 9 (September 1928): 10.

[26] *New York Times* (September 27, 1923, February 17, 1924); Samuel Crowther, "Henry Ford: Why I Bought the Wayside Inn," *Country Life* 47, no. 6 (April 1925): 44; Wayside Inn Diary, May 13, 1930 (manuscript, Wayside Inn, Sudbury, Mass.).

[27] *New York Times* (March 4, 1928, April 13, 1930).

Fig. 10. Laboratory, Wayside Inn Boys School, South Sudbury, Mass. ca. 1928; destroyed. (Wayside Inn.)

to "live in apparent harmony with one another and with the eighteenth-century pine, pewter and Puritanism of their surroundings." Actually, the surroundings were themselves meant to be instructive of American values. The collective diary kept in the inn acknowledged that "the Inn is an Americanization school for everyone."[28] Yet today, when America's ethnic diversity seems something to be cherished rather than homogenized, few traces of the Wayside Inn Boys School remain.

The Americanization movement flourished when architectural design was eclectic—a matter of choice—and there was no unanimity con-

[28] *New York Times* (March 4, 1928, April 13, 1930); Wayside Inn Diary, April 9 and May 13, 1930.

cerning the appropriate style for buildings where Americanization was carried on. Mary Simkhovitch, in her *Settlement Primer*, gave advice on the planning of settlement houses, insisting that they be "hospitable and homelike," but she did not require that they be colonial revival. Sinclair Lewis, in his 1932 novel *Ann Vickers*, had his heroine decry settlements as "cultural comfort stations, rearing their brick Gothic among the speakeasies and hand laundries." Perhaps he had in mind Jane Addams's Hull House in Chicago, the best-known settlement house in America. Planned by Pond and Pond, Hull House was modeled after Toynbee Hall, London, both architecturally and in social organization. Also in Chicago was the Abraham Lincoln Center (1903) designed by Frank Lloyd Wright and Dwight Heald Perkins without reference to historical precedent.[29]

Settlement and Americanization work went on in new and old structures of various styles. It is no wonder that Allen Davis has concluded that most settlements "grew haphazardly" while trying "to create a homelike environment."[30] Still, for many Americans of old stock like Simkhovitch, *homelike* implied the old American home of a particular neighborhood. And some Americanization leaders—notably Cardinal Mundelein and Henry Ford—were keenly aware of the value of colonial design in the patriotic education of the immigrant.

[29] Simkhovitch, 'Settlement Primer, p. 9; Sinclair Lewis, *Ann Vickers* (New York: Collier and Son, 1932), p. 238; Allen B. Pond, "The Settlement House," *Brickbuilder* 11, nos. 7–9 (July–September 1902); William Allin Storrer, *The Architecture of Frank Lloyd Wright: A Complete Catalogue* (Cambridge, Mass.: MIT Press, 1979), p. 95.

[30] Davis, *Spearheads for Reform*, pp. 17, 32.

Index

Page numbers in **boldface** refer to illustrations.